Selfish Genes and Christian Ethics

Theological and Ethical Reflections on Evolutionary Biology

Neil Messer

scm press

British Library Cataloguing in Publication data

A catalogue record for this book is available
from the British Library

978 0 334 02996 0

First published in 2007 by SCM Press
9–17 St Alban's Place,
London N1 0NX

www.scm-canterburypress.co.uk

SCM Press is a division of
SCM-Canterbury Press Ltd

Typeset by Regent Typesetting, London
Printed and bound in Great Britain by
William Clowes Ltd, Beccles, Suffolk

Contents

Preface   vii

Chapter 1   Introduction   1

Part 1   Mapping the Territory   19

Chapter 2   Evolution and Ethics   21
  1 'Evolution and Ethics' in context   22
  2 The argument of 'Evolution and Ethics'   27
  3 The issues raised by 'Evolution and Ethics'   32
    a Explanation   32
    b Justification   34
    c Content   35
    d Moral capability and its limits   36
    e Theodicy   38
    f Redesigning ourselves and the world   40

Chapter 3   Redrawing the Map   42

**Part 2   Evolutionary Ethics and the Command of
God the Creator**   63

Chapter 4   The 'Evolution of Ethics' and the Doctrine
of Creation   65
  Introduction   65
  1 The 'evolution of ethics'   65
  2 Creation and evolution   74

Contents

3   Human creatures   79

4   Human being as moral being   83

Chapter 5   The 'Ethics of Evolution' and the Call
of God   97

   1   The 'ethics of evolution'   97
       a   Spencer, Huxley and Moore   97
       b   Evolutionary ethics in recent debate   99

   2   'Is' and 'ought' revisited   104

   3   Altruism and the love of neighbour   109

Part 3   Freedom, Sin and Salvation   131

Chapter 6   Evolution, Freedom and Moral Failure   133

   1   A 'tenacious and powerful enemy'?   133
       a   A morally problematic inheritance?   133
           i   Male violence   133
           ii   Maternal care and neglect of high-risk infants 136
           iii   Debunking morality   138
           iv   But are we 'good natured' after all?   139
       b   Evaluation   140

   2   Determinism, freedom and responsibility   145
       a   Determinisms: genetic, biological, environmental, social 145
       b   Is biology destiny?   147
       c   Is determinism compatible with freedom?   151
       d   Does 'ought' imply 'can'?   156

   3   Responding to moral failure   158

Chapter 7   Salvation and Sin (1): Holy Love and
Original Sin   163

   1   Holy love and the 'cruciality of the cross'   166

   2   Pride, sloth and falsehood   169
       a   Humility and pride   169
       b   Exaltation and sloth   174
       c   The victor and the true witness   178

   3   Original sin   184

Contents

Chapter 8   Salvation and Sin (2): Theodicy and Hope   196

  1 The justification of God   196

  2 Transformed relationships and the redemption of our
bodies   203

  3 Ultimate hope and penultimate responsibility   207

    a The ultimate and the penultimate   207

    b 'Already' and 'Not yet'   209

    c A cosmic and universal hope   211

Chapter 9   Working Out Our Own Salvation?   216

  1 Medicine, technology and the Baconian project   216

    a Human genetic modification   218

    b Human cloning and embryonic stem cell technology   220

    c Genetically modified crops   222

  2 Technological projects and the Christian narrative   226

  3 Diagnostic questions   229

    a Is the project good news to the poor?   229

    b Is the project an attempt to be 'like God', or does it
conform to the image of God?   231

    c What attitude does the project embody towards
the material world (including our own bodies)?   233

    d What attitude does the project embody towards past
failures?   234

  4 Assessing the projects   235

    a Genetically modified crops   235

    b Health   237

    c Human cloning and stem cell technology   238

    d Human genetic manipulation   242

Chapter 10   Conclusion   246

  1 Incorporating whatever is well-founded in the
accounts on which reductionists draw   246

  2 Handling issues evidence with which reductionist
views have difficulty   247

  3 Clarifying, challenging and reshaping moral concepts
and experience   248

Contents

Bibliography   251

Index of Names and Subjects   267

Preface

This book has, in a sense, been a long time in the making. My interest in the kind of question explored here dates back to my school days. A few years later, by the time I was a research student in molecular biology, I had begun to feel frustratingly ill-equipped to think about the theological and ethical puzzles posed by the biological sciences. Then a call to ordained ministry led to theological studies in Cambridge and London, and to the opportunity to think more fully about such things. Much of my writing over the past few years has been concerned with questions that arise at this frontier between the biological sciences and theological ethics, and this book is no exception. As will become obvious, though, the ecclesial and theological traditions by which I have been formed have made me dissatisfied with some of the ways in which this frontier territory is often explored, so this book is an attempt to deploy some theological resources less frequently brought to bear on the questions discussed here. However, this should not be taken to indicate any lack of appreciation for the work of those who have explored this ground before me. I have learned much even from those with whom I have disagreed most sharply in this book, and without their work I could not have done my own.

This book, I have said, has been a long time in the making, and I have incurred many debts in the making of it. Many teachers, colleagues and friends have, over the years, encouraged me to think and write about the issues with which it is concerned, and have helped me in various ways to do so. More recently, when I began to plan the book, Susan Parsons gave me invaluable advice and encouragement. Discussions with various colleagues and friends, particularly Nigel Biggar, helped me to get my ideas into focus and encouraged me to think that they were worth working on. The Department of Theology and Religious Studies in Lampeter has proved a highly congenial place to do this kind of work, and I have gained much from conversations and discussions with colleagues here, particularly Simon Oliver. Much of the research and writing was done during two periods of study leave, from July to December 2004 and from December 2005 to February 2006. I am grateful to the University of

Wales, Lampeter, for granting me that leave, and to colleagues, particularly Mark Cartledge, Michael Elliott, Simon Oliver and Paula Yates, who shouldered extra burdens while I was away.

Parts of the book have been presented as conference and seminar papers. A very early version of Chapter 2 and an early draft of Chapters 4 and 5 were presented to the Association of Teachers of Moral Theology in November 2003 and November 2005 respectively. Chapter 9 started life at the annual conference of the Science and Religion Forum in July 2004, and later versions were subsequently presented to conferences at Westminster College, Cambridge, and in Lampeter. Early versions of Chapter 2 and the last part of Chapter 5 were road-tested on departmental seminars in the Departments of Theology and Religious Studies and Philosophy, respectively, in Lampeter. I am grateful for the invitations that led to some of these presentations, and for helpful comments and discussion on each occasion. David Clough, Dave Leal, Simon Oliver and Jacqui Stewart each read and commented on some or all of the draft. I am most grateful to them for their comments, from which I have learned much. I remain, of course, fully responsible for whatever, through stubbornness, stupidity or haste, I have failed to learn.

I thank Barbara Laing and her colleagues at SCM Press for their enthusiasm in taking on this project and their help in seeing it through to publication. I acknowledge, with thanks, permission from the Continuum International Publishing Group Ltd to quote extensively from the English translation of Karl Barth's *Church Dogmatics*, vol. IV.1 (1956).

My most heartfelt thanks, as ever, are to my wife Janet, who has been a constant support and encouragement, and to my children Fiona and Rebecca, for the encouragement that they give just by being around. All three have been more good-natured than I had a right to expect about the time I have spent shut away in my study completing the typescript. I think they are almost as pleased as I am to see it finished.

Neil Messer
University of Wales, Lampeter
August 2006

I remarked above that I have learned much even from those with whom I have disagreed most sharply. Since one of those whom I had in mind was Arthur Peacocke, whose death was announced shortly after the typescript had been delivered to the publisher, I should like to take this opportunity to express my respect for his pioneering role in the field of science and theology, and my personal appreciation for his kindness and generosity – from which I, like others, have benefited on occasion.

December 2006

I

Introduction

To rank Charles Darwin's theory of natural selection as one of the most influential intellectual developments of modern times is hardly to make a controversial claim. With the publication of *The Origin of Species*,[1] he laid the foundations of the theory which has become the working paradigm of more or less all of modern biology, as the geneticist (and Orthodox Christian) Theodosius Dobzhansky affirmed when he wrote that 'nothing in biology makes sense except in the light of evolution'.[2] But it is not only the world of professional biologists that has felt the profound effects of Darwinism. The abundance of evolutionary discussion, theorizing and speculation in popular science writing and journalism testifies to the wide-ranging impact of Darwin's theory on modern Western culture and intellectual life. And although Darwin, for tactical reasons, almost totally avoided mention of *human* evolution in the *Origin*, much of this discussion, theorizing and speculation is preoccupied with the implications of evolution for aspects of human life. Not surprisingly, evolutionary theory interests us, above all, for what we hope (or fear) that it will tell us about ourselves.[3]

---

1 Charles Darwin, *The Origin of Species by Means of Natural Selection; or, The Preservation of Favoured Races in the Struggle for Life*, ed. by J. W. Burrow, London: Penguin, 1968; repr. 1985 (orig. pub. London: John Murray, 1859). As is well known, a version of the theory of natural selection was independently worked out by Alfred Russel Wallace, who communicated it to Darwin in 1858, unaware that the latter had been at work on the theory for many years. The upshot was that, at the instigation of Darwin's allies Sir Charles Lyell and Joseph Hooker, Wallace's paper was presented to the Linnaean Society together with two short papers of Darwin's from 1844 and 1857 – thus acknowledging Wallace's work while carefully establishing Darwin's priority. Darwin then rushed the *Origin* into print the following year. On the Darwin–Wallace episode, see, further, Adrian Desmond and James Moore, *Darwin*, London: Penguin, 1992, pp. 466–72.

2 Theodosius Dobzhansky, 'Nothing in Biology Makes Sense except in the Light of Evolution', *American Biology Teacher*, 35 (1973), pp. 125–9; reprinted in Mark Ridley (ed.), *Evolution* (Oxford Readers), Oxford: Oxford University Press, 1997, pp. 378–87.

3 For a few recent examples, chosen more or less at random, see: Anon., 'Did Humans and Chimps Once Merge?', *New Scientist*, 20 May 2006, p. 14; Anon.,

In particular, one widespread preoccupation is the significance of evolution for ethics. As I shall describe in Chapter 2, from Darwin's time onwards, evolutionary theorists have speculated about the origins of human morality and about what, if anything, knowledge of those origins might imply about our life in the world as moral beings and agents. Such theorizing received a new impetus from the 1960s onwards with the developments in theoretical biology that gave rise to the controversial fields of sociobiology and, later, evolutionary psychology. A burgeoning literature, both popular and technical, bears witness to the ongoing interest in evolution and ethics, and scholars from outside the biological fold with a professional interest in ethics and morality have not been slow to enter the fray. It is with that discussion and debate that this book is concerned, though I shall wish to call into question the terms of the debate as they are commonly set out in the literature.

Evolutionary biology is often supposed to be in conflict with 'religion' in general and with Christian beliefs about human life and the world in particular. One aspect of this supposed conflict, particularly relevant to this book, is that evolutionary accounts of morality are thought to be in some sense a threat to a Christian moral vision. Whatever the reasons why this supposition is so widespread, one of the main concerns of this book is to show that Christian theology is well able to engage critically and constructively with discussions of evolution and ethics, and to assimilate insights from biology into a Christian moral vision that is both broader and richer than anything biology alone can supply. That said, it is not intended first and foremost as a work of apologetics, in the conventional sense of a defence of Christian claims in response to challenges from contemporary culture – in this case, from biology or from speculations arising from biology. There are many distinguished examples of apologetic responses, in that sense, to challenges made in the name of evolutionary biology,[4] but my main aim is somewhat different. To be sure, in Chapter 3 I shall explain briefly why I think that the

---

'Hobbit Brain "Too Small" to Be New Species', *New Scientist*, 27 May 2006, p. 15; Andrew Brown, 'The Human Factor', *The Guardian*, 29 July 2006; James Flint, 'Don't Worry, Be Happy' (review of Jonathan Haight, *The Happiness Hypothesis*), *The Guardian*, 22 July 2006; Paul Rincon, 'Fossils Fill Gaps in Human Lineage', BBC News, 12 April 2006, online at http://news.bbc.co.uk/go/pr/fr/-/1/hi/sci/tech/4900946. stm (accessed 2 August 2006).

4 See, e.g.: John F. Haught, *God after Darwin: A Theology of Evolution*, Boulder, CO: Westview, 2000; Alister McGrath, *Dawkins' God: Genes, Memes and the Meaning of Life*, Oxford: Blackwell, 2005; Kenneth R. Miller, *Finding Darwin's God: A Scientist's Search for Common Ground between God and Evolution*, New York: Perennial (HarperCollins), 2002; Keith Ward, *God, Chance and Necessity*, Oxford: Oneworld, 1996.

supposedly Darwinian challenge to Christian belief articulated with particular vigour by the likes of Richard Dawkins and Daniel Dennett is badly mistaken. However, my primary concern is not to show that a Christian doctrine of creation is defensible in the face of a neo-Darwinian theory of origins, nor more generally that Christian faith is credible in a scientific age. Indeed, as the book progresses, I shall express a certain amount of dissatisfaction with styles of Christian engagement that, preoccupied with demonstrating the credibility of Christianity in the face of modern science, accept more than they ought of the terms on which secular Darwinist attacks on Christian belief are set up. Accordingly, I shall also suggest that a Christian theological engagement with the evolution-and-ethics literature need not and should not do what it too frequently does, namely, accept the standard ways of framing the debates and questions in that literature.

My central aim in this book is to articulate – from within, as it were – a theological and moral vision formed by one particular Christian tradition, and to show how rich are the resources offered by that tradition for a critical and constructive engagement with debates about evolution and ethics. I shall claim that this tradition should not be content to accept the terms of those debates as they are standardly set up, but should be ready to reframe the questions and make creative responses that can appropriate insights from evolutionary biology without being subsumed by the latter. Such a critical and creative theological engagement with the evolution-and-ethics field calls for the development of some large theological themes, as will become clear in subsequent chapters. Consequently, while I am working from within one specific Christian tradition (the Reformed Protestant tradition), I cannot expect to achieve anything like a representative coverage even of that one tradition. All I can do is to choose a small number of wise guides, mostly from within that tradition or informed by it, and take my cue from them in developing my own theological response to the questions about evolution and ethics.

One thing I do not propose to do is to enter the fray of debates about creationism and intelligent design.[5] Though these debates are periodically noisy and attention-grabbing, I regard them as something of a sideshow to the real engagement of Christian theology with evolutionary theory. I shall explain very briefly in Chapter 3 why I consider creationism to be as misconceived in its way as the reductionism of

---

5 I use the term 'creationism', here and elsewhere, in the conventional sense of a claim that the early chapters of the book of Genesis are to be taken literally as a scientific account of the origins of the world and human life.

Dawkins and Dennett – indeed, I shall suggest that in an important sense, each is the reflection of the other. Some commentators treat the 'intelligent design' (ID) theory of Michael Behe, William Dembski and others as little more than a stalking-horse for creationism.[6] That over-simplifies the case, since proponents of ID take pains to distance them-selves from creationism, and are willing to accept scientific conclusions (for example, about the age of the earth and the relationships between species) that creationists reject.[7] However, its critics argue that its aims and aspirations have much in common with those of creationism,[8] in which case it risks running into similar theological difficulties. Be that as it may, proponents of ID insist that it is a strictly scientific theory; commentators who are well placed to assess its scientific merits (includ-ing Christian scientists, who could be expected not to hold a brief for any putative secular-humanist conspiracy to suppress anti-Darwinian dissent) conclude that, thus far, it has failed to make its scientific case.[9]

The main body of this book is in three parts. Part 1, Mapping the Territory, begins with an attempt to characterize the main issues in play in current discussions of evolutionary biology and ethics. I do this by way of one of the earliest sustained discussions of the topic, T. H. Huxley's 1893 lecture 'Evolution and Ethics'. It might seem strange to use an essay from the end of the nineteenth century to structure my dis-cussion of a debate that is current at the beginning of the twenty-first, but my contention is that the questions raised explicitly or implicitly by Huxley's essay are those that remain in play, to varying extents, in current debates. In Chapter 3, I propose that a Christian theological engagement with these questions offers a promising and fruitful alter-native to the reductive vision exemplified by Daniel Dennett's presenta-tion of Darwinism as a 'universal acid' that eats its way through every area of human understanding.[10] Having surveyed various possible ways of relating Christian doctrine to biological science in developing a theo-logical account, I choose an approach influenced by Karl Barth, in which Christian doctrine sets the terms of the encounter and insights

---

6 For a recent introduction to ID, see William A. Dembski, *Intelligent Design: The Bridge between Science and Theology*, Downers Grove, IL: InterVarsity Press, 1999.

7 Dembski, *Intelligent Design*, pp. 247–52.

8 See, e.g., Howard J. Van Till, 'Are Bacterial Flagella Intelligently Designed? Reflections on the Rhetoric of the Modern ID Movement', *Science and Christian Belief*, 15.2 (2003), pp. 117–40 (pp. 121–2); Miller, *Finding Darwin's God*, pp. 163–91.

9 Van Till, 'Are Bacterial Flagella Intelligently Designed?'; Miller, *Finding Darwin's God*, pp. 129–61.

10 Daniel C. Dennett, *Darwin's Dangerous Idea: Evolution and the Meanings of Life*, London: Penguin, 1996.

from biology are critically appropriated. Such an approach will not simply accept Huxley's mapping of the territory, but will seek to redraw the map.

The remaining two parts of the book are an exploration of how the contemporary discussion of evolution and ethics might be transformed by an encounter with a moral and theological vision shaped by some key figures within the Reformed tradition of Christianity – particularly, as I have already suggested, Karl Barth and some of those influenced by him. In Part 2, I bring three of the questions mapped in Chapter 2 – about the explanation of human morality, the justification of moral claims and the substantive content of ethics – into engagement with the Christian doctrine of creation. In Chapter 4, I survey a range of proposed evolutionary explanations of the existence and features of human morality, and argue that a theological understanding of humans and the world as God's creation suggests an account of morality that can incorporate insights from biology, but that is by no means reducible to the latter. However, I also argue that 'morality', insofar as it is understood as a merely human project to know and to do the good, is not at home in this theological vision: in the words of Dietrich Bonhoeffer, Christian ethics can be 'considered an ethic only as the critique of all ethics'.[11] In Chapter 5, I argue that the issue of the relationship between 'is' and 'ought', which lies at the heart of the question about the evolutionary justification of moral norms, can be helpfully reframed by locating it within a Christian understanding of the world as created for a good end. One way of articulating this understanding would be by some version of natural law, but I claim that Barth's ethic of 'the command of God the Creator' has some advantages over versions of natural law theory that have been deployed in recent discussions of evolution and ethics. This claim is explored by way of a discussion of altruism and the love of neighbour, which also serves to illustrate the kind of difference that a theological treatment might make to evolutionary arguments about the *content* of moral obligation.

In the final part, I explore more fully what is alluded to at various points in Part 2: that humans and the world are to be understood theologically as flawed by sin and evil, but as reconciled and redeemed by God, in Christ, in the power of the Spirit. In Chapter 6 I survey a range of arguments that suggest, in effect, that our evolutionary history has left us with morally problematic tendencies and dispositions. This claim raises questions about determinism, freedom and responsibility, which

---

11 Dietrich Bonhoeffer, *Ethics: Dietrich Bonhoeffer Works*, vol. 6, ET ed. by Clifford J. Green, Minneapolis: Fortress, 2005, p. 300.

are discussed in the remainder of the chapter. In Chapters 7 and 8, I attempt to relocate this discussion within the Christian doctrines of salvation and sin. I develop an account of sin based on the work of Barth, Alistair McFadyen and others; I explore various possible correlations between this account and the evolutionary claims surveyed in Chapter 6, and argue that, in all cases, re-describing our problem as sin places putative evolutionary insights in a broader and more comprehensive picture. I explore what 'original sin' might mean in the light of evolutionary history, and suggest that some authors' difficulties with it can be attributed to the tendency to restrict sin-talk to too narrowly 'moral' a frame of reference, as McFadyen puts it.[12] Talk of original sin raises the issue of theodicy, and at the beginning of Chapter 8 I make some brief suggestions as to how that issue may most helpfully be addressed. In the remainder of the chapter, I sketch some aspects of the transforming work both accomplished and promised in Christ, and of its significance for human life in the world. Finally, in Chapter 9, I turn to practical outworking, specifically to the moral evaluation of technological projects directed to the improvement of the world and ourselves. I argue that if our evaluation of such projects is relocated within a theological narrative of creation, sin and salvation, that theological understanding can suggest 'diagnostic questions' by which technological projects can be morally assessed.

The reader might find it helpful to have a brief account of the evolutionary theory which gives rise to the specific questions explored in this book. Accordingly, the remainder of this introductory chapter is given over to a brief sketch of some salient features of evolutionary biology since Darwin.

By the time of the *Origin*'s publication in 1859, evolutionary theories were not new, though they remained controversial and much of the scientific establishment was reluctant to accept them. Among the antecedents to Darwin's theory were the very speculative version proposed by his grandfather Erasmus in the 1790s and the theory published by Jean-Baptiste Lamarck in 1809, the year of Darwin's birth. Nowadays, commentators often regard the discovery of a plausible mechanism of evolutionary change as Darwin's most important contribution.[13] The

---

12 Alistair McFadyen, *Bound to Sin: Abuse, Holocaust and the Christian Doctrine of Sin*, Cambridge: Cambridge University Press, 2000, pp. 19–21 and *passim*.

13 It should be noted, though, that what seemed most distinctive – and threatening – to many of his contemporaries was his conclusion that all forms of life are related to one another by descent from a common ancestor. I thank Jacqui Stewart for pointing this out to me.

theory is at heart very simple – his friend and ally T. H. Huxley later recalled that his first reaction to it had been 'How extremely stupid of me not to have thought of that!'[14] – and Darwin himself summarized its essential points as follows:

> If, during the long course of ages and under varying conditions of life, organic beings vary at all in the several parts of their organisation, and I think this cannot be disputed; if there be, owing to the high geometrical powers of increase of each species, at some age, season or year, a severe struggle for life, and this certainly cannot be disputed; then, considering the infinite complexity of the relations of all organic beings to each other and to their conditions of existence, causing an infinite diversity in structure, constitution and habits, to be advantageous to them, I think it would be a most extraordinary fact if no variation ever had occurred useful to each being's own welfare ... But if variations useful to any organic being do occur, assuredly individuals thus characterised will have the best chance of being preserved in the struggle for life; and from the strong principle of inheritance they will tend to produce offspring similarly characterised. This principle of preservation, I have called, for the sake of brevity, Natural Selection.[15]

Darwin held that 'Natural Selection has been the main but not exclusive means of modification.'[16] Others to which he drew attention included *sexual selection*, or differential success in gaining access to mates,[17] and *correlation of growth*, in which one change, that is directly selected for, also brings about other changes that are not themselves directly selected for.[18] He also believed that modification could come about by what he called 'pangenesis'. This was similar to the view, associated with Lamarck, that changes which take place in an individual during its lifetime can be transmitted to its offspring. August Weismann, later in the

---

14 Thomas Henry Huxley, 'On the Reception of the Origin of Species' (1887), online at http://alepho.clarku.edu/huxley/Book/Recep.html (accessed 14 July 2006).

15 *Origin*, pp. 169–70.

16 *Origin*, p. 69.

17 *Origin*, pp. 136–8. Darwin believed that this was more or less entirely a matter of male competition for females, for which he has been much taken to task by feminist commentators: see Charles Darwin, *The Descent of Man, and Selection in Relation to Sex*, London: John Murray, 1871, repr. with introduction by John Tyler Bonner and Robert M. May, Princeton, NJ: Princeton University Press, 1981, pp. 271–9, and, for a critique, Sarah Blaffer Hrdy, *Mother Nature: A History of Mothers, Infants, and Natural Selection*, New York: Pantheon, 1999, pp. 12–23.

18 *Origin*, pp. 182–8.

nineteenth century, is generally credited with laying 'pangenesis' to rest by showing that variations that arise elsewhere in the body cannot be translated back into the 'germ-plasm' (those cells and tissues involved in sexual reproduction).[19]

One major gap in Darwin's account was the lack of a plausible theory of inheritance, without which he could not show how advantageous variations could be passed on to their bearers' offspring. The current view in his day was that characteristics from both parents were blended in the offspring, but, as he realized, such 'blending inheritance' would quickly result in the loss of variation as differences between individuals became averaged out in their descendants. Unknown to Darwin and his colleagues, the Austrian monk Gregor Mendel was working on inheritance around the time of the *Origin*'s publication. Mendel proposed a 'particulate' theory in which discrete units of inheritance (which later came to be called 'genes') are passed on from parents to offspring. Variation is caused by the existence in the population of different versions ('alleles') of the same gene. If offspring receive different alleles from their two parents, the two versions are not blended, but remain distinct and can be handed on to those individuals' descendants in their turn. Mendel's theory remained virtually unknown until the beginning of the twentieth century. When it was rediscovered, it was initially thought to support a rival evolutionary theory in which evolution was caused by spontaneous genetic changes (mutations) that brought about relatively large, sudden changes in the organism. On this view, natural selection acting on small continuous variations would be more or less irrelevant to evolution. However, in the 1920s and 1930s, population geneticists such as R. A. Fisher, Sewall Wright and J. B. S. Haldane showed that Mendelian inheritance could give rise to small continuous variations, that Darwinian natural selection *required* a Mendelian form of inheritance in order to work and that, over time, natural selection acting on small variations could give rise to large evolutionary changes.[20]

---

19 For a brief description of pangenesis, see Darwin, *Descent*, p. 280; on Weismann, see John Maynard Smith, 'Weismann and Modern Biology', *Oxford Surveys in Evolutionary Biology*, 6 (1989), pp. 1–12, reprinted in Ridley, *Evolution* (Oxford Readers), pp. 17–22; see also Francisco J. Ayala, 'The Evolution of Life: An Overview', in Robert John Russell, William R. Stoeger, SJ, and Francisco J. Ayala (eds.), *Evolutionary and Molecular Biology: Scientific Perspectives on Divine Action*, Vatican City State: Vatican Observatory / Berkeley, CA: Center for Theology and the Natural Sciences, 1998, pp. 21–57 (p. 25).

20 See, e.g.: R. A. Fisher, 'The Nature of Inheritance', from *The Genetical Theory of Natural Selection*, Oxford: Oxford University Press, 1930. Sewall Wright, 'The Roles of Mutation, Inbreeding, Crossbreeding, and Selection in Evolution', *Proceedings of the VI International Congress of Genetics*, 1 (1932), pp. 356–66 and J. B. S.

This synthesis of Darwinian with Mendelian theory has been known as the 'modern synthesis' since Julian Huxley coined the term in the 1940s. Early work in population genetics, particularly that of Wright, also suggested the importance of 'genetic drift' (the accumulation of random genetic mutations that have little or no effect on the organism's fitness and are therefore not subject to selection pressures) as an additional mechanism of evolutionary change, alongside natural selection. Dispute continues among biologists as to the relative importance of selection and genetic drift in evolution.

The development of molecular genetics since the discovery of the structure of DNA (deoxyribonucleic acid) in 1953 has added an enormous amount of detailed information to this picture. For example, it has shown how genetic information is encoded in the sequence of nucleotides, the molecular 'building blocks' that are strung together in a DNA macromolecule, and how that information is translated into the sequences of the many thousands of different kinds of protein molecule that perform the vast range of functions necessary for the growth, development and maintenance of a living organism. It has shown how various kinds of random mutation can arise in DNA sequences, and how these can sometimes result in phenotypic changes (that is, changes in the structure or function of the organism) by giving rise to structural and functional changes in proteins. Molecular genetics also allows equivalent (homologous) DNA and protein sequences in different species to be compared, and such comparisons provide evidence of evolutionary relationships between species. One particular way of tracing evolutionary relationships is suggested by the 'neutral theory' of molecular evolution, proposed by the geneticist Motoo Kimura in 1968, which holds that most genetic mutations are adaptively 'neutral' – that is, they are neither advantageous nor disadvantageous to the organism.[21] If this is so, then there will be no selection pressure acting for or against the accumulation of most DNA sequence changes, in which case they can be expected to accumulate at a roughly constant rate. Comparing the equivalent sequences in different species will give an

Haldane, 'Disease and Evolution', *La Richercha Scientifica*, 19, suppl. (1949), pp. 68–76, reprinted in Ridley, *Evolution* (Oxford Readers), pp. 22–32, 32–40 and 41–7, respectively; also, for overviews, Ayala, 'The Evolution of Life', pp. 25–6, and Stephen Jay Gould, *The Structure of Evolutionary Theory*, Cambridge, MA: Harvard University Press, 2002, pp. 503–18.

21 For a summary and discussion, see Motoo Kimura, 'Recent Development of the Neutral Theory Viewed from the Wrightian Tradition of Population Genetics', *Proceedings of the National Academy of Sciences of the USA*, 88 (1991), pp. 69–73, reprinted in Ridley, *Evolution* (Oxford Readers), pp. 88–94.

indication of the time since their evolutionary lineages diverged: the accumulation of genetic mutations acts as a 'molecular clock' of evolution. The evidence suggests that the 'molecular clock' is not entirely accurate, but nonetheless provides reliable evidence of evolutionary relationships.[22] The neutral theory also has wider implications for the understanding of evolution, particularly about the relative importance of natural selection and genetic drift as drivers of evolutionary change. The neutral theory and its implications remain an area of controversy within evolutionary biology.[23]

Another area of controversy relevant to this book is the question of *levels of selection*. There is some ambiguity in early evolutionary writers, including Darwin, about the level at which natural selection operates. Darwin's own summary of the theory, quoted earlier, suggests that natural selection promotes variations that are advantageous to *individuals* that possess them, but elsewhere he seems to entertain the possibility of 'group selection': that natural selection can promote characteristics favourable to whole *groups*, even if those characteristics are not advantageous to the individuals that display them.[24] In the early 1960s, V. C. Wynne-Edwards proposed a group-selectionist account of evolution, but the publication a few years later of George Williams's influential *Adaptation and Natural Selection* led to the general rejection of group selection as a significant factor in evolution: most evolutionists agree that it will usually have far too weak an effect to be a significant factor in evolution compared with the much stronger effect of individual selection.[25] In the 1970s, Richard Dawkins took Williams's argument a stage further and argued that the *gene* should be regarded as the fundamental level of selection. Although early on he presented this argument simply as a shift in perspective that could yield useful insights, his more recent accounts have tended to make stronger claims for this 'gene's-eye'

---

22 Ayala, 'The Evolution of Life', pp. 52–5.

23 See Tomoko Ohta, 'The Current Significance and Standing of Neutral and Nearly Neutral Theories', *BioEssays*, 18 (1996), pp. 673–7, and Martin Kreitman, 'The Neutral Theory Is Dead. Long Live the Neutral Theory', *BioEssays*, 18 (1996), pp. 678–82; both reprinted in Ridley, *Evolution* (Oxford Readers), pp. 94–100 and 100–8 respectively; also Mark Ridley, *Evolution*, 3rd edn, Oxford: Blackwell, 2003, ch. 7, and online material on the neutral theory at http://www.blackwellpublishing. com/ridley/tutorials/Molecular_evolution_and_neutral_theory1.asp (accessed 16 July 2006).

24 One context, particularly relevant to this book, in which he makes the latter suggestion, is in his discussion of the evolution of morality: see, e.g., *Descent*, pp. 166–7.

25 George C. Williams, *Adaptation and Natural Selection*, Oxford: Oxford University Press, 1966; for a summary and discussion, see Gould, *Structure*, pp. 554–6.

view of evolution.[26] Dawkins's gene-selectionism gave rise to his most famous, most criticized and probably most frequently misunderstood metaphor: 'a predominant quality to be expected in a successful gene is *ruthless selfishness*'.[27] By this Dawkins meant that a gene that is successful at surviving and producing copies of itself will be one that can produce effects that are advantageous to it. 'Success' for most genes these days requires cooperation with thousands of other genes to build 'survival machines' – microorganisms, plants and animals, including humans – that do an effective job of replicating and spreading the genes that have 'built' them. Very often, the 'selfishness' of animals' genes will give rise to selfish behaviour in individual animals, but not always: one of the sources of Dawkins's account was William Hamilton's theory, which will be discussed in Chapter 4, that a 'gene for' altruistic behaviour towards kin could in some circumstances survive and spread in a population. In Dawkins's language, it might 'achieve its own selfish goals' by promoting altruistic behaviour on the part of its 'survival machine'.[28]

Since the publication of *The Selfish Gene*, Dawkins has frequently been accused of – among other things – using the metaphor of 'selfishness' in a careless and equivocal manner liable to confuse and mislead, presenting models of behaviour that are over-simplified abstractions with little empirical support, and defining the concept of 'the gene' in a way not well supported by more carefully done genetics. He and others have equally vigorously defended the selfish-gene view of evolution as an expression of evolutionary orthodoxy, and a perfectly mainstream example of the way in which biologists use models and theoretical abstractions to simplify complex problems.[29] More generally, Williams's argument that levels of selection above the individual are insignificant for evolution, though widely accepted since the 1960s, has recently been called into question by various authors. As I shall describe in Chapter 4, some evolutionists have recently argued that group selection *could* have

26 Richard Dawkins, *The Selfish Gene*, 2nd edn, Oxford: Oxford University Press, 1989 (1976), pp. x–xi.
27 Dawkins, *The Selfish Gene*, p. 2 (emphasis added).
28 *The Selfish Gene*, pp. xi, 2, 20. The scare-quotes around the words 'gene for', here and in subsequent chapters, indicate that the 'genes' in theoretical discussions such as Hamilton's are theoretical abstractions devised for the purposes of mathematical modelling, not identifiable stretches of DNA that could be extracted and sequenced.
29 For an early and particularly trenchant critique, see Mary Midgley, 'Gene-juggling', *Philosophy*, 54 (1979), pp. 439–58; see also Dawkins's reply, 'In Defence of Selfish Genes', *Philosophy*, 56 (1979), pp. 556–73, and Midgley's response, 'Selfish Genes and Social Darwinism', *Philosophy*, 58 (1983), pp. 365–77. All are online at http://www.royalinstitutephilosophy.org/articles/ (accessed 13 August 2006).

been a significant factor in human evolution, and could, among other things, account for aspects of human morality. More generally, Steven Jay Gould and others have argued for a hierarchical view in which evolution operates at a number of levels, including those of the gene, the cell, the organism, the group and the species.[30]

What of human origins?[31] Our nearest living relatives are the great apes, and in particular chimpanzees and bonobos, which are more closely related to humans than they are to gorillas or orang-utans. Molecular genetic evidence suggests that the human and chimpanzee lineages diverged around 5–6 million years (Myr) ago. A number of fossils of early hominid species have been found, the oldest (*Ardipithecus ramidus*) around 4.4 Myr old. However, Camilo Cela-Conde observes that it is very difficult to reconstruct the evolutionary relationships between these early hominid species unambiguously and to work out the details of our own species' direct ancestry.[32] The genus *Homo* (which includes our own species, *Homo sapiens*) appeared in the fossil record 1.8 Myr ago with the first remains of *Homo erectus*. Prior to *H. erectus*, hominids seem to have been confined to Africa, but *H. erectus* fossils have also been found in Asia, the Middle East and Europe. The transition from *H. erectus* to *H. sapiens* is thought to have occurred around 400,000 years ago. There is also fossil evidence in Europe and the Middle East for the presence of Neanderthal hominids (*H. neanderthalensis*) from 200,000 years ago until around 40,000 years ago. The relationship between Neanderthals and modern humans is unclear, though there is evidence that the latter are not the direct descendants of Neanderthals. There is also disagreement as to the origins of modern humans. Some scientists hold that a transition from *H. erectus* to archaic and then modern forms of *H. sapiens* took place in various parts of the world, which would have required migration and interbreeding from time to time between populations in widely separated regions. However, a variety of molecular biological evidence leads others to believe that all modern humans are descended from a small population in Africa (or perhaps the Middle East) very roughly 200,000 years ago.

Since the beginnings of Darwinism, evolutionists have theorized about the origins of human behaviour and culture as well as physical charac-

---

30 Gould, *Structure*, pp. 681–714; see also Niles Eldredge, *Reinventing Darwin: The Great Evolutionary Debate*, London: Phoenix, 1996.

31 For what follows, see Ayala, 'The Evolution of Life', pp. 55–7, and Camilo J. Cela-Conde, 'The Hominid Evolutionary Journey: A Summary', in Russell *et al.*, *Evolutionary and Molecular Biology*, pp. 59–78.

32 Cela-Conde, 'The Hominid Evolutionary Journey', pp. 63–9.

teristics. Such theorizing took a new turn from the 1960s onwards with the work of theoretical biologists such as William Hamilton and Robert Trivers, who proposed mathematical models for the evolution of various behavioural traits in humans and other animals. As is well known, one major focus of their work was the evolution of altruistic behaviour, and I shall return to their theories about altruism in later chapters. In a series of books first published in the 1970s, the entomologist Edward O. Wilson coined the term 'sociobiology' to describe this evolutionary approach to animal and human behaviour,[33] and claimed that it could transform our self-understanding:

> Without it, the humanities and social sciences are the limited descriptors of surface phenomena . . . With it, human nature can be laid open as an object of fully empirical research . . . and our self-conception can be enormously and truthfully enriched.[34]

The discipline of sociobiology has been controversial from the outset, though it has attracted many adherents, not all inclined to make such ambitious or reductive claims as those found in Wilson's early books. Sociobiology has also encouraged the development of other similar approaches to behaviour and culture, notably evolutionary psychology (EP).[35] In common with Wilsonian sociobiology, the ambition of EP is to explain human psychology, behaviour and culture in terms of the interaction of our genes with our environment. However, it makes a number of distinctive claims, including the following:[36] (1) the human mind is made up of a large number of quite specific functions, often referred to in the EP literature as 'mental modules' or 'mental organs', and understood largely as information-processing mechanisms;[37]

---

33 Edward O. Wilson, *The Insect Societies*, Cambridge, MA: Harvard University Press, 1971; *Sociobiology: The New Synthesis*, abridged edn, Cambridge, MA: Harvard University Press, 1980 (1975); *On Human Nature*, Cambridge, MA: Harvard University Press, 1978.

34 Wilson, *On Human Nature*, p. 2.

35 For a collection of papers presented as a manifesto for EP, see Jerome H. Barkow, Leda Cosmides and John Tooby (eds.), *The Adapted Mind: Evolutionary Psychology and the Generation of Culture*, New York: Oxford University Press, 1992. Note that evolutionary psychologists often take pains to distinguish their discipline from sociobiology, while acknowledging that the two have much in common: see, e.g., Steven Pinker, *How the Mind Works*, London: Penguin, 1998, pp. 41–2.

36 See John Tooby and Leda Cosmides, 'The Psychological Foundations of Culture', in Barkow *et al.*, *The Adapted Mind*, pp. 19–136, and Pinker, *How the Mind Works*, pp. 3–58.

37 Pinker spells out the importance of the 'computational theory of mind' for EP: *How the Mind Works*, pp. 21–7.

(2) these functions are universal across all human societies and cultures; (3) they have evolved as adaptations in response to specific selection pressures acting on our evolutionary ancestors; (4) by far the most significant period for the evolution of the human mind is the Pleistocene (1.8 Myr–10,000 years ago), during which our ancestors lived as hunter-gatherers – mental functions have evolved to be adaptive for Pleistocene hunter-gatherer life, which means that they are *not* necessarily adaptive for life in agricultural, industrial or post-industrial societies;[38] (5) the rich complexity and diversity of human social behaviour and culture arises, not because humans are 'blank slates' or from the general flexibility of the human mind, but because behaviour and culture are 'generated by an incredibly intricate, contingent set of functional programs that use and process information from the world, including information that is provided both intentionally and unintentionally by other human beings'.[39]

Some of these specific claims of EP – for example, the notion of 'mental modules', the strictly computational model of the mind and the view that the Pleistocene was *the* overwhelmingly important 'environment of evolutionary adaptation' – have been called into question.[40] More generally, some biologists, social scientists and philosophers have developed a number of criticisms that apply more or less equally to sociobiology, EP and similar attempts to connect human evolutionary history with human psychology, behaviour and culture. Some of the most important criticisms of such theories can briefly be summarized as follows:[41]

I *They present a simplistic picture of the relationship between genes and behaviour, thereby promoting an equally simplistic biological determinism.* This is particularly evident in the language of 'a gene for' some behaviour or other – altruism, adultery, etc. – which is sometimes used quite deliberately by theoretical biologists as a simplification for

---

38 Leda Cosmides, John Tooby and Jerome H. Barkow, 'Introduction: Evolutionary Psychology and Conceptual Integration', in Barkow *et al.*, *The Adapted Mind*, pp. 3–15 (pp. 5–6).

39 Tooby and Cosmides, 'The Psychological Foundations of Culture', p. 24.

40 See, e.g., Barbara Herrnstein Smith, 'Sewing Up the Mind: The Claims of Evolutionary Psychology', in Hilary Rose and Steven Rose (eds.), *Alas Poor Darwin: Arguments against Evolutionary Psychology*, London: Jonathan Cape, 2000, pp. 129–43; Annette Karmiloff-Smith, 'Why Babies' Brains Are Not Swiss Army Knives', in Rose and Rose, *Alas Poor Darwin*, pp. 144–56; Hrdy, *Mother Nature*, pp. 96–117.

41 For what follows, see, e.g.: Eldredge, *Reinventing Darwin*; Gould, *Structure*, Part II; Rose and Rose, *Alas, Poor Darwin*; Steven Rose, *Lifelines: Life beyond the Gene*, 2nd edn, London: Vintage, 2005.

the purposes of mathematical modelling, and sometimes much more carelessly by popular writers on evolution. (It should be noted that evolutionary psychologists distance themselves from this language, arguing that genes do not produce behaviour, and behaviour does not evolve: behaviour is generated by *minds*, and *minds* are the product of genes, interacting with one another and with the environment, which have evolved to be the way they are under the influence of natural selection.)[42] Critics of reductionist and determinist evolutionary theorizing emphasize the complexity and subtlety of the relationship between genotype and phenotype:[43] almost any phenotypic feature, and certainly any behavioural feature, is influenced by a large number of genes. Gene sequences themselves are subject to complex processes of cutting, splicing and editing; the expression of genes, which depends on a highly sophisticated set of cellular 'machinery', is very precisely regulated according to cell type and developmental stage, so that gene products are made when, where and in the quantities in which they are needed. An individual's phenotype will be influenced not only by his or her genes but also by the course taken by his or her embryonic and foetal development, which is affected by a wide variety of factors. Human behaviour, of course, is crucially dependent on the human brain, an organ of phenomenal complexity and developmental plasticity, whose development, both before and after birth, is influenced in subtle and profound ways not only by genes and developmental pathways but also by the particular, contingent features of the individual's interactions with others and with his or her physical and living 'environment'.

2   *They rely on an over-simplified 'adaptationist' view of evolution.* No-one disputes that adaptive change under the influence of natural selection is *part* of what drives evolution; the issue is the relative importance of adaptation and other causes of evolutionary change. Sociobiologists and evolutionary psychologists tend to assume that most or all evolutionary change is the result of adaptation in direct response to selection pressures (the existence of other, non-adaptive, causes of evolutionary change is acknowledged, but their significance is played down). This assumption underlies the EP approach of 'reverse engineering', in which one observes a particular behaviour, infers the existence

---

42 See Pinker, *How the Mind Works*, p. 42.

43 'Genotype' is standardly defined as 'all or part of the genetic constitution of an individual or group', and 'phenotype' as 'the observable properties of an organism that are produced by the interaction of the genotype and the environment': *MedLine Plus Medical Dictionary*, online at http://www.nlm.nih.gov/medlineplus/mplusdictionary. html (accessed 18 July 2006).

of a 'mental module' that gives rise to that behaviour and asks what challenge in the ancestral environment that 'module' was 'designed' by natural selection to meet. Adaptationism is often said to be the neo-Darwinian 'orthodoxy'. If so, it is an orthodoxy that has been vigorously challenged over the years by critics such as Stephen Jay Gould, who argues for a 'pluralist' view of evolution that gives full weight to other causes of evolutionary change.[44] These include genetic drift, 'architectural' constraints imposed by the organism's 'body plan' and its embryonic development (there might simply not be that much scope for variation in the way that a four-limbed terrestrial vertebrate, for example, is put together), non-adaptive side-effects of other adaptive changes (which is part of what Darwin meant by 'correlation of growth') and 'exaptation' – that is, the later, adaptive 'co-option' and use of features that originally resulted from other adaptive or non-adaptive causes (a good example is the flattened head of a species of African tree-dwelling lizard, which seems to have arisen as an adaptation for hunting and hiding under tree bark, and later been co-opted as an aerofoil surface that helps the lizard glide between trees).[45]

3 *The empirical support for sociobiological and evolutionary-psychological theories is poor.* Some, for instance, depend on highly speculative reconstructions of human evolutionary history, for which relevant data may be hard to come by; others are not specific enough to yield testable predictions, making them hard to refute, but also scientifically uninformative; still others do fit the available data well, but their proponents have not shown that they explain the data better than alternative hypotheses. Popular sociobiological and EP literature, in particular, is castigated for incautious theorizing and speculation that sometimes amounts to little more than 'Just So' storytelling.

4 *They give unsatisfactory accounts of human behaviour.*[46] For example, dynamic interactions between individuals are reified by giving them a label that classifies them as static, fixed phenomena ('aggression', 'altruism' and so forth). Tendentious parallels are sometimes made between the behaviour of humans and that of other animals – as I shall note in Chapter 6, for instance, there is controversy about the use of

---

44 The founding charter of Gould's pluralist approach could be identified as S. J. Gould and R. C. Lewontin, 'The Spandrels of San Marco and the Panglossian Paradigm: A Critique of the Adaptationist Programme', *Proceedings of the Royal Society of London*, series B, 205 (1979), pp. 581–98, reprinted in Ridley, *Evolution* (Oxford Readers), pp. 139–54.

45 See Gould, *Structure*, pp. 1235–6.

46 On this point, see especially Rose, *Lifelines*, pp. 278–99.

terms like 'rape', 'battering' and 'infanticide' to describe non-human animal behaviours.[47] Furthermore, very different kinds of human inter-action in widely varying social contexts (for instance, 'aggressive out-bursts, arson, attempted rape and exhibitionism')[48] are lumped together as examples of the same phenomenon ('aggression', in this example) and held to be the products of the same genetic cause, biochemical abnormality, mental module or evolutionary adaptation.

5   *They obscure the distinction between proximal and distal causes of social problems.*[49] It may be that part of the explanation for the fact that some people in particular circumstances behave as they do (vio-lently and aggressively, for example) lies in some aspect of human evolutionary history. But that is not to say that the evolutionary history amounts to a *cause* of the behaviour – it might just have made the behav-iour *possible*. To focus attention on evolutionary causes or explanations runs the risk of ignoring much more obvious and direct 'proximal' causes. This could have various bad results. One is the stigmatization of individuals or groups who are believed to be predisposed by their genes or their biochemistry towards some problematic kind of behaviour. Another is that attention might be diverted away from the most obvious and promising means of addressing the problem: limiting the avail-ability of firearms, for example, might be a much more effective way of reducing the homicide rate than speculating about the evolutionary roots of violence among young men.

Some critics, such as Steven Rose, hold that these features of socio-biological and evolutionary psychological theories make it all too easy for such theories to be put to ideological uses in which the theory is shaped by social stereotypes and prejudices, and is then used to justify those same stereotypes and prejudices.[50] It is beyond the scope of this book to attempt to adjudicate on the scientific disagreements between sociobiologists, evolutionary psychologists and their critics. However, some of the criticisms summarized here will be in the background of my discussion of evolutionary theories about altruism in Chapter 4, and in Chapter 6 I shall assess some specific claims about the evolutionary roots of various morally problematic kinds of behaviour in the light of

---

47 See below, p. 134, n. 4.

48 Rose, *Lifelines*, p. 281, citing H. G. Brunner *et al.*, 'Abnormal Behavior Associated with a Point Mutation in the Structural Gene for Monoamine Oxidase A', *Science*, 262 (1993), pp. 578–80.

49 See especially Rose, *Lifelines*, pp. 296–9.

50 See Rose, *Lifelines*, pp. 278–99.

these criticisms, asking to what extent the claims under discussion stand or fall by the validity of the critique.

As I have already observed, the evolutionary origins of morality and the significance of evolution for ethics have been a preoccupation of evolutionists interested in human behaviour ever since Darwin.[51] To some aspects of the long and complex discussion of these matters, I now turn.

---

51 Since many of my sources do not make a clear distinction between 'ethics' and 'morality', I shall not attempt to distinguish between these two terms in an entirely consistent or hard-and-fast way either, though, so far as the context allows, I shall tend to reserve the term 'ethics' for the study of, or reflection upon, morality. In order to avoid sowing too much confusion, I shall do my best to avoid undue equivocation and ambiguity in my use of these terms.

Part 1

Mapping the Territory

2

Evolution and Ethics

What, if anything, is the significance of evolutionary biology for ethics? In 1990, the philosopher James Rachels complained that the majority of his colleagues had largely ignored Darwinism, believing it irrelevant to philosophy.[1] Whatever the truth of his complaint at that time, recent years have seen a spate of writing and speculation on the moral significance of human evolution. In this literature, a number of different issues are raised, but are not always clearly articulated or differentiated from one another. The present chapter is a mapping exercise, an attempt to characterize as clearly as possible the various issues for ethics that are raised in the literature on evolution and ethics.

To bring some clarity to this sometimes diffuse discussion, I shall take as my guide one of the earliest sustained accounts of the ethical significance of evolution, Thomas Henry Huxley's Romanes Lecture of 1893, 'Evolution and Ethics'.[2] This may seem a surprising choice, since there is much in the picture of human origins now offered by evolutionary biology that Huxley did not, and could not, know about: for example, he did not know of Mendel's work on inheritance and pre-dated the 'modern synthesis' of Darwinism with Mendelian genetics, and the contributions of molecular biology and theoretical biology outlined in the last chapter did not begin until more than half a century after Huxley's death. Furthermore, there may be some justice in David Goslee's claim that Huxley's own answers to the questions he raised about evolution and ethics were marked by internal tension and equivocation.[3] Nonetheless, the Romanes Lecture strikingly and presciently anticipates most, if not all, of the major issues that can be found in discussions of evolution

---

1 James Rachels, *Created from Animals: The Moral Implications of Darwinism*, Oxford: Oxford University Press, 1990, p. 2.

2 Thomas Henry Huxley, 'Evolution and Ethics' (The Romanes Lecture, 1893), in *Evolution and Ethics and Other Essays (Collected Essays,* vol. 9), London: Macmillan, 1894, pp. 46–116; also online at http://alepho.clarku.edu/huxley/CE9/ (accessed 14 December 2005).

3 David Goslee, 'Evolution, Ethics and Equivocation: T. H. Huxley's Conflicted Legacy', *Zygon*, 39.1 (2004), pp. 137–60.

and ethics a century later. Later in this chapter, the argument of the lecture will be summarized and the questions it raises identified; before doing either of these things, however, it is worth briefly setting 'Evolution and Ethics' in the intellectual context of its time.

I 'Evolution and Ethics' in context

Darwin studiously avoided mentioning human evolution in the *Origin*, except for a throwaway remark in the concluding chapter: 'Psychology will be based on a new foundation, that of the necessary acquirement of each mental power and capacity by gradation. Light will be thrown on the origin of man and his history.'[4] However, it seems clear that this omission was for tactical reasons, to ease the *Origin*'s reception and avoid the controversy that would have attended direct speculation about the origin and nature of humankind. Darwin's notebooks show that he had human origins in view from the beginnings of his work on evolution.[5] His contemporaries were not slow to make the connection, as evidenced by the famous and much-mythologized British Association debate in Oxford in 1860, whose high point is supposed to have been a titanic clash between Huxley and Samuel Wilberforce, the Bishop of Oxford, on the subject of human ancestry from apes.[6] In fact, Darwin's

---

4 Charles Darwin, *The Origin of Species by Means of Natural Selection, or the Preservation of Favoured Races in the Struggle for Life*, 1st edn, ed. with an introduction by J. W. Burrow, London: Penguin, 1968 (1859), p. 458.

5 Adrian Desmond and James Moore, *Darwin*, London: Penguin, 1992, pp. 243–4.

6 Historians frequently point out that contemporary accounts of the debate are so scarce and contradictory that it is extremely difficult to know what really happened: see, e.g., John Hedley Brooke, 'The Huxley–Wilberforce Debate: Why Did It Happen?', *Science and Christian Belief*, 13.2 (2001), pp. 127–41, also online with a discussion at http://www.st-edmunds.cam.ac.uk/cis/brooke/index.html (accessed 14 December 2005). Adrian Desmond reports the version given in a letter of Huxley from 1860: Wilberforce asked him whether he traced his descent from apes on his grandfather's or grandmother's side; 'If then, said I, the question is put to me would I rather have a miserable ape for a grandfather or a man highly endowed by nature and possessed of great means of influence & yet who employs these faculties & that influence for the mere purpose of introducing ridicule into a grave scientific discussion, I unhesitatingly affirm my preference for the ape', T. H. Huxley to Frederick Dyster, 9 September 1860, quoted by Adrian Desmond, *Huxley: From Devil's Disciple to Evolution's High Priest*, London: Penguin, 1998, p. 279. But Joseph Hooker's account of the same event made Huxley's part insignificant and Hooker himself the victor over Wilberforce: Brooke, 'The Huxley–Wilberforce Debate', p. 128; Desmond, *Huxley*, p. 280. The simple version of the myth, in which Huxley routed Soapy Sam and the forces of ecclesiastical obscurantism, is still repeated all too uncritically by some who should know better: see, e.g., Rachels, *Created from Animals*, pp. 47–9. For a recent

theory of natural selection and his throwaway remarks about human origins fitted neatly into debates about human evolution that were already underway by the late 1850s. As Huxley noted in the preface to the 1894 edition of his book *Man's Place in Nature* (originally published in 1863), by the end of the 1850s he was already convinced, on the grounds of comparative anatomy, of the close relationship between humans and the great apes.[7] Much of *Man's Place in Nature* is taken up with detailed anatomical, palaeontological and other evidence for this relationship, and Darwinian natural selection is presented towards the end of the second chapter as the only theory that can plausibly account for it.[8] Also by the end of the 1850s, Herbert Spencer had sketched out his grand project to unify the disciplines of biology, psychology, sociology and ethics on the basis of a theory of evolution – a project subsequently worked out at great length in his *System of Synthetic Philosophy*.[9] Spencer first outlined his concept of evolution in 1857,[10] and, although he incorporated Darwin's theory of natural selection into his account after the publication of the *Origin*, his evolutionary theory remained at least as much Lamarckian as Darwinian throughout the *Synthetic Philosophy*.[11] It was Spencer, not Darwin, who coined the phrase 'the survival of the fittest' (though Darwin incorporated it into later editions of the *Origin*), and Spencer was one of the first to speculate about the relevance of evolution and the survival of the fittest to ethics, society and politics. Notoriously, the survival of the fittest was one of the grounds (though only one) on which he advocated an extreme *laissez-faire* individualism and opposed social welfare for the poor: the latter would 'interfere with the natural order of things' by which 'society is constantly excreting its unhealthy, imbecile, slow, vacillating, faithless

---

reconsideration of the debate, see J. R. Lucas and Janet Browne, 'The Huxley–Wilberforce Debate Revisited', 6 November 2003, online at http://users.ox.ac.uk/~jrlucas/revisit.html (accessed 4 August 2006).

7 Huxley, *Man's Place in Nature* (*Collected Essays*, vol. 7), London: Macmillan, 1894, pp. vi–ix, online at http://alepho.clarku.edu/huxley/CE7/ (accessed 14 December 2005).

8 Huxley, *Man's Place*, pp. 147–50.

9 Herbert Spencer, *The System of Synthetic Philosophy*, 10 vols, London and Edinburgh: Williams and Norgate, 1860–93.

10 Spencer, 'Progress: Its Law and Causes', *The Westminster Review*, 67 (April 1857), abridged version online at http://www.fordham.edu/halsall/mod/spencer-darwin.html (accessed 14 December 2005).

11 'Lamarckian', not so much in the sense of holding that acquired characteristics could be inherited, as in the sense – much more central to Lamarck's own evolutionary theory, and denied by Darwinism – that the evolutionary process is progressive, having inherent in it a drive towards ever more perfect forms of life.

members'.[12] It was this strain in Spencer's thought that earned him the dubious reputation of the 'father of social Darwinism' (though the term 'social Darwinism' originated in France somewhat later and did not come into use in Britain until the mid 1890s)[13] and endeared him to American businessmen like Andrew Carnegie and John D. Rockefeller, eager to justify *laissez-faire* capitalism by appeal to the survival of the fittest. But there was more to Spencer's thought on evolution and ethics than just the survival of the fittest. His *Data of Ethics* contains one of the earliest sustained attempts to develop an ethical system on the basis of evolution,[14] an attempt which will be discussed further in Chapter 5.

Spencer was by no means alone in speculating about the relevance of evolution to social and political life. As early as the 1860s, a number of evolutionists were considering the significance of natural selection for these matters.[15] For example, Alfred Russel Wallace, the co-discoverer with Darwin of the theory of natural selection, believed that those human populations whose members were rational and altruistic would thereby gain a selective advantage over others, with the result that these qualities would spread and prevail. (Reflecting the widespread racism of his colonialist times, he also believed that this process would result in the extinction of native populations in the Americas and Australasia, thanks to the 'superior' intellectual and moral qualities of European colonists.)[16] Again, Darwin's cousin Francis Galton argued at some length that intelligence and character were hereditary, but feared that the intelligent, hard-working and forward-looking were being outbred in modern society by the stupid, idle and reckless, and that the general quality of the population would therefore decline over time.[17] Others

---

12 Spencer, *Social Statics; or the Conditions Essential to Human Happiness Specified and the First of Them Developed*, London: Chapman, 1851, pp. 323–4, quoted by Michael Ruse, *Can a Darwinian Be a Christian? The Relationship between Science and Religion*, Cambridge: Cambridge University Press, 2001, p. 171.

13 Desmond, *Huxley*, p. 575.

14 Herbert Spencer, *The Data of Ethics*, London: Williams and Norgate, 1884 (1879), pp. 3–46.

15 Diane B. Paul, 'Darwin, Social Darwinism and Eugenics', in Jonathan Hodge and Gregory Radick (eds), *The Cambridge Companion to Darwin*, Cambridge: Cambridge University Press, 2003, pp. 214–39 (pp. 215–17).

16 Alfred Russel Wallace, 'The Origin of Human Races and the Antiquity of Man Deduced From the Theory of "Natural Selection"', *Journal of the Anthropological Society of London*, 2 (1864), pp. clviii–clxxxvii, online at http://www.wku.edu/~smithch/wallace/S093.htm (accessed 14 December 2005).

17 Francis Galton, 'Hereditary Talent and Character', *Macmillan's Magazine*, 12 (1865), pp. 157–66, 318–27, online at http://galton.org/essays/1860-1869/galton-1865-hereditary-talent.pdf (accessed 14 December 2005); Paul, 'Darwin, Social Darwinism and Eugenics', pp. 216–17.

speculating along similar lines included Walter Bagehot and William Greg.[18] In the *Descent of Man*, Darwin addressed himself to this discussion, responding explicitly to Wallace, Galton, Bagehot and Greg.[19] He agreed with Wallace that intelligence and morality would have conferred a selective advantage on humans during our evolutionary history, but also with Galton and others that, in civilized societies, medicine and social care preserved many of the 'weak in body or mind' who would otherwise have died out, and that 'this must be highly injurious to the race of man'.[20] However, neither Darwin nor Galton advocated coercive measures to prevent the 'weak' from 'propagat[ing] their kind'; Darwin argued that to do so would require us to suppress that 'sympathy' which is one of the most valuable parts of our evolutionary inheritance. Rather, they both hoped that a change in social mores would slowly alter the balance of the population in the kind of direction they considered favourable.[21] Diane Paul has argued that coercive and violent programmes of 'eugenics' came later, only related to Darwin's thought by strange and tortuous routes.[22]

Huxley himself first entered the territory of the moral and social implications of evolution well before the date of the Romanes Lecture. In particular, in his 1888 essay 'The Struggle for Existence in Human Society', he argued that primitive human existence, like that of other animals, had been a 'Hobbesian war of each against all';[23] even if industrialized societies managed to create the conditions of peace, population growth would inevitably result in competition for scarce resources and

---

18 Paul, 'Darwin, Social Darwinism and Eugenics', p. 217.

19 Charles Darwin, *The Descent of Man, and Selection in Relation to Sex*, London: John Murray, 1871, repr. with introduction by John Tyler Bonner and Robert M. May, Princeton, NJ: Princeton University Press, 1981, pp. 158–84.

20 Darwin, *Descent*, p. 168. One contrast implicit in these discussions, but not clearly articulated until the later twentieth century, is between what would now be called individual-selectionist and group-selectionist approaches: Wallace's argument, for example, is broadly group-selectionist, whereas Galton's is individual-selectionist.

21 *Descent*, pp. 168–9; Paul, 'Darwin, Social Darwinism and Eugenics', pp. 218–23.

22 Paul, 'Darwin, Social Darwinism and Eugenics', pp. 231–7. For a different emphasis, see Stephen R. L. Clark, *Biology and Christian Ethics*, Cambridge: Cambridge University Press, 2000, who, though he agrees (p. 197) with Paul's specific point, tends to place more stress on the problematic relationships between Darwinism and various dubious kinds of ideological thinking. Anthony O'Hear is even less inclined to exonerate Darwin of giving aid and comfort to racist eugenics: *Beyond Evolution: The Limits of Evolutionary Explanation*, Oxford: Oxford University Press, 1997, pp. 133–6.

23 Thomas Henry Huxley, 'The Struggle for Existence in Human Society', in *Evolution and Ethics and Other Essays (Collected Essays*, vol. 9), pp. 195–236 (p. 204). See also his 1886 essay 'Science and Morals', in *Collected Essays*, vol. 9, pp. 117–46.

would reinstate this Malthusian struggle for existence. Spencer, as we have seen, based a moral and political case for individualism and *laissez-faire* on this ground. By contrast Huxley, apparently under the influence of Hume, refused to read moral norms off this supposedly natural state of affairs, and began to differentiate between the 'ethical' and the 'natural': nature, which gave rise to pain and misery as well as beauty and pleasure, was 'non-moral'.[24] Accordingly, his response to the 'struggle for existence in human society' was diametrically opposed to Spencer's: he called for public health and welfare provision and a system of technical education supported by local taxation. He advocated these measures both in order to mitigate the worst effects of the struggle for existence within British urban populations and to equip the British population as well as possible in that struggle as it manifested itself in international economic competition.[25] This essay was one of the markers of his increasing distance from Spencer; their long-standing friendship was ended abruptly the following year by a letter of Huxley to *The Times* attacking Spencer's political and social views.[26] Huxley's bleak view of the struggle for existence set him apart also from the émigré Russian anarchist Prince Petr Kropotkin, who was beginning to develop his well-known argument that mutual aid was a more important factor than individual self-assertion in the evolution of both animals and humans.[27] Kropotkin, like Spencer, was willing to draw ethical conclusions from his claims about evolution, but his conclusions were the very opposite of Spencer's:

> In the practice of mutual aid, which we can retrace to the earliest beginnings of evolution, we thus find the positive and undoubted

24 Huxley, 'The Struggle for Existence', pp. 196–7. On the illegitimacy of reading moral conclusions off nature, cf. David Hume, *A Treatise of Human Nature*, ed. by L. A. Selby-Bigge, rev. by P. H. Nidditch, Oxford: Clarendon Press, 1978 (1739–40), p. 469. Hume's influence on Huxley is evident in the latter's *Hume: With Helps to the Study of Berkeley* (*Collected Essays*, vol. 6), London: Macmillan, 1894 (1878), online at http://alepho.clarku.edu/huxley/CE6/index.html (accessed 14 December 2005).

25 The occasion for the essay was a public lecture in support of the city of Manchester's scheme to raise a local tax to fund technical education. Adrian Desmond draws attention to the complex background to this essay: Huxley was 'rationalizing pain in an industrial nation and policing the masses with Malthusian biology', yet also beginning to revolt morally against the bleak vision of nature that he inferred from evolution – bleakness that, according to Desmond, owed much to Huxley's grief over the insanity and death of his beloved daughter Mady; Desmond, *Huxley*, pp. 557–61.

26 Desmond, *Huxley*, pp. 573–4.

27 Petr Kropotkin, *Mutual Aid: A Factor of Evolution*, London: Heinemann, 1902, online at http://socserv2.socsci.mcmaster.ca/~econ/ugcm/3113/kropotkin/mutaid.txt (accessed 15 December 2005).

origin of our ethical conceptions; and we can affirm that in the ethical progress of man, mutual support not mutual struggle – has had the leading part. In its wide extension, even at the present time, we also see the best guarantee of a still loftier evolution of our race.[28]

Huxley disagreed, but sympathetically.[29]

In 1892, Huxley was invited by his friend George Romanes to deliver the second of the annual lectures endowed by the latter at Oxford University. The first Romanes Lecturer, in 1893, was to be Huxley's long-standing adversary William Gladstone, and Romanes was particularly anxious that Huxley should be the one to follow Gladstone. Though the statute establishing the lectures excluded religion and politics as subjects, Romanes suggested that 'much may be consigned under "science" and "philosophy"'.[30] Huxley was attracted both by the prospect of taking on his old opponent once again and by the opportunity to place on record his opposition to Spencer, and so proposed to lecture on 'Evolution and Ethics'. The lecture not only provoked a lively debate at the time but also set the agenda for much of the discussion of evolution and ethics in the subsequent century.[31] To the argument of that lecture I now turn.

2   The argument of 'Evolution and Ethics'

Huxley, ever the communicator and popularizer, begins his lecture with an illustration drawn from the children's story 'Jack and the Beanstalk'. In the life of a bean plant, he says, we see a cyclical process in which an inert-seeming bean gives rise to a great plant, but the plant then withers and dies away, leaving only some more beans, as apparently inert as the first. He treats this cycle as a type of the cyclical process of evolutionary

28 Kropotkin, *Mutual Aid*, 'Conclusion'.
29 Desmond, *Huxley*, pp. 564–5.
30 Quoted by Desmond, *Huxley*, p. 591.
31 Early reaction to the Romanes Lecture included reviews by an anonymous reviewer ('The Romanes Lecture', *The Oxford Magazine*, 11 (24 May 1893), pp. 380–1), Leslie Stephen ('Ethics and the Struggle for Existence', *Contemporary Review*, 64 (August 1893), pp. 157–70) and Andrew Seth ('Man's Place in the Cosmos', *Blackwood's Edinburgh Magazine*, 154 (December 1893), pp. 823–34), all online at http://alepho.clarku.edu/huxley/bib2.html (accessed 16 December 2005). Huxley responded in the 'Prolegomena', published along with the Romanes Lecture in *Collected Essays*, vol. 9, available online at http://alepho.clarku.edu/huxley/CE9/E-EProl.html (accessed 15 December 2005). For discussion of the reviews and Huxley's response, see Goslee, 'Evolution, Ethics and Equivocation'.

change characteristic of the cosmos, in which growth and flourishing are followed by decline and decay. This process has given rise to great beauty and wonder, but also to great pain and suffering. Humankind, like other living things, is a product of the evolutionary process, and has prospered during evolutionary history by means of 'those qualities which he [*sc.* "man"] shares with the ape and the tiger; his exceptional physical organization; his cunning, his sociability, his curiosity, and his imitativeness; his ruthless and ferocious destructiveness when his anger is roused by opposition'.[32] But as humanity has become 'civilized' (or at any rate, as we have become 'ethical'), those qualities, which previously worked to the advantage of our species, have become 'defects'.

We are not the first, says Huxley, to ponder the significance of the cosmic evolutionary process for ethics: other civilizations and their thinkers have been here before us and have confronted 'the same dread problem of evil':

> They have also seen that the cosmic process is evolution; that it is full of wonder, full of beauty, and, at the same time, full of pain. They have sought to discover the bearing of these great facts on ethics; *to find out whether there is, or is not, a sanction for morality in the ways of the cosmos*. (p. 53, emphasis added)

The two ancient systems of thought that confronted this problem were Buddhism (together with Hinduism before it) and Stoicism. Huxley states the ethical problem with which they, like the civilization of ancient Israel, wrestled, as follows. *Justice* is one of the earliest ethical principles to emerge as civilization develops: human societies cannot do without it. Like Kropotkin, he observes that mutual trust and co-operation are needed even in the animal world, for example in wolf packs. Early human societies also depended on mutual trust and co-operation, and developed social sanctions against those of their members who violated that trust. As civilizations developed, these systems of social enforcement of trust and co-operation were refined into notions of punishment and reward according to desert. But justice, understood in this way, seems to be absent from the cosmic evolutionary process:

> If there is one thing plainer than another, it is that neither the pleasures nor the pains of life . . . are distributed according to desert . . . Thus, brought before the tribunal of ethics, the cosmos might well

---

32 Huxley, 'Evolution and Ethics', pp. 51–2. Further page references to this work in this and the next section are given in brackets in the text.

seem to stand condemned. The conscience of man revolted against the moral indifference of nature, and the microcosmic atom should have found the illimitable macrocosm guilty. But few, or none, ventured to record that verdict. (pp. 58–9)

According to Huxley, the ancient Indian response to this problem (first in Hinduism, then intensified in Buddhism) was to seek release from 'the illusive phantasmagoria of life': 'to refuse any longer to be the instruments of the evolutionary process, and withdraw from the struggle for existence' (p. 63). The Greek and Roman Stoics, in contrast, developed the view that 'the cosmos is the effect of an immanent, omnipotent, and infinitely beneficent cause', and therefore that 'the existence in it of real evil, still less of necessarily inherent evil, is plainly inadmissible' (p. 71). Therefore they had to account for the experience of evil in the world. This they did, he says, by developing *theodicies* that said 'firstly, that there is no such thing as evil; secondly, that if there is, it is the necessary correlate of good; and moreover, that it is either due to our own fault, or inflicted for our benefit' (pp. 71–2). The Stoics, as he reads them, held the view that, in Alexander Pope's words, 'whatever is is right', and that humans should 'live according to nature' (pp. 72, 73). But they were forced to admit the existence of evil in the world, which meant that 'even a passable approximation to that ideal was to be attained only at the cost of renunciation of the world and mortification, not only of the flesh, but of all human affections' (p. 76). Thus, the 'optimism' of the Stoics and the 'pessimism' of Buddhism amounted to much the same thing in the end: 'By the Tiber, as by the Ganges, ethical man admits that the cosmos is too strong for him; and, destroying every bond which ties him to it by ascetic discipline, he seeks salvation in absolute renunciation' (p. 77).

Huxley then turns to the modern debate, and rejects the extremes of 'optimism' and 'pessimism', both of which lead to ethical passivity and quietism, in favour of the commonsensical view that there are both good and evil in the world, and that human action is able to tip the balance towards greater good or greater evil. If that is the case, can an understanding of evolution help us in our efforts to tip the balance towards the good? Or, as he puts it:

Hence the pressing interest of the question, to what extent modern progress in natural knowledge, and, more especially, the general outcome of that progress in the doctrine of evolution, is competent to help us in the great work of helping one another? (p. 79)

He answers his own question with a resounding rebuttal of the 'ethics of evolution' advocated by Spencer and others. When they speculate about the 'ethics of evolution', he says, they are really talking about the 'evolution of ethics'. He has no difficulty in agreeing with them that evolutionary theory can, or will be able to, explain 'the origin of the moral sentiments',[33] but observes that 'the immoral sentiments have no less been evolved' (p. 79). This means that the Stoical injunction to 'follow nature' cannot give us any criteria for distinguishing between the moral and the immoral. Making explicit the Humean separation of 'ought' from 'is' that he earlier hinted at in 'The Struggle for Existence', he insists that

> Cosmic evolution may teach us how the good and the evil tendencies of man may have come about; but, in itself, it is incompetent to furnish any better reason why what we call good is preferable to what we call evil than we had before. (p. 80)

Huxley goes on to complain, in effect, that Spencer and other advocates of 'the ethics of evolution' fall foul of Hume's strictures against deriving an 'ought' from an 'is': they smuggle an element of evaluation into supposedly factual premises about evolution by using the phrase 'the survival of the fittest'. 'Fittest', in their writing, is made to mean something like 'best' or 'most perfect', whereas Huxley insists that, in an evolutionary context, it can only properly mean that which is most likely to survive under the prevailing conditions. When we consider humans, he thinks it is clear that 'fittest' does not mean morally 'best'. Humans have evolved by means of a struggle for existence in which '[t]he strongest, the most self-assertive, tend to tread down the weaker' (p. 81). We are still subject to the forces and influences that shaped this evolutionary struggle, but ethics, so far from taking its cue from these tendencies (as the advocates of 'the ethics of evolution' suggest) is *opposed* to them:

---

33 Huxley does not give a clear account of his own criteria for ethical judgement, but his use of the language of the 'moral sentiments' hints at metaethical debts to Hume and Adam Smith. The former debt is explicitly acknowledged in the final chapter of his essay on Hume (*Collected Essays*, vol. 6, pp. 228–40), and the latter in the more extended discussion of the evolution of the moral sentiments in the 'Prolegomena' (*Collected Essays*, vol. 9, pp. 26–33). These influences lead Michael Ruse to claim Huxley as a forerunner of his own ethical scepticism, though, as he acknowledges, Huxley's expressed views can hardly be taken as a whole-hearted endorsement of scepticism: Michael Ruse, 'Evolutionary Ethics in the Twentieth Century: Julian Sorrell Huxley and George Gaylord Simpson', in Jane Maienschein and Michael Ruse (eds.), *Biology and the Foundations of Ethics*, Cambridge: Cambridge University Press, 1999, pp. 198–224 (pp. 219–20).

the practice of that which is ethically best – what we call goodness or virtue – involves a course of action which, in all respects, is opposed to that which leads to success in the cosmic struggle for existence . . . its influence is directed, not so much to the survival of the fittest, as to the fitting of as many as possible to survive. (pp. 81–2)

This means that our evolved nature will not help us in our efforts to live ethically: rejecting the responses he has earlier attributed to Buddhism and Stoicism, Huxley exhorts his audience, 'Let us understand, once for all, that the ethical progress of society depends, not on imitating the cosmic process, still less in running away from it, but in combating it' (p. 83).

What is entailed by 'combating' the cosmic process? Huxley principally has in view the development of culture and 'civilization', by which societies place limits on the exercise of the instincts we share with 'the ape and the tiger' and enforce those limits by means of social and legal sanctions: that 'social progress' which 'means a checking of the cosmic process at every step and the substitution for it of another, which may be called the ethical process' (p. 81). But he also looks ahead to imagine a more direct application of science and technology in the service of ethics:

much may be done to change the nature of man himself. The intelligence which converted the brother of the wolf into the faithful guardian of the flock ought to be able to do something towards curbing the instincts of savagery in civilized man. (p. 85)

Huxley is no Panglossian. Commentators, rightly or wrongly, attribute the bleakness of his cosmic vision in 'The Struggle for Existence in Human Society' to traces of Calvinism inherited from his radical Dissenting background.[34] Whatever the truth of this, the Huxley of 'Evolution and Ethics' is clear that 'ethical man' has a fight on his (or her?) hands: 'Ethical nature may count upon having to reckon with a tenacious and powerful enemy as long as the world lasts' (p. 85). But he is now willing to express some cautious optimism about humanity's chances in the struggle: he sees 'no limit' to the scope of human efforts to 'modify the conditions of existence' (p. 85), and is even willing, as we have just seen, to speculate about more direct attempts to modify human nature. He closes with a call to arms: maturity means leaving behind the youthful illusion that we can and should attempt to escape from pain and sorrow, and instead being willing to fight the good fight,

---

34 Desmond, *Huxley*, pp. 559–61, 622–6.

'cherishing the good that falls in our way, and bearing the evil, in and around us, with stout hearts set on diminishing it' (p. 86).

3 The issues raised by 'Evolution and Ethics'

Huxley's treatment of evolution and ethics was the object of much discussion at the time, and has continued to attract scholarly commentary in the intervening years. Some contemporary reviewers drew attention to the internal tensions in his argument, suggesting that the position he wished to maintain between ethical idealism and materialism was inherently unstable and likely to collapse into one or the other.[35] More recent comment has sought also to contextualize Huxley and the Romanes Lecture personally, socially, culturally and politically. For example, the struggles and tragedies of his family life are said to have informed his vision of the savagery of nature and deterred him from utopian schemes to weed out the 'unfit' from society; or again, it is argued that his separation of 'ethical nature' from a 'cosmic nature' marked by competition and struggle allowed him to distance himself, not only from the *laissez-faire* individualism of Spencer, but also from Kropotkin's socialism, and served as a rationalization for his paternalistic brand of capitalism.[36] My present interest, however, is not primarily in these forms of analysis, but in his framing of the questions about evolution and ethics. As I have already suggested, the Romanes Lecture is one of the earliest reasonably clear statements of issues that have continued to preoccupy students of evolution and ethics in the intervening century. Six such issues may be identified that are raised, explicitly or implicitly, by Huxley's lecture.[37]

a Explanation

Can an evolutionary explanation be given for the existence and the particular characteristics of human morality?[38] By the time of 'Evolution

---

35 For a collapse into naturalism, see Stephen, 'Ethics and the Struggle for Existence'; into idealism, Seth, 'Man's Place'; for discussion, see Goslee, 'Evolution, Ethics and Equivocation', pp. 144–9.

36 Goslee, 'Evolution, Ethics and Equivocation'; Desmond, *Huxley*, pp. 583–9.

37 In what follows, I shall allude briefly to recent and current discussions that have taken up the issues raised by Huxley. These discussions will be described more fully in subsequent chapters.

38 Huxley tends to use the word 'ethics' to mean what I am referring to as 'morality': as I observed in Chapter 1 (n. 51), the two terms are often not clearly distinguished in these discussions.

and Ethics', there had already been considerable speculation about the evolutionary origins of morality. For example, Darwin devoted more than a chapter of the *Descent* to the evolution of the 'moral sense' and 'moral faculties'.[39] Huxley remarked of those who theorized in this way, 'I have little doubt, for my own part, that they are on the right track' (p. 79). But this endorsement points to a tension in his argument, as his reviewers were not slow to notice: he portrayed the evolutionary process as 'gladiatorial', one of 'ruthless self-assertion' and 'thrusting aside, or treading down, all competitors'; how then could such a process give rise to a morality that 'demands self-restraint' and 'requires that the individual shall not merely respect, but help, his fellows' (p. 82)? As Huxley himself later put it, 'ethical nature, while born of cosmic nature, is necessarily at enmity with its parent . . . this seeming paradox is a truth, as great as it is plain'.[40]

In more recent discussions, in the wake of the 'modern synthesis' of Darwinism with Mendelian genetics, this 'seeming paradox' has been expressed more sharply by focusing on the puzzle of altruistic behaviour – that is, behaviour by one individual that promotes others' interests rather than its own, perhaps even at the expense of its own. The theories of kin selection and reciprocal altruism, which will be outlined in Chapter 4, offer theoretical solutions to this puzzle by showing how 'genes for' altruistic behaviour towards kin and others could, under some circumstances, survive and spread in populations. On the strength of these theories, sociobiologists such as E. O. Wilson have answered the question of explanation in thoroughly reductionist terms: morality should eventually be entirely explicable in terms of the interaction of our genes with our environment.[41] Wilson's reductionism attracted a variety of stringent criticisms; in response to these, more recent authors such as Daniel Dennett have proposed more sophisticated reductionist schemes. Dennett still believes that a totally reductionist account, in which Darwinian 'descent with modification' is a universal explanatory principle, is possible but, in order to explain morality in these terms, he supplements biological evolution with Richard Dawkins's notion of 'memes' – ideas, thoughts, beliefs and so forth that evolve by means of a process of cultural selection analogous to the biological selection process identified by Darwin. As I shall note in Chapters 3 and 4, however, philosophers such as Mary Midgley and Holmes Rolston III find

---

39 Darwin, *Descent*, pp. 70–106, 161–7.

40 Huxley, *Collected Essays*, vol. 9, p. viii.

41 Edward O. Wilson, *On Human Nature*, Cambridge, MA: Harvard University Press, 1978, p. 167.

the concept of 'memes' uninformative and incoherent, and oppose the reductionism of Dennett and others.[42]

b   Justification

Is it possible to construct an 'ethic of evolution' – that is, to draw normative moral conclusions from putative facts about evolution? As I noted earlier, one of Huxley's chief complaints against evolutionary ethicists like Spencer was that they confused the 'evolution of ethics' with the 'ethics of evolution'; in other words, they failed to distinguish between questions of explanation and of justification. Huxley agreed with them about evolutionary explanation, but followed Hume in denying that they were entitled to derive a moral 'ought' from a biological 'is'. A little later, G. E. Moore developed a similar critique, finding Spencer guilty of what he called the 'naturalistic fallacy'.[43] Since the beginning of the twentieth century, Moore's critique of the naturalistic fallacy has commanded wide agreement. That, however, has not stopped some scientists and philosophers, who could be labelled 'naturalists', trying to base moral conclusions on facts about evolution. As I shall describe in more detail in Chapter 5, some – such as T. H. Huxley's grandson Julian and, more recently, E. O. Wilson – have more or less ignored the problem of the naturalistic fallacy. Others, such as the philosopher Robert J. Richards, do not ignore the problem, but nonetheless claim that it is possible to base moral conclusions on factual premises about evolution without committing a fallacy.[44]

A second group, who might, following Michael Ruse's self-description, be called 'sceptics', agrees that evolutionary biology can *explain* the phenomenon of morality, but denies that there can be any objective *justification* of moral claims. We have the moral instincts and beliefs that we do (for example, that we should co-operate with, and behave altruistically towards, one another) because those instincts and convic-

---

42 Mary Midgley, *The Ethical Primate: Humans, Freedom and Morality*, London: Routledge, 1994; id., 'Why Memes?', in Hilary Rose and Steven Rose (eds.), *Alas, Poor Darwin: Arguments against Evolutionary Psychology*, London: Jonathan Cape, 2000, pp. 67–84; Holmes Rolston III, *Genes, Genesis and God: Values and Their Origins in Natural and Human History*, Cambridge: Cambridge University Press, 1999 (p. 291).

43 G. E. Moore, *Principia Ethica*, Cambridge: Cambridge University Press, 1959 (1903), pp. 48–58.

44 Robert J. Richards, 'A Defense of Evolutionary Ethics', *Biology and Philosophy*, 1 (1986), pp. 265–93; reprinted as Appendix 2 of his *Darwin and the Emergence of Evolutionary Theories of Mind and Behavior*, Chicago: University of Chicago Press, 1987.

tions conferred a selective advantage upon our evolutionary ancestors; that is all. Ruse claims T. H. Huxley and the mid-twentieth-century palaeontologist G. G. Simpson as antecedents of his own sceptical stance, though he acknowledges that the evidence in support of his claim is at best ambiguous.[45]

A third kind of response to the question about justification is to *critique* all evolutionary ethics, whether of the 'naturalist' or the 'sceptical' kind. A leading critic is Peter G. Woolcock, who argues that Ruse's sceptical account gives fewer grounds for optimism about the persistence of morality than the latter thinks, and that 'naturalists' like Richards fail to avoid the naturalistic fallacy. He concludes by pulling a form of Rawlsian contractarianism out of the hat as his own favoured solution to the problem of moral justification.[46]

c   Content

What implications, if any, does evolutionary biology have for the content of normative ethics? As we have seen, early Darwinians and other evolutionary theorists were not slow to try and draw substantive moral conclusions from evolutionary theory. Michael Ruse portrays a bewilderingly diverse range of normative moral judgements that Victorian evolutionists sought to justify by appeal to evolution: from Spencer's anti-collectivism to Wallace's socialism and Kropotkin's anarchism; from the patriarchy of many evolutionists to Wallace's feminism; from Ernst Haeckel's militarism to Spencer's pacifism.[47] In his Romanes Lecture, Huxley did not attempt a systematic presentation of the content of ethics, but much of the last part of the lecture is a sustained attack on Spencerian individualism, and although Spencer was nowhere named, the intention was not lost on Huxley's target.[48]

Notwithstanding twentieth-century strictures against the naturalistic fallacy, those who have nonetheless attempted some form of evolutionary ethics have not been short of substantive, as well as methodological, proposals. To give just two examples, Julian Huxley made human control over the conditions of life in the world his key principle and

45 Ruse, 'Evolutionary Ethics in the Twentieth Century', p. 218; see also his *Taking Darwin Seriously*, Oxford: Blackwell, 1986, and 'The Significance of Evolution', in Peter Singer (ed.), *A Companion to Ethics*, Oxford: Blackwell, 1991, pp. 500–10.

46 Peter G. Woolcock, 'The Case against Evolutionary Ethics Today', in Maienschein and Ruse, *Biology and the Foundation of Ethics*, pp. 276–306.

47 Michael Ruse, *Can a Darwinian Be a Christian? The Relationship between Science and Religion*, Cambridge: Cambridge University Press, 2001, pp. 170–81.

48 Goslee, 'Evolution, Ethics and Equivocation', p. 146.

favoured state planning as a means to that end, and Edward O. Wilson argued that the central moral principles to be derived from a 'biologized' ethic would be tolerance, respect for human and bio-diversity, and universal human rights.[49] Many of the normative proposals that have been advanced would seem to fall foul of the naturalistic fallacy – if indeed it is a fallacy – but some philosophers approach the question of the significance of evolution for the content of ethics more indirectly. For example, James Rachels rejects any version of evolutionary ethics conducted after the manner of Spencer. Instead, he argues that the greatest significance of Darwinism for morality is that it undermines theistic and other supports of the doctrine of human dignity (that is, the notion that humans are set apart from animals and have a special moral status). The ethic he believes to be most consistent with Darwinism is *moral individualism*: 'an equal concern for the welfare of all beings' regardless of their species, 'with distinctions made among them only when there are relevant differences that justify differences in treatment'.[50] He holds that this view implies, among other things, the acceptance of suicide and euthanasia, vegetarianism, and the rejection of some, perhaps all, animal experimentation.

d Moral capability and its limits

In our efforts to live as we know (or believe) we ought, does our evolutionary inheritance help or hinder us, or is it simply irrelevant? T. H. Huxley was in no doubt that our evolutionary heritage is a significant moral problem for us: in the Romanes Lecture, he warned that the nature bequeathed to us by evolution bears the mark of 'the ape and the tiger'; ethical progress depends on 'combating' that nature, pitting the 'microcosm' of human ethics and culture against the 'macrocosm' (pp. 51–2, 83). Some of his early readers, including Leslie Stephen, feared that, if that is the contest to which we are committed, the 'microcosm' is bound to have the worst of it.[51] Huxley himself, though, was by no means an unqualified pessimist: true, he warned that '[e]thical nature may count upon having to reckon with a tenacious and powerful enemy as long as the world lasts', but nonetheless he saw 'no limit to the extent to which intelligence and will, guided by sound principles of investiga-

---

49 Ruse, 'Evolutionary Ethics in the Twentieth Century', pp. 200–8; Wilson, *On Human Nature*, pp. 196–9.
50 Rachels, *Created from Animals*, p. 222.
51 Stephen, 'Ethics and the Struggle for Existence', p. 157.

tion, and organized in common effort, may modify the conditions of existence' (p. 85).

Some recent authors stand firmly in the Huxleian tradition on this question. For example, Richard Dawkins began and ended the book that made famous his 'gene's eye' view of evolution with comments about ethics and society that (apart from the language of genes and replicators) could almost have come from the pages of the Romanes Lecture. Like Huxley, the Dawkins of *The Selfish Gene* identified ethical progress with the effort to combat nature:

> Be warned that if you wish, as I do, to build a society in which individuals cooperate generously and unselfishly towards a common good, you can expect little help from biological nature . . . Let us understand what our own selfish genes are up to, because we may then at least have the chance to upset their designs, something that no other species has ever aspired to.[52]

And, like Huxley, he believed that our intelligence (in particular, our capacity for conscious foresight) gives us hope in the struggle:

> even if we look on the dark side and assume that individual man is fundamentally selfish, our conscious foresight – our capacity to simulate the future in imagination – could save us from the worst selfish excesses of the blind replicators . . . We are built as gene machines and cultured as meme machines, but we have the power to turn against our creators. We, alone on earth, can rebel against the tyranny of the selfish replicators.[53]

Others, though, read the same evidence somewhat differently. I have already cited Michael Ruse as a self-identified 'ethical sceptic', but despite his sceptical metaethic, he is sanguine about the prospects for morality: our moral instincts are so valuable to us, and have been so deeply embedded in us during our evolutionary history, that we can be confident that they will persist.[54] In this respect, he seems to be less the heir of Huxley than of Kropotkin, who believed that ethical behaviour is a matter not of combating nature but of recovering our primal instinct for 'mutual aid' in the face of social conditions that tend to

---

52 Richard Dawkins, *The Selfish Gene*, 2nd edn, Oxford and New York: Oxford University Press, 1989, p. 3.
53 Dawkins, *The Selfish Gene*, pp. 200–1.
54 Ruse, 'The Significance of Evolution', pp. 507–8.

suppress it.[55] Another optimistic answer, on more empirical grounds, comes from the primatologist Frans de Waal, who argues that many components of human morality can be found at least in embryo among our primate relatives.[56] However, he offers only a qualified optimism: many less admirable human traits can also, he thinks, be found among the other great apes.

e Theodicy

What moral assessment, if any, should we make of the evolutionary history of life on earth? In the Romanes Lecture, Huxley drew a sharp contrast between 'ethical nature' and 'cosmic nature', remarking that 'brought before the tribunal of ethics, the cosmos might well seem to stand condemned' (p. 59). There seem to be two related aspects to his complaint against the cosmos: that the evolutionary process depends on the 'ruthless' and 'gladiatorial' struggle for existence (p. 84), the cause of untold pain and suffering, and that the principle of justice, by which pleasure and pain should be apportioned according to desert, and without which human societies could not function, is absent from this cosmic process (pp. 57–9). The statute barring the discussion of religion and politics in the Romanes Lectures prevented Huxley from drawing explicitly theological conclusions from these observations. However, his contemptuous treatment of the theodicies of the Stoics, and by extension all theodicies, made it fairly clear that he believed the prevalence of 'pain and sorrow and wrong' in the world to be a serious difficulty for the belief that 'the cosmos is the effect of an immanent, omnipotent, and infinitely beneficent cause' (pp. 71–3). In earlier essays he was able to be more direct: for example, the opening pages of 'The Struggle for Existence in Human Society' echo Hume's *Dialogues* in presenting the problem of evil as a compelling argument against natural theology.[57] Huxley argued that the existence of pain and suffering, as well as beauty and pleasure, in the world, not only undermine natural theology, but also render illegitimate any attempt to discern moral meaning in nature. If we see a deer pursued by wolves, 'the fact that the deer suffers, while the wolf inflicts suffering, engages our moral

---

55 Kropotkin, *Mutual Aid*; Desmond, *Huxley*, pp. 564–5.

56 Frans B. M. de Waal, *Good Natured: The Origins of Right and Wrong in Humans and Other Animals*, Cambridge, MA: Harvard University Press, 1996.

57 Huxley, 'The Struggle for Existence', pp. 195–202; David Hume, *Dialogues Concerning Natural Religion*, ed. Stanley Tweyman, London: Routledge, 1991, parts 10, 11 (pp. 152–71).

sympathies'; but both are the products of nature, in which case we are bound to conclude that 'the goodness of the right hand which helps the deer, and the wickedness of the left hand which eggs on the wolf, will neutralize one another: and the course of nature will appear to be neither moral nor immoral, but non-moral'.[58]

Huxley was not alone in drawing these moral and theological conclusions. In response to the Harvard botanist Asa Gray (one of Darwin's strongest American supporters, and an orthodox Christian who urged him to understand natural selection as an aspect of God's providential ordering of the world), Darwin wrote:

> I own that I cannot see as plainly as others do, and as I should wish to do, evidence of design and beneficence on all sides of us. There seems to me too much misery in the world. I cannot persuade myself that a beneficent and omnipotent God would have designedly created the Ichneumonidae with the express intention of their feeding within the living bodies of Caterpillars, or that a cat should play with mice.[59]

Stephen Jay Gould reads Darwin's letter to Gray as a skilfully argued defence of something like his (Gould's) own 'NOMA' position, that science and religion are 'non-overlapping magisteria', neither of which should be used to pronounce on questions properly addressed by the other.[60] Others, such as David Hull, read the kind of evidence adduced by Darwin as powerful support for an argument against the existence of a loving, omnipotent God: 'The God of the Galapagos is careless, wasteful, indifferent, almost diabolical. He is certainly not the sort of God to whom anyone would be inclined to pray.'[61] And George Williams argued in 1988 that Huxley did not go far enough: in the light of modern sociobiology and ethology, nature must be regarded not as nonmoral, but as immoral.[62] To many Christians concerned to demonstrate

---

58 Huxley, 'The Struggle for Existence', p. 197.

59 Charles Darwin to Asa Gray, 22 May 1860, in Francis Darwin (ed.), *The Life and Letters of Charles Darwin*, 2 vols, New York, Appleton, 1905, vol. 2, p. 105; online at http://pages.britishlibrary.net/charles.darwin/texts/letters/letters2_02.html (accessed 21 December 2005).

60 Stephen Jay Gould, *Rocks of Ages: Science and Religion in the Fullness of Life*, London: Vintage, 2002, pp. 191–207.

61 David L. Hull, 'God of the Galapagos', *Nature*, 352 (1991), pp. 485–6 (p. 486), quoted by Christopher Southgate, 'God and Evolutionary Evil: Theodicy in the Light of Darwinism', *Zygon*, 37.4 (2002), pp. 803–22 (p. 804).

62 George C. Williams, 'Huxley's Evolution and Ethics in Sociobiological Perspective', *Zygon*, 23.4 (1988), pp. 383–407. For a critical discussion, see the responses by Sarah Blaffer Hrdy, Michael Ruse, Ralph Wendell Burhoe and John B. Cobb, Jr., and the reply by Williams, *Zygon*, 23.4 (1988), pp. 409–38.

that Darwinism is compatible with belief in a loving, omnipotent Creator, the problem of evolutionary evil has seemed to be a challenge that they must take up, and in recent years there have been numerous attempts to produce evolutionary theodicies more robust than those pilloried by Huxley.[63]

f   Redesigning ourselves and the world

If, as Huxley thought, the 'ethical progress of society' depends on combating the 'cosmic process', what means may legitimately be used in that combat? Huxley's main focus, as I observed in the last section, was on social and cultural means, such as the development of laws that restrain the kinds of behaviour associated with 'the ape and the tiger'. But as I noted, he also speculated about the use of scientific and technological interventions to change human nature itself: 'The intelligence which converted the brother of the wolf into the faithful guardian of the flock ought to be able to do something towards curbing the instincts of savagery in civilized man' (p. 85). He did not make it clear what he meant by this speculative aside, though the analogy of the wolf and the dog suggests some form of selective breeding or eugenics. Certainly the idea of eugenics was in the air, and some of his reviewers were willing enough to speculate about 'suppressing' the 'unfit' members of society.[64] But Huxley himself, like Darwin a quarter of a century earlier, was uneasy about such eugenic projects: humans were not intelligent or wise enough to be capable of reliably distinguishing the 'fit' from the 'unfit', and the practice of suppression would also require the practitioners to suppress in themselves those feelings of 'natural affection and sympathy' to an extent that would be morally disastrous.[65] The appalling history of 'eugenics' in the twentieth century gives ample reason to think that these were not idle fears.

Worries about repeating that history are among the factors that lead many people to make a sharp distinction between social and technological means of addressing the moral problems of human society: addressing these problems by education or by changing social conditions seems fairly uncontroversial, but commentators are often more inclined to worry about the prospect of using, for example, drugs or

---

63 For a critical survey of recent evolutionary theodicies and for constructive proposals, see Southgate, 'God and Evolutionary Evil'. Southgate's proposals will be discussed further in Chapter 8.

64 See, e.g., Stephen, 'Ethics and the Struggle for Existence', esp. p. 170.

65 Huxley, 'Prolegomena', pp. 33–40.

genetic engineering to achieve the same ends. However, some authors are willing to challenge this distinction and contemplate technological attempts to change human nature. For example, Janet Radcliffe Richards argues that the distinction between social and technological intervention is a relic of a world-view in which nature is teleologically ordered and it is wrong to interfere with that ordering; on a Darwinian view of nature, the distinction does not make sense, and any intervention must be assessed on its merits – which, for Richards, seems to boil down to a consequentialist calculus of benefits, harms and risks.[66] In similar vein, Jonathan Glover argued some years ago that a prohibition on interfering with nature was not sufficient reason for refusing to change the nature of our species, if doing so would help us to avoid repeating the horrors of the twentieth century.[67] Many of the same technologies, such as genetic manipulation, that are the objects of speculation about the future prospects for redesigning ourselves could also be used to manipulate other living creatures and other parts of the natural world technologically. Indeed, in some cases, they are already being used more or less routinely in such ways. So the question about redesigning *ourselves* in an attempt to curb some of the problematic aspects of our own nature can be extended to include the legitimacy of redesigning aspects of the *world around us* in the attempt to deal with the consequences of human wrongdoing or to meet other kinds of human need.

I have identified six issues that can be discerned in Huxley's Romanes Lecture and that appear, with various degrees of prominence, in more recent discussions of evolution and ethics. All six will reappear in some form in the later chapters of this book. But they will not all be addressed in the ways in which they have been formulated in this chapter. In the next chapter, I shall argue that the Romanes Lecture was not a neutral way of framing the issues of evolution and ethics (indeed, it is doubtful whether any way of framing them could be neutral) and shall question the assumptions implicit in the way that Huxley framed the questions. I shall suggest that a theological engagement with these issues will reframe the agenda – or, to use my earlier metaphor, will redraw the map of evolution and ethics.

---

66 Janet Radcliffe Richards, *Human Nature after Darwin: A Philosophical Introduction*, London: Routledge, 2000, pp. 252–6.

67 Jonathan Glover, *What Sort of People Should There Be? Genetic Engineering, Brain Control and Their Impact on Our Future World*, Harmondsworth: Pelican, 1984, pp. 55–6.

3

Redrawing the Map

In Chapter 2, I identified six questions that can be discerned in T. H. Huxley's 1893 essay 'Evolution and Ethics' and that have continued to preoccupy writers on evolution and ethics to the present day, and sketched something of the range of possible answers that can be found in the literature.[1]

In response to the question of *explanation*, a variety of 'reductionist' answers claim that the phenomenon of morality can be explained without remainder by some process of Darwinian descent with modification: some reductionists, like E. O. Wilson in his early sociobiological books, claim that it can be entirely explained by processes of *biological* evolution, whereas others, like Dennett, also invoke processes of *cultural* descent with modification involving constructs such as 'memes'. Others, such as Holmes Rolston and Mary Midgley, find the concept of 'memes' unconvincing, and seek to give accounts of the emergence of a morality that is thoroughly biological in its origins, but that, as it develops, transcends biology and cannot be reduced to it. On the question of *justification*, I identified three broad groups of responses: first, those that I labelled 'naturalist' hold that in some way moral conclusions can be justified by appeal to putative facts about evolution; second, those (including himself) whom Michael Ruse identifies as 'sceptics' deny that either evolution or anything else can supply an ultimate justification of moral claims; third, critics of both naturalistic and sceptical ways of linking evolution and ethics, such as Peter Woolcock, hold that we shall have to look elsewhere for justifications of moral conclusions, but that such justifications can be found. On the question of *content*, there has been no shortage of normative proposals, justified by direct appeals to evolution, in the writings of biologists such as Julian Huxley and E. O. Wilson. Some philosophers, such as James Rachels, who find such proposals uncon-

---

1 In what follows, I shall refer quite frequently to 'Huxley's questions', by which I shall mean the questions that, I argued in the previous chapter, are raised either explicitly or implicitly in the Romanes Lecture.

vincing, nonetheless argue in more indirect ways that evolutionary biology does have implications for the content of ethics. For Rachels, these implications are centred on undermining the notion that humans have a special moral status distinct from, and superior to, that of other living beings.

Regarding the question of our *moral capability and its limits*, some recent authors, such as Dawkins in *The Selfish Gene*, echo T. H. Huxley's pessimism: if we wish to live morally, we cannot expect much help from our biological nature – indeed, to live as we ought might require a 'rebellion' against our selfish genes and memes. Others, such as Frans de Waal, hold that the roots of our moral instincts and beliefs can be found in our primate relatives, and infer from this that our endeavours to live and act well go with, not against, the grain of our evolutionary inheritance, at least some of the time. In response to the question of *theodicy*, or more broadly the moral evaluation of the evolutionary process, it is frequently argued that the suffering and waste inherent in the evolutionary process, and the 'ruthless selfishness' that Dawkins and others attribute to genes and perhaps memes, are the opposite of what one would expect if the world were the creation of a good, loving and omnipotent God. Some echo Huxley in denying that any moral meaning can be attributed to the evolutionary process; others, like George Williams, go further and call it immoral. In response, many Christian believers have attempted to argue in various ways that our understanding of the evolutionary process *can* be reconciled with belief in a good, loving and omnipotent Creator. On the final question, about *redesigning ourselves*, some authors in recent decades have argued for the moral legitimacy of using technology to change ourselves so as to overcome our moral limitations and failings, should it ever become possible to do so effectively and safely.

The attempts that I have surveyed to answer Huxley's questions are not all free from careless argument and muddle, and there is plenty of scope for further philosophical work on these positions in an attempt to tidy up some of the remaining confusion. Valuable though that work would be, it will not be a major preoccupation of this book. However, I do wish to observe at this stage that not all possible combinations of answers to the six questions seem equally viable. For example, it seems difficult to combine a 'reductionist' view of explanation with a 'naturalist' view of moral justification. E. O. Wilson attempted such a combination in his project of 'biologizing' ethics, and has frequently been taken to task for a variety of philosophical errors, including the naturalistic fallacy. Daniel Dennett acknowledges that Wilson's 'biologized' ethic was unconvincing. However, he argues that Wilson's error was not naturalism as such, 'but, rather, any simple-minded attempt to rush from facts to values'. A more 'circumspect' naturalism that 'attempt[s] to unify our world-view so that our ethical principles don't clash irrationally with the way the world *is*' would not be a fallacy. It is not entirely clear, though, how this claim is justified. The reason Dennett himself gives runs as follows:

> From what can 'ought' be derived? The most compelling answer is this: ethics must be *somehow* based on an appreciation of human nature – on a sense of what a human being is or might be, and on what a human being might want to have or want to be . . . No one could seriously deny that ethics is responsive to such facts about human nature. We may just disagree about where to look for the most telling facts about human nature – in novels, in religious texts, in psychological experiments, in biological or anthropological investigations.[2]

But this seems to short-circuit the argument by smuggling in hints of evaluation under cover of phrases like 'what a human being . . . might be . . . or want to be'. The category of things Dennett is prepared to consider as 'facts' about human nature seems to be much broader than those that critics of the 'naturalistic fallacy' have in mind. A reductionist view of the explanation of morality would seem to fit more easily with a sceptical view of moral justification, such as that of Michael Ruse, or perhaps with a critical stance, like that of Peter Woolcock, towards any attempt to connect normative ethics with evolution.

Again, moral 'scepticism' of the sort favoured by Michael Ruse seems to sit uneasily with optimism about human moral capacities. Ruse is an optimist: he believes that even though '[m]orality is no more than a collective illusion fobbed off on us by our genes for reproductive ends',[3] it will persist in human society, both because we have a deep-seated genetic predisposition to act morally and because morality is as useful to us in evolutionary terms as our eyes.[4] As Woolcock points out, however, even if we do have a predisposition to act morally, it hardly amounts to

---

2 Daniel C. Dennett, *Darwin's Dangerous Idea: Evolution and the Meanings of Life*, London: Penguin, 1996, p. 468.

3 Michael Ruse, 'The Significance of Evolution', in Peter Singer (ed.), *A Companion to Ethics*, Oxford: Blackwell, 1993, pp. 500–10 (p. 506).

4 Michael Ruse, *Taking Darwin Seriously*, Oxford: Blackwell, 1986, p. 256; cited by Peter G. Woolcock, 'The Case against Evolutionary Ethics Today', in Jane Maienschein and Michael Ruse (eds.), *Biology and the Foundation of Ethics*, Cambridge: Cambridge University Press, 1999, pp. 276–306 (p. 288).

a guarantee that we will continue to do so.[5] Ruse's second argument is also less than reassuring, because it seems to rest on a confusion as to what might be meant by calling a trait evolutionarily 'useful'. On a reductionist biological account (to which Ruse is highly sympathetic), an adaptation will persist and spread, not necessarily if it is useful to individuals that possess it, but if it is effective at getting the genes that code for it passed on to the next generation. Indeed, the puzzle to which the theories of kin selection and reciprocal altruism were addressed was precisely how a 'gene for' behaviour *disadvantageous* to its possessor might persist and spread. A further potential difficulty with Ruse's optimism is that – as is often pointed out – the genetic traits that we possess now are those that were adaptive during the period of our evolutionary *past* when our ancestors were subject to relevant selection pressures. There is no guarantee that they are still useful or adaptive to us *now*, and therefore that they will persist in the future.

It might also be wondered whether attempts like Wilson's to argue from a reductionist view of explanation to a fairly conventional view of moral content are convincing. As Paul Farber suggests, a cautionary tale may be found in the history of evolutionary ethics: many nineteenth- and twentieth-century writers on evolutionary ethics 'read [their] own values into nature only to discover them there'.[6] For example, the French writer Jean de Lanessan, by contrast with his Anglo-American contemporaries, attempted to derive from evolution a 'natural morality' that coincided with the values of the Third Republic. Michael Ruse makes a similar point about Julian Huxley, who attempted to justify, on the basis of his account of evolutionary progress, a claim about the moral importance of human independence and control over the conditions of our life, but in fact simply read *into* his account of evolution the values that he wanted to derive from it.[7] Farber's conclusion is that

> Contemporary authors who look to evolution for knowledge applicable to ethics need to be mindful of past attempts to use evolution as a foundation for ethical systems, and thereby may avoid duplicating the mistakes of the past.[8]

---

5 'The Case against Evolutionary Ethics Today', pp. 288–9.

6 Paul Lawrence Farber, 'French Evolutionary Ethics during the Third Republic: Jean de Lanessan', in Maienschein and Ruse, *Biology and the Foundations of Ethics*, pp. 84–97 (p. 95).

7 Michael Ruse, 'Evolutionary Ethics in the Twentieth Century: Julian Sorrell Huxley and George Gaylord Simpson', in Maienschein and Ruse, *Biology and the Foundations of Ethics*, pp. 200–12.

8 Farber, 'French Evolutionary Ethics', p. 96.

But this cautionary tale might give grounds for suspicion of any attempt to justify the conventional values of one's time by appeal to some account of evolution, particularly if that account offers a reductionist explanation of morality and other human capacities. If one begins with a reductionist form of evolutionary explanation, it may be that a much more radically deconstructive account of the content of ethics, such as James Rachels's, follows more easily therefrom.

I am not attempting to argue that certain combinations of answers to Huxley's questions are necessary, or that others are impossible. For example, I am not trying to show that reductionism *entails* a radical deconstruction of traditional moral beliefs, that reductionist explanations of morality *cannot* be combined with naturalistic methods of justifying moral claims, or that scepticism is *incompatible* with optimism about human moral capabilities. To show any of these things would require a lengthier analysis than space permits. All I am expressing is a suspicion that some combinations of positions, such as reductionism with naturalism, and scepticism with optimism, are much harder to support than others.

Alasdair MacIntyre's well-known analysis of the fragmentation of moral discourse in modernity might support this suspicion and suggest why it should be so.[9] MacIntyre argues that the 'Enlightenment project' in ethics is an attempt to justify moral language and conclusions by means of a form of reasoning detached from the older and richer tradition which gave rise to that language and within which it makes sense. The choice that faces us can be summarized as 'Nietzsche or Aristotle': to follow Nietzsche – who according to MacIntyre understood the failure of the Enlightenment project more clearly than any of his contemporaries – in abandoning the attempt to justify the moral language and concepts that we have inherited from our forebears, or to recover the tradition from which our moral language has come, a tradition whose 'intellectual core', as MacIntyre puts it, is Aristotelian.[10]

It could be that something like this choice faces us in relation to evolutionary biology and ethics. Daniel Dennett has famously likened Darwinism to a 'universal acid' that corrodes its way through everything it touches. No aspect of our thought or culture is left unchanged when exposed to this 'acid', though Dennett is optimistic enough to believe that a surprising amount is still recognizable.[11] However, this may be

---

9 Alasdair MacIntyre, *After Virtue: A Study in Moral Theory*, 2nd edn, London: Duckworth, 1985.
10 *After Virtue*, p. 117.
11 Dennett, *Darwin's Dangerous Idea*, p. 521.

over-optimistic. To argue that a reductionist view of human nature and the world, in which Darwinian descent with modification explains everything without remainder, is an adequate source from which '"ought" [can] be derived',[12] or to hold, like Wilson, that moral norms like universal human rights can be inferred from such a reductionist view, is to try to defend, on the basis of an anthropology corroded by Dennett's 'universal acid', moral language and concepts that have their origins in a very different and much richer anthropology.[13] It is not at all clear that the new anthropology and the old moral concepts can be made to cohere. It may be that, if a reductionist view is right, it will require a radical revision of our moral language and concepts – perhaps more radical even than authors such as Rachels imagine.

Many reductionists suppose that Christianity is one of the older traditions displaced by a reductionist evolutionary account, and that it is the source of many of the moral concepts corroded by the 'universal acid' of Darwinism.[14] Later in this chapter, I shall suggest that it is a mistake to believe that evolutionary biology entails a reductionist account opposed to Christianity. If I am right about that, then the Christian moral tradition is at any rate not ruled out as an alternative to reductionism. Should it then prove possible to articulate an account of that tradition that can incorporate whatever is well-founded in the evolutionary accounts on which reductionists draw, that will give grounds for thinking that (*pace* Dennett and others) Darwinism does not imply a preference for reductionism. If it turns out that there are issues and evidence that reductionist accounts have trouble handling convincingly, but that this Christian account is better able to handle, that will give grounds for thinking that the latter is *preferable* to reductionist accounts. If it also turns out that some of the moral concepts and experi-

---

12 *Darwin's Dangerous Idea*, p. 468.

13 It might, of course, be argued that the notion of universal human rights is itself a product of the Enlightenment project and accordingly, in MacIntyre's terms, incoherent. But this does not really affect the substance of the suggestion that I am making. On such a critical view, post-Enlightenment theories of rights are presumably attempts to justify inherited notions of the value and proper treatment of human beings that can more coherently be articulated as part of the tradition from which they originated. If that is so, then a notion of universal human rights based on Wilson's reductionist anthropology would be even less coherent than one based on any standard post-Enlightenment theory.

14 So, e.g., Dennett, *Darwin's Dangerous Idea*; James Rachels, *Created from Animals: The Moral Implications of Darwinism*, Oxford: Oxford University Press, 1990; Edward O. Wilson, *Consilience: The Unity of Knowledge*, London: Abacus, 1999, pp. 265–96. For a recent attempt at *rapprochement*, see Michael Ruse, *Can a Darwinian Be a Christian? The Relationship between Science and Religion*, Cambridge: Cambridge University Press, 2001.

ence discussed in the evolution-and-ethics literature display incoherence or confusion, and that this Christian account is able to clarify, challenge and reshape those concepts, that will suggest that the Christian cannot only make a robust contribution to discussions of evolution and ethics as those discussions are commonly framed, but can reframe the discussions in richer and more fruitful ways.

The most obvious way to show that such an account can be developed is to develop it. Accordingly, Parts 2 and 3 of this book are intended to be 'one long argument' (to borrow Darwin's description of the *Origin*)[15] that proceeds by articulating one particular account of a Christian tradition, an account rooted in Reformed Protestantism, and attempting to show how it can do the three kinds of conceptual work that I have just outlined: incorporating whatever is well-founded in evolutionary accounts of human origins, handling issues and evidence with which reductionist accounts have difficulty, and clarifying, challenging and reshaping moral concepts and experience that show signs of confusion and incoherence. This will not amount to a knock-down argument against reductionism or in favour of Christian ethics – as James Rachels in effect acknowledges in his presentation of the opposite case, knock-down arguments are hard to come by in this discussion[16] – but is intended to build a cumulative case that this Christian moral tradition has more to offer than reductionism in response to the ethical questions raised by evolutionary biology.

What kind of theological engagement with the evolution-and-ethics literature is in view? It might be said that there is in fact no encounter or engagement between biology and theology, properly understood: the two are complementary but separate, not coming into contact unless one or other moves outside its proper disciplinary boundaries. This was the position taken, for example, by the late Stephen Jay Gould in his proposal that science, on the one hand, and 'religion and ethics', on the other, are 'non-overlapping magisteria', or NOMA.[17] For example, it could be said that science should restrict itself to questions of explanation, leaving questions about meaning and value to theology. However, it is notoriously difficult to establish and maintain some agreed boundary that would divide the two territories and, in any case, from the

---

15 Charles Darwin, *The Origin of Species by Means of Natural Selection; or, The Preservation of Favoured Races in the Struggle for Life*, ed. by J. W. Burrow, London: Penguin, 1968; repr. 1985 (orig. pub. London: John Murray, 1859), p. 435.

16 Cf. *Created from Animals*, e.g. pp. 91–8, 126–8.

17 Stephen Jay Gould, *Rocks of Ages: Science and Religion in the Fullness of Life*, London: Vintage, 2002.

theological side it would seem unsatisfactory to separate them so sharply that neither has anything to say about the other. The world about which theology has something to say is the same world that is investigated by biology, and if theology refuses to engage with biological descriptions of that world it risks becoming disembodied and developing a quasi-Gnostic detachment from the material world.

If there is to be an engagement between biological and theological accounts of moral being and acting, how might that engagement be set up? In effect, the project to be attempted in Parts 2 and 3 is to articulate a Christian moral anthropology. Among the putative sources of that anthropology are aspects of Christian doctrine,[18] on the one hand, and of the natural sciences (specifically evolutionary biology), on the other. What part should each play in shaping the account that is developed? In a typology that owes more than a little to Hans Frei, five kinds of answer can be imagined:[19]

1 Only science contributes to the account, and the contribution of Christian doctrine is dismissed;

2 Both science and Christian doctrine contribute to the account; its

---

18 'Christian doctrine' is, of course, a far from straightforward category. In this discussion I am using it as a rough shorthand for the central convictions of the Christian Church, formed by its Scriptures, by its reflection on those Scriptures and by its communal praxis during the course of its history, in the hope that this rough-and-ready definition lends sufficient clarity for my present purposes.

19 Hans W. Frei, *Types of Christian Theology*, ed. by George Hunsinger and William H. Placher, New Haven, CT: Yale University Press, 1992; see also David Ford, 'On Being Theologically Hospitable to Jesus Christ: Hans Frei's Achievement', *Journal of Theological Studies*, NS, 46.2 (1995), pp. 532–46. A number of typologies have been proposed for interactions between science and religion. Perhaps the most widely used is Ian Barbour's fourfold scheme of Conflict, Independence, Dialogue and Integration: for a brief recent statement, see Ian Barbour, *Nature, Human Nature and God*, London: SPCK, 2002; for a critical discussion, see Geoffrey Cantor and Chris Kenny, 'Barbour's Fourfold Way: Problems with His Taxonomy of Science–Religion Relationships', *Zygon*, 36.4 (2001), pp. 765–81, and, for a reply, Ian G. Barbour, 'On Typologies for Relating Science and Religion', *Zygon*, 37.2 (2002), pp. 345–59. For my present purposes, the typology that I have adapted from Frei seems more suitable than others such as Barbour's, for two reasons. First, I am not asking about the relationship between two monolithic entities, 'science' and 'religion', but about the contributions that might be made to a Christian theological anthropology by sources 'internal' (Christian doctrine) and 'external' (biology) to Christian faith and practice, a question closer to Frei's than to Barbour's. Secondly, the typology outlined here allows for a more fine-grained differentiation between the middle positions in my scheme, which is helpful in setting out the terms of my own exposition. It should be obvious enough that I am proposing this typology simply for the relatively modest purposes of my present discussion, and am not attempting anything like a general taxonomy of 'science and religion'.

shape is determined by the scientific contribution, and the input from Christian doctrine must be adjusted to fit the outlines determined by the scientific contribution;

3 Both science and Christian doctrine contribute, and neither has sole control over the shape of the account;

4 Both science and Christian doctrine contribute; the shape of the account is determined by Christian doctrine, and the scientific contribution is critically appropriated to that doctrinally shaped account;

5 Only the contribution of Christian doctrine is admitted, the scientific contribution being denied or dismissed.

An example of the first type is the biological reductionism exemplified by Dennett. Since the purpose of this book is to explore the possibility of an *alternative* to reductionism, the option offered by Dennett hardly seems promising. I suggested earlier that if it proves possible to articulate a richer account that meets the conditions I proposed, that will in itself be a reason for rejecting the reductionist view. However, it is worth briefly offering a more direct response to Dennett's reductionism at this stage, since he seems to think that his account delivers a knockout punch to any Christian view of the world and human life.[20] Leaving aside his rather knockabout rhetorical strategy of insult and ridicule,[21] his serious argument amounts to a series of claims about *explanation*. He begins by remarking that belief in God has often been invoked to answer teleological or 'why' questions about the universe (in Aristotelian terms, questions about final causes), but that it fails to put a stop to the infinite

---

20 Dennett frequently writes in a general way of religion, 'faith' or 'the hypothesis of God' (see, e.g., *Darwin's Dangerous Idea*, pp. 154–6) in a way that could run the risk of obscuring the very large differences between faith traditions, although he is clearly not unaware of these differences and does at times refer to specific religious traditions by name (e.g. pp. 511–20). It seems from his autobiographical comments (pp. 17–18) that his formative experience of religion was Christian and, when he discusses 'faith' or the 'hypothesis of God', what he appears to have in mind is some version of Christian faith (or at any rate, an understanding of 'faith' that would be much more familiar to a Christian, a Jew or a Muslim than – say – a Hindu or a Buddhist). Since the account I am developing in this book is rooted in my own Christian tradition, and since it is likely to be more fruitful to discuss the particularities of one tradition than to make broad and potentially inaccurate generalizations about 'religious belief' in general, I shall treat Dennett's arguments as arguments against *Christian* belief and respond to them as such.

21 See, e.g., his treatment of Teilhard de Chardin in *Darwin's Dangerous Idea*, pp. 320–1: in a little over a page of ridicule, around seven lines of serious argument can be discerned, and these could be roughly paraphrased as 'Teilhard and Darwinism cannot both be right, and we *know* Darwinism is right, so Teilhard must be wrong.' One does not have to be an admirer of Teilhard to think that this does not amount to a very serious piece of argumentation.

regress to which such questions give rise. Because of this, he says, people often substitute 'how' questions (questions about efficient causes) for the 'why' questions to which they are unable to find satisfactory answers. He claims, somewhat implausibly, that ancient cosmogonies such as 'the book of Genesis' and modern theories such as the Big Bang are, alike, attempts to answer such 'how' questions.[22] He believes that Darwinism both answers the 'how' questions and, more importantly, '[shows] us a new way to make sense of "why" questions',[23] a way that he thinks is greatly superior to belief in God. With reference to 'how' questions, he attempts to show how Darwinian ideas can be extended from Darwin's own theory 'downwards', to the emergence of life from non-life and order from chaos, and 'upwards', to account for the emergence of consciousness, intelligence and culture from unintelligent matter. He argues that this capacity for extension makes it a superior explanatory hypothesis to the 'hypothesis of God' in accounting for the organized complexity of life.[24] Some of his extensions of Darwinism are plausible, some less so – for example, his attempt to extend it 'upwards' relies heavily on the tendentious concept of 'memes', to which I shall return in Chapter 4 – and Stephen Jay Gould has called his attempt to turn Darwinism into a Theory of Everything 'Darwinian fundamentalism'.[25] But whether or not Dennett is right to think that descent with modification is the only kind of causal hypothesis needed to account for life, his claim that it is a better kind of explanatory hypothesis than 'the hypothesis of God' misses the point. It is a commonplace in discussions of science and theology that belief in a creator God is emphatically not an explanatory hypothesis of the same kind as scientific hypotheses like Darwinism, to be invoked to fill the explanatory gaps in our scientific knowledge of the world.[26]

---

22 *Darwin's Dangerous Idea*, p. 24. The claim is carelessly phrased: presumably he is referring to the two creation narratives (not *a* cosmogony) found in the early chapters of Genesis, since the bulk of the book does not even superficially resemble a cosmogony. But even with reference to Genesis 1–3, it is not obvious that they are attempts to answer the same questions that the Big Bang theory addresses: see, e.g., Gordon J. Wenham, *Genesis 1–15* (Word Biblical Commentary, 1), Waco, TX: Word, 1987, pp. xlv–liii, 11–40, 55–91, for discussion of questions that seem to have preoccupied the writers and editors of the Genesis creation narratives but do not interest modern cosmologists.

23 *Darwin's Dangerous Idea*, p. 25.

24 *Darwin's Dangerous Idea*, pp. 150–5.

25 Stephen Jay Gould, 'Evolution: The Pleasures of Pluralism', *New York Review of Books*, 26 June 1997, pp. 47–52, online at http://www.stephenjaygould.org/reviews/gould_pluralism.html (accessed 10 August 2006).

26 Belief in a 'God of the gaps' is routinely repudiated by writers on science and theology: for some recent examples, see R. J. Berry, *God's Book of Works: The Nature and*

Dennett not only claims, however, that Darwinism can answer all our 'how' questions. He also believes that it can supply better answers than the traditional religious ones to the teleological or 'why' questions, and this claim might appear to pose a more serious challenge to the Christian doctrine of creation. What he appears to mean is that Darwin shows how it is possible to have design without an intelligent Designer: biological evolution is a process by which unintelligent algorithms produce solutions to design problems. This means that something can 'exist for a reason without its being *somebody's* reason'.[27] In other words, for Dennett, the Darwinian answer to any 'why' question is: because it was the best available solution to some design problem or other. He thinks that this kind of 'because' answer is preferable to others, such as those offered by belief in a divine Creator, because the latter either 'go round and round in circles or spiral off in an infinite regress of mysteries'.[28]

But it is not clear that Darwinism answers the same kind of 'why' question as belief in a divine Creator, any more than it was clear that belief in God is an inferior version of the kind of explanatory hypothesis supplied by the natural sciences. Dennett's treatment of both 'how' and 'why' questions manifests a particularly hard-line assumption about the univocity of language. This is starkly illustrated by a passage from Richard Dawkins, quoted with approval by Dennett, in which Dawkins dismisses the notion that the existence of God is required to explain the existence of the biochemical machinery of self-replication that would enable more complex forms of life to evolve:

[A]ny God capable of intelligently designing something as complex as the DNA/protein replicating machine must have been at least as complex and organized as that machine itself. Far more so if we suppose him *additionally* capable of such advanced functions as listening to prayers and forgiving sins. To explain the origin of the DNA/protein machine by invoking a supernatural Designer is to explain precisely nothing, for it leaves unexplained the origin of the Designer.[29]

Theology of Nature, London: T&T Clark (Continuum), 2003, p. 18 n. 3; Arthur Peacocke, *Theology for a Scientific Age*, 2nd enlarged edn, London: SCM Press, 1993, p. 153; John Polkinghorne, *Faith, Science and Understanding*, London: SPCK, 2000, pp. 66–8. I shall suggest below, however, that some approaches to the science–theology dialogue risk making a mistake similar to Dennett's in this matter.

27 *Darwin's Dangerous Idea*, p. 25, emphasis original.

28 *Darwin's Dangerous Idea*, p. 25.

29 Richard Dawkins, *The Blind Watchmaker*, Harlow: Longman, 1986, p. 141 (emphasis original); quoted in part by Dennett, *Darwin's Dangerous Idea*, p. 153.

If this is to be understood as an argument against the existence of the God who is spoken of in Christian theology, it is a long way wide of the mark. The God in whom Dawkins, on the evidence of this passage, does not believe is a being like us, only greater: more intelligent, more complex and so on. But this is not the God in whom Christians believe. The utter transcendence of God has commonly been taken by Christian theologians to mean that when the same language is predicated of Creator and creatures, it cannot be used univocally. To do so would be to deny the difference between Creator and creation, either deifying the creation or reducing God to a being like us, but bigger.[30] Nor is it true, though, that terms predicated both of God and of creatures are used wholly equivocally, since, as Trevor Hart puts it, that would render any statement about God 'meaningless . . . and tantamount to an untruth'.[31] Rather, there has to be some form of *analogy* between terms as they are used of God and the same terms as they are used of creatures. To say this much, of course, is to do no more than hint at a complex area of theological debate and an equally complex piece of intellectual history.[32] But the point for my present purposes is that the arguments of Dawkins and Dennett that I have been discussing here seem completely innocent of *any* concept of analogy – indeed, of any recognition that language might function in other ways than the simplest kind of univocity. If that notion of univocity is mistaken – and recent studies argue that even in the natural sciences, let alone theology, our language is irreducibly metaphorical, and far more complex than Dawkins and Dennett seem to assume[33] – then Dennett has not succeeded in showing that Darwinism and the Christian doctrine of creation are rival teleologies. If he has not, we need not agree with him that acceptance of Darwinism requires rejection of the Christian doctrine of creation.[34]

---

30 Trevor Hart, *Regarding Karl Barth: Essays toward a Reading of His Theology*, Carlisle: Paternoster, 1999, p. 175.

31 Hart, *Regarding Karl Barth*, p. 185.

32 Aspects of the theological debate are brought into focus by Barth's critique of Thomas Aquinas' doctrine of the *analogia entis* and his own preference for the *analogia fidei*: see, e.g., Thomas Aquinas, *Summa Theologiae*, I.13.2–6; Karl Barth, *Church Dogmatics*, ET ed. by G. W. Bromiley and T. F. Torrance, Edinburgh: T&T Clark, 1956–75, vol. II.1, pp. 224–33; and, for a brief commentary, Hart, *Regarding Karl Barth*, pp. 173–94. The intellectual history includes the late mediaeval replacement, by John Duns Scotus and William of Ockham, of Thomas' doctrine of analogy with a doctrine of univocity: for a brief discussion, see Colin E. Gunton, *The Triune Creator: A Historical and Systematic Study*, Grand Rapids: Eerdmans, 1998, pp. 117–25.

33 See, e.g., Colin E. Gunton, *The Actuality of Atonement: A Study of Metaphor, Rationality and the Christian Tradition*, Edinburgh: T&T Clark, 1988, pp. 27–52.

34 The line of argument in the last few paragraphs was suggested in part by Simon

The fifth position in my typology – *only the contribution of Christian doctrine is admitted, the scientific contribution being denied or dismissed* – is most obviously exemplified by 'creationism', as that term is commonly understood.[35] This is not entirely straightforward, since creationism makes apparently scientific claims. However, the apparently scientific claims made by 'creation science' can only be understood as scientific in a fairly unconventional way. What creationism does is to reject, on the grounds of a particular reading of Christian doctrine, the account of human life and the world that the biological sciences produce by following their own methods and procedures, and replace it with one devised *a priori* to fit that doctrinal stance.[36] Creationism is thus more or less the mirror image of Dennett's reductionism: the latter makes theological claims (albeit more or less entirely negative ones) in much the same way in which creationism makes scientific ones. Unsurprisingly, it is fairly clear from the creationist literature that creationists make the same mistaken assumption as reductionists like Dennett: that Darwinian evolution and the Christian doctrine of creation are rival explanatory hypotheses of the same type.

The two extreme positions in my typology, biological reductionism and creationism, both exclude any possibility of a serious engagement between evolutionary biology and theology, requiring instead the supplanting of one by the other. It seems, then, that any serious attempt to develop a theological account of moral being and acting in response to Huxley's questions will have to proceed along the lines of one of my middle three types.

The second is one in which *both science and Christian doctrine contribute to the account; its shape is determined by the scientific contribution, and the input from Christian doctrine must be adjusted to fit the outlines determined by the natural sciences.* Something like this rela-

---

Oliver, 'What Can Theology Offer to Religious Studies?' in M. Warrier and S. Oliver (eds.), *Theology and Religious Studies: An Exploration of Disciplinary Boundaries*, forthcoming, 2007, and by discussion following the presentation of that essay as a seminar paper at the University of Wales, Lampeter, in February 2006.

35 See, e.g., Henry M. Morris (ed.), *Scientific Creationism*, San Diego, CA: Creation-Life, 1974.

36 This is particularly clear in the 'Preface' to Morris, *Scientific Creationism*, which begins with a complaint about the harmful effects supposed to follow from the teaching of evolution in schools, and continues: 'Evolutionist teaching is not only harmful sociologically, but it is false scientifically and historically. Man and his world are *not* products of an evolutionary process but, rather, are special creations of God. According to the Biblical record, God Himself wrote with his own hands these words: "For in six days the Lord made heaven and earth, and all that in them is . . ."' (p. iii, emphasis original).

tionship between natural science and Christian doctrine has been advocated by Arthur Peacocke in various works. For example, in a recent article, he presents the natural sciences as the outstanding example of rational enquiry, valid and relevant in all places and cultures, and well able to withstand the challenges of postmodernity.[37] He repeatedly contrasts this with what he takes to be the parlous reputation of theology: 'For many decades now – and certainly during my adult life in *academe* – the Western intellectual world has not been convinced that theology is a pursuit that can be engaged in with intellectual honesty and integrity.'[38] Theology's lack of intellectual integrity is held to be evident in that, instead of conforming to the standards of honest and rigorous enquiry set by the natural sciences, it closes down any such enquiry by fideistic appeals to the Bible, Church authority or *a priori* truths.[39] If theologians are to have any credibility in the modern world, they must kick such intellectually dubious habits and instead adopt the criteria of rational enquiry that obtain in the natural sciences. What this amounts to is that theology must adopt the practice of inference to the best explanation (IBE). Peacocke's criteria of the best explanation are 'comprehensiveness', 'fruitfulness', 'general cogency and plausibility', 'internal coherence and consistency' and 'simplicity or elegance'.[40] The data to be explained include not only particular physical phenomena and the nature of the material world but also the religious experiences of communities of faith (including those recorded by Jews and Christians in the Bible) and the very existence and comprehensibility of the world. With such a variety of things to be explained, 'explanation' must be understood in broader terms than simply an account of physical cause-and-effect within the causal structures of the world: Peacocke follows Keith Ward in taking it to mean 'that which renders intelligible'.[41] Notwithstanding this qualification, however, it appears that he broadly shares with Dawkins and Dennett the assumption that a claim about the existence or activity of God is *the same kind of explanatory hypothesis*

---

37 Arthur Peacocke, 'Science and the Future of Theology: Critical Issues', *Zygon*, 35.1 (2000), pp. 119–40. See also his *Paths from Science towards God: The End of all Our Exploring*, Oxford: Oneworld, 2001.

38 Peacocke, 'Science and the Future of Theology', p. 120.

39 'Science and the Future of Theology', pp. 130–1. It must be said that Peacocke's critique of the present state of theology includes more than a little caricature of the way in which theologians go about their business now and have done in the past, as John Polkinghorne has also noted: *Science and the Trinity: The Christian Encounter with Reality*, London: SPCK, 2004, pp. 23–5.

40 Peacocke, 'Science and the Future of Theology', pp. 128–9.

41 Peacocke, *Theology for a Scientific Age*, p. 98, quoting Keith Ward, *The Concept of God*, Oxford: Blackwell, 1974, p. 148.

as a natural scientific theory.[42] Thus, he quotes Clayton and Knapp with approval:

> On this view, many Christian beliefs are potential explanations: they tell me why certain data that need to be explained are the way they are; they account for certain facts about human existence. When I believe them, I believe they do a better job of explaining the data than other explanatory hypotheses of which I am aware.[43]

He claims that this procedure will allow us to infer, from the reality of the world as disclosed by the natural sciences, the existence of 'an *Ultimate Reality, God*',[44] and to make a series of inferences about the characteristics and actions of such a God.[45]

But it is not clear that Peacocke's version of 'IBE' takes us as far as he thinks. He proposes that the existence of the world and its comprehensibility to us are most simply and economically explained by postulating the existence of a creator God.[46] *Given the existence* of this God, Peacocke draws a series of inferences about God's characteristics and actions – God is one, but a diversity-in-unity, personal or more than personal, omnipotent, omnipresent, both transcendent and immanent, and so on – by a combination of metaphysical arguments and inferences from the character of the world.[47] But these further inferences are conditional on the prior assumption that this God exists. For example, Peacocke infers from the interplay of 'chance' and 'necessity' that makes biological evolution possible that '*[f]or a theist*, God must now be seen as creating in the world through what we call "chance" operating within the created order'.[48] Accordingly, he resists the quite different conclusions that the atheist molecular biologist Jacques Monod famously drew from the same phenomenon.[49] But he can only do so

---

42 This is not to suggest that he ignores the importance of metaphor for theological language – see, e.g., *Paths*, pp. 152–3 – but his account of explanation still seems prone to the notion of univocity that also causes problems for materialists such as Dawkins and Dennett.

43 P. Clayton and S. Knapp, 'Rationality and Christian Self-Conceptions', in W. M. Richardson and W. J. Wildman (eds.), *Religion and Science: History, Method, Dialogue*, London and New York: Routledge, 1996, p. 134; quoted by Peacocke, *Paths*, p. 29.

44 Peacocke, *Paths*, p. 129, emphasis original.

45 *Paths*, pp. 39–125, 129–30; cf. the similar discussion in his *Theology for a Scientific Age*, pp. 99–183.

46 *Theology for a Scientific Age*, pp. 101–4; *Paths*, pp. 39–41.

47 *Theology for a Scientific Age*, pp. 108–83; *Paths*, pp. 40–115.

48 *Paths*, p. 77, emphasis added.

49 *Theology for a Scientific Age*, pp. 115–19.

because of his *prior* choice of theism: the phenomenon itself does not provide evidence that will support his case and refute Monod.

It might seem that the 'data' of religious experience support a stronger argument in favour of the postulate of God. But this is not necessarily so: materialists have not been slow to propose naturalistic explanations of religious phenomena.[50] Two considerations remain that might tip the scales in favour of the postulate of God as the best explanation: the existence of the world and its comprehensibility. The second, however, is undermined by Peacocke's fondness for evolutionary epistemology,[51] since such an epistemology would lend itself to being used in a materialist schema to show how the world could be comprehensible to us *without* its being the creation of a rational divine Mind. So only the 'mystery of existence' question, 'Why is there anything at all?',[52] seems to tip the balance away from a purely materialist explanation. On this, Dennett at least half-agrees with Peacocke, conceding that the mystery of existence may be the one outstanding question that the otherwise universal 'acid' of Darwinism cannot attack. Dennett deals with this problem by wondering whether it is an intelligible question at all.[53] Peacocke might, with some justice, find this an unsatisfactory response.[54] But the question remains, why is *Peacocke's* kind of God necessary to explain the mystery of existence? Why not the God of deism, since naturalistic causal processes are sufficient to explain everything within the natural world? Or why not a pantheistic deity like Spinoza's *Deus sive natura*, a concept that even Dennett is prepared to entertain, since it makes no difference whatever to his materialism?[55] In short, Peacocke's apologetic strategy is an attempt to beat materialists such as Dennett at their own game, but it seems to me that if the game is played on this field, by these rules, it may turn out that Dennett, not Peacocke, has the best of it after all. In my comments about Dennett I argued, in effect, that Christian theologians should *decline* his choice of turf and rules. This is not – as Peacocke might protest – a fideistic abandonment of rational enquiry, but a recognition, with philosophers such as MacIntyre, that the

---

50 E.g. David Sloan Wilson, *Darwin's Cathedral: Evolution, Religion, and the Nature of Society*, Chicago, IL: University of Chicago Press, 2002.

51 By 'evolutionary epistemology' is meant the theory that our perceptions of the world are likely to correspond reasonably well to reality, since the ability to have such perceptions would have conferred a selective advantage on our ancestors; Peacocke, 'Science and the Future of Theology', pp. 125–7.

52 Peacocke, *Paths*, p. 39.

53 Dennett, *Darwin's Dangerous Idea*, pp. 180–1.

54 Cf. *Theology for a Scientific Age*, pp. 87–8.

55 Dennett, *Darwin's Dangerous Idea*, p. 520.

standards and criteria of rational enquiry are *internal to traditions*.[56] That is not to say that different traditions and disciplines of enquiry cannot engage with one another, only that it is a fantasy to think that some neutral ground – or level playing field – can be found on which to stage the encounter.[57] Dennett's playing field is no more level than anyone else's.

My third type of account is one to which *both science and Christian doctrine contribute, neither having sole control over its shape.* Some of John Polkinghorne's writings, particularly his 1993–4 Gifford Lectures, *Science and Christian Belief*,[58] would seem to be a distinguished example of theology done in this way. In those lectures, Polkinghorne describes himself as a 'bottom-up thinker' who prefers to begin, not with grand conceptual schemes, but with the 'data' on the basis of which theories are constructed – whether the physical phenomena and experimental results which the theories of the physical sciences are constructed to explain, or the faith experience that underlies the theologizing of the Christian community. He holds that the Christian believer, like the natural scientist, is engaged in the search for 'motivated belief', though the kind of evidence that can appropriately be taken to motivate belief will differ greatly according to the subject matter. A very different kind of evidence is appropriate to a theological 'exploration into God' from that appropriate to the construction of a theory in particle physics.

The central question of his Gifford Lectures is 'whether the strange and exciting claims of orthodox Christianity are tenable in a scientific age'.[59] Accordingly, he structures his exploration around the Nicene Creed; the 'warp' of his theological tapestry is 'the engagement with the record of Christian tradition', while 'the woof is the engagement with contemporary understandings of ourselves and the universe we inhabit'.[60] In practice this results in a variety of forms of encounter. For example, the chapter on 'Knowledge', expounding the word 'believe' in the first line of the creed, is (as one might expect) largely a discussion of epistemology, advocating (among other things) critical realism, Michael Polanyi's concept of 'tacit knowledge', and a certain kind of natural

---

56 See, e.g., Alasdair MacIntyre, *Whose Justice? Which Rationality?*, London: Duckworth, 1988.

57 See MacIntyre, *Whose Justice?*, pp. 349–88, for a proposal as to how such engagements should take place.

58 John Polkinghorne, *Science and Christian Belief: Theological Reflections of a Bottom-Up Thinker*, London: SPCK, 1994. As I shall suggest, however, there is some ambiguity in their assignment to this category.

59 Polkinghorne, *Science and Christian Belief*, p. 7.

60 *Science and Christian Belief*, p. 6.

theology. The chapter on 'Creation' takes the account of origins given by cosmology and evolutionary biology, and addresses various questions raised by the attempt to combine theological claims about creation with this scientific account. Among those questions are how we are to understand God's providential interaction with the world, and what we are to make of the problem of evil. Again, the chapter on 'Eschatology' begins with cosmological predictions about the eventual fate of the universe, and raises a variety of theological questions about how we are to articulate the future hope promised in the New Testament and Christian tradition in the light of those predictions. By contrast, in chapters on the historical Jesus, the crucifixion and resurrection, and Christology, the engagement is almost entirely with the New Testament, biblical scholarship and (to a limited extent) systematic theological discussion of the atonement and the person of Christ. Occasional analogies are made with scientific theories and methods, but – understandably enough – the natural sciences do not have a very high profile in these chapters.

This approach certainly seems to allow for a richer encounter between Christian doctrine and natural science than my second type, in which theology all too easily finds itself forced onto the Procrustean bed of a certain type of scientific rationality. Polkinghorne agrees with Arthur Peacocke about the value of inference to the best explanation in the science–theology dialogue,[61] but his insistence that 'the kind of evidence considered, and the kind of understanding attained, must be conformed to the Reality about which one is attempting to speak'[62] makes him hospitable to a wider range of approaches and methods of enquiry than Peacocke seems to be, and creates more space within which theology can speak in its own distinctive voice.

Nonetheless, I wonder how stable this third type of theological account turns out to be. In a more recent book, Polkinghorne remarks that, in the past, the agenda of the science-and-religion dialogue has often been 'set from the science side', but that an agenda set by cosmology, particle physics, evolutionary biology and so on does not get to the heart of the matter:

> the central source of my own belief in God does not lie in such matters. Rather, it is to be found in my encounter with the figure of Jesus Christ, as I meet him in scripture, in the Church and in the sacraments. For me, it is Trinitarian belief that is truly persuasive belief.[63]

---

61 Polkinghorne, *Science and the Trinity*, pp. 24, 26–9.
62 *Science and Christian Belief*, p. 4.
63 *Science and the Trinity*, pp. xii, xiii. Having contrasted Arthur Peacocke's

The book in which he writes these words is presented as a contribution to the science-and-theology dialogue in which the agenda is set by theological, not scientific, themes and concerns. The shift in emphasis that he thus identifies in his own work might lead us to wonder whether the kind of science-and-theology dialogue in which neither partner controls the agenda can be sustained, or whether such an encounter will inevitably tend to drift towards either the second or the fourth type, with one or other dialogue partner dominating the shape of the encounter. Indeed, although I characterized Polkinghorne's Gifford Lectures as an example of the third type of encounter, the fact that they are structured according to the articles of the Nicene Creed might already signal the beginnings of a shift towards the fourth.

It seems, then, that the methodological decision to be made at this point in my discussion comes down to a choice between my second and fourth types of theological account. There may, as Polkinghorne suggests, be value in the second type, though my critical remarks about Peacocke suggest that it has certain inherent dangers, particularly a tendency to rule out *a priori* some of theology's most characteristic (and, I would say, appropriate) modes of speech and enquiry. Be that as it may, for the task I have set myself in this book – to articulate a theological account of moral being and acting that can incorporate biological insights while offering an intellectually and morally fruitful alternative to biological reductionism – it seems clear that the fourth type is the better suited. What is needed is a theological account in which Christian doctrine is able to speak in its own distinctive voice, and in which insights from biology are taken seriously, but not uncritically.

I suggest that a model for this fourth type of encounter – in which *both science and Christian doctrine contribute to the account, its shape being determined by Christian doctrine, and the scientific contribution being critically appropriated to that doctrinally shaped account* – can be found in the theology of Karl Barth. Barth might seem an odd choice of theological dialogue partner for a Christian engagement with biology. He does not, by and large, enjoy a high standing in the science-and-religion world. He and his approach are sometimes dismissed out of

---

approach unfavourably with Polkinghorne's, I must acknowledge that in some of his writings Peacocke makes a similar point: see, e.g., *Theology for a Scientific Age*, pp. 94–8. Nonetheless, the emphasis of Peacocke's approach, stated increasingly forcefully in his more recent writings, does seem to be on the need for Christian communities to *revise* the faith and theology that they have learned from Scripture, the Church and the sacraments in response to the challenges put to them by the natural sciences.

hand.[64] Where his theology is taken more seriously, it is still often regarded as unhelpful for the dialogue of science and theology, for a variety of reasons. One is his uncompromising opposition to natural theology;[65] another is that he notoriously refused to engage with the natural sciences, holding (for example) that they were irrelevant to the doctrine of creation as such.[66] But I shall attempt to show in subsequent chapters that, notwithstanding his own failure to engage with science, his theological method offers great scope for just the kind of critical appropriation of insights from other disciplines that I wish to attempt.[67] Given Barth's massive theological influence in the last century, it seems worth investigating the resources that might be found in his theology for a critical and constructive engagement with biology in the area that this book explores.

What would this type of theological engagement with biology look like? It would not simply accept Huxley's agenda as given. In this respect, it would differ from some of the theological treatments that have been offered hitherto, which do more or less accept Huxley's framing of the questions. For example, a recent collection of essays by scientists, philosophers and theologians, co-edited by a biologist and a philosophical theologian, is structured around what are essentially three of Huxley's questions: explanation, justification and theodicy.[68]

The trouble with simply accepting Huxley's agenda is that his framing of the questions is not neutral – indeed, it is doubtful whether any could be, since anyone's framing of the questions is bound to be guided by their basic assumptions about the kind of world to which the questions refer. Huxley's cosmos, as I observed in Chapter 2, is amoral. The evolutionary process produces great beauty and wonder, but also great pain and suffering: nature's 'right hand' helps the deer run from the

---

64 See, e.g., Peacocke's brief and disparaging reference to 'neo-Barthians', 'Science and the Future of Theology', p. 120.

65 See, e.g., Celia Deane-Drummond, *Biology and Theology Today*, London: SCM Press, 2001, p. 42; Polkinghorne, *Science and Christian Belief*, pp. 42–3; also the latter's discussion of Thomas Torrance's divergence from Barth on this point: Polkinghorne, *Faith, Science and Understanding*, London: SPCK, 2000, pp. 177–9.

66 Barth, *Church Dogmatics*, vol. III.1, pp. ix–x; for critiques on this point, see Polkinghorne, *Faith, Science and Understanding*, pp. 177–9; Philip Clayton, *God and Contemporary Science*, Edinburgh: Edinburgh University Press, 1997, pp. 66–7.

67 See, further, Nigel Biggar, *The Hastening That Waits: Karl Barth's Ethics*, Oxford: Oxford University Press, 1993, pp. 146–61.

68 Philip Clayton and Jeffrey Schloss (eds.), *Evolution and Ethics: Human Morality in Biological and Religious Perspective*, Grand Rapids: Eerdmans, 2004. For the framing of the questions, see especially Jeffrey P. Schloss, 'Introduction: Evolutionary Ethics and Christian Morality' (pp. 1–24).

wolf, while 'the left hand . . . eggs on the wolf'.[69] Justice, the basic value of human society and ethics, is absent from nature.[70] Huxley follows Hume in making a sharp separation between fact and value: values are not to be discerned in nature, nor deduced from facts about it, but are only to be found in *human* life and thought. The cosmic process is indifferent, perhaps even hostile, to human efforts to live and act well: 'ethical nature, while born of cosmic nature, is necessarily at enmity with its parent',[71] and the cosmos threatens to be 'too strong' for 'ethical man'.[72]

By contrast, an understanding of the cosmos not as amoral, but as God's good creation, of our moral problem not merely as the persistent traces of 'the ape and the tiger', but as the sin by which we alienate ourselves from God, from one another and from the creation, and of our hope as lying not merely in our efforts to combat nature, but in the reconciling love of God in Jesus Christ, might not merely propose different answers to Huxley's questions, but frame the questions themselves differently. If we understand things in this way, we will not be content to accept Huxley's moral map of the world, but will wish to redraw the map. Our priorities will be different: following a theological survey, some parts of the territory will prove to be bigger, others smaller, than Huxley draws them. For example, questions of explanation might be less prominent, while questions of content and moral capability might loom larger. Furthermore, some features of the landscape will look different: Huxley's question about justification becomes a question about the ethical implications of the doctrine of creation; the question about moral capability and its limits becomes a question about sin and 'fallenness'; the question about redesigning ourselves must be placed in the context of the salvation and eschatological hope that are God's gifts to us in Christ. The remainder of this book is an attempt to show in more detail how one particular account of ourselves and the world, shaped by Christian doctrine (in particular, the doctrines of creation, sin and salvation) might critically appropriate insights from biology, reframe Huxley's questions and suggest interesting and fruitful answers.

---

69 Thomas Henry Huxley, 'The Struggle for Existence in Human Society', in *Collected Essays*, vol. 9, pp. 195–236 (p. 197).

70 Thomas Henry Huxley, 'Evolution and Ethics' (The Romanes Lecture, 1893), in *Evolution and Ethics and Other Essays* (*Collected Essays*, vol. 9), London: Macmillan, 1894, pp. 56–9.

71 *Collected Essays*, vol. 9, p. viii.

72 'Evolution and Ethics', p. 77.

Part 2

Evolutionary Ethics and the Command of God the Creator

4

The 'Evolution of Ethics' and the Doctrine of Creation

Introduction

At the end of the last chapter, I claimed that a Christian theological engagement with Huxley's questions about evolution and ethics will not be content with attempting to devise persuasive answers to the questions as they have been framed in Huxley's terms, but can both reframe the questions and offer interesting and fruitful answers to those reframed questions. In this chapter, I shall test this claim in relation to Huxley's first question, concerning the explanation of morality: can evolutionary biology supply an explanation of the origins of human morality, or an account of what Huxley called the 'evolution of ethics'?

1 The 'evolution of ethics'

Evolutionary biologists' discussions of this question frequently focus on the puzzle of altruistic behaviour, which they define as behaviour by one individual that enhances others' chances of survival and reproduction at a cost to the altruist's own. Examples of altruistic behaviour, in this sense, in the animal kingdom have long been known. One of the most frequently discussed cases is that of the social insects: the order Hymenoptera (which includes bees, wasps and ants) contains several species with highly organized social structures. These insect societies exhibit numerous examples of altruistic behaviour: for example, in some species, most females do not themselves reproduce, instead performing activities which help the queen to produce as many offspring as possible.

It is worth noting in passing that confusion is sometimes evident in the literature between this technical sense of 'altruism' and everyday uses of the word that make it mean something like 'behaviour directed at help-

65

ing others for their own sake'.[1] The two senses of the word, obviously enough, have something in common: both are concerned with one individual's promotion of another's interests rather than its own. But there are also contrasts between the everyday and technical senses of 'altruism', including the place of voluntariness, intention and motivation. Biologists officially concern themselves only with the effects of the behaviour – behaviour which, in many of the textbook cases, seems to be entirely instinctive – whereas it is often held that to count as altruistic in the everyday sense, an act must (among other things) be voluntary and must be motivated by concern or regard for others.[2]

In the 1960s, the theoretical biologist William Hamilton proposed a famous solution to the puzzle of altruism (in the technical sense) which has become known as 'kin selection'.[3] A 'gene'[4] that leads an individual to act altruistically towards his or her kin, even if this reduces the individual's chance of reproducing, will spread in a population if it brings about a sufficient improvement in the beneficiaries' chances of reproducing. This is because there is a significant likelihood that the beneficiaries, being genetically related to the altruist, will carry copies of the same gene – and the more closely related they are, the higher the probability. The social insects offer a particularly clear example, because a peculiarity of their genetics means that females are more closely genetically related to their sisters than to any other individuals, including their own offspring.[5] This means that the most efficient way for any female to propagate her own genes may well be to assist her mother to have as many (female) offspring as possible. This evolutionary logic, however, is

---

1 Robert Paul Churchill and Erin Street, 'Is There a Paradox of Altruism?', in Jonathan Seglow (ed.), *The Ethics of Altruism*, London: Frank Cass, 2004, pp. 87–105 (p. 89).

2 Churchill and Street, 'Is There a Paradox of Altruism?', pp. 88–9; see also Jurgen de Wispelaere, 'Altruism, Impartiality and Moral Demands', in Seglow, *The Ethics of Altruism*, pp. 9–33 (p. 11), who *restricts* the definition of altruism to a motivational disposition to further the good of others. For a more complex taxonomy distinguishing six different senses of the word 'altruism', see Holmes Rolston III, *Genes, Genesis and God: Values and their Origins in Natural and Human History*, Cambridge: Cambridge University Press, 1999, pp. 272–4, n. 11.

3 William D. Hamilton, 'The Evolution of Altruistic Behaviour', *American Naturalist*, 97 (1963), pp. 354–6, and 'The Genetical Evolution of Social Behaviour', parts I and II, *Journal of Theoretical Biology*, 7 (1964), pp. 1–52, both reprinted with commentary in Hamilton, *The Narrow Roads of Gene Land: The Collected Papers of W. D. Hamilton*, vol. 1, Oxford: W. H. Freeman, 1996, pp. 1–82.

4 As in previous chapters, the scare-quotes signal that these 'genes' are theoretical constructs.

5 Niles Eldredge, *Reinventing Darwin: The Great Evolutionary Debate*, London: Phoenix, 1996, pp. 207–8.

not limited to social insects: there have been many attempts to apply it to other animals, including mammals, and popular writers speculate extensively about its application to human relationships.[6]

Following the publication of Hamilton's papers on kin selection, others theorized about the evolutionary origins of altruism that extends beyond kin. Most famously, in the early 1970s, Robert Trivers published his theory of 'reciprocal altruism' – essentially a sophisticated theoretical articulation of the folk wisdom that if you scratch my back, I'll scratch yours.[7] Trivers used the mathematical discipline of game theory to argue that altruistic behaviour can be promoted by natural selection if the favour is likely to be returned. Reciprocal altruism received further theoretical support in the 1970s from computer simulations by Robert Axelrod and others which suggested that strategies of reciprocal co-operation could be 'evolutionarily stable' – that is, impervious to subversion by 'free-riders'.[8] Studies of animal, particularly primate, behaviour since the 1970s have supplied empirical evidence of reciprocity.[9]

Most commentators agree, however, that human altruism is not reducible without remainder to kin selection and reciprocity. There have been various attempts to develop evolutionary explanations for what we might call 'genuine' (i.e. non-kin, non-reciprocal) altruism. One possibility, summarized by Helena Cronin, is *manipulation*.[10] Natural selection could favour a 'gene for' behaviour that made some individuals successful at manipulating others to act in the manipulators' reproductive interests rather than their own – for example, a 'gene' that made young cuckoos successful at inducing their hosts to care for them at the expense of the hosts' own young. In this scenario, natural selection acts on the 'gene for' the cuckoo's manipulative behaviour; genuine altruism (in the technical sense defined at the beginning of this section) is displayed by the host that falls victim to the manipulation. This is,

---

6 E.g. Robert Wright, *The Moral Animal: Evolutionary Psychology and Everyday Life*, London: Abacus, 1996, pp. 155–88.

7 Robert L. Trivers, 'The Evolution of Reciprocal Altruism', *Quarterly Review of Biology*, 46 (1971), pp. 35–56.

8 Reviewed, e.g., by Richard Dawkins, *The Blind Watchmaker*, 2nd edn, Oxford: Oxford University Press, 1989, pp. 202–33.

9 Frans B. M. de Waal, *Good Natured: The Origins of Right and Wrong in Humans and Other Animals*, Cambridge, MA, and London: Harvard University Press, 1996, pp. 133–62.

10 Helena Cronin, *The Ant and the Peacock: Altruism and Sexual Selection from Darwin to Today*, Cambridge: Cambridge University Press, 1991, pp. 261–4. See also Lee Cronk, 'Evolutionary Theories of Morality and the Manipulative Use of Signals', *Zygon*, 29.1 (1994), pp. 81–101.

therefore, a scenario in which natural selection has given rise to a 'gene' that produces a genuinely altruistic behavioural phenotype, albeit in a rather indirect way: the 'gene' is in the cuckoo's genome, but its phenotype is displayed by its host, whose behaviour is regarded for this purpose as part of the 'extended phenotype' of the *cuckoo's* 'genes'.[11] This might not be a state of affairs that lasts very long in evolutionary terms: it could be expected that natural selection would strongly favour the development of resistance to manipulation in the 'sucker' species, so that an evolutionary arms race ensued between 'manipulators' and 'suckers'. But this might not happen, because the evolutionary cost to the 'sucker' might not be particularly high, and it could turn out to be more costly in evolutionary terms to develop defences against manipulation:

> spending a season rearing a cuckoo needn't be fatal to reproductive success and might anyway be a rare event for any individual member of the host species. By contrast, we can expect the cuckoos to put up an impressive evolutionary fight because for them this race is a matter of life and death . . . So the cuckoos probably owe some of their victory to the 'life–dinner principle': 'The rabbit runs faster than the fox, because the rabbit is running for his life while the fox is only running for his dinner'.[12]

Though Cronin's chief example is the cuckoo, which manipulates members of another species, she also suggests that manipulation between members of the same species could be selected for. When it comes to explaining the roots of human altruism, however, she focuses on the role of reciprocity and has little directly to say about manipulation.[13]

Loren Haarsma summarizes a second kind of hypothesis: 'that altruism and morality are adaptive and have a genetic basis'.[14] If this is taken

---

11 Richard Dawkins, *The Extended Phenotype: The Gene as the Unit of Natural Selection*, Oxford: W. H. Freeman, 1982.

12 Cronin, *The Ant and the Peacock*, p. 262, quoting Dawkins, *The Extended Phenotype*, p. 65.

13 Cronin, *The Ant and the Peacock*, pp. 335–42.

14 Loren Haarsma, 'Evolution and Divine Revelation', in Philip Clayton and Jeffrey Schloss (eds.), *Evolution and Ethics: Human Morality in Biological and Religious Perspective*, Grand Rapids: Eerdmans, 2004, pp. 153–70 (p. 155). Note that Haarsma cites both Cronin and Cronk as advocates of this hypothesis, but if he means that they believe genuine altruism to be adaptive for the individual displaying the adaptive behaviour, then he would appear to be mistaken. To be sure, Cronin follows Richard Dawkins in holding a 'gene's eye view' of natural selection in which manipulation is adaptive *for the 'gene'* that causes it, but that evolutionary advantage is gained by causing behaviour at a distance, in another individual – the 'sucker' – that is *maladaptive* for the latter, and its genes.

to mean that altruism, in the technical sense described earlier, is adaptive, then it is hard to see how this view avoids self-contradiction: it amounts to the claim that a 'gene for' behaviour that reduces the individual's reproductive chances (or those of its 'genes') increases the reproductive chances of that individual (or its 'genes'). If, in contrast, it is to be understood as the more general claim that altruism is one aspect of a morality that has a genetic basis and that improves the reproductive chances of moral individuals (or their 'genes'), then this hypothesis collapses into another of the views summarized by Haarsma: 'that altruism beyond kin and beyond reciprocation is a non-adaptive side effect of other adaptive traits' that themselves have a genetic basis.[15] For example, it might be that humans evolved the mental equipment and psychological dispositions necessary for reciprocal altruism because reciprocity was adaptive for our evolutionary ancestors, but, once this psychological equipment had evolved, it could give rise to new behaviours, such as genuine altruism, in new contexts.[16] Or, more generally, the course of our evolution as a social species might have favoured the development of traits such as sympathy and the capacity to predict the outcomes of our actions; once these capacities had developed, genuine altruism and other aspects of morality could arise out of them.[17]

These explanations are all either individual-selectionist or (in the case of authors like Dawkins and Cronin) gene-selectionist: that is to say, they hold, respectively, either that it is individuals or that it is genes that are subject to evolutionary selection pressures. As such, they follow the widespread current consensus, noted in Chapter 1, against group selectionism.[18] However, a few recent authors, such as Christopher Boehm, have challenged this consensus and argued that human altruism and other 'prosocial' traits could have evolved by a process of genetic group selection.[19] The standard objection to group-selectionist evolutionary explanations is that unless there is very little variation *within* groups, great variation *between* groups and a high rate of group extinction, any

---

15 Haarsma, 'Evolution and Divine Revelation', p. 155.

16 So, e.g., Cronin, *The Ant and the Peacock*, pp. 325–42.

17 On sympathy and other 'social instincts', see Charles Darwin, *The Descent of Man, and Selection in Relation to Sex*, London: John Murray, 1871, repr. with introduction by John Tyler Bonner and Robert M. May, Princeton, NJ: Princeton University Press, 1981, vol. 1, pp. 97–106, and Mary Midgley, *The Ethical Primate: Humans, Freedom and Morality*, London: Routledge, 1994, pp. 141–53.

18 See above, pp. 10–11.

19 Christopher Boehm, 'Explaining the Prosocial Side of Moral Communities', in Clayton and Schloss, *Evolution and Ethics*, pp. 78–100; see also Elliott Sober and David Sloan Wilson, *Unto Others: The Evolution and Psychology of Unselfish Behavior*, Cambridge, MA: Harvard University Press, 1998.

evolutionary effects caused by natural selection acting at the group level will be masked by the much greater effects of individual (or gene) selection. The conditions required for group selection to play a significant role are generally held to be highly improbable. Boehm acknowledges that this is true in general, but proposes that in early human evolution these conditions were met. In particular, on the basis of analogies with present-day non-literate communities, he holds that early human communities had cultural means of enforcing within-group conformity to the majority moral norm of the group, thus helping to create the conditions in which genetically based variations in moral behaviour *between* groups could significantly affect the survival and reproduction rates of those groups' members. Thus, he believes, a careful group-selectionism that takes account of the standard critiques can rehabilitate the more 'genetically naïve' group-selectionist explanation of morality advanced by Darwin.[20]

Peter Richerson and Robert Boyd, like Boehm, refer back to Darwin's group-selectionist account of the evolution of morality. Unlike Boehm, however, they concur with the majority view that any large evolutionary effect due to *genetic* group selection is implausible. Instead, they propose an account in which a range of *cultural* group selection processes influenced the evolution of morality: that is to say, cultures that have manifested behavioural traits such as genuine altruism have tended to flourish and spread by a variety of means, while cultures that have not have tended to die out.[21] Like Darwin, they trace the origins of human morality to the capacity for sympathy, a capacity that could have arisen by means of genetic evolutionary processes; they hold that once our species developed this capacity, that set in train a process of cultural evolution that has enabled us to defy the 'evolutionary law of gravity' stated by Hamilton's theory of kin selection.[22]

Early sociobiologists such as E. O. Wilson took their cue from the theories of Hamilton, Trivers and others in proposing a simple kind of reductionist answer to the question about the explanation of morality: it should eventually be explicable without remainder in terms of the

---

20 Boehm, 'Explaining the Prosocial Side', p. 81; see Darwin, *Descent*, vol. 1, pp. 166–7.

21 Peter J. Richerson and Robert Boyd, 'Darwinian Evolutionary Ethics: Between Patriotism and Sympathy', in Clayton and Schloss, *Evolution and Ethics*, pp. 50–77. They make the point that unlike genetic evolution, cultural evolution depends on neither the reproductive failure nor the death of individuals: one culture can flourish and another die out, for example, if the members of one group join another and assimilate culturally to the latter.

22 Richerson and Boyd, 'Darwinian Evolutionary Ethics', p. 72.

interactions of genes with their environment.[23] Some of the proposed explanations of genuine altruism that I have outlined would lend themselves fairly straightforwardly to such a reductionist scheme (though probably none of them actually *entails* a reductionist view of the Wilsonian kind). In particular, Cronin's proposal about manipulation and at least some versions of the 'non-adaptive side-effect' hypothesis could fit into a reductionist view quite straightforwardly. Boehm's genetic group-selectionist hypothesis fits a simple reductionist scheme less easily, because it depends on cultural as well as genetic mechanisms to make group selection work. To be sure, Wilson and his collaborators have attempted to assimilate cultural mechanisms to their reductionism in various ways. One of Wilson's best-known metaphors is of genes 'hold[ing] culture on a leash'.[24] However, as critics such as Holmes Rolston have pointed out, it is neither entirely clear what might be meant by this metaphor, nor at all certain that culture is under the kind of genetic influence that the metaphor of 'leashing' seems to imply.[25] In later works, Wilson has attempted to give a more nuanced account of the relationship between genes and culture with the concept of gene–culture co-evolution, whereby culture brings about changes in behaviour that are subsequently reinforced by genetic changes.[26] However, as Rolston points out, cultural change in human societies can be orders of magnitude faster than genetic evolutionary change, so it is hard to envisage how these processes could keep in step with one another.[27]

In response to such critiques of Wilson, others such as Daniel Dennett have attempted to salvage reductionism in their evolutionary explanations by proposing more complex, but still reductionist, schemes. Dennett acknowledges that early sociobiologists like Wilson were guilty of 'greedy reductionism', of trying to explain too much in one go.[28] His

23 Edward O. Wilson, *On Human Nature*, Cambridge, MA: Harvard University Press, 1978, p. 167; for a recent reiteration of his view, see Wilson, *Consilience: The Unity of Knowledge*, London: Abacus, 1998, pp. 280–5. It should be noted there is a tendency for such claims to elide the differences between *behaviour* such as altruism (in the biological sense) and *morality*, a system of values that govern the *evaluation* of behaviour. I thank Jacqui Stewart for drawing this point to my attention.

24 E.g. Wilson, *On Human Nature*, p. 167.

25 Rolston, *Genes, Genesis and God*, pp. 120–4.

26 Charles J. Lumsden and Edward O. Wilson, *Genes, Mind and Culture*, Cambridge, MA: Harvard University Press, 1981; see John Maddox *et al.*, 'Discussion: Genes, Mind and Culture', *Zygon*, 19.2 (1984), pp. 213–32.

27 Rolston, *Genes, Genesis and God*, pp. 128–30.

28 Daniel C. Dennett, *Darwin's Dangerous Idea: Evolution and the Meanings of Life*, London: Penguin, 1996, pp. 467–81.

own 'good reductionism' relies on the claim that the Darwinian process of descent with modification is a universal algorithm that can be run on many different kinds of hardware.[29] Neo-Darwinian evolutionary biology describes how the algorithm runs in biological systems by means of the inheritance and mutation of *genes*. But the same algorithm, Dennett thinks, can give rise to psychological and social change, in a way that can account for human motivation, behaviour and culture, by acting on *memes*, or units of cultural inheritance.[30] Thus, descent with modification becomes a theory of everything that can explain all biological, psychological and cultural phenomena without remainder.

As I have noted in earlier chapters, however, many commentators find the 'memology' of Dennett and others unconvincing. Mary Midgley suggests that it owes its appeal to the verbal analogy between 'genes' and 'memes', which suggests a promise that memology will place the humanities on the same kind of objective footing as the natural sciences; the analogy, however, is spurious and apt to mislead, because 'thought and culture are not the sort of thing that can have distinct units at all. They do not have a granular structure for the same reason that ocean currents do not have one – namely, because they are not stuffs but patterns.'[31] Others, including a number of evolutionary biologists, have also argued that there are more disanalogies than analogies between genetic evolution and cultural change.[32] Once the spurious parallels are removed from the picture, all that seems to remain is that ideas and practices are invented, handed on, tested, modified and sometimes discarded; and that, as Rolston remarks, is something that we have known for millennia.[33]

Some critics of reductionist explanations seek to give accounts of a morality that is biological in its origins, but that has transcended those biological origins and is not reducible to them. For example, Midgley, following Darwin in the *Descent*, develops an account in which 'social instincts' such as sympathy are central.[34] She points to the evidence

---

29 *Darwin's Dangerous Idea*, pp. 48–60.

30 *Darwin's Dangerous Idea*, pp. 335–69; see also Susan Blackmore, *The Meme Machine*, Oxford: Oxford University Press, 1999, esp. pp. 147–74.

31 Mary Midgley, 'Why Memes?', in Hilary Rose and Steven Rose (eds.), *Alas Poor Darwin: Arguments against Evolutionary Psychology*, London: Jonathan Cape, 2000, pp. 67–84 (pp. 67–8).

32 See, e.g., Rolston, *Genes, Genesis and God*, pp. 145–8; Stephen Jay Gould, 'Evolution: The Pleasures of Pluralism', *New York Review of Books*, 26 June 1997, pp. 47–52, available online at http://www.stephenjaygould.org/reviews/gould_pluralism.html (accessed 10 August 2006).

33 Rolston, *Genes, Genesis and God*, p. 146.

34 Midgley, *The Ethical Primate*, pp. 128–53; Darwin, *Descent*, vol. 1, pp. 70–106.

for the existence of such instincts, at least in rudimentary form, in our primate relatives,[35] and argues that, in our species, these social instincts are 'quieter' but more persistent than our other motives, and lead us to adopt a moral stance that is 'roughly generalized by the Golden Rule'. The proposal of Darwin's that she has developed, she says,

> is not just one more philistine piece of reductivism. It is an attempt to make sense of morality as it actually is, while regarding it as something which has evolved, and to explain the oddities of its actual working from its evolutionary history.[36]

Rolston, too, wishes to give an account of morality that has its roots in our evolutionary history, but transcends those roots. While he does not deny that rudimentary forms of sociality can be found among our close evolutionary relatives and are likely to have existed among our evolutionary ancestors, the development of ethics proper required the emergence of culture in human evolutionary history: 'Far from a killjoy reduction of ethics to nothing but biology, we have discovered that ethics is naturalized only at the start by way of anticipation and launching; afterward it is conceived and socialized in culture.'[37] But he goes further than Midgley, suggesting that the emergence of ethics is a sign of transcendence: 'As it matures, we are left wondering whether it does not even move beyond, glimpsing universals. The genesis of ethics . . . reveals transcendent powers come to expression point on Earth.'[38] This account of ethics forms part of his project of natural theology, whereby the emergence of 'value' during the natural history of the Earth, its development and flourishing, and the remarkable 'breakthroughs' or 'information explosions' that have occurred at intervals during that history provide a warrant for faith in a 'God [who] perennially underlies the causal forces in the world, and . . . gives meaning to the world'.[39]

An even more sceptical stance towards the explanatory power of evolutionary theories in respect of morality is taken by Anthony O'Hear.[40] He argues that, if human social life were subject to Darwinian principles, many of the moral virtues that are most familiar to us would not exist,

---

35 Cf. de Waal, *Good Natured*.
36 Midgley, *The Ethical Primate*, pp. 144, 145.
37 Rolston, *Genes, Genesis and God*, p. 291.
38 *Genes, Genesis and God*, p. 291.
39 *Genes, Genesis and God*, p. 368.
40 Anthony O'Hear, *Beyond Evolution: The Limits of Evolutionary Explanation*, Oxford: Oxford University Press, 1997, pp. 101–74.

because they would be strongly selected against. He also rejects the meme-based cultural evolutionary scheme of Dennett, and cultural group-selectionist explanations similar to Richerson and Boyd's,[41] on the grounds that once humans have developed the capacity for rational reflection about their behaviour the persistence of moral beliefs or traditions can no longer be explained simply in terms of their survival value to the group or the capacity of their memes to out-compete others: 'As self-conscious agents, there are occasions when we cannot avoid reflecting on our moral and political intuitions, just as at times we cannot avoid considering the truth of our moral beliefs.'[42] In other words, morality as we experience and practise it in real human communities 'may presuppose another, non-Darwinian world for [its] intelligibility',[43] and O'Hear thinks that this claim holds true even in the face of the attempts by Dennett and others to extend Darwinian forms of explanation beyond the biological to the social and cultural spheres.[44]

In short, a wide range of evolutionary proposals has been advanced to account for the fact that humans are beings who experience themselves as subject to moral demands and constraints, but (as might be expected) there is no consensus as to the plausibility or explanatory power of these proposals. In the following sections, I shall attempt to sketch out what might result if this debate about the possibilities and limits of a biological explanation of morality is brought into contact with a Christian understanding of humans and the world as God's creation.

2 Creation and evolution

In a recent survey, Colin Gunton draws attention to a number of important and distinctive features of the Christian doctrine of creation that, among other things, have a bearing on its relationship to scientific accounts of human origins.[45] First, it is a *credal affirmation*: 'We believe

---

41 O'Hear's example of cultural group-selectionism is based on F. A. Hayek, *The Fatal Conceit*, London: Routledge, 1988.

42 O'Hear, *Beyond Evolution*, p. 154.

43 *Beyond Evolution*, p. 143.

44 For a further critique of reductionist and determinist attempts to apply biology to human behaviour, with particular reference to the ethological ideas of Konrad Lorenz and others (which, she argues, were both scientifically flawed and distorted by the ideological climate of Nazi Germany), see Jacqui A. Stewart, *Reconstructing Science and Theology in Postmodernity: Pannenberg, Ethics and the Human Sciences*, Aldershot: Ashgate, 2000, pp. 49–58.

45 Colin E. Gunton, *The Triune Creator: A Historical and Systematic Study*, Grand Rapids, MI, and Cambridge: Eerdmans, 1998.

in one God, the Father, the Almighty, maker of heaven and earth, of all that is, seen and unseen.' This means, as Gunton puts it, that it is 'not something self-evident or the discovery of disinterested reason, but part of the fabric of Christian response to revelation'.[46] He thus distances the doctrine of creation from any form of natural theology. Evidence of the Creator may be everywhere in the world, as Paul says (Romans 1.18–23); but Paul also appears to think that the evidence is universally ignored or misread, which is attributed by many of his readers to 'the human heart's universal tendency to fabricate idols'.[47]

The fact that the Christian doctrine of creation is a credal affirmation has other important implications. One, to which I shall return shortly, is that it is a different kind of statement from scientific statements about the world. To say, 'We believe in God . . . maker of heaven and earth' is to make a different *kind* of claim than when one says that the universe originated in the Big Bang, or that life on earth is the product of evolution by natural selection. Another is that the doctrine of creation is inextricably linked to other Christian doctrines and credal affirmations: Gunton draws attention in particular to its close connections with redemption and eschatology. This connection between creation, redemption and eschatology means among other things that (unlike scientific accounts) the Christian doctrine of creation offers a teleological understanding of the world. Gunton draws on Irenaeus of Lyons to argue that creation is to be understood as a 'project': what God has made is, in an unqualified sense, good; yet there is also a sense in which it has still to be completed, because it is destined for eschatological perfection. On this view, the significance of sin and evil is that they divert the creation from its eschatological goal; redemption can then be understood as its redirection towards the eschatological fulfilment for which God destined it.[48]

The second relevant feature of the Christian doctrine of creation is that God created the world out of nothing, rather than merely fashioning it from pre-existing matter. This affirmation is not to be found, explicitly at any rate, in the biblical sources of the doctrine of creation, but was a crucial development in the early history of Christian thought. Influential characters in this part of the story include Irenaeus, Athanasius, Basil of Caesarea and Augustine of Hippo. The doctrine of *creatio ex nihilo* sets up an 'absolute ontological distinction', as Gunton

---

46 *The Triune Creator*, p. 8.
47 *The Triune Creator*, p. 7, citing John Calvin, *Institutes*, I.5.
48 *The Triune Creator*, pp. 55–6.

puts it, between Creator and creature;[49] this is important, not only for a proper account of God's power and freedom in creation, but also to safeguard the identity of the creation. If the creation is identified too closely with the being of God, there is a danger that it will come to be seen merely as some sort of extension of God's being, and its own reality denied or downplayed.

The doctrine of *creatio ex nihilo* also suggests the temporal and finite nature of the creation: it had a beginning and will have an end. Thus the doctrine of creation is not simply a way of saying that the world is dependent upon God for its existence. Talk of the creation is 'tensed': God created the heavens and the earth 'in the beginning'; the universe is sustained by God's power and love; God will in due time bring all things to fulfilment in Christ. But the significance of this temporal language is not straightforward, because it raises the difficult question of the relationship between the eternal Creator and the temporal creation.[50] This question cannot be discussed at length here, but a few brief points may be made. To begin with, the Creator is eternal, not limited or self-limited by time as we experience it, and it would be unwise to try and safeguard the reality of time or the freedom of human action in history by projecting our temporal limitations back onto God, as sometimes seems to happen in discussions of science and theology.[51] Nonetheless, as Barth argues, it may also be unwise to describe the eternal God as 'timeless': it might be better, as Gunton puts it, to speak of God's eternity 'as, so to speak, directed to the creation of time'.[52] Christian orthodoxy (as distinct from deism) of course affirms the continuing engagement of the eternal God with the temporal creation, and this engagement is brought to its sharpest focus in the Incarnation, the closest possible interaction of the eternal God with historical human existence in the world.

In any event, our historical time is part of God's creation, and this lies behind the insight, going back to Augustine, that it makes no sense to

---

49 *The Triune Creator*, p. 67.

50 *The Triune Creator*, pp. 79–92; see also, e.g., Karl Barth, *Church Dogmatics*, ET ed. by G. W. Bromiley and T. F. Torrance, Edinburgh: T&T Clark, 1956–75 (hereafter *CD*), vol. III.1, pp. 42–76; Wolfhart Pannenberg, 'Eternity, Time and the Trinitarian God', *CTI Reflections*, 3 (1999), pp. 49–61; Russell Stannard, 'God in and beyond Space and Time', in Philip Clayton and Arthur Peacocke (eds.), *In Whom We Live and Move and Have Our Being: Panentheistic Reflections on God's Presence in a Scientific World*, Grand Rapids, MI: Eerdmans, 2004, pp. 109–20.

51 See, e.g., Ian Barbour, *Nature, Human Nature and God*, London: SPCK, 2002, pp. 105–8.

52 Gunton, *The Triune Creator*, p. 91, citing Barth, *CD* II.1, pp. 615–18.

ask what God was doing before the creation of the world.[53] There was no 'before', *if* 'before' is understood in terms of the historical time that we inhabit. This means that both the 'beginning' and the 'end', as Christian theology understands them, are beyond the reach of scientific and historical investigation: the Big Bang was not the 'moment of creation', notwithstanding the tendency of popular scientific literature so to describe it; nor will the heat death of the universe be the eschaton. That is why, as Barth insists, the story of creation 'in the beginning' cannot be told by means of history, but instead requires what he calls 'saga'.[54] It also reinforces the point made earlier, that the Christian doctrine of creation is a different kind of discourse from scientific statements about the world. To put the matter this way reinforces the point made in Chapter 3, that it is a great mistake to assume (with scientific reductionists such as Daniel Dennett and creationists such as Henry Morris) that belief in a creator God is an explanatory hypothesis of the same kind as Darwinian evolutionary theory. Of course, it is easy to point out that this assumption is mistaken, but harder to specify the different kinds of question that a scientific account of origins and the Christian doctrine of creation address. Nonetheless, it is important to be aware at any rate that there *is* a difference, and to be alert to the potential for confusion.

The third feature of the Christian doctrine of creation to which Gunton draws attention is that creation is the work of the God who is Father, Son and Holy Spirit. Among other things, this feature makes it possible to speak of the creation as contingent rather than necessary. God had no need to create the universe to meet any need of God's: 'prior to' the creation, so to say, God is 'already' a Trinity of Persons united in perfect communion and love. Therefore, the creation of the world can be understood as an act of sheer gratuitous love on God's part, and when God pronounces the creation 'very good' (Gen. 1.31) this must be taken to mean that it is good *in and for itself*, not merely instrumentally. The contingency and goodness of the creation have important implications for the natural sciences. Its contingency suggests that, if we wish to understand the material world, we shall need to employ scientific means. God was not bound to create the universe, nor to create *this* universe as opposed to some other one. The created order could have been other than it is. Therefore if we wish to know what it is like, we

---

53 Augustine, *Confessions*, XI.10–30, in Whitney J. Oates (ed.), *Basic Writings of St Augustine*, vol. 1, New York: Random House, 1948, pp. 189–203.
54 Barth, *CD* III.1, pp. 76–94.

shall not be able to find out by reasoning *a priori* about the kind of world that God must have made: empirical investigation of the world that God has actually made will be needed. The goodness of the creation suggests one motivation for doing so – not, to be sure, the only reason why science is worth doing, but at any rate a reason to think that the investigation of the world is likely to prove rewarding.

Creation as the work of the triune God also suggests an understanding of the *mediation* of God's creative work. Gunton draws attention to the well-known image of Irenaeus, that God created the world by means of his 'two hands', the Son and the Spirit.[55] This image, which might on the face of it appear naively anthropomorphic, is actually both sophisticated and significant in several respects. Part of its significance is that God had no need of intermediaries to do the work of creating the world. Irenaeus thus sets himself against Gnostic views that set up hierarchies of intermediate beings and take such a dim view of the material world that salvation must mean rescue *from* the material rather than salvation *in and with* it. The image of God's two hands also enables Irenaeus to emphasize that *creatio ex nihilo* is an act, not just of divine power and will, but also of gratuitous love; according to Gunton, this emphasis is neglected in the work of later writers like Tertullian and Augustine, whose talk of *creatio ex nihilo* tends to be separated from the Trinitarian context in which Irenaeus sets it. Irenaeus' view, furthermore, has important implications for the relation of God to the world. As Gunton puts it,

> Irenaeus' God is ontologically transcendent, as creator of everything else that exists. But by virtue of his triune nature, God the Father is able to enter into personal relations with the created order by the mediating activity of his two hands, the Son and the Spirit, who are as truly God as he is God.[56]

This makes possible a nuanced account of the relationship between God and the creation, an account that can avoid the opposite errors of placing so much stress on creation's closeness to God that it becomes difficult to speak of the creation's identity and freedom (as in pantheistic and perhaps panentheistic accounts) and of emphasizing God's transcendence in such a way that it becomes difficult to give an account of God's involvement with the world (as in theologies that tend towards deism). In other words, this way of conceiving the Trinitarian mediation

---

55 Gunton, *The Triune Creator*, pp. 52–6, 61–4.
56 *The Triune Creator*, p. 60.

of creation allows us to speak of a creator God who is both *utterly other* than the creation and *continuously and intimately involved* with it, but whose involvement nonetheless *leaves the creation free* to be itself in response to its Creator.

3 Human creatures

The theological discussion of what it means to be a human creature has been dominated, in the history of Christian thought, by attempts to expound the doctrine of the *imago Dei*: the affirmation that humans are made in the image and likeness of God (Gen. 1.26–7). It has often been said in recent years that attempts to locate the *imago Dei* primarily in the structure of the individual human soul or in some characteristic that sets us apart from the non-human creation are, at least, in need of revision and extension.[57] Recent writing has tended instead to give a *relational or social* account of the *imago*. Christoph Schwöbel has argued that, in this respect, it has reflected a more general trend in anthropological reflection, to think of human being in terms of relationships – whether to the physical and biological world, to one another in social relations, to the cultural milieu in which one participates, or to oneself in self-relation. For Schwöbel, what distinguishes a Christian anthropology from others is that it identifies the defining relationship, which gives shape and direction to all the others, as 'the relationship of the triune God to humanity'.[58] Later, I shall have one or two caveats to enter about this presentation of the matter, but there is undoubtedly much to be said for it.

One persuasive account of the *imago Dei* in relational terms has been developed by Alistair McFadyen. He explores what it means to be made in the image of God, describing 'vertical' and 'horizontal' dimensions of the image: the 'vertical' dimension is that human beings are created for relationship with God, a relationship which is 'structured from God's side as dialogue'. That is to say, God addresses us in a way which leaves us free either to respond with gratitude and praise or to refuse such response. Insofar as we respond to God in such a way, our life 'has an

---

57 See, e.g., Gunton, *The Triune Creator*, pp. 193–211; Kevin Vanhoozer, 'Human Being, Individual and Social', in Colin E. Gunton (ed.), *The Cambridge Companion to Christian Doctrine*, Cambridge: Cambridge University Press, 1997, pp. 158–88.

58 Christoph Schwöbel, 'Human Being as Relational Being: Twelve Theses for a Christian Anthropology', in Christoph Schwöbel and Colin E. Gunton (eds.), *Persons, Divine and Human: King's College Essays in Theological Anthropology*, Edinburgh: T&T Clark, 1991, pp. 141–65 (p. 143).

undistorted structure', but distortion is introduced into our life when we refuse the dialogue to which God invites us. Such undistorted or distorted forms of relationship with God constitute, over time, a 'history of communication' whose 'sedimentation' forms our personal identity.[59]

God's relationship of dialogue with us also calls for our response in the 'horizontal' dimension, that is to say, in our interpersonal and social relationships. Here, McFadyen draws on Jürgen Moltmann's Trinitarian theology to argue that the image of God in human beings must be understood in relational terms:

> Just as the Persons of the Trinity receive and maintain their identities through relation, and relations of a certain quality, then so would human persons only receive and maintain their identities through relations with others and would stand fully in God's image whenever these identities and relations achieved a certain quality.[60]

By analogy with the relationships between the persons of the Trinity and the 'vertical' divine–human relationship, McFadyen argues that human relations which fully reflect God's image are *dialogical*, leaving the other free and un-coerced, and '*ex-centric*', that is to say outward-looking and centred on the other rather than on oneself. Like the vertical relationship with God, our relationships with one another in the horizontal dimension contribute to that sedimentation of communications which shapes our personal identity. Patterns of communication which are distorted by being in some measure coercive, self-centred and so on (in other words, sinful) cause our identity to develop in distorted ways, thereby limiting our freedom to relate to others in undistorted ways. Social structures as well as individual relationships can be distorted. In this fallen world, we are all born into such distorted patterns and structures, and in this sense are the inheritors of original sin. In such a world, God offers the possibility of redemption through Christ, which McFadyen discusses in terms of Jesus' call of the disciples. The call of Christ comes to us as perfectly undistorted communication (dialogical rather than coercive, and other-centred rather than self-centred). The call invites *us* to respond in an undistorted way: 'Follow me' is an invitation to shift the central focus of our lives from ourselves to Christ and

---

59 Alistair I. McFadyen, *The Call to Personhood: A Christian Theory of the Individual in Social Relationships*, Cambridge: Cambridge University Press, 1990; quotations from pp. 19, 23.

60 McFadyen, *The Call to Personhood*, p. 31.

others.[61] This experience is made real in the Church, where the presence of Christ is experienced. The energy of the Holy Spirit is made available to those who respond to the call of Christ, holding out the possibility of living in transformed ways in this still-distorted world.

In somewhat similar vein to McFadyen, Kevin Vanhoozer has attempted to rework a traditional Christian anthropology in terms of the self as speech-agent: 'God creates human persons by calling them forth out of nothing to the dignity of fellowship.'[62] We come to know ourselves as selves by virtue of the encounters in which others call us by name. Our personal identity is to be understood in historical and relational terms: it is underwritten not by an unchanging substance but by faithfulness and constancy in the history of our communicative activity. Notwithstanding biological or social constraints that may limit our freedom of movement, we have both freedom and moral responsibility in our communicative action, and Vanhoozer characterizes the life of Christian faith, too, in terms of communicative action:

> Christian existence is a matter of the relation a speaker bears to his own words. Faithfulness may be defined as the religious relation to one's own words; the life of faith is the life of faithful speech . . . The church . . . exists as a gathered people by virtue of the divine call . . . To be human is to participate in the covenant of divine discourse as a faithful hearer and speaker.[63]

Undoubtedly there is much to be affirmed in these accounts. They offer an enormously valuable corrective to the rationalism and individualism that are found in some other accounts of personhood and the *imago*, and they emphasize that human identity is to be found in relation to God. If there is a problem with them, however, it lies in the persistent danger that they become to a greater or lesser extent disembodied. McFadyen, to be sure, wishes 'to take physical embodiment with appropriate seriousness',[64] and it is true that embodiment is a necessary (but

---

61 It should be obvious from what follows, particularly the discussion of sin as sloth in Chapter 7, that this is not to be construed as a command to become 'doormats', allowing our selfhood to be dissipated in the service of others. It is, rather, a call to turn away from distorted forms of human life, such as the solipsism of living for oneself first and foremost – a form of life turned in on itself (*incurvatus in se*, to use Luther's phrase) – to the true humanity that is to be found in communion with God and one another. I am grateful to Kurt Remele for prompting me to enter this clarification.

62 Vanhoozer, 'Human Being', p. 180.

63 'Human Being', pp. 182–3.

64 McFadyen, *The Call to Personhood*, p. 78.

not sufficient) condition for communicative agency: it seems impossible to conceive of any kind of human communication that does not depend in *some* way on human bodies (be that on voices, faces, hands or whatever). But to suggest that 'the reality of persons is . . . *primarily* social'[65] risks overstating the case. Certainly, if it were suggested that speech-agency is *the* crucial and distinctive characteristic of human persons, this would seem to offer a rather attenuated picture of human personal being, living and relationships.[66] If it is true that Christian worship is an anticipation of the destiny that God intends for human creatures and for the whole creation, this would certainly seem to set a question mark against accounts of personhood as communication in which the latter is narrowly understood in terms of speech-agency. Certainly, one of the central acts of Christian worship, namely, the proclamation of the Word, can obviously be described as a speech-act; but the other equally central acts, the sacraments of baptism and the Eucharist, have to do not only with speech but also with eating and drinking, with broken flesh and spilled blood, with death and burial in the earth (or in water) and with rising to new (but still embodied) life. In the Eucharist we *communicate* in ways that involve speech, to be sure, but that are centred on the physical actions of material bodies.

One thing that a critical appropriation of biology into the Christian doctrine of creation can do for us is to remind us to give due weight to the fact that human personhood in the image of God is physically embodied existence in a material world. As John Zizioulas has remarked, whatever else Darwinism does or does not do for us, it reminds us of our continuity with the animals.[67] A similar point was made by Mary Midgley some years ago in her oft-quoted remark that '[w]e are not just rather like animals; we *are* animals'.[68] An account of human evolution might help us to understand the significance of the Genesis creation narratives when they tell us that God formed the

---

65 *The Call to Personhood*, p. 78, emphasis added.

66 It might seem plausible to scholars, who earn their living by means of speech-acts, that these are *the* characteristic form of human being and agency, but it seems harder to describe other forms of human activity in the same way. Building a house, making a garden, cooking a meal or driving a bus, for example, could certainly be described as forms of communicative activity, but to subsume them under the heading of speech-acts would entail stretching the meaning of 'speech' to an implausible degree.

67 John D. Zizioulas, 'Preserving God's Creation. Three Lectures on Theology and Ecology. I', *King's Theological Review*, 12 (1989), pp. 1–5, cited by Gunton, *The Triune Creator*, pp. 186–7, 205.

68 Mary Midgley, *Beast and Man*, rev. edn, London: Routledge, 1995 (1978), p. xxxiii.

human being from the dust of the earth (Gen. 2.7) and that humankind was created, like other animals, on the sixth day (Gen. 1.24–31). In other words, it can – almost literally – help us to *flesh out* what it means to be embodied creatures. It can thereby offer an antidote to an *over-*emphasis on relationality in understanding human personhood: it can caution us against imagining that relationships are the only thing that have formed us, or attempting to subsume everything that can be said about humanity under the heading of 'relationships'.[69] This means, furthermore, that an evolutionary biological account of human origins can remind us that our embodiment (the *sine qua non* of our creaturely existence in the material world) inevitably opens up to us some possibilities for living and acting in the world and closes off others. As Midgley suggests, it is a mistake to think 'that we are wholly flexible, that our freedom offers unlimited new directions', and that we can and should 'create or invent our own values, instead of taking goals as in some sense given'.[70] An account of human evolution might help us to understand where some of the limits to our flexibility and our possibilities lie – particularly since it is often suggested that human sociality itself has at least some of its roots in the contingent features of our evolutionary history, in which case our evolutionary inheritance could be one of the factors that predisposes us to some patterns of sociality rather than others. However, the question of how we should evaluate our limits, and what moral conclusions (if any) can be drawn from them, is far from straightforward to answer; I shall return to various aspects of this issue in subsequent chapters.

4 Human being as moral being

On almost any account of what it is to be human, *morality* is an important part of the picture. That is certainly true of a Christian theological anthropology, but more needs to be said about both what is meant by 'morality' and what part it plays in a Christian account of human being.

It is clear from section 1 that evolutionary accounts of human origins also have plenty to say about morality, and some (though not all) are

---

69 Cf. Schwöbel, 'Human Being', pp. 141–2, where he seems to attempt to present every kind of anthropology as relational: thus, for example, biological anthropology is an account of 'the relationship of human beings to other parts of the animal world and to its common microbiological structures'. In a sense, of course, this is true, but only if the word 'relationship' is used in a rather different sense from the senses it bears when we are talking about personal relationships between humans, or of humans to God.

70 Midgley, *The Ethical Primate*, pp. 150–3, 159 (p. 150).

confident of being able to give a complete explanation of our having a morality of the kind that we do. Some evolutionary explanations have a tendency to reduce 'morality' to a relatively small number of behaviours and traits, exemplified by *altruism*: there is sometimes a tendency to assume that if altruism can be explained in evolutionary terms, it should also be possible to explain the other behaviours and traits that make up morality. But from a theological standpoint, how satisfactory is this as an account of what we mean by morality? Within the framework of a Christian theological anthropology, what is meant by it, and is it the kind of thing that *could* be susceptible to a natural scientific (for example, evolutionary) explanation?

If we attempt to outline the understanding of morality that might be suggested by the doctrine of creation and the theological anthropology outlined above, several features suggest themselves.

1 The Christian doctrine of creation includes *an evaluative comment on the material world, from the very outset*: 'God saw everything that he had made, and indeed, it was very good' (Gen. 1.31). Furthermore, the Genesis creation narratives paint a picture in which the good of humankind is supported by the material world. We are, so to say, at home here. In this respect, a Christian view of creation stands in contrast to modern estimates of the material world, which, as Gerald McKenny has argued, have tended increasingly since the eighteenth century to see it as indifferent to the human good, and as needing to be subdued in the service of the latter.[71] There is no need to project philosophico-theological puzzles such as the Euthyphro dilemma onto this text: it is fairly clear that, for its author, Israel's God is good, and the creation is good because it reflects the purposes of the good God who

---

71 Gerald P. McKenny, *To Relieve the Human Condition: Bioethics, Technology and the Body*, Albany, NY: State University of New York Press, 1997, pp. 18–19. This subjugation of nature in the service of human ends is a central part of what McKenny characterizes as the 'Baconian project', which will be discussed further in Chapter 9. As I suggested in Chapter 2, this view of the cosmos is well reflected in Huxley's 'Evolution and Ethics' and in some of his other writings: see above, pp. 38–40 (ch. 2, section 3e). For an even more negative estimate of the material world, see George C. Williams, 'Huxley's Evolution and Ethics in Sociobiological Perspective', *Zygon*, 23.4 (1988), pp. 383–407. Of course, the Priestly creation narrative from which I have quoted also includes the command to 'subdue' the earth; but as I shall argue later, when read within the framework of a Christian anthropology and doctrine of creation, the command to subdue the earth and have dominion over it needs to be understood in terms of humanity's 'priestly' vocation of enabling the creation to be itself in response to its divinely ordered destiny. This gives a very different picture from that of humanity bending an indifferent nature to our own ends.

made it.[72] This is not yet a moral evaluation, but it is morally relevant, and suggests the outlines of a moral picture: the goodness of the creation consists in its conforming to the purposes of its good Creator. For humans, who are able to reflect and deliberate on their lives and actions, this conformity to God's good purposes will be in some measure a matter of personal character and decision. Moral living and acting have something to do with 'going with the grain', as it were, of the way God has created the world; human lives, decisions and actions will be good if they conform to the purposes for which God has created the world; human treatment of the non-human creation will be good insofar as it enables the creation to fulfil its created purposes.

This is not to say, of course, that an understanding of the good for humans and the material world – much less detailed moral prescriptions – can simply be read off our observations of the world or ourselves. Following Gunton, I noted earlier that the doctrine of creation is a credal affirmation, part of the fabric of human response to God's self-revelation in Christ. We do not know the world as creation merely by looking at it, nor by investigating it scientifically; we need to be taught by the Creator that the world is God's good creation. And that suggests that mere scientific inspection of the world will not disclose to us what it means to 'go with the grain' of God's purposes in creation. The question of how we *might* know what it means will be taken up later; for the present, the point is simply that, *pace* those modern commentators such as George Williams who make a thoroughly negative moral estimate of the material world, in theological perspective a kind of goodness that has moral significance is part of the structure of things from the outset.

Furthermore, I argued earlier that a Christian doctrine of creation offers a teleology, in a way that a natural scientific account of the universe cannot. If the world is understood – credally, in response to revelation – as God's 'project' (Gunton's word), created good and destined for perfection, this adds to what I have already said about the moral structure of the way things are. The good, for humans and the whole creation, is whatever is oriented to the destiny of the created order; evil is whatever diverts us or the creation from that destiny. Again, these things cannot be learned from scientific observations of the world or of human life, because scientific observation and theorizing are in the nature of the case confined to created time, whereas the creation

---

72 So, e.g., Wenham, *Genesis 1–15* (Word Biblical Commentary, 1), Waco, TX: Word, 1987, p. 18.

and the ultimate destiny of the world have to do with the action of the eternal God beyond the confines of temporal creaturely existence. How we might learn about these things will, again, be taken up later.

It will be noticed that the account I have outlined proceeds in more or less the opposite direction from Holmes Rolston's natural theology, to which I referred briefly in section 1. Rolston begins by claiming that 'value' is present wherever there is life – microbial, plant or animal, sentient or non-sentient. Any living organism is 'self-actualizing', and in growing, metabolizing, repairing injuries, reproducing and so on, it 'defends' the value inherent in it:

> As an heir to its portion of the diversity and complexity generated in evolutionary natural history, any particular organism, with its genes, defends that organism's good inhering in itself, in its 'self' – a somatic though not a psychological 'self' – which in reproduction is passed in part to an offspring 'self', which is also such good defended in kin.[73]

As humans appear in evolutionary history, and as culture develops and breaks free of the 'leash' of the genes, *moral* value emerges from the non-moral value that pervades the living world. The climax of this evolutionary story of the emergence of value is that we are led to conclude that 'the world is sacred', a conclusion embraced 'even [by] so resolute a naturalist as Daniel Dennett'.[74] 'But then', continues Rolston,

> why not say that here, if anywhere, is the brooding Spirit of God? One needs an adequate explanation for generating the sacred out of the secular. Indeed, why not even go on to say that this genesis of value is the genesis of grace, since the root idea in 'grace' . . . is pleasing, favorable, praiseworthy; essentially, again, the idea of something valuable, now also a given.[75]

If this is to be taken as an argument from the existence of value in the natural world to belief in God as its most plausible explanation, then it has certain difficulties. First, is it so obvious that 'value' is intrinsically *present* in the natural world? Rolston chides those who deny that non-sentient beings can value anything for stipulating rather than arguing for this point.[76] But it could be said that his own attribution of 'values'

---

73 Rolston, *Genes, Genesis and God*, pp. 39–40.
74 *Genes, Genesis and God*, p. 362, quoting Dennett, *Darwin's Dangerous Idea*, p. 520.
75 *Genes, Genesis and God*, p. 362.
76 *Genes, Genesis and God*, p. 39.

to all living things is also a stipulation – that he posits what he then invokes the existence of God to explain – and if his opponents do not accept the stipulation, it is unlikely that they will be persuaded by the explanation. Second, there is a danger of unhelpful shifts in the meaning of the word 'value'. Non-moral value is held to be present throughout the biological world, and even non-sentient animals and plants are said to 'value' what promotes their good. When humans evolve, they develop *moral* values, which then impel them to respect the non-moral value of nature.[77]

> Nature is amoral, but that is not to disparage it. That is to set aside irrelevant categories for its interpretation. Amoral nature is fundamentally and radically the ground, the root out of which arise all the particular values manifest in organisms and ecosystems. This includes all human values, even though, when they come, human values rise higher than their precedents in spontaneous nature.[78]

But this leaves rather obscure the relationship between the non-moral *value* that is attributed to nature, the non-moral *valuing* that even plants are said to do, and the *moral* value and valuing that emerge in human history. For all that Rolston rightly takes sociobiologists to task for making confusing shifts in the meanings of words like 'altruism' and 'selfishness',[79] there is a risk that his own shifting use of the language of value could also, at times, obscure more than it illuminates.

Rolston's natural-theological project is, perhaps, vulnerable to the critique of natural theology voiced some years ago by T. F. Torrance: insistent that the proper method of a science must be determined by the nature of its object, Torrance held that because the Object of theological enquiry is God, the methods of natural science are inappropriate for 'scientific theology'. This led him to a methodological (though not, as he was careful to emphasize, a metaphysical) rejection of natural theology:

> Both natural science and scientific theology operate through a methodological exclusion of one another, for by their very nature they move in opposite directions . . . Natural science starts from premises that do not include God, and moves in an opposite direction to theology in accordance with the nature of its subject-matter, but 'natural theology' starts from the same premises and the same

---

77 *Genes, Genesis and God*, p. 280.
78 *Genes, Genesis and God*, pp. 286–7.
79 *Genes, Genesis and God*, pp. 272–6.

phenomena as natural science and seeks to move towards God, and in so doing brings itself into conflict with natural science and with pure theology, proving to be a source of confusion to both if not an actual obstacle in their progress.[80]

The account that I sketched earlier of the goodness of creation is an attempt to proceed in the direction recommended by Torrance. If, instead of positing the existence of 'value' and using it to argue for the existence of God, we begin with the credal affirmation that the good Creator judges the creation to be 'very good', this enables us to give an account in which the relationship between the non-moral goodness of the world and the moral goodness of good human action and character is somewhat clearer.

2   The Christian anthropology outlined in the last section suggests *an account of the formation of personal identity that might lend itself to an understanding of moral formation*. According to McFadyen and others, personal identity is formed by the 'sedimentation' of our 'communication history': our encounters and relationships with God and with one another lay down a deposit, as it were, that constitutes the particular selves that we are. This suggests that our personal identities are dynamic, always changing as a result of new relationships and episodes in our 'communication history', and that we are constantly involved in shaping our own and one another's identities, in either 'undistorted' or 'distorted' ways. However, at the heart of our identity is our 'deep self', the product of our earliest, most enduring and most significant relations, the settled core of our identity that is not easily subject to flux or shifting.

There are striking parallels between this account of personhood and those contemporary accounts of virtue ethics that, following MacIntyre, stress the importance of moral communities in forming the character and virtue of their members.[81] A moral community in the MacIntyrean sense has an identity shaped by a narrative and a tradition. The tradition is embodied and rehearsed in the community's shared discourse and practices; it shapes the community's rationality and conception of the good life; and it is itself constantly subject to argument and re-negotiation among the community's members. The community provides the

---

80 Thomas F. Torrance, *Theological Science*, London: Oxford University Press, 1969, pp. 102–3.

81 Alasdair MacIntyre, *After Virtue: A Study in Moral Theory*, 2nd edn, London: Duckworth, 1985, pp. 218–25.

locus within which its members learn and grow in virtue, by participating in significant relationships that help 'sediment' their personal and moral identity, by following the example of others, by participating in the community's corporate practices and by coming to inhabit its tradition as their own. Thus it is within a moral community that the 'sedimentation' of its members' personal identities and moral characters takes place.

This is not to say, of course, that any given community is necessarily a good thing just because it is the kind of community that shapes its members' personal and moral identities. It is quite possible for a community to live by a narrative and a tradition so distorted that its moral rationality and character become thoroughly corrupted, and the moral character that is 'sedimented' in its members is vicious rather than virtuous. Indeed, any moral community in this world will in some measure be distorted and corrupted, since, as I observed earlier, we are all formed in some measure by distorted relationships, and pass on distorted forms of relationship to others in our turn. For this reason, as I shall argue later, talk of virtue ethics in a Christian theological context must be firmly located (so to say) after Easter and Pentecost.

3   This Christian anthropology also suggests a *structure of call and response* in the human moral life lived before God. We are constituted as persons by God's gracious call to us, which establishes a covenant relationship with us and invites, but never coerces, the appropriate response of love, faithfulness and worship to God. As Vanhoozer puts it, 'God evokes human creatures through his creative, saving and sanctifying activity and calls them to faithful fellowship. Humans, as communicative and covenantal creatures, respond to this call, sometimes appropriately . . ., sometimes inappropriately . . .'.[82] Similarly, we are bound together with one another in the 'inclusive covenant' that encompasses all human creatures, and in many overlapping 'special covenants' with particular persons or communities, which might include, for example, marriage and family life, political community, and the relationships between professionals and those whom they serve – for example in health care.[83] Like the 'vertical' covenant relationship that is

---

82 Vanhoozer, 'Human Being', p. 103.

83 Joseph L. Allen, *Love and Conflict: A Covenantal Model of Christian Ethics*, Lanham, MD: University Press of America, 1995 (1984); William F. May, 'The Medical Covenant: An Ethics of Obligation or Virtue?', in Gerald P. McKenny and Jonathan R. Sande (eds.), *Theological Analyses of the Clinical Encounter*, Dordrecht: Kluwer, 1994, pp. 29–44.

established by God's gracious address to us, these 'horizontal' covenant relationships have about them a structure of call and response: my neighbour's mere presence to me determines to some extent what would count as my appropriate response to her,[84] and particular features of our relationship (for example, her need for health care, if I am a health professional and she is one of my patients) may further determine the shape of the response that is called forth from me. Indeed, biblical texts such as the parable of the sheep and the goats (Matt. 25.31–46) suggest a close relationship between the 'vertical' and the 'horizontal': there is a sense in which the call of my neighbour, particularly my neighbour in need, *is* the call of Christ to me. And the form of God's address to us (dialogical, not coercive; centred on the other, not self-centred) suggests something central about the form of *human* covenant relationships that conform to the *imago Dei*.

4   The Christian doctrine of creation and theological anthropology sketched here also suggest *an account of human relationships with the non-human creation*. This must be characterized, first, in terms of *solidarity*: the theme of the 'ontological homogeneity' of creation, first fully articulated by Basil of Caesarea,[85] suggests that the basic relation in which we stand to all other created things is that of fellow-creature. Within this basic stance, there can be different degrees of closeness: the writers of the Genesis creation narratives emphasize our close kinship to the other animals, created like us on the sixth day (Gen. 1.24–6), or formed like us from the dust of the earth (2.18–20).[86]

Our relationship with the non-human creation must also be characterized in terms of *responsibility*: here, difficult and controversial concepts such as dominion, stewardship and priesthood come into play. These notions are problematic in more than one way: first, they might seem incredible in the light of modern scientific knowledge of the vastness of the universe and the smallness of humanity. It is hard to imagine, for example, how humanity's priestly role for the creation might be exercised in respect of Alpha Centauri. However, if our concern is with the structure of the human moral life lived before God, it seems a wise procedure to leave these abstract and somewhat impractical objections on one side, at least for the present: our first concern should be with our

---

84 This might include, as a fairly basic obligation, the Kantian precept of treating her as an end in herself, never merely as a means – though not exactly for Kant's reasons.

85 Gunton, *The Triune Creator*, pp. 71–3.

86 Cf. Barth, *CD* III.4, pp. 348–56.

responsibilities in respect of those parts of the material creation that are within our reach. Secondly, however, the concepts of dominion, stewardship and priesthood are problematic even when restricted to this narrower field: many writers on ecological ethics find some or all of them unacceptable for expressing the proper relation between humans and the rest of the material world. Ruth Page, for example, believes that no matter how hard Christians try to reinvent the concept of 'dominion' as responsible care, it cannot be rehabilitated from its connotations of the violent subjection of the non-human world; she is, however, cautiously supportive of some notions of 'stewardship' and 'priest-hood'.[87] Stephen Clark, in contrast, dismisses talk of stewardship as 'fashionable cant' that tempts us to think of the world in dangerously anthropocentric terms.[88]

These concepts certainly have their dangers, and could no doubt be co-opted to legitimate the human abuse of the non-human world – though the extent and the precise nature of the part that they have played in the genesis of the current ecological crisis is much disputed.[89] But if we attempt to take seriously the relevant biblical texts and the tradition that has been built upon them, we are bound to say that part of humanity's vocation from God entails a particular position in the created world and responsibility for it, of a sort towards which the concepts of dominion, stewardship and priesthood are attempts to point. Gunton, for example, argues that 'dominion' should not be understood as domination or exploitation (the parallel images of gardening and of naming the animals in Genesis 2 rule that out); rather, the 'dominion' to which God calls humanity is 'a calling to be and to act in such a way as to enable the created order to be itself as a response of praise to its

---

87 Ruth Page, *God and the Web of Creation*, London: SCM Press, 1996, pp. 122–30, 158–64. Her predominant model of the relationship between humans and non-human nature is 'companionship': pp. 154–8. If what I have said about human solidarity with the non-human creation is correct, this is surely right, but, as she recognizes, it does not do away with the need to find ways to speak of human *responsibility* for the non-human world.

88 Stephen R. L. Clark, *How to Think about the Earth: Philosophical and Theological Models for Ecology*, London: Mowbray, 1993, pp. 53, 106–16. He also gives short shrift to the use of 'priesthood' language in this context: 'Those Christian environmentalists who . . . speak of man (*sic*) as "the world's high priest" should . . . remember what priests, in Greece and Israel, actually did' (p. 17).

89 The classic statement for the prosecution is Lynn White, Jr, 'The Historical Roots of our Ecologic Crisis', *Science*, 155 (1967), pp. 1203–7. Aspects of his thesis have been much argued about: for brief recent discussions see, e.g., Ian Barbour, *Nature, Human Nature and God*, London: SPCK, 2002, pp. 121–2, and Colin A. Russell, 'Where Science and History Meet: Some Fresh Challenges to the Christian Faith?', *Science and Christian Belief*, 13.2 (2001), pp. 113–25 (pp. 121–2).

maker'.[90] But Gunton, like many others, goes on to emphasize that the role of humanity in relation to the rest of creation must, in the light of texts such as Colossians 1.15–20, be understood christologically:

> Genesis makes the human race both the crown of, and uniquely responsible for, the shape that creation takes. By speaking of Jesus Christ as the true image of God, the New Testament shows that this responsibility is realised only in and through him.[91]

5   At various points, my accounts of the doctrine of creation and of theological anthropology have also pointed towards the Christian doctrines of *salvation and sin*.[92] In the New Testament, the language of the *imago Dei* is used principally in relation to Christ (as in the passage from Colossians just cited) – an indication that, within a Christian theological frame of reference, we know ourselves as persons first and foremost in relation to Christ, which is to say, in the light of his incarnation, earthly ministry, death on the cross and resurrection. In the light of the New Testament witness to the life, death and resurrection of Christ, we know ourselves as sinners for whose sake he died and was raised from the dead.

This knowledge of ourselves – as sinners redeemed through Christ's death and resurrection – both enriches and complicates the account of human being as moral being that I have sketched out thus far. If we think about moral formation, for example, in terms of McFadyen's account of the sedimentation of our communication history, it reminds us that our communication with God and with one another is never free from distortion. Although God's loving address to us invites our response of love, faithfulness and worship, we habitually refuse that response. In place of encounters with one another that are dialogical and other-centred, we frequently find ourselves relating to one another in *distorted* ways: ways that are coercive or manipulative of others, or that tend to co-opt them to serve our own ends. Furthermore, this distortion does not only affect individual relationships, but also social structures. We are all born into networks of relationships and social

---

90 Gunton, *The Triune Creator*, p. 12.

91 *The Triune Creator*, pp. 12–13.

92 I follow others' examples in speaking of 'salvation and sin', rather than 'sin and salvation', to draw attention to Barth's point that it would be theologically illegitimate to try and construct a doctrine of sin in advance of a doctrine of salvation, as if we could truly know what our need is independently of what God has done in Christ to meet that need: *CD* IV.1, pp. 138–42. This point will be developed further in Chapters 7 and 8.

structures that manifest these distortions in various ways, so that the 'sedimentation' of our personal identity is distorted in various ways, and we in our turn pass on those forms of distortion to others. This is one way in which the Christian language of original sin can be understood.[93] It is also conceivable that we are predisposed to some forms of distorted relationship by the particular, contingent course that our evolutionary history has taken; thus it could conceivably make sense to speak of a biological 'inheritance' of sin, or at any rate of a predisposition to sin.[94] Our moral formation in this world, in other words, is inevitably in some measure vicious rather than virtuous. Such distortion not only inhibits our capacity for undistorted relations and the sedimentation of virtuous character; it also clouds our moral judgement, so that, of ourselves, we lack the capacity not only to *be* truly good people but also to understand what it *is* to be truly good.

Accordingly, to understand ourselves as sinners redeemed by God in Christ radically calls into question the project of ethics, understood as a merely human attempt to know the good, to do good and to become good. Ethics as a merely human project can be understood as an example of the human pride, characterized by Barth, that makes us want to be our own judges and our own helpers, thereby alienating ourselves from God who is our truly just and merciful judge and the true source of our help.[95] Commenting on the serpent's promise in Genesis 3.5, 'You will be like God, knowing good and evil', Barth acidly comments, 'What the serpent has in mind is the establishment of ethics.'[96] Likewise, Dietrich Bonhoeffer begins one of the fragments of his unfinished *Ethics* thus:

> The knowledge of good and evil appears to be the goal of all ethical reflection. The first task of Christian ethics is to [invalidate] that knowledge. This attack on the presuppositions of all other ethics is so unique that it is questionable whether it even makes sense to speak of

---

93 See McFadyen, *Bound to Sin*, for a fuller account of original sin, understood at root as idolatry: the basic refusal to orient our being and energies to God in a response of love, joy and praise. This will be discussed further in Chapter 7.

94 See Richard Wrangham and Dale Peterson, *Demonic Males: Apes and the Origins of Human Violence*, London: Bloomsbury, 1997, for one such evolutionary proposal. Talk of an inheritance of sin or of predisposition to sin in this way should, of course, be clearly distinguished from the highly unfortunate (and thoroughly distorted) ways in which such talk has been used at times in the history of the Christian tradition, to the disparagement of bodies, women and sex. The connections between human evolution and the Christian doctrine of sin will be explored further in Part 3.

95 Barth, *CD* IV.1, pp. 445–78.

96 *CD* IV.1, p. 448.

a Christian ethics at all. If it is nevertheless done, then this can only mean that Christian ethics claims to articulate the origin of the whole ethical enterprise, and thus to be considered an ethic only as the critique of all ethics.[97]

This is one reason why it is so important that the New Testament uses the language of *imago Dei* first and foremost of Christ. It is not in our own human life in and of itself, but in the person of Jesus Christ, that we can reliably know what it is to be a human person made in the image of God; it is from him that we learn what undistorted communication that reflects the image of God looks like: 'Christ himself is God's call to proper forms of identity and of relation with God and others, to proper forms of responsibility. But Christ Himself [*sic*] is also the paradigm of the intended form of response.'[98] His call, 'Follow me', is at once God's undistorted – and transformative – address to us and an invitation to join the community of his disciples, whose life together is (or should be) characterized by similarly undistorted forms of relationship. For this reason, talk of covenant relationships in Christian ethics must take its bearings from the *new* covenant inaugurated by Christ's death, the covenant with which Christians identify themselves afresh every time they celebrate the Eucharist together.

The Church, however egregiously it sometimes fails to live up to its identity, is the community constituted by this new covenant relationship, and it is called in its life together (most of all, in its worship) to be an anticipation of the destiny which God promises to all people through the making of this new covenant.[99] That being the case, if the Church is to be

---

97 Dietrich Bonhoeffer, *Ethics: Dietrich Bonhoeffer Works*, vol. 6, ET ed. by Clifford J. Green, Minneapolis: Fortress, 2005, pp. 299–300. I have followed Neville Horton Smith's earlier translation from the sixth German edition (London: Collins, 1963, p. 17) in rendering *aufheben*, in the second sentence of the passage quoted, 'to invalidate' instead of *Ethics*'s rather weak 'to supersede'. My thanks to Kathy Ehrensperger and Ulrike Vollmer for helping me to understand Bonhoeffer's German at this point.

98 McFadyen, *The Call to Personhood*, p. 47.

99 This understanding of the Church's calling is partially, but not fully, captured by Joseph Allen in his covenantal account of Christian ethics, cited earlier: *Love and Conflict*, pp. 283–310. By treating the Church as one of the many forms of 'special covenant' that are established in the world by God's gracious action, he is able to say that it is a special covenant, formed by divine election, with the particular vocation of witnessing to 'the reality of the inclusive covenant as God has made it known through Jesus Christ' (p. 293); however, by identifying the Church as a 'special covenant' to which only some people belong, as opposed to the 'inclusive covenant' which is for all people, he makes it difficult to say that the Church is called to be an *anticipation* of the transformed relationships with God and one another to which all are called by God.

understood as a 'community of character' in which its members can learn and grow in virtue,[100] then it is clear that virtue and character can no longer be understood as parts of a merely human project of ethics. The narrative that forms the character of the Church is the narrative of God's saving activity in and through Jesus Christ; the central practices of this community are to proclaim the good news of that saving work and to break bread and drink wine together 'in remembrance (*anamnēsis*) of him'. Furthermore, the practices of preaching, baptism and Eucharist all bear witness in various ways that the Church could not be the Church were it not for the empowering and transformative presence of the Holy Spirit. So the virtues that are formed, and the moral character that is sedimented, within this 'community of character' are to be understood as aspects of 'sanctification': the work of God's grace in Christ, in the power of the Spirit, remaking and redirecting the lives and relationships of disciples as they respond to the call to follow Christ; a foretaste of God's work in Christ to redirect humanity and the whole creation towards the destiny for which the creation was made.[101]

I have described several aspects of the account of morality that is suggested by the doctrine of creation and Christian anthropology sketched out earlier. Many of these points bear on chapters where I shall discuss, among other things, the possibility of an evolutionary justification of moral norms, the significance of evolution for the content of moral obligation and the relevance of evolution to discussions of moral failure and sin. What, though, is their significance for the question under discussion in this chapter, namely, the possibility of an evolutionary *explanation* of ethics?

---

100 So Stanley Hauerwas, *A Community of Character: Toward a Constructive Christian Social Ethic*, Notre Dame, IN: University of Notre Dame Press, 1981.

101 This view of the Church's role is obviously influenced by Hauerwas, and as such might seem vulnerable to the often-voiced critique that Hauerwas's 'Church' is an idealized construct very different from the empirical realities of actual Christian churches: see, e.g., Robin Gill, *Churchgoing and Christian Ethics*, Cambridge: Cambridge University Press, 1999, pp. 13–30, and, for a response, Samuel Wells, 'How Common Worship Forms Local Character', *Studies in Christian Ethics*, 15.1 (2002), pp. 66–74. No doubt there is more work to be done, for example, in attending to the empirical reality of the Church and in specifying more precisely the gap between that reality and 'the church that should exist if we were more courageous and faithful' (*A Community of Character*, p. 6). However, for my present purpose, it is sufficient to maintain what does not seem unduly controversial: (i) that the Church is called to play a vital part in the moral formation of its members, a kind of moral formation whose character is defined by the Church's distinctive narrative and liturgical practice, (ii) that the empowerment of the Spirit is promised to enable the Church to live up to its calling, and (iii) that it often fails, but that there are occasions when, and ways in which, it does not fail – as both Gill and Wells, in different ways, report.

Even from the thumbnail sketches I have given, it is clear that the moral picture suggested by these Christian doctrines is more richly textured than many of the evolutionary accounts canvassed in the literature. There are, for sure, points of contact with evolutionary accounts of human nature. For example, my account of the social formation of personal and moral identity has points of contact with biological accounts of the evolution of *Homo sapiens* as a social species, as well as with social-scientific accounts of communicative action and the formation of personal identity. It is also possible that a theologically driven account of the ends or goals of human life will have features in common with a biological account of the selection pressures that have shaped human nature during our evolutionary history (though if, as the Christian tradition has habitually claimed, our *ultimate* end is life in union with God, the natural sciences will in the nature of the case have nothing to say about this one way or the other). But my account also suggests that talk of morality is not fully at home in a scientific narrative of human origins, and if we attempt to speak of morality solely within a scientific narrative we shall have an attenuated picture of it. There is a great danger of circularity in the more reductionist attempts to explain morality in evolutionary terms: 'morality' is equated with those features (such as altruistic behaviour) for which plausible evolutionary explanations can be given, and it is then proclaimed that evolutionary biology can explain 'morality' without remainder. By contrast, I have sketched a picture in which (among other things) human morality has its origins in the goodness of God's creation, is shaped by the God-given ends and goals of human life, includes a responsibility (extending well beyond enlightened self-interest) for the non-human creation, and is subject to radical questioning and re-conception in the light of the death and resurrection of Christ. Morality so understood would not seem to lend itself to evolutionary explanations in any simple way, which at any rate signals that, if the map is not drawn in a way that pre-judges the issue in favour of reductionist accounts, their explanatory power is by no means as obvious as it may appear. Of course, my account has also suggested that morality is not comfortably at home in a theological narrative, either – if by 'morality' is understood a merely human project to know what is good and to better ourselves. The concept of morality and the project of ethics are only at home in the theological narrative that I have sketched out once they have been 'taken captive to obey Christ' (2 Cor. 10.5).

5

The 'Ethics of Evolution' and the Call of God

In his Romanes Lecture, as I described in Chapter 2, T. H. Huxley took to task those (such as Herbert Spencer) who confused 'the ethics of evolution' with 'the evolution of ethics'. Huxley was quite prepared to agree with Spencer and others that an account could be given of the *evolution of ethics* – that an evolutionary explanation could be given for humans having the kind of morality that we do. He disagreed with Spencer, however, about the *ethics of evolution*: that is, about whether moral conclusions can be drawn from facts about evolution, or moral norms inferred from evolution, and if so, how. This latter set of questions – those that I described in Chapter 2 as questions about moral *justification* – are in view throughout this chapter; in the last section I shall also address the third issue identified in Chapter 2, the implications of evolution for the *content* of ethics.

1 The 'ethics of evolution'

a Spencer, Huxley and Moore

Herbert Spencer, as I noted in Chapter 2, is nowadays frequently identified as the 'father of social Darwinism'. Leaving aside that doubtful distinction, his lengthy writings do also contain one of the first sustained attempts to develop an ethic on the basis of evolutionary biology.[1] Never entirely shaking off a Lamarckian view of evolutionary progress, he holds that in evolution there is a progression from the lower to the higher. The 'limit', or pinnacle, of this evolutionary progress, is

---

1 Spencer, *The Data of Ethics*, London: Williams and Norgate, 1884 (1879), pp. 3–46; see also James Rachels, *Created from Animals: The Moral Implications of Darwinism*, Oxford: Oxford University Press, 1990, pp. 62–70, for a summary and discussion.

(naturally) seen in human beings. The most fully evolved conduct, exhibited by humans, is that which increases the length and quality of their lives, promotes the birth and nurture of offspring and results in 'permanently peaceful societies'. But Spencer then asks what we mean by the terms 'good' and 'bad', and argues that we call an object 'good' if it fulfils its prescribed ends. A knife is good if it cuts well; an umbrella is bad if it fails to keep us dry. So with human conduct: the good is that which is well adjusted to ends. He appeals to everyday experience to show that we customarily apply the term 'good' to conduct which promotes each of the three groups of ends he has previously identified – self-preservation, procreation and the creation of permanently peaceful societies – and 'bad' to conduct which opposes these ends. He concludes that 'the conduct to which we apply the name good, is the relatively more evolved conduct; and the bad is the name we apply to conduct which is relatively less evolved'; the conduct we identify as best is that which 'fulfils all three classes of ends at the same time'.[2]

If Spencer was one of the earliest thinkers to affirm the possibility of an evolutionary ethic, T. H. Huxley was one of the earliest to deny it, arguing in the Romanes Lecture that 'Cosmic evolution may teach us how the good and the evil tendencies of man may have come about; but, in itself, it is incompetent to furnish any better reason why what we call good is preferable to what we call evil than we had before';[3] I suggested in Chapter 2 that he learned this line of argument, and the sharp distinction between 'is' and 'ought' on which it depends, from David Hume, who famously problematized the relationship of 'is' and 'ought' in his *Treatise of Human Nature*.[4] At the beginning of the twentieth century, the problem was restated (without reference to Hume) by G. E. Moore, who argued that thinkers such as Spencer who identified 'good' with some other property (such as 'more evolved') committed what he called the 'naturalistic fallacy'.[5] Moore's treatment of the naturalistic fallacy depends in part on the so-called 'open-question' argument. If 'good' can be defined in terms of some natural property, such as 'conducive to happiness', then the question 'Is conduct that is conducive to happiness *good*?' will be equivalent to a question such as 'Is a bachelor

---

2 Spencer, *The Data of Ethics*, pp. 25, 26.

3 Thomas Henry Huxley, 'Evolution and Ethics' (The Romanes Lecture, 1893), in *Evolution and Ethics and Other Essays* (*Collected Essays*, vol. 9), London: Macmillan, 1894, pp. 46–116 (pp. 79–80).

4 David Hume, *A Treatise of Human Nature*, ed. by L. A. Selby-Bigge, rev. by P. H. Nidditch, Oxford: Clarendon Press, 1978 (1739–40), p. 469.

5 George Edward Moore, *Principia Ethica*, Cambridge: Cambridge University Press, 1903, pp. 37–58.

unmarried?' The latter is a *closed question*, whose answer we know simply by knowing the meanings of the words. But that is not true of the former question: it remains an *open question* whether conduct conducive to happiness is good, so 'conducive to happiness' cannot be a *definition* of 'good'.[6]

b Evolutionary ethics in recent debate

Some authors have wished to defend Spencer against Moore's attack. For example, James Rachels argues that Moore's objection to Spencer may have been less telling than Moore thought, because Spencer could be construed as proposing, not a *definition* of the word 'good', but a *criterion for judging* what is good. If so, the open-question argument does not apply.[7] Such defences notwithstanding, Moore succeeded in considerably dampening the general enthusiasm for Spencerian evolutionary ethics for much of the twentieth century. However, even after Moore, there have still been those whom I identified in Chapter 2 as evolutionary 'naturalists': those who have wished in some way to base moral norms on putative facts about evolution. Some of these have simply ignored the problem of the naturalistic fallacy. For example, E. O. Wilson, in his early sociobiological writings, called for 'ethics to be removed temporarily from the hands of the philosophers and biologized',[8] a programme that would conflate a biological explanation of moral beliefs and judgements with an attempt to derive normative moral conclusions from this 'biology of ethics'. Some of the normative conclusions in Wilson's early work were piecemeal comments on particular social issues, such as gender roles, which in some cases amounted to fairly stereotyped conservative conclusions read off factual claims about human evolution.[9] However, he also attempted to identify the

---

6 See, further, Rachels, *Created from Animals*, pp. 66–70; also Peter G. Woolcock, 'The Case against Evolutionary Ethics Today', in Jane Maienschein and Michael Ruse (eds.), *Biology and the Foundations of Ethics*, Cambridge: Cambridge University Press, 1999, pp. 276–306 (pp. 283–4).

7 Rachels, *Created from Animals*, pp. 69–70. Moore acknowledged that Spencer's account, being loosely expressed, would bear this interpretation; but he thought that in those places where Spencer appeared to use 'more evolved' as a criterion rather than a definition, he identified 'good' with 'pleasant'; thus, on that reading, he was a hedonist and, as such, still committed the naturalistic fallacy.

8 Edward O. Wilson, *Sociobiology*, abridged edn, Cambridge, MA: Harvard University Press, 1980, p. 287.

9 E. O. Wilson, *On Human Nature*, Cambridge, MA: Harvard University Press, 1978, pp. 124–41; note, however, that some of the conclusions drawn in this way were 'liberal' rather than 'conservative', for example his comments about homosexuality,

core components of a 'code of moral values' based on the 'biology of ethics': one was the survival of the human gene pool, which would require us to renounce tribalism and selfishness; a second was the protection of human genetic diversity; a third was universal human rights.[10] Earlier in the twentieth century, Julian Huxley, Thomas Henry's grandson and the first Director of the United Nations Educational, Scientific and Cultural Organization (UNESCO), found in evolution a tendency towards ever higher levels of organization, to the point

> where the world-stuff (now moulded into human shape) finds that it experiences some of the new possibilities as having value in or for themselves; and further that among these it assigns higher and lower degrees of value, the higher values being those which are more intrinsically or more permanently satisfying, or which involve a greater degree of perfection . . . this is the *most desirable* direction of evolution, and accordingly . . . our ethical standards must fit into its dynamic framework. In other words, it is ethically right to aim at whatever will promote the increasingly full realization of increasingly higher values.[11]

He was taken to task by C. D. Broad for ignoring the problem of 'is' and 'ought'.[12] More recently, Michael Ruse has argued that he was guilty of the circularity that has beset many projects of evolutionary ethics: he simply read into evolution what he wished to infer from it.[13]

Not all evolutionary naturalists have ignored the problem of 'is' and 'ought'. Some, however, have suggested that it is no fallacy to attempt

---

pp. 142–8. Critics have frequently identified a contrast in Wilson's early sociobiological work between his carefully documented and solidly based discussions of non-human animals (particularly insects, his own area of scientific expertise) and the less solid foundation of some of his remarks about human society.

10 *On Human Nature*, pp. 196–8. In later writings, he has extended the principle of the protection of genetic diversity to the preservation of *bio*diversity: see Michael Ruse, 'Evolutionary Ethics in the Twentieth Century: Julian Sorrell Huxley and George Gaylord Simpson', in Maienschein and Ruse, *Biology and the Foundations of Ethics*, pp. 198–224 (p. 208).

11 Julian Huxley, 'Evolutionary Ethics' (The Romanes Lecture, 1943), in T. H. Huxley and Julian Huxley, *Evolution and Ethics: 1893–1943*, London: Pilot Press, 1947, pp. 103–51 (p. 125), emphasis original.

12 C. D. Broad, 'Critical Notice of Julian Huxley's *Evolutionary Ethics*', *Mind*, 53 (1944), pp. 344–67, also online at http://www.ditext.com/broad/huxley.html (accessed 16 August 2006).

13 Ruse, 'Evolutionary Ethics', p. 211; as noted in Chapter 3, an earlier example of such circularity is given by Paul Lawrence Farber, 'French Evolutionary Ethics during the Third Republic: Jean de Lanessan', in Maienschein and Ruse, *Biology and the Foundations of Ethics*, pp. 84–97.

to derive 'ought' from 'is'. For example, Daniel Dennett claims that 'the fallacy is not naturalism but, rather, any simple-minded attempt to rush from facts to values', and that a more 'circumspect' naturalism that 'attempt[s] to unify our world-view so that our ethical principles don't clash irrationally with the way the world *is*' is not a fallacy.[14] I suggested in Chapter 3, however, that his own defence of this claim falls somewhat short of being comprehensive and convincing. A more sustained defence of evolutionary ethics is offered by Robert Richards.[15] He supposes, for the sake of his argument, that humans have evolved a 'moral sense' by means of processes such as kin selection. This moral sense prompts us to seek the welfare of the community, and to recognize that all our fellow-humans come within the scope of our moral concern. In any particular social context, the insight provided by the moral sense will give the community a criterion by which to judge which forms of behaviour are to be morally approved. Richards claims that this evolutionary ethic avoids committing the naturalistic fallacy, in the latter's usual form, because it does not appeal to evolutionary facts to sanction a particular kind of social arrangement or development. He does freely acknowledge that his system attempts to 'derive its norms from facts',[16] but argues that this in itself is not a fallacy.

It is not clear, though, that he succeeds in showing how a *moral* ought can be derived from facts about evolution. He 'stipulates' (his word) that 'community welfare is the highest moral good'.[17] The arguments that he offers in support of this stipulation are variations on the following:

> the evidence shows that evolution has, as a matter of fact, constructed human beings to act for the community good; but to act for the community good is what we mean by being moral. Since, therefore, human beings are moral beings – an unavoidable condition produced by evolution – each ought to act for the community good.[18]

But it is not clear that this gets us further than Michael Ruse's 'sceptical' position, discussed below: that evolution has made us beings of a kind

---

14 Daniel C. Dennett, *Darwin's Dangerous Idea: Evolution and the Meanings of Life*, London: Penguin, 1996, p. 468.

15 Robert J. Richards, 'A Defense of Evolutionary Ethics', *Biology and Philosophy*, 1 (1986), pp. 265–93; reprinted as Appendix 2 of his *Darwin and the Emergence of Evolutionary Theories of Mind and Behavior*, Chicago; University of Chicago Press, 1987, pp. 595–627. The latter source is the one cited in the following discussion.

16 Richards, 'A Defense', p. 620.

17 'A Defense', p. 620.

18 'A Defense', pp. 623–4.

who think we ought to act altruistically, but no ultimate justification can be given for the claim that we ought. Richards does succeed in showing that if this *is* how evolution has made us, then a 'causal' or predictive 'ought' follows, by analogy with the claim that 'lightning has flashed, so it ought to thunder'.[19] He holds that what marks out the claim about community welfare as a *moral*, not merely causal, 'ought' is simply that 'the activities of heeding the community good and approving of altruistic behavior constitute what we mean and (if [this version of evolutionary ethics] is correct) must mean by "being moral"'.[20] But this seems to make something like the move criticized by Moore, identifying a natural property (being disposed to act for the community welfare) with 'good' in the moral sense. It is not clear, then, that Richards *has* avoided committing the 'naturalistic fallacy' as characterized by Moore, but this does not necessarily matter to him. As I have already noted, he argues that no ethical system can avoid some sort of appeal to empirical facts to justify moral norms; '[c]onsequently, either the naturalistic fallacy is no fallacy, or no ethical system can be justified'.[21]

The second of these alternatives, though unappealing to Richards, is argued for by Michael Ruse, who explains that according to an 'ethical skeptic' such as himself,

> [ethics] has evolved to make us good cooperators, because given the kinds of beings we humans are, cooperation is a good adaptive strategy in the struggle for existence. But there is nothing beyond this, and certainly no solid ground of proof. We have a moral sense because it is adaptively advantageous to have it, but ultimately . . . there is nothing that it is sensing![22]

It might seem that once the secret gets out that 'morality is a collective illusion foisted upon us by our genes',[23] the morality whose authority we have hitherto recognized will lose all hold on us. However, Ruse does not think so. Morality will not be effective in making us good cooperators unless we are convinced that it lays objective obligations upon us, and consequently it has proved adaptive for us to be so convinced. The

---

19 'A Defense', p. 625.
20 'A Defense', p. 625.
21 'A Defense', p. 620.
22 Ruse, 'Evolutionary Ethics', pp. 198–224 (p. 218).
23 Ruse, *Taking Darwin Seriously: A Naturalistic Approach to Philosophy*, Oxford: Blackwell, 1986, p. 253.

belief that morality has an objective reference may be a 'collective illusion', but it is one that is deeply rooted in our human nature, and we could not simply choose to ignore what we have hitherto perceived as our moral obligations. Moreover, says Ruse, morality is 'an effective adaptation'; why should we wish to throw it over, 'any more than we should put out our eyes?'[24] It should be noted that if Ruse is right to think that our moral sense is an evolutionary adaptation, that only means that it was adaptive to us during our evolutionary *history*: it might seem intuitively plausible that it continues to be in our collective interests to obey the dictates of our moral sense, but evolution supplies no guarantee that this is so. Furthermore, Peter Woolcock questions Ruse's confidence that we *would* continue to take notice of the moral sense once the cat was out of the bag: if we became convinced that our deep-seated disposition to believe in the objectivity of moral norms was an illusion, then it could be that our self-interest would motivate us to train ourselves out of any residual inclination to take notice of our moral sense.[25] Even if these questions are left on one side, the most that Ruse offers is not a *categorical* justification of moral norms (one that has a claim on us regardless of our feelings or wishes), but a *hypothetical* justification such as: *If* we seek to ensure the survival and flourishing of our species, *then* we ought to obey the dictates of our moral sense.

Woolcock himself is unpersuaded both by evolutionary sceptics such as Ruse and evolutionary ethicists such as Richards. His own response to the debate is to propose a social contract theory whereby, given 'a genetic disposition to believe privately what we offer as the public reasons for our actions' (in other words, a 'disposition to socialization') and 'the general features of rationality', we are likely to find that 'people will act as if morality were objective'.[26] This is because, when called upon to justify our actions in public, we shall find that egoistic reasons, even if they were the true motives of our actions, will not be acceptable to others. We shall therefore have to learn to justify our actions by appealing to altruistic reasons, and our 'disposition to social-ization' will lead us to internalize those reasons. As the circle of people before whom we have to justify our actions widens, so will the scope of our altruism. It should be noted, though, that this account only offers reasons for thinking that 'people will act *as if* morality were objective',

---

24 Ruse, *Taking Darwin Seriously*, p. 253.
25 Woolcock, 'The Case against Evolutionary Ethics Today', pp. 288–9.
26 Woolcock, 'The Case against Evolutionary Ethics Today', p. 302.

not for believing that categorical justifications of moral norms are true. Perhaps, therefore, Woolcock's account as well as Ruse's bears out Richards's claim that if it is always a fallacy to derive norms from facts, then 'no ethical system can be [categorically] justified'.[27]

Richards argues persuasively that the categorical justification of moral norms is bound to require some kind of appeal to empirical facts, but the objections tabled by Hume, Moore and recent critics such as Woolcock seem to place formidable difficulties in the way of such appeals. Perhaps this *impasse* requires us to look in a different way at the relationship of 'is' and 'ought', as I shall attempt to do in the next section.

2 'Is' and 'ought' revisited

Attempts to construct a 'naturalistic' ethic, for example by inferring moral norms from facts about evolution, would seem to require at least three conditions: first, the existence of nature as a given, independent of our apprehension of it; secondly, that we are able to discover facts about it; thirdly, that we can devise a rationally defensible procedure for inferring moral norms from the facts that we have discovered. The first of these conditions might perhaps be threatened by extreme social constructivist views of nature, but even if we reject such views and accept, as Peter Scott puts it, that 'the structures and processes of nature are real and "excess to thought"',[28] problems arise with the second and third.

The second is called into question by the thought that our perceptions of nature are to some extent socially constructed: as Scott puts it, 'The engagement with . . . nature, through our socially formed discourses, is by a range of social practices in our habitation: knowledge of nature is always thereby perspectival and emerges in particular praxes.'[29] If there is no 'pure' knowledge of nature free from social and cultural conditioning, then attempts to find out what nature is like in order to derive moral norms from that knowledge will be fraught with difficulty, since there is every likelihood that some ideological construct or other will shape an understanding of nature that will then be invoked to support that same ideology. This is the circularity that has already been noted in relation to nineteenth- and twentieth-century attempts at evolutionary

---

27 Richards, 'A Defense', p. 620.

28 Peter Scott, *A Political Theology of Nature*, Cambridge: Cambridge University Press, 2003, p. 6.

29 Scott, *A Political Theology*, p. 6; see also John Habgood, *The Concept of Nature*, London: Darton, Longman and Todd, 2002, pp. 14–19, 61–6.

ethics, whose authors often read into evolution what they wished to infer from it. It is the kind of argumentative move that, for example, can underpin the ideological use of appeals to nature to support patriarchal moral claims. In Chapter 7, I shall outline the trenchant critique directed by feminist sociobiologist Sarah Blaffer Hrdy at such patriarchal ideological moves in relation to evolution.[30]

The third requirement of a 'naturalistic' evolutionary ethic is the feasibility of inferring moral norms from facts about nature. It is this move, of course, that has been challenged by Hume, Moore and more recent critics of evolutionary ethics. However, the challenge may not be as powerful as it seems. As Alasdair MacIntyre points out, it depends on a sharp separation of *fact* and *value*.[31] According to MacIntyre, this tendency to separate fact from value took hold in the eighteenth century (though others have argued that its roots go back further). Although many thinkers since then have believed that the separation of fact and value is logically necessary, MacIntyre challenges this view. He believes that it was a symptom of that major shift in moral thinking which he calls the 'Enlightenment project'; before the eighteenth century it would not have seemed obvious that facts and values are distinct and separate from one another. For example, according to Thomas Aquinas' account of natural law, we can draw conclusions about how we ought to behave from observations of ourselves and the world.[32] In a sense, natural law arguments move from an 'is' to an 'ought', but they do so in a very different way from a Spencerian evolutionary ethic. The crucial difference is that in Thomas's natural law theory the facts themselves are not neutral but value-laden. The theory claims that human beings have been created by God with particular ends or purposes. This is a factual claim about the kind of thing a human being is: when we say 'human being', part of what we mean is 'a being that exists for these ends'. But this factual claim has an evaluative claim built in: a human being is the kind of being whose good consists in fulfilling these ends. Given Thomas's first principle of practical reason – 'that good is to be sought and done, evil to be avoided'[33] – it follows that right actions are those that help us to fulfil our ends.

---

30 Sarah Blaffer Hrdy, *Mother Nature: A History of Mothers, Infants, and Natural Selection*, New York: Pantheon, 1999.

31 Alasdair MacIntyre, *After Virtue: A Study in Moral Theory*, 2nd edn, London: Duckworth, 1985, pp. 56–9.

32 Thomas Aquinas, *Summa Theologiae*, ET ed. by Thomas Gilby, OP, London: Eyre and Spottiswoode, 1964–76 (hereafter *ST*), I-II.94.

33 *ST* I-II.94.2.

I have identified two difficulties with drawing moral conclusions from putative facts about nature: the danger of using socially constructed notions of nature to support ideological conclusions, and the so-called 'naturalistic fallacy'. But MacIntyre's comments about the relation of 'ought' and 'is' help to point us towards a way of making connections between the way the world is and moral judgements that can avoid both difficulties.

That way is to understand the world, including embodied human life, as *creation*. As I emphasized in Chapter 4, to understand humans and the world in this way is to make a credal affirmation, which among other things enables us to speak *teleologically* of ourselves and the world – to say that we and the world are God's 'project' directed towards an ultimate end – which we could not do on the basis of scientific observation. It is this teleological understanding that allows us to draw moral conclusions from factual claims, since a description of the world as creation includes the evaluative claims that it has been created 'very good' and that it is directed to a good purpose. Good life and action in the world, on this account, are those that go 'with the grain' of the goodness of creation and the good ends towards which it is directed. But, as I argued in Chapter 4, our understanding of what it means to go 'with the grain' of God's good purposes for the creation can never simply be read off our scientific understandings of the world or derived from those understandings. If this is so, it rules out the kinds of evolutionary ethics discussed in the previous section. Ruling out attempts to derive moral conclusions from accounts of nature can help safeguard us against the danger, identified earlier, of grounding our ethics on ideological constructions of nature.

Instead, our knowledge about the ways of being and acting in the world that go 'with the grain' of God's creative purposes must be rooted in the biblical witness to the creative activity of God and the Christian tradition's reflection on that biblical witness. Something like what I mean is suggested by Karl Barth's account of 'ethics as the command of God the Creator'.[34] The language of 'command', of course, has various unhappy resonances, as many of Barth's critics have pointed out: for example, it can appear theologically voluntarist, ethically intuitionist and perhaps arbitrary (in the everyday sense of capricious) and unpredictable.[35] In these respects, it might seem to compare unfavourably

---

34 Karl Barth, *Church Dogmatics*, ET ed. by G. W. Bromiley and T. F. Torrance, Edinburgh: T&T Clark, 1956–75 (hereafter *CD*), vol. III.4.
35 See Nigel Biggar, *The Hastening That Waits: Karl Barth's Ethics*, Oxford:

with Thomist natural law theory, to which I have already alluded. I shall suggest in the next section, however, that Barth's divine command ethic is not prone to some of the faults that are often attributed to such ethics, and that in some respects it is preferable to some of the contemporary readings of natural law theory that have been deployed in critical engagements with evolutionary biology.

Such an ethic of the command of God might seem inhospitable to the account of virtue and character that I associated in Chapter 4 with a relational Christian anthropology. However, as Nigel Biggar argues, 'the act of responding to God's command does not fill the whole of Barth's ethical stage. It may be the climax but it is not the whole story.'[36] Certainly, Barth is reluctant to speak of the virtues, because he does not wish to support the notion of a human being as 'an independent entity – an absolute substance – which simply "possesses" certain "properties"'.[37] Any account in which natural virtue could be either known about or achieved independently of God's grace in Christ would hardly have his support. But this is not the kind of account that I have been sketching. Following McFadyen, I made clear in Chapter 4 that, in a fallen world, our communication history is always distorted in various ways, and the moral character 'sedimented' from that history is in some measure vicious rather than virtuous. Within a Christian theological anthropology, the defining relationship must be God's gracious call to us in Christ – the call that summons us to new ways of living in relationship with God and one another, that shows us what a human life transformed by God's grace looks like and that makes such transformed ways of living possible for us. If we are to speak of character and virtue in the context of this theological anthropology, it must be the character and virtue made possible by the saving work of Christ and the sanctifying work of the Spirit. In fact, as Biggar argues, Barth is willing to discuss 'human goodness and virtuous dispositions' on these terms,[38] and in volume III.4 of the *Dogmatics* he gives an account of the formation of character in terms of our response to God's call.[39] All of this is to suggest that the kind of divine command ethic that I am advocating here does not exclude an account of the moral life, lived in response to that command, in terms of character and virtue.

Clarendon Press, 1993, pp. 19–25, for a summary of such criticism; see also Oliver O'Donovan, *Resurrection and Moral Order: An Outline for Evangelical Ethics*, 2nd edn, Leicester: Apollos, 1994, pp. 86–7.

36 Biggar, *Hastening*, p. 129.

37 *Hastening*, p. 131.

38 *Hastening*, pp. 132–3, citing Barth, *CD* I.2, p. 790.

39 *CD* III.4, pp. 387–90; for discussion, see Biggar, *Hastening*, pp. 133–9.

It might, however, seem as though a divine command ethic of the sort developed by Barth is at least as vulnerable to the dangers of ideologically motivated projections of our own interests and prejudices as the naturalistic ethics that I have criticized. As Biggar notes, one objection to Barth's ethic is that, because of its particularity and unpredictability, it 'precludes public accountability [and] cannot help but close the door on self-criticism too', and therefore, ironically, that it promotes 'the ideological kind of ethics that it was originally designed to preclude'.[40] This has to be admitted as a danger – indeed, as I shall suggest in the next section, there are reasons to think that Barth did not always succeed in avoiding it – but there are features of his method that help to guard against it. One is his treatment of *Grenzfälle*, those 'borderline cases' or exceptional situations in which God's command takes highly unusual forms.[41] At times, his discussion of borderline cases has a highly voluntarist tone that might seem to undermine the possibility of moral reasoning altogether.[42] However, as Biggar argues, he does not always take such an extreme voluntarist line, and it is possible to understand a *Grenzfall* not as 'the trangression or suspension of the rule but rather an unusual mode of keeping it' that causes us, not to set aside our moral reasoning, but to extend or refine it; thus, Barth's concept of the *Grenzfall* can be understood as a way of '[making] systematic ethics systematically open to correction'.[43] Another safeguard against ideological distortion might be found in Barth's approach to Scripture in ethics: as Biggar notes, he is determined to guard against self-justifying or manipulative uses of the Bible, such as selective proof-texting or treating it as no more than a moral rule-book.[44] Accordingly, he privileges biblical *narrative* as a more comprehensive mode of witness to God's command than individual texts, rules or principles.[45]

In the next section, I shall explore how an ethic of 'the command of God the creator' might reframe the discussion of one particular concrete theme that is prominent in the evolution-and-ethics literature. Doing this will enable me to draw out a little further the points of contact and

---

40 Biggar, *Hastening*, pp. 24–5.

41 Some of the best-known examples occur in his discussion of the protection of life (*CD* III.4, pp. 397–470), where he considers exceptional cases where the taking of a human life might be commanded. Another example, in the context of his discussion of parents and children, will be noted in the next section.

42 See, e.g., *CD* III.4, pp. 411–13.

43 Biggar, *Hastening*, pp. 34, 35.

44 *CD* II.2, pp. 675–6, 704; see Biggar, *Hastening*, pp. 103–5.

45 *CD* II.2, p. 672.

contrast between Barth's divine command ethic and some versions of natural law theory that are frequently brought to bear on such themes. That discussion will also provide an illustrative example of the way in which a theological engagement with the evolution-and-ethics discussion can reframe, and constructively address, the third issue that I identified in Chapter 2: the implications of evolutionary biology for the *content* of our moral obligation.

3   Altruism and the love of neighbour

It will be clear from earlier chapters that in recent discussions of evolution and ethics *altruism* has a prominent place. It looms large in the discussion of the issues that I have already discussed, namely, questions about the explanation of morality and about the justification of moral norms. When we come to consider the *content* of moral obligation (the third issue identified in Chapter 2), altruism seems to function in two different ways.

First, it is often treated as a moral obligation – perhaps one among many, perhaps a particularly important one, perhaps a summation of all our moral obligations. Questions then arise about the nature and extent of that obligation. Can we learn anything about the priorities and limits of altruistic concern from our evolutionary history: might we, for example, have an obligation to show more costly altruism towards kin, friends and neighbours than towards strangers? (It is said that the biologist J. B. S. Haldane, asked whether he would lay down his life for his brother, responded that he would not for one brother, but would for two brothers or eight first cousins. That quip neatly sums up the arithmetic of the kin selection theory outlined in Chapter 4.) Or is the lesson the reverse, as Peter Singer argues: that sociobiology debunks our tendency to favour kin over strangers, by showing this tendency to be a product of our evolutionary history rather than an insight into a universal moral truth?[46] Secondly, though, altruism occupies a more basic place in some discussions: it is treated as a necessary condition of any *moral* way of life whatsoever, and therefore, by implication, of any detailed delineation of our moral norms, obligations and so forth. Our basic choice is between altruism and egoism, and only if we choose an altruistic stance will we recognize the force of any moral claims on us. So, for example, Peter Woolcock identifies the basic challenge facing any evolutionary ethic as that of supplying an 'altruism guarantee' – a

---

46 Peter Singer, 'Ethics and Sociobiology', *Zygon*, 19.2 (1984), pp. 141–58.

compelling reason why we should choose an altruistic stance rather than an egoistic one.[47]

The use of altruism as an illustrative example, then, would seem to offer a helpful focus to the more general question, identified in Chapter 2, of the implications of evolution for the content of our ethics. It might appear that the more general issue could helpfully be explored by way of specific questions about altruism: is there anything to be learned from our evolutionary history about the nature and extent of the altruism required of us? And what is the place of altruism in the moral life – is it one moral obligation among many, is it a particularly important obligation, does it sum up all our moral duties or is it a necessary condition of any moral life, properly understood?

As I have repeatedly claimed, however, Christians engaging theologically with the discussion of evolution and ethics should not assume that they will be satisfied with addressing the questions as they are commonly put in the literature. They are likely to find that they need to reframe the questions. So how might theology engage with the questions that I have just identified about altruism and the content of the moral life? One obvious connection, made by many authors, is between altruism and the command to love one's neighbour as oneself. Some treat altruism as more or less equivalent to neighbour-love: in a recent multi-author collection by scientists, philosophers and theologians, both editors and several of the contributors make this assumption.[48] One of the editors, Philip Clayton, in a section of his concluding chapter that carries the heading 'Altruism or Love', remarks, 'With altruism, we reach the crucial question for religious ethics.'[49] His co-editor, Jeffrey Schloss, equates the biological 'question of altruism or cooperative sacrifice' with 'the issue of sacrificial love [which] is also of paramount importance to religious understandings of morality. In the Christian tradition, it is considered the ultimate telos of human existence, the summation and fulfilment of all moral obligation.'[50] Both of these quotations include claims about the place of neighbour-love in a Christian understanding of the moral life, to which I shall return later. But for the moment, what interests me is that they equate altruism with neighbour-love in a fairly straightforward way.

---

47 Woolcock, 'The Case Against Evolutionary Ethics Today'.

48 Philip Clayton and Jeffrey Schloss (eds.), *Evolution and Ethics: Human Morality in Biological and Religious Perspective*, Grand Rapids, MI: Eerdmans, 2004.

49 Clayton, 'Biology and Purpose', in Clayton and Schloss, *Evolution and Ethics*, pp. 318–36 (p. 333).

50 Schloss, 'Evolutionary Ethics and Christian Morality', in Clayton and Schloss, *Evolution and Ethics*, pp. 1–24 (p. 10).

Colin Grant, by contrast, seems to call into question such simple equations of altruism with neighbour-love. Following others, he identifies various forms of paradox that seem to be inherent in altruism, all of which have to do with tensions in the way that the relationship of self to the other is set up.[51] Altruism seems to require a forgetfulness of self, a focus on the other's interests rather than my own. Yet if I have an altruistic motivation to seek the other's good and an empathic concern about the other's distress, then it seems that altruistic motivation turns out to be self-interested after all: the pleasure I take in others' well-being is *my* pleasure, and the distress I feel at others' suffering is *my* distress, from which *I* seek relief by helping them. If I am supposed to be forgetful of myself, the self that is supposed to forget itself keeps intruding in the picture, and there is always a tendency towards a self-righteous preoccupation with my own altruistic performance. Though solutions can be proposed to at least some forms of the paradox of altruism,[52] Grant claims that the paradox persists and makes the concept of altruism 'elusive'. Yet the notion 'points to something in human life that is too important to be dismissed simply because of its elusiveness'.[53] He holds that the internal tensions and paradoxes in the concept of altruism arise from the fact that it is a modern invention (usually credited to Auguste Comte), a secularized version of the Christian concept of *agapē*, or disinterested love. He concludes that 'true altruism is religious' – that the paradoxes can be resolved and altruism seen to be a genuine possibility when we recognize its transcendent ground:

> The mutual caring that morality advocates is feasible because it is not simply a moral ideal or an immediate social possibility, but because it is underwritten by reality in its deepest dimensions. Our failure to realize this moral ideal in life as we live it is not a reason to abandon its pursuit because our basis is not finally in ourselves, but in God who offers renewal through forgiveness.[54]

I am very much inclined to agree with Grant that some of the puzzles and internal tensions of altruism arise because it is a secularized version of *agapē*, but it seems to me that he fails to follow this line of thought

---

51 Colin Grant, *Altruism and Christian Ethics*, Cambridge: Cambridge University Press, 2001, pp. 77–88.

52 See, e.g., Robert Paul Churchill and Erin Street, 'Is There a Paradox of Altruism?', in Jonathan Seglow (ed.), *The Ethics of Altruism*, London: Frank Cass, 2004, pp. 87–105.

53 Grant, *Altruism*, p. 85.

54 Grant, *Altruism*, p. 248.

through to its proper conclusion. He recognizes that, on a Christian view, the source of *agapē* is God, and *agapē* is only a possibility for humans at all because of the overflowing love of God toward us. But his understanding of what is meant by *agapē*, human or divine, remains shaped to an important degree by the secularized accounts of altruism with which he began. Thus, he finds himself worrying about whether God is really an altruist or an egoist. Christian theology has tradition- ally insisted that God's love for us arises not from any neediness in God, but out of God's 'aseity', or ontological self-sufficiency; but does this make God basically self-centred rather than altruistic? 'It would be supremely ironic if the identification of God in the absolutely altruistic terms of *agapē* ultimately reflected an assumption of God characterised by narcissistic egoism.'[55]

Such strangely anthropomorphic God-talk is surely a sign that some- thing has gone wrong. The problem seems to be that Grant has failed to appreciate the full significance of a critique of the concept of altruism that he himself cites. As I have noted, the word 'altruism' is generally reckoned to have been invented by Comte, who identified 'the subordi- nation of egoism to altruism' as 'the chief problem of human life'.[56] But, as Alasdair MacIntyre has argued, it is not just the word, but also the opposition of altruism to egoism, that is characteristically modern, in that it expresses a notion of human beings as individuals whose goods are always potentially in competition with the goods of others. Before the seventeenth century, he says, the problem could not have been set up in this way. On the view of human good that prevailed up to that time,

> [t]here is no way of my pursuing my good which is necessarily antagonistic to you pursuing yours because *the* good is neither mine peculiarly nor yours peculiarly – goods are not private property . . . The egoist is thus, in the ancient and medieval world, always someone who has made a fundamental mistake about where his own good lies and someone who has thus and to that extent excluded himself from human relationships.[57]

MacIntyre's critique of Comte makes it clear that, when Grant worries about whether God is an altruist or an egoist, he is in effect asking

---

55 Grant, *Altruism*, pp. 199–200.
56 Auguste Comte, *Système de Politique Positive* (1851–4), in G. Lenzer (ed.), *Auguste Comte and Positivism: The Essential Writings*, Chicago, IL: University of Chicago Press, 1983, p. 400, quoted by Keith Graham, 'Altruism, Self-Interest and the Indistinctness of Persons', in Seglow, *The Ethics of Altruism*, pp. 49–67 (p. 49).
57 MacIntyre, *After Virtue*, pp. 228–9.

whether or not God is prepared to put our good before God's own if our good comes into conflict with God's. When the question is put like that, it sits very awkwardly – to say the least – with the ways in which Christians have usually wanted to talk about God. Grant, in other words, has underestimated the extent to which altruism is a *peculiarly* modern concept that cannot be treated as an accurate translation of earlier Christian notions of love, divine or human.

The oddness of asking whether God is an altruist or an egoist can be drawn out further by looking a little more closely at Grant's treatment of divine aseity.[58] He describes with approval the tendency in recent theology to be dissatisfied with describing God's love as *agapē*, or disinterested love originating in divine self-sufficiency. Utterly disinterested love, it is said, is not real love: genuine love is characterized by relationships of mutuality in which both parties need, desire, give and receive. If God is truly to be described as loving, God's love for the creation must include an element of *eros* – needy, desiring love – as well as *agapē*. Yet Grant recognizes an obvious difficulty with this. If God creates, and loves the creation, out of need and desire rather than self-sufficiency, then God would seem to be loving the creation instrumentally rather than for its own sake.[59] This, again, would seem to make God an egoist rather than an altruist. So either way, God turns out not to be a true altruist after all.

In an attempt to resolve this dilemma, Grant is drawn to process theology with its dipolar God characterized on the one hand by transcendent independence, absoluteness, infinity, changelessness and so on, and on the other by dependence, relativity, finitude and change.[60] Presumably *agapē*, the disinterested love originating in God's self-sufficiency, is associated with the 'absolute' pole of God, and *eros*, or needy, dependent love, with God's 'relative' pole. Yet it is hard to see how this helps: if both kinds of love are under suspicion of being ultimately egoistic, then combining both in the two poles of one God hardly seems to absolve God of the charge of egoism.

Part of the problem seems to be that much of this talk of God's love operates by anthropomorphically projecting the human experience of love onto God. But if Christians wish to speak *theologically* about love, the movement must surely be in the opposite direction. We know what God's love is, not by projecting our experience of love onto God, but by

---

58 See, esp., Grant, *Altruism*, pp. 190–217.

59 *Altruism*, pp. 203–4, citing Paul Fiddes, *The Creative Suffering of God*, Oxford: Oxford University Press, 1989, p. 74.

60 *Altruism*, pp. 206–17.

God's self-revelation in Jesus Christ. Likewise, if 'Love your neighbour as yourself' is to be understood as the command of God to us, we shall have to learn what that love looks like in the light of God's love for us, not the other way around. This is, of course, a very simple characterization of a complex theological dynamic. There is much more to be said about how this theological movement works: how, for example, we disentangle God's self-revelation, mediated as it is by human words and actions, from our projections of our own experience onto God. Nonetheless, it seems to me that theological reasoning does have to proceed in this basic direction.

So, for example, if we begin from the affirmation of faith to which Christians are committed – that the God who is made known in and through Jesus Christ is a Trinity of Persons in communion – then Grant's worries about whether God is an altruist or an egoist are put in a very different light. (Grant himself recognizes that a Trinitarian understanding of God is needed to resolve some of the dilemmas in the account that he develops, but a doctrine of the Trinity does not fit very comfortably onto the Procrustean bed of process theology.)[61] As Colin Gunton has argued, if the Creator of heaven and earth is from all eternity a Trinity of Persons, then it becomes possible to speak of a kind of divine self-sufficiency that is not narcissistic self-absorption but (as it were) 'already', prior to the creation, a dynamic of perfect communion and love; not, though, an eternally closed circle, but a dynamic of communion with its own outward momentum, so to say, that brings the creation into being and reaches out to it in love.[62] So the integrity and freedom of the creation are underwritten, because God's purpose in creating is not instrumental, to make up any divine lack or need, but, at the same time, it is possible to speak of God's delight in creation: 'God saw everything that he had made, and indeed, it was very good' (Gen. 1.31).[63]

Again, if we try to answer the question, 'What does it *mean* to love our neighbours as ourselves?', by attending to the distinctive sources of Christian faith, we will not simply say, 'Altruism.' As an account like that of Paul Ramsey shows, we will find ourselves saying something more complex, more richly textured and altogether more interesting.[64]

---

61 *Altruism*, pp. 212–17.

62 See, e.g., Colin E. Gunton, *Act and Being: Towards a Theology of the Divine Attributes*, London: SCM Press, 2002, pp. 104, 125–33.

63 Gunton, *The Triune Creator: A Historical and Systematic Study*, Grand Rapids, MI: Eerdmans, 1998, pp. 9–10.

64 Paul Ramsey, *Basic Christian Ethics*, new edn with foreword by Stanley Hauerwas and D. Stephen Long (Library of Theological Ethics), Louisville: Westminster/John Knox, 1993 (1950).

An ethic determined by the Bible and the tradition shaped by the Bible, he believes, will be grounded in God's covenanting activity towards humankind, and particularly in two basic notions: first, 'God's righteousness and love' and, second, the eschatological fulfilment of this righteousness and love in the 'Kingdom of God' whose coming was announced by Jesus.[65] The proper response to this covenant love of God, as it is made known in Jesus' proclamation of the Kingdom, is what Ramsey calls 'obedient love', which at heart amounts to disinterested love of neighbour. In *Basic Christian Ethics*, this understanding of Christian love informs an exposition of diverse themes and issues, enabling him (among other things) to develop an account of Christian freedom in opposition to rigid legalism, and – thirty years before MacIntyre's 'recovery of virtue' – at least the rudiments of an account of virtue ethics. In later works, partly in opposition to the situationist ethics of Joseph Fletcher, it becomes incorporated into his concept of 'love transforming natural law'.[66] This core concept of Christian love informs his reworking of just war theory,[67] his pioneering treatment of medical ethics,[68] and much more besides. Of course, there are plenty of respects in which Ramsey's account is open to challenge, correction and extension in the light of the sources he himself identifies as central.[69] But the range, subtlety and fruitfulness of thought that can be informed by this central theme of 'obedient love' shows just how much more Christians can and must say than 'altruism' when they ask themselves about love's meaning.

I have suggested, then, that when Christians ask about the relevance of evolution for the content of moral obligation, they should not be content simply to translate neighbour-love into altruism and ask about the relevance of evolution for altruism. The questions I stated earlier must be recast: first, *does evolution have anything to teach us about the Christian imperative to love one's neighbour as oneself?* Second, *what is the place of neighbour-love in a Christian theological vision of the moral life?*

---

65 *Basic Christian Ethics*, p. 2.

66 For a summary and discussion, see D. Stephen Long, *Tragedy, Tradition, Transformism: The Ethics of Paul Ramsey*, Boulder, CO: Westview, 1995, e.g. pp. 54–64, 83–94.

67 Ramsey, *War and the Christian Conscience: How Shall Modern War Be Conducted Justly?*, Durham, NC: Duke University Press, 1961.

68 Ramsey, *The Patient as Person: Explorations in Medical Ethics*, New Haven, CT: Yale University Press, 1970.

69 For a sympathetic critique, see Long, *Tragedy, Tradition, Transformism*.

One kind of answer to the first of these questions is offered by Stephen Pope. He wishes to follow the example of Thomas Aquinas in '[grounding] his notion of love in a developed, scientifically grounded theory of human nature'.[70] His motivation is that, in the Thomist tradition with which he aligns himself, 'grace does not destroy nature but perfects it'.[71] Thomas used the best science available to him, namely Aristotelian biology; Pope wants to use sociobiology in a functionally equivalent way to Thomas's use of Aristotle. A critical appropriation of sociobiological accounts of human sociality, he argues, will serve as a corrective to some of the deficiencies in recent Catholic accounts of love. These accounts tend to focus either on personalist accounts of interpersonal mutuality and the 'I–Thou' encounter or on the call of liberation theology to solidarity with all people, especially the world's poor and oppressed. Pope's complaint against these accounts is that, for all their strengths, they 'fail to deal with, and, in many cases, even to recognize, the need to discriminate between various objects of love and to prioritize the moral responsibilities attending various relationships'.[72] He holds that by attending to natural loyalties and affections, Thomas Aquinas was able to avoid this deficiency. He hopes that an updated Catholic account of the 'ordering of love' incorporating modern biological insights into human nature will likewise also be able to avoid it. Thus, for example, he argues that while kin selection theory cannot supply a blueprint for the ordering of human affections or directly guide our concrete moral decisions, it can make a positive contribution in several respects. It encourages realism about the limits to human love, the persistence of conflict and the pervasiveness of partiality in human relations. It corrects an unbalanced emphasis on love as 'purely conscious and deliberate'.[73] And it points to the importance of natural ties of marriage and family; indeed, these natural relationships, when they work as they should, provide the environment that children need if they are ever to *develop* the capacities for I–Thou encounter and wider social concern on which personalist and liberationist accounts of love rely.

Colin Grant finds Pope's argument a disturbing example of the '[d]ismissal of altruism, and substitution of more circumscribed visions'; Pope, he charges, 'basically accepts sociobiology's "naturalization" of

---

70 Stephen J. Pope, *The Evolution of Altruism and the Ordering of Love*, Washington, DC: Georgetown University Press, 1994, p. 50.

71 *ST* I.1.8 ad 2.

72 Pope, *The Evolution of Altruism*, p. 42.

73 *The Evolution of Altruism*, p. 132.

altruism'.[74] This is hardly a fair criticism. Pope is clear that he does not wish to read an ethic of love uncritically off a sociobiological account of human nature. Thus, he rehearses some of the standard criticisms of sociobiology, such as its tendency to crude reductionism, determinism and egoism.[75] He also acknowledges some of the points of tension between the understanding of natural affections disclosed by socio-biology and a New Testament ethic that 'radically relativizes' natural loyalties and affections in the light of the Gospel.[76] Nonetheless, I wonder whether he is *sufficiently* critical, or at any rate critical in the right kind of way, in appropriating evolutionary insights. For one thing, as he acknowledges,[77] his account does not address in any detail the relationship of 'is' to 'ought', so it remains a little unclear to what extent, and in what way, he means a sociobiological account of human sociality to shape a Christian ethic of love. Furthermore, although he acknowledges the radical challenge that some strands of the New Testament pose for his biologically grounded account of the ordering of love, he tends to note the challenge and then move fairly swiftly on to safer ground. It is true that to some extent these difficulties arise from the deliberately limited scope of his project. He intends his book to be an initial and modest contribution to the much larger project of articu-lating a contemporary Catholic account of the ordering of love. He explicitly identifies both of the difficulties I have raised – a philosophical explication of the relationship between 'ought' and 'is', and a fuller engagement with the Bible – as unfinished business which that larger project would have to tackle. But it is possible that a sustained attempt to do so would not resolve, but heighten, some of the tensions in his account. It could be that these tensions are traceable to the use he makes of the Thomist axiom that 'grace perfects nature'.[78]

Pope's employment of this axiom certainly allows a much more nuanced reading of Thomas than some treatments of the latter in the

---

74 Grant, *Altruism*, p. xv.
75 Pope, *The Evolution of Altruism*, pp. 99–114.
76 *The Evolution of Altruism*, p. 143.
77 *The Evolution of Altruism*, p. 158.
78 What follows should not be taken to mean that I wish to deny the axiom, only to read it differently from some ways in which it is sometimes understood. As Eugene F. Rogers puts it, 'we ought to define nature in terms of grace because it takes Jesus Christ to tell us what nature is': *Thomas Aquinas and Karl Barth: Sacred Doctrine and the Natural Knowledge of God*, Notre Dame, IN: University of Notre Dame Press, 1999, p. 190. Rogers argues that this is how *ST* I.1 should be read, and he also explicitly identifies this reading with Barth's principle, cited below, that creation is the external basis of the covenant, and the covenant is the internal basis of the creation (*CD* III.1, §41.2, 3).

context of evolution and ethics, such as a recent essay in which Larry Arnhart presents Darwin as an intellectual heir of Thomas.[79] Darwin held that humans have a 'moral sense' which developed during our evolutionary history because it proved adaptive to our ancestors, and Arnhart identifies Darwin's moral-sense theory in quite a simple way with Thomist natural law. He believes that his Darwinian-Thomist view is consistent with 'biblical religion', because 'human morality expresses the natural inclinations of the human animal as belonging to a natural world created by God, who saw his creation as entirely good'.[80] He does not seriously entertain the possibility that even natural inclinations whose origins lie in God's good creation might now be an unreliable guide to the good because, for example, they might have become disordered by human sin.[81] Pope certainly does entertain that possibility. He notes that our natural human affections, as made known by sociobiology, have some potential for evil as well as good, and must be extended or even challenged by a Christian ethic: 'in some ways, then, the ethic of love works against nature, *at least as the sociobiologists depict it*'.[82] That last qualification, though, is significant, because it hints that if the sociobiological picture of nature is inconsistent with a Christian ethic of love, it must be because sociobiology is giving us a one-sided picture of nature. Pope still appears to think that if we can understand our natural inclinations properly they will offer us a broadly reliable guide to our good.

Understanding our natural inclinations properly might be more difficult than we sometimes think, if, as I suggested in the previous section, our concepts of nature are inevitably in some measure socially constructed, and therefore vulnerable to various forms of ideologically driven distortion. One concrete example noted earlier was the claim of feminist biologists such as Sarah Hrdy that a male-dominated biological profession has often read patriarchal notions of gender roles and relationships into its understanding of human evolution, which was

---

79 Larry Arnhart, 'The Darwinian Moral Sense and Biblical Religion', in Clayton and Schloss, *Evolution and Ethics*, pp. 204–20.

80 Arnhart, 'The Darwinian Moral Sense', p. 204.

81 In his *Darwinian Natural Right: The Biological Ethics of Human Nature*, Albany, NY, State University of New York Press, 1998, pp. 254–5, Arnhart summarily dismisses this view as a kind of 'Augustinian asceticism' diametrically opposed to the Aristotelian-Darwinist naturalism that he wishes to promote. But to co-opt Thomas to the latter is surely a one-sided reading of him, ignoring (for example) Alasdair MacIntyre's argument that one of his great and distinctive achievements was a *synthesis* of the Aristotelian and Augustinian traditions: *Whose Justice? Which Rationality?*, London: Duckworth, 1988, pp. 164–82.

82 Pope, *The Evolution of Altruism*, p. 155 (emphasis added).

then used to lend support to those accounts of gender roles. This could be seen as one instance of the more general possibility that human sin so distorts our moral vision that we cannot reliably discover for ourselves what we need to know about God and the good.[83] Pope's position can certainly acknowledge the difficulty of understanding our natural inclinations rightly, though the natural law tradition on which he draws has tended to be optimistic about the capacity of human reason to discern the good, original sin notwithstanding. A more far-reaching difficulty for Pope's view, though, is that while it is quite possible that sociobiology does give a partial or distorted picture of human nature, to rely on this possibility to resolve any tensions between biology and a Christian understanding of the human good would be a risky strategy. We have to reckon with the possibility that biology, or some other form of empirical investigation, could yield *reliable* information about human nature that, if incorporated into a natural law framework of the kind Pope advocates, would stand in sharp tension with aspects of a traditional Christian ethic. In other words, we have to take seriously the possibility that Arnhart refuses to entertain, and about which Pope seems ambivalent, at best: that even if we understand our natural inclinations properly, they will not necessarily (so to say) tell us the truth about our good.

This possibility is articulated, for example, in the divine command ethic that John Hare develops from his reading of the late mediaeval philosopher and theologian John Duns Scotus.[84] There are two reasons why it might be so. One is that, though the *end* towards which God calls us – loving union with God – is necessary, the route by which God calls us to reach that end is *contingent*. God could have ordained a different route for us. (It is this notion of contingency, of course, which attracts the charge that Scotus' account makes ethics arbitrary and could lead to an understanding of God as a tyrant whose every whim must be obeyed. Hare argues at some length that Scotus' concept of 'supervenience'

---

83 Arnhart rejects this possibility in a cursory discussion in which he implies that it depends on a 'Gnostic dualism that would deny the goodness of natural human inclinations' ('The Darwinian Moral Sense', p. 207). He lines up not only Thomas but also Calvin in support of the opposite view that sin does not destroy our natural knowledge of right and wrong. This seems rather a crude polarization, among other things eliding the not insignificant differences between Thomas and Calvin.

84 John E. Hare, *God's Call: Moral Realism, God's Commands, and Human Autonomy*, Grand Rapids: Eerdmans, 2001, pp. 49–85; id., 'Is There an Evolutionary Foundation for Human Morality?', in Clayton and Schloss, *Evolution and Ethics*, pp. 187–203.

enables him to avoid arbitrariness, in the everyday sense.[85] As Hare puts it, 'the moral goodness or badness of an act supervenes on the act itself',[86] by which he means that moral evaluation of the act is *grounded* in the nature of the act, but is not *entailed* by it. Put more generally, 'the moral law towards the neighbor does not *follow* from our nature, but it *fits* it spectacularly well'.)[87] The other reason that our natural inclinations might mislead us is that, because of human sin, those inclinations (or 'affections') are disordered. We have two basic kinds of affection, the 'affection for advantage', which inclines us to our own benefit, and the 'affection for justice', which inclines us to seek the good for its own sake. Both are good, the products of God's good creation; our problem, though, is that we are born with a tendency to rank them wrongly, putting the affection for advantage before the affection for justice. This results in a kind of 'incoherence' in the moral life, and means that we are not necessarily naturally inclined towards the moral goods towards which God calls us. Such an account of divine command ethics rules out versions of natural law theory – including, as Hare forcefully points out, Arnhart's – that try to deduce conclusions about the good from our natural inclinations. It would, however, allow for an account of natural law in which God's command 'fits' our nature, so that '[w]hat is right is also what makes for flourishing as a human being'.[88] This account would be close to Barth's ethic of the command of God the Creator, as Nigel Biggar understands it: the task of such an ethic is 'to describe right human action in terms of that conformity to the given structure of their creaturely being for which God's sanctifying command liberates humans'.[89]

---

85 Hare, *God's Call*, pp. 62–78. The impression of arbitrariness can be reinforced, as Hare notes, by the fact that Scotus uses the word *arbitrium* in connection with God's commandments; however, to translate this as 'arbitrary' in the everyday sense is misleading; its meaning is closer to the less familiar legal sense of 'arbitrary' meaning 'discretionary'.

86 *God's Call*, p. 66.

87 *God's Call*, p. 75.

88 *God's Call*, p. 77.

89 Biggar, *Hastening*, p. 49; cf. pp. 41–2, where he identifies Barth with a tradition that includes (among others) Aquinas, Duns Scotus and Calvin, in which 'God's command [is] the expression of a divine will that is governed by the divine *Ratio* or Wisdom', against the radical voluntarism of William of Occam. It should be noted that David Clough takes Biggar to task for paying insufficient attention to the dialectical structure of Barth's ethics: Barth always holds in tension the need to think systematically about ethics with the ever-present possibility that God's command will '[contradict] what we thought we knew'; Clough, *Ethics in Crisis: Interpreting Barth's Ethics*, Aldershot: Ashgate, 2005, pp. 114–18 (p. 117). According to Clough, Biggar's account tends to collapse this tension in the direction of system and predictability, thereby tend-

I have suggested that Pope is committed to the notion that our natural inclinations, properly understood, will give us a broadly reliable guide to the good; one problem with this is that human sin might place greater obstacles than we sometimes imagine in the way of our understanding our natural inclinations rightly; another is the possibility that biology (or some other form of empirical investigation) will disclose natural inclinations that are contrary to Christian accounts of the good. Another way of expressing these difficulties is to ask whether Pope's account sufficiently acknowledges the difference between 'nature' and 'creation'. The latter, I argued earlier, is a theological category: when Christians claim that the material world (including our own bodies) is 'very good' because it is the creation of a good and loving God, and that our good consists in conforming to the ends for which we have been created, they are making theological claims. And if we want to know about the ends for which God has created us, and what ways of living are oriented towards our ultimate good, we are asking theological questions. Now of course it is perfectly possible to argue that enough traces of God's good purpose are detectable in the world, and that our created minds have sufficient capacity to detect those traces, that we can learn much of what we need to know from an honest investigation of nature. As is well known, such a view can indeed claim a certain amount of support from the New Testament, particularly Paul's account in the letter to the Romans of Gentiles who have the requirements of God's law 'written on their hearts' (Rom. 2.12–16). But as I observed in Chapter 4, there are strong strands of Christian thought that have read those texts rather differently and have insisted that, if our finite and sinful minds are ever to learn what we need to know of God's good purposes in creation, we shall need help. Such a line of thought is expressed powerfully by the theologian who has already been one of my major conversation partners in this book, Karl Barth.

Barth's principle is not that grace perfects nature, but that *creation is the external basis of the covenant and the covenant is the internal basis of creation.*[90] This way of putting it stems from his resolutely Christo-

---

ing to play down the very features that give Barth's ethics its vitality and vigour. For my purposes, it is not necessary to adjudicate this disagreement: what is necessary for the present argument is, first, that the divine command is not arbitrary (in the everyday sense) because it is grounded in God's faithfulness and constancy; secondly, that we have not only the possibility, but also the responsibility, of deliberating systematically about our moral responsibilities; but thirdly, that the conclusions we reach are necessarily provisional, always open to question, challenge and even contradiction by God's command. On these points, Biggar and Clough, if I understand them rightly, agree.

90 Barth, *CD* III.1, §41.2, 3.

centric approach to theology: whatever theology knows about God, humanity and the world, it knows by virtue of God's self-revelation in Jesus Christ. So the God who created us and the world is not some alien God, but the God whom we already know in Christ. God the Creator is the God who, from all eternity, wills to be *with us* and *for us* in Jesus Christ. This, among other things, gives us grounds for affirming the goodness of creation and God's love for it: as Kathryn Tanner puts it,

> If the Father who creates is the Father of Jesus, this act of creation must be seen as one of free loving beneficence, a Fatherly act of favour . . . one may be sure that the world exists as a good gift if the God who creates is the God of Jesus Christ.[91]

It also expresses the relationship between creation and God's reconciling and redeeming work: creation is, as it were, the 'theatre' in which God's reconciling work takes place.[92] This need not, however, reduce it to a mere prelude, of no importance except as a means to an end. God's act of creating the world is itself an act of grace – of God's free, unconstrained and undeserved love. As Barth puts it, 'creation in itself and as such – as and because it has its roots in the grace of God in Jesus Christ – is already marked as a form of the divine Yes, which is the quintessence of all His works'.[93]

How does all this help us with our ethical questions? 'The task of theological ethics', says Barth, 'is to understand the Word of God as the Command of God.'[94] Thus ethics is always intimately bound up with Christian doctrine, and every area of doctrine has ethical implications. In the last part of his doctrine of creation, Barth thematizes ethics as 'the Command of God the Creator'. The creative purpose of God, enacted in the creation, implies a command or call from God to us to be the creatures God intends us to be. This command comes to us as good news: it validates our creaturely being, and sets us free to be all that God means us to be. But how do we know what that is? Not by empirical investigation of human nature: that can only yield what Barth calls 'working hypotheses of human self-understanding'.[95] These have their value, as we shall see; but for Barth it is Jesus Christ who shows us what

---

91 Kathryn Tanner, 'Creation and Providence', in John Webster (ed.), *The Cambridge Companion to Karl Barth*, Cambridge: Cambridge University Press, 2000, pp. 111–26 (pp. 118–19).

92 Tanner, 'Creation and Providence', p. 118.

93 Barth, *CD* III.4, p. 40.

94 *CD* III.4, p. 4.

95 *CD* III.4, p. 44.

it is to be truly human, and therefore shows us the shape of the command of the Creator.

There are four dimensions to this command, four principal ways in which God's command sets us free to be truly human creatures. We are set free for relationship with God, for relationship with one another, to be creatures of this particular – human – kind, and, finally, we are set free, as finite creatures, to live within our spatial and temporal limits, within which we can live out our particular vocations. Since the focus of this section is on human sociality, it is with the second of these aspects – freedom in fellowship – that I shall be concerned.

Barth identifies three aspects under which he considers freedom in fellowship: men and women, parents and children, and our relationships with 'near and distant neighbours'. The first of these aspects is the most basic to Barth's account, and the one to which he gives most space. To be human is to exist in relationship with others who are sufficiently like us that we can be in relationship, yet sufficiently different to be genuinely other than us, not simply replicas of us. Barth thinks that the male–female relationship is the paradigm of a relationship with another who is like me yet different.[96] To be human is to be male or female, and our proper response to God's command in this sphere is to be what we are, not (for example) to try and transcend our sex in some kind of over-spiritualized androgyny. Marriage is at the heart of his account, and he has much to say about sex and gender, though his treatment of 'man and woman' is not restricted to 'sexual ethics' narrowly understood.

To be informed by Barth's method is not, of course, to be slavishly committed to his conclusions. His treatment of 'man and woman' includes the notorious 'A and B' passage in which he likens man and woman to the letters A and B and claims (albeit with caveats and qualifications) that women are subordinate to men: 'A precedes B, and B follows A. Order means succession . . . It means super- and subordination.'[97] As some commentators argue, this stratification of men and women is in tension with, if not contradictory to, his basic point about the importance of otherness in human relations. As Wolf Krötke puts it, 'it is much more reasonable to conceive the *mutual communication* of equally human human beings in their otherness as the "basic form of humanity"'.[98] This self-contradiction, if such it be, is particu-

---

96 CD III.2, pp. 285–324.
97 CD III.4, p. 169.
98 Wolf Krötke, 'The Humanity of the Human Person in Karl Barth's Anthropology', trans. by Philip G. Ziegler, in Webster, *Cambridge Companion to Karl Barth*, pp. 159–76 (p. 169; emphasis added).

larly ironic, because Barth prefaces his own argument with a rejection of theological treatments such as Emil Brunner's that absolutize particular patterns (in Brunner's case, socially conservative ones) of gender roles and relationships.[99] He arguably then proceeds to fall into a similar ideological trap himself. As I suggested in the last section, though, what is worth noting is that Barth's approach, alert as it is to our constant tendency to confuse our own images and constructs with God's revelation, contains within itself rich resources for suspicion, self-criticism and self-correction.

The second kind of relationship that Barth considers is that of parents and children, and here, in a sense, he *relativizes* ties of blood and kinship.[100] The point about the command to honour our fathers and mothers (Exod. 20.12), as he sees it, is that children are called to recognize their parents as God's representatives to them, the 'bearers and mediators of [God's] promise'; it is not the genetic relationship as such, but the 'oversight and responsibility' implied by that relationship, that is of theological and ethical significance.[101] Barth, always concerned to emphasize God's sovereign freedom to command, allows the possibility that obedience to Christ could lead children away from their parents, or even parents from their children, though a situation in which this happened would be one of those *Grenzfälle*, or exceptional cases, in which the command of God takes highly unusual forms.[102]

The third aspect of freedom in fellowship is our relationships with near and distant neighbours.[103] The relationships of men and women, and of parents with children, are given features of the kind of creature that God has made us. Other human relationships, by contrast, are not 'given' in this way, but contingent. (This means, incidentally, that Barth refuses to accord 'the family' any special status as a category for study in this context.)[104] But for all their contingency, the command of the Creator does include such relationships. God's call to me as my Creator is always a call that comes to me *somewhere* – as a member of a particular people, with a particular language, geographical location and shared history in common. These are my 'near neighbours'. But there is a wider circle to which I also belong, encompassing all my fellow-

---

99 CD III.4, pp. 152–3, citing Emil Brunner, *Man in Revolt: A Christian Anthropology*, trans. Olive Wyon, London: Lutterworth, 1939, p. 358.

100 CD III.4, pp. 240–85.

101 CD III.4, p. 243.

102 CD III.4, pp. 260–1, 285.

103 CD III.4, pp. 285–323.

104 CD III.4, pp. 241–2, 286.

humans – my 'distant neighbours' who are nonetheless still my neighbours. Barth has some important things to say about the relationship between these two circles of 'near' and 'distant' neighbours.[105] First, there is no clear-cut distinction between near and distant. Secondly, God's call has, as it were, an outward momentum to it: I am always being called to *expand* the circle of my loyalties and concerns. There are obvious points of contact here with the widespread concern in the evolution and ethics literature to find ways of extending the naturally tribal limits of our care for one another. Barth's reasons for extending the boundaries, though, are very different from those in much of the literature, which often do not go very far beyond the pragmatic worry that tribalism equipped with modern weapons could be dangerous to the future of our species.[106] Thirdly, since the particular configuration of our near and distant neighbours is 'reversible, fluid and removable',[107] no particular social arrangement or political entity should be absolutized.[108]

Given Barth's resolutely Christocentric method, it might seem that he leaves no room for an interdisciplinary conversation with evolutionary biology, of the sort that we have seen in accounts like Stephen Pope's.[109] But this judgement would be premature. As I have noted, Barth holds that scientific and other forms of investigation into human nature yield only 'working hypotheses of man's self-understanding', as distinct from the real knowledge we have of ourselves as those 'to whom God is gracious in Jesus Christ'.[110] But he nonetheless thinks that these 'working hypotheses' have their proper place within this knowledge. As Nigel Biggar puts it,

> Barth insists that a properly theological anthropology will not simply
> repudiate 'the phenomena of the human recognisable to every human

105 *CD* III.4, pp. 300–4.

106 See, e.g., Peter J. Richerson and Robert Boyd, 'Darwinian Evolutionary Ethics: Beyond Patriotism and Sympathy', in Clayton and Schloss, *Evolution and Ethics*, pp. 50–77.

107 *CD* III.4, p. 302.

108 Cf. *CD* III.4, p. 292: '[W]e have to remember that no particular place, . . . no particular form of life, is holy, just as no man is holy. God alone is holy.' It is worth remembering the context in which Barth wrote this, soon after the Second World War, when memories of the Nazi ideology of blood and soil, which absolutized Hitler and the Third Reich in just the way criticized by Barth, were still fresh. The latter's strategy of theological resistance to such ideologies during the 1930s and 1940s, as is well known, involved a resolute denial that we can claim any knowledge of the divine ordering of the world independently of Christ: see *CD* III.4, pp. 305–9.

109 Indeed, Barth himself famously thought that natural science was irrelevant to the Christian doctrine of creation as such: *CD* III.1, pp. ix–x.

110 *CD* III.4, p. 41.

eye and every thinking mind'. But it will qualify and order such 'general knowledge' with a necessarily theological account of real human being – that is, human being as creature, pardoned sinner, and child of the Father.[111]

It is true that Barth failed to engage in a very serious or sustained way with empirical data in his consideration of some concrete moral problems – a failure that, as Biggar observes, may have had something to do with faults in his methodology, but may have been at least partly because he saw his primary task in this area as articulating the ethical implications of Christian theology, leaving the detailed analysis of concrete problems to others.[112] Be that as it may, there is undoubtedly room within an account of human sociality following Barth's approach for the critical appropriation of insights from evolutionary biology. In some respects, this critical appropriation will resemble that attempted by Stephen Pope and other natural law theorists. Evolutionary biology might have an important contribution to make to a detailed picture of our particular human loyalties and affections – with the caveat, also entered by Pope, that the scientific claims made in these discussions are frequently tentative and sometimes highly controversial. Insofar as the science is reliable, it will be able to 'flesh out' our understanding of our relationships with one another as men and women, as parents and children, and with our near and distant neighbours. It could help us to understand better the particular, contingent contexts in which we hear God's call to 'freedom in fellowship'. But like Pope's, such an account will regard this knowledge as morally ambiguous. Loyalties to which our evolutionary history might have predisposed us are not necessarily those to which God calls us: we might be called to transcend our natural bonds of affection. As I have shown, Barth, like Pope, is concerned to challenge the tribalism which sociobiology claims is a product of human evolution.

Though my account, following Barth, clearly has common features and points of contact with Pope's natural law approach, there are also important methodological and substantive contrasts. Methodologically, it differs in that we know about the particular loyalties to which we are called, not by an investigation of human nature and natural inclinations, but from the knowledge of real human being that we have in and through Christ. Substantively, the account that I have sketched is more likely to relativize our natural ties and affections in the light of our self-

111 Biggar, *Hastening*, p. 156, quoting Barth, *CD* III.2, p. 199.
112 Biggar, *Hastening*, pp. 156–60.

knowledge in Christ. As I noted earlier, for example, Barth is relatively uninterested in 'the family' as a category for investigation, preferring to ask about the 'neighbours' among whom I hear God's call. Pope certainly wishes to repudiate the idea expressed in Haldane's quip about two brothers and eight first cousins,[113] but Barth's divine command ethic might equip us better than Pope's natural law approach to do so.

I have concentrated mainly on the first of the two questions that I identified earlier: does evolution have anything to teach us about neighbour-love? I have answered that question with a qualified 'Yes'. I end this section with some brief comments about the second question: what is the place of neighbour-love in a Christian theological vision of the moral life? Though this is not directly a question about evolution and Christian ethics, an answer to it is often presupposed – for example, by Jeffrey Schloss, whom I quoted earlier, who equates altruism in a fairly straightforward way with neighbour-love and describes the latter as 'the ultimate telos of human existence, the summation and fulfilment of all moral obligation'.[114] Strictly speaking, in the Christian tradition, the *telos* of human existence is more commonly reckoned to be eternal life with God, but Schloss is by no means alone in regarding neighbour-love as the summation of all Christian moral obligation. In so doing, of course, he is heir to a long tradition that, indeed, claims some support from the New Testament. 'The commandments, "You shall not commit adultery; You shall not murder; You shall not steal; You shall not covet"; and any other commandment, are summed up in this word, "Love your neighbour as yourself"', says Paul (Rom. 13.9). And a theologian like Paul Ramsey shows how rich and subtle a system of ethics can be built on this one great command. Yet even in the New Testament, this is by no means the whole picture: there are several major strands of New Testament literature in whose accounts of the moral life neighbour-love hardly features. As Richard Hays remarks, to make neighbour-love our chief hermeneutical lens 'might produce more distortion than clarity in our construal of the New Testament's ethical witness'.[115] That witness is too complex and diverse to be subsumed without remainder under the heading of love. And indeed, the kind of ethical reflection in response to that witness that we find in a thinker like Karl Barth does some justice to this diversity and complexity. As we saw earlier, 'freedom in fellowship' is only one dimension of our response

---

113 Pope, *The Evolution of Atruism*, pp. 145–6.

114 See above, note 50.

115 Richard B. Hays, *The Moral Vision of the New Testament: Community, Cross, New Creation*, Edinburgh: T&T Clark, 1997, p. 203.

to the command of God the Creator, and the canvas would become broader still if we also considered 'the one command of God' under the aspects of the command of God the Reconciler and the command of God the Redeemer.[116] In short, when a theological ethic that conceptualizes its task as '[understanding] the Word of God as the command of God'[117] encounters a discussion of evolution and ethics frequently obsessed with altruism, it will not only say that there is much more to Christian love of neighbour than altruism. It will also put neighbour-love itself firmly in its place: as an important part of a Christian moral vision, to be sure, but by no means all that there is to be said about the life that we are called to live in response to the love of God made known in Jesus Christ.

This chapter has been concerned with two issues: first, whether (and if so, how) moral norms might be justified on the basis of putative facts about human evolution; secondly, what implications, if any, evolutionary biology has for the content of moral obligation. The first issue, as commonly stated, hinges on the problem of inferring 'ought' from 'is'. I have attempted to show that if this debate is brought into engagement with a Christian doctrine of creation, the question can be reframed so that it is no longer a matter of justifying moral conclusions on the basis of empirical facts. Rather, moral judgements follow from an understanding of humans and the world as having been created good and with a purpose. Insights into human origins and nature gained from evolutionary biology have a contribution to make to our understanding of the kind of creature we are – the way we have been made and the ends towards which our creaturely nature is ordered – but to make that contribution, they must be critically appropriated into the broader and richer context of a Christian theological anthropology. The discussion of altruism and neighbour-love in the last part of the chapter has allowed me to specify in a little more detail how this reframing of the issue of moral justification might work. It has also offered an opportunity to show how one particular moral norm, much discussed in debates about evolution and ethics, might be transformed by a Christian theological engagement with those debates.

---

116 'The Command of God the Reconciler' was to have been the conclusion of Barth's doctrine of reconciliation (*CD* IV.4), left unfinished at his death. Lecture fragments of his ethics of reconciliation are published in English as *The Christian Life*, trans. Geoffrey Bromiley, new edn, London: T&T Clark, 2004 (1981). 'The Command of God the Redeemer' would have been the final part of vol. V of *CD*, which Barth did not live to write.

117 *CD* III.4, p. 4.

At various points in this and the last chapter, I have noted in passing that part of the theological anthropology that must be developed in response to these issues is an understanding of human sin. In the next part of the book, I shall attempt to show, among other things, how a Christian understanding of sin might reframe and address the issues about the morally problematic aspects of human nature and the world that I identified in Chapter 2.

Part 3

Freedom, Sin and Salvation

6

Evolution, Freedom and Moral Failure

1   A 'tenacious and powerful enemy'?

The fourth issue raised by T. H. Huxley's Romanes Lecture was the one that earlier I rather clumsily labelled 'our moral capability and its limits'. As I noted in Chapter 2, Huxley believed that our evolutionary history has left us with a moral problem: he warned that '[e]thical nature may count upon having to reckon with a tenacious and powerful enemy as long as the world lasts', though he by no means thought that the fight was hopeless.[1] Was he right to think that evolution has given us a nature that in some respects is a 'tenacious' enemy of the 'ethical nature' which we also have within us? In order to investigate this issue further, it will be helpful to look in a little more detail at the kind of claim that is made about the moral problems with which evolution might have left us. In this section, I shall outline and discuss some examples of such claims.

a   A morally problematic inheritance?

i   Male violence

One such claim is made by Richard Wrangham and Dale Peterson in respect of male violence and aggression.[2] They appeal to a variety of anthropological evidence to support the claim that violence between males, lethal aggression towards other groups and sexual aggression towards females are more or less universal features of the human male behavioural repertoire. Without advocating a simplistic biological determinism – indeed, they reject the opposition of nature and nurture as an error traceable to Francis Galton, and affirm that human behav-

---

1 Thomas Henry Huxley, 'Evolution and Ethics', in *Collected Essays*, vol. 9, London: Macmillan, 1894, pp. 46–116 (p. 85).

2 Richard Wrangham and Dale Peterson, *Demonic Males: Apes and the Origins of Human Violence*, London: Bloomsbury, 1997.

iour arises from a complex interaction of biology and culture[3] – they do hold that human male violence has roots in the history of human biological evolution. Some aspects of human male violence, they argue, are unusual in the animal kingdom, but do have parallels among our closest evolutionary relatives, the great apes: killing members of other groups of conspecifics is not uncommon among chimpanzees; male violence towards females and coerced mating are known in several great ape species; male gorillas and (less frequently) chimpanzees kill infants fathered by other males.[4] From these parallels, and from what little evidence is available from the fossil record, they infer that male violence has been a feature of hominid behaviour at least since the human and chimpanzee lineages diverged, 'making modern humans the dazed survivors of a continuous, 5-million-year habit of lethal aggression'.[5]

Wrangham and Peterson attribute chimpanzee male violence to two particular features of chimpanzees' social organization, both of which (they speculate) could have been promoted by contingent features of their diet and the ecology of their environment. One is male bonding: males stay in the social group and territory where they were born, whereas females leave the group of their birth and attach themselves to other groups to mate and rear young. This means that the lasting feature of a chimpanzee social group is the relationships among the males, not

---

3 *Demonic Males*, pp. 83–107.

4 See, e.g., *Demonic Males*, pp. 1–27, 127–52. The killing of conspecifics from other groups is highly unusual in the animal kingdom, but killing of infants and male violence towards females is more widespread: for the former, see, e.g., Sarah Blaffer Hrdy, *Mother Nature: A History of Mothers, Infants, and Natural Selection*, New York: Pantheon, 1999, pp. 32–6, 89–90. To describe male violence towards females and infants, Wrangham and Peterson use – and defend – the language of 'relationship violence', 'rape', 'battering' and 'infanticide', thus suggesting links with aspects of human male violence towards women and children. It should be noted that such use of language is not infrequently criticized for obscuring important differences between human and non-human behaviours and – even if that is not the intention of those who use the language – risking the legitimation of male violence: see, e.g., Hilary Rose and Steven Rose (eds.), *Alas Poor Darwin: Arguments against Evolutionary Psychology*, London: Jonathan Cape, 2000, pp. 2–3. Wrangham and Peterson certainly do not wish to legitimate such behaviour – the burden of their argument is that it is important to understand the roots of male violence in order to control and overcome it – but they defend their use of apparently anthropomorphic language on the grounds that if there might be genuine parallels, they should not be ignored: see *Demonic Males*, p. 284 n. 6. For a more general defence of the critical use of anthropomorphic language in the study of animal behaviour, see Frans B. M. de Waal, *Good Natured: the Origins of Right and Wrong in Humans and Other Animals*, Cambridge, MA: Harvard University Press, 1996, pp. 62–6.

5 Wrangham and Peterson, *Demonic Males*, p. 63.

those of females. The other is what they call 'party-gang' organization:[6] rather than forming relatively large and stable troops (as, for example, gorillas do), chimpanzees organize themselves into smaller groups whose size fluctuates much more than the size of troops. These features, they propose, encourage male status-seeking and the formation of what have been called 'political' coalitions;[7] they also encourage inter-group aggression, since it is not uncommon for one group to encounter an isolated individual or a much smaller group that can be attacked without much risk to the attacker. Wrangham and Peterson hypothesize that human males, like their chimpanzee relatives, have been bequeathed an emotional disposition to seek and maintain high status, if necessary using force and violence to do so: in other words, *male pride* is part of the human evolutionary inheritance. They also argue that human sociality has some important similarities to chimpanzee social organization, and that this has left men with an emotional predisposition to strong 'ingroup–outgroup bias': loyalty to one's own group and hostility to other groups.[8]

However, Wrangham and Peterson do not believe that the evolutionary inheritance of our species is ineluctable, and, as evidence that it is not, they point to the chimpanzees' closest relative, the bonobos.[9] The latter have a similar social structure to chimpanzees, but the lethal aggression and other forms of extreme violence frequently seen among chimpanzees do not seem to be significant features of bonobo social life. Wrangham and Peterson propose that this is because of crucial differences in social structure, perhaps promoted by ecological differences in the two species' habitats during their evolutionary history. Bonobo groups tend to be larger, and more stable and uniform in size, than chimpanzee groups; they often have a higher proportion of females, and the females form stronger and more lasting bonds and coalitions than do female chimpanzees.[10] There is also less intense competition for mates among bonobo males than among chimpanzee males, because bonobo females' ovulation is concealed, so that males cannot tell

---

6 *Demonic Males*, pp. 165–8.

7 See Frans B. M. de Waal, *Chimpanzee Politics: Power and Sex among the Apes*, New York: Harper and Row, 1982.

8 For pride, see Wrangham and Peterson, *Demonic Males*, pp. 190–3; for ingroup–outgroup bias, pp. 193–8.

9 *Demonic Males*, pp. 200–30.

10 Among other things, sex between bonobo females seems to be frequently used as a means of strengthening female bonds and coalitions; more generally, bonobos are celebrated in popular scientific literature for the vigour and variety of their sex-lives, a fact which leads Steven Pinker to propose that their motto is 'Make love not war': *How the Mind Works*, London: Penguin, 1998, p. 371.

whether a particular female is fertile. Since there is less competition among males for access to fertile females, status-seeking and competition for dominance are less evident in male bonobo life. The lesson Wrangham and Peterson draw for human life from the comparison of chimpanzees and bonobos is that men are likely to have a deep-seated propensity to status-seeking pride and groupish aggression for the foreseeable future, but that the more social power and influence is exercised by women, and the stronger the female coalitions that are formed in human societies, the more these proud and aggressive male tendencies can be curbed. They believe that liberal democracy, for all its faults, holds out the best hope of meeting these conditions.[11]

ii Maternal care and neglect of high-risk infants

Evolutionary psychologists habitually study forms of behaviour that are claimed to be both ubiquitous and commonplace. However, they sometimes also comment on extreme but rare forms of human behaviour, and claim that these too can be explained in terms of universal mental adaptations interacting with extreme conditions in the individual's physical, social or cultural environment. One example is Janet Mann's study of maternal behaviour towards prematurely born twins with extremely low birth-weights.[12] Mann's starting point was Robert Trivers's theory of parental investment, which predicts that natural selection will favour parents who use their resources so as to rear the greatest number of offspring that survive to reproduction.[13] From Trivers's theory, Mann developed the following hypothesis. Investment of resources in one child may limit the ability of the parents to invest resources in other actual or potential children. A child is 'of low reproductive value' if he or she is at high risk of diseases or disabilities that

---

11 Wrangham and Peterson, *Demonic Males*, pp. 231–51.

12 Janet Mann, 'Nurturance or Negligence: Maternal Psychology and Behavioral Preference among Preterm Twins', in Jerome H. Barkow, Leda Cosmides and John Tooby (eds.), *The Adapted Mind: Evolutionary Psychology and the Generation of Culture*, New York: Oxford University Press, 1992, pp. 367–90. It should be noted that Mann's paper is limited to proposing a scientific explanation of the behaviour that she discusses – she does not enter into the realm of moral evaluation or critique. To read this paper as an example of the claim that some aspects of our evolutionary inheritance predispose us to behave in morally problematic ways is an inference that I have drawn from Mann's claims, not one that she herself explicitly makes.

13 Robert L. Trivers, 'Parental Investment and Sexual Selection', in Bernard Campbell (ed.), *Sexual Selection and the Descent of Man 1871–1971*, Chicago, IL: Aldine, 1972, pp. 136–79, also online at http://orion.oac.uci.edu/~dbell/Trivers.pdf (accessed 21 August 2006).

will either make him or her unlikely to survive to reproductive age or seriously impair his or her chances of reproductive success. Trivers's theory predicts that natural selection will have favoured parents who are able to detect whether their children are at risk of such diseases or disabilities, and who respond in one of two ways: either increasing their level of care to meet the child's greater needs or minimizing their care so as to reduce the resources expended on the at-risk child. Which course is followed will be influenced by the circumstances: where resources are scarce and conditions difficult, the cost-cutting minimal-care option will be more likely than when resources are plentiful. The option very unlikely to be favoured by natural selection is moderate care such as would be adequate for a healthy child, since this level of care will not suffice for a very sick child, but will still divert significant resources away from other actual or potential children.

Mann tested this hypothesis by studying a sample (a small one, as she acknowledges) of extremely low-birth-weight twins and their mothers.[14] Such twins, she says, provide a 'natural experiment' for testing her hypothesis, because their high level of need makes great demands on parental resources and because it often happens that one twin is born healthier than the other. In two cases, she found that mothers failed even to provide adequate levels of basic care, such as feeding and changing; in both cases, the mothers were very 'resource poor' and were from the lowest socioeconomic classes represented in the study. In all other cases, basic care was adequate, but Mann reports that in their 'positive maternal behaviors' such as holding, soothing and playing with the child, all her mothers showed a preference for the healthier of their twins by the time the infants were eight months old. She argues that these experimental results support her hypothesis and the Trivers parental-investment theory from which it was derived. In short, she claims that the theory and her experimental results suggest that a predisposition to neglect one's child under certain circumstances proved adaptive, and was therefore selected for, during human evolutionary history. In similar vein, others have also proposed that the neglect, abandonment and even, in extreme cases, killing of infants by mothers who lacked the resources to rear them could have proved adaptive during human evolutionary history.[15]

---

14 Fathers were not included in this study: Mann comments that '[p]aternal care is certainly relevant (even crucial), but cannot be adequately addressed within the limitations of this paper' ('Nurturance or Negligence', p. 387).

15 E.g. Hrdy, *Mother Nature*, pp. 288–317; Pinker, *How the Mind Works*, pp. 440–5.

iii Debunking morality

A somewhat different kind of moral critique of our evolutionary inheritance is suggested by writers such as George Williams. In a commentary from 1988 on Huxley's 'Evolution and Ethics', Williams agrees with Huxley's negative evaluation of the evolutionary process, but holds that when Huxley attributed 'moral indifference' to the cosmic process he did not go far enough: 'gross immorality' is Williams's verdict on nature.[16] This conclusion is inferred partly from the existence in nature of behaviours that Williams calls 'patently pernicious',[17] including those forms of violence, abuse and neglect discussed by Wrangham and Peterson, Mann, Hrdy and others. However, he also argues that even those aspects of our evolutionary inheritance that might appear more praiseworthy are in fact anything but. Referring to the theories of kin selection, reciprocity and manipulation that I surveyed in Chapter 4, he comments:

> As a general rule today a biologist seeing one animal doing something to benefit another assumes that it is manipulated by the other individual or that it is being subtly selfish. Its selfishness would always be defined in relation to its single ultimate interest, the replication of its own genes. Nothing resembling the Golden Rule or other widely preached ethical principle is operating in living nature. It could scarcely be otherwise. Evolution is guided by a force that maximizes genetic selfishness.[18]

Group-selectionist accounts of moral behaviour, he believes, would fare no better in terms of moral evaluation, since they would merely substitute competition between groups, in which the members of one group pursued their collective interest at the expense of those outside the group, for competition between individuals. Popular evolutionary writers, notably Robert Wright, have enthusiastically followed and extended Williams's train of thought, speculating that natural selection during our evolutionary history has favoured tendencies towards cheating, hypocrisy (because it is in my interests both to cheat and to maintain the kind of good reputation that will induce others to do me favours) and

---

16 George C. Williams, 'Huxley's Evolution and Ethics in Sociobiological Perspective', *Zygon*, 23.4 (1988), pp. 383–407 (p. 384).

17 Williams, 'Huxley's Evolution and Ethics', p. 392.

18 'Huxley's Evolution and Ethics', p. 391.

self-deception (because it is often in my interests to deceive others, and I will be able to do so much more effectively if I am sincerely convinced of whatever I am trying to persuade them to believe).[19]

Williams agrees with those who theorize that in human evolution, kin selection, reciprocity and manipulation have given rise to genuine morality. However, this does not mitigate his verdict of 'gross immorality' against the evolutionary process: morality is 'an accidental capability produced, in its boundless stupidity, by a biological process that is normally opposed to the expression of such a capability'.[20] This capability that nature has accidentally and stupidly bestowed upon us, though, presents us with the moral demand also recognized by Huxley and by Richard Dawkins: to combat the 'cosmic process' or to 'rebel against the tyranny of the selfish replicators'.[21]

iv But are we 'good natured' after all?

A more optimistic view of our moral capabilities comes from the primatologist Frans de Waal: rejecting what he calls the 'Calvinist sociobiology' of Dawkins, Williams and others, he argues in effect that our biological nature can support many of our highest moral aspirations.[22] He identifies several features of human morality – sympathy, the making of social rules, reciprocity, peacemaking and the avoidance of conflict – and presents evidence drawn from his own extensive and close observation of primates that these characteristics can be found (some of the time and to some extent) in our closest evolutionary relatives. In short, he claims that at least the beginnings of morality can be found in non-human animals, and he is scathing of biologists who readily use terms such as 'spiteful', 'greedy' and 'murderous' of animals but resist the language of 'friendship' and 'reconciliation' as overly anthropomorphic.[23] However, de Waal's observations do not support unqualified

---

19 Robert Wright, *The Moral Animal: Evolutionary Psychology and Everyday Life*, New York: Abacus, 1996, pp. 263–326.

20 Williams, 'Reply to Comments on "Huxley's Evolution and Ethics in Sociobiological Perspective"', *Zygon*, 23.4 (1988), pp. 437–8 (p. 438).

21 Huxley, 'Evolution and Ethics', p. 83; Richard Dawkins, *The Selfish Gene*, 2nd edn, Oxford: Oxford University Press, 1989, pp. 200–1.

22 Frans B. M. de Waal, *Good Natured: The Origins of Right and Wrong in Humans and Other Animals*, Cambridge, MA, and London: Harvard University Press, 1996. 'Calvinist' here seems to be used as a fairly non-specific term of disapproval, only loosely linked to any specific claims that might be found in Calvin's theology.

23 *Good Natured*, pp. 18–20.

optimism: alongside sympathy we find fear, indifference, hostility and *Schadenfreude*.[24]

One of de Waal's aims is to challenge our sense of vast superiority over other animals. Another is to emphasize that our morality is rooted in our biological nature, not disembodied and detached from it.[25] At times he makes this point with a certain amount of caricature, but his considered conclusion appears to be that

> The distinction between right and wrong is made by people on the basis of how they would like their society to function. It arises from interpersonal negotiation in a particular environment, and derives its sense of obligation and guilt from the internalisation of these processes. Moral reasoning is done by *us*, not by natural selection.
>
> At the same time it should be obvious that human morality cannot be infinitely flexible. Of our own design are neither the tools of morality nor the basic needs and desires that form the substance with which it works. Natural tendencies may not amount to moral imperatives, but they do figure in our decision-making. Thus, while some moral rules reinforce species-typical predispositions and others suppress them, none blithely ignore them.[26]

Some aspects of de Waal's view of ethics are obscure, but on the question in view in the present chapter he is clear enough: our biological nature inevitably influences and constrains our moral behaviour, sometimes supporting and sometimes hindering our efforts to live according to the moral rules and standards we recognize.

b Evaluation

What are we to make of the diverse claims about our moral capability and its limits stated or implied by the sources I have surveyed? In Chapter 1, I noted a variety of criticisms levelled at sociobiology and evolutionary psychology by some biologists, social scientists and philosophers;[27] should those criticisms be justified, how vulnerable would the claims surveyed above be to them?

---

24 *Good Natured*, pp. 83–8.
25 *Good Natured*, pp. 209–18.
26 *Good Natured*, p. 39.
27 See above, pp. 14–17. See also Jacqui Stewart's critique of earlier attempts to apply reductionist and determinist biological ideas to human behaviour: above, Chapter 4, n. 44.

1   *They present a simplistic picture of the relationship between genes and behaviour, thereby promoting an equally simplistic biological determinism.* Determinism will be a major focus of the remainder of this chapter, allowing this challenge to be explored more fully. For now I shall simply observe that not all of the claims surveyed here depend on either the hard biological determinism or the simplistic account of causal relationships between genes and behaviour criticized by Rose and others. Of the main sources cited above, the paper by Williams – drawing as it does on fairly clear-cut readings of kin selection and reciprocity theory – seems the most deterministic in tone; yet Williams explicitly calls for the free and responsible exercise of human choice in opposition to the selfish tendencies favoured by our evolutionary legacy. Mann, likewise, emphasizes the power of the capacities and predispositions that she holds to be products of our evolutionary history, yet does not seem to regard our behaviour as absolutely determined by them. Wrangham and Peterson, as I noted, affirm the complexity of the causes of human behaviour, and disavow any simplistic link between genes and behaviour. Their model is that evolution has given rise to certain characteristic temperaments and emotional dispositions in humans; problematic forms of behaviour and social structure, such as patriarchy, come about 'not as a direct mapping of genes onto behaviour, but out of the particular strategies that men (and women) invent for achieving their emotional goals. And the strategies are highly flexible, as every different culture shows.'[28] If this is how they understand the relationship between evolution and behaviour, they would seem to be largely in agreement with de Waal, and with other commentators such as Mary Midgley, that humans are neither 'gene machines' nor completely blank sheets of paper: our evolutionary history has left us with certain species-typical tendencies and dispositions.[29]

---

28 Wrangham and Peterson, *Demonic Males*, p. 125.

29 Mary Midgley, *The Ethical Primate: Humans, Freedom and Morality*, London: Routledge, 1994, pp. 128–53. The language of 'gene machines' and 'blank paper' is drawn proximately from Janet Radcliffe Richards's typology of views about the scope of evolutionary explanation of human nature: *Human Nature after Darwin: A Philosophical Introduction*, London: Routledge, 2000, pp. 54–6. Sociobiologists and evolutionary psychologists are categorized as 'gene-machine Darwinists', while critics such as Rose and Gould, who accept a materialist evolutionary account of human origins but deny that biological evolution can shed much light on the details of human emotions, behaviour or culture, are described as 'blank-paper Darwinists'. I shall use Richards's terminology from time to time in this chapter, with the caveat that it is a simplified shorthand for two extreme positions on a spectrum that may include intermediate positions such as the views that I have here attributed to Midgley and to Wrangham and Peterson.

2 *They rely on an over-simplified 'adaptationist' view of evolution.*
Among the claims surveyed here, those of Williams and Mann are certainly drawn from quite strongly adaptationist readings of evolutionary
theory. By contrast, while Wrangham and Peterson describe sociobiology as the 'conventional wisdom in biological science because it
explains animal behavior so well',[30] and while they posit an explanation
for male violence in terms of evolutionary adaptations, this would
not seem to commit them to the view attacked by Eldredge, Rose and
others, that adaptation under the influence of natural selection is the
only motor of evolutionary change. Since, as Eldredge puts it, 'no
rational evolutionary biologist feels that most change is not adaptive, or
that adaptive change is not caused by natural selection',[31] it is hard to
see that *all* claims of the sort surveyed in this section stand or fall by the
outcome of the arguments about adaptationism around his evolutionary 'High Table'.

3 *The empirical support for sociobiological and evolutionary-psychological theories is poor.* There are various aspects to this critique. One is
that sociobiologists and evolutionary psychologists devise 'Just So'
stories – plausible but untested speculations. A second is that some of
their theories are not specific enough to be testable against experimental
data, and are therefore scientifically uninformative. Thirdly, it is said
that sociobiologists and evolutionary psychologists sometimes demonstrate a good fit between their theories and the data, but fail to show
that rival hypotheses would not explain the same data at least as well.
The various accounts that I have surveyed, being of different kinds and
produced with different aims, vary widely in the strength and nature of
their empirical foundations. De Waal's book is a sustained attempt to
present empirical evidence for behaviour in other animals that corre-
sponds to some extent to aspects of human morality; it is, accordingly,
based on a wealth of experimental observation. By contrast, Wrangham
and Peterson are attempting an historical reconstruction of the putative
evolutionary origins of human violence. While they draw widely on
ethological and palaeontological evidence, they acknowledge that
aspects of their reconstruction are highly speculative, since the relevant
evidence is scarce and hard to obtain. Insofar as ethical or theological
arguments about the limits of our moral capabilities draw on hypo-

---

30 Wrangham and Peterson, *Demonic Males*, pp. 22–3.
31 Niles Eldredge, *Reinventing Darwin: The Great Evolutionary Debate*, London:
Phoenix, 1996, p. 56.

theses such as Wrangham and Peterson's, they will necessarily have a certain provisionality about them.

4 *They give unsatisfactory accounts of human behaviour,* for example by making unjustified parallels between the behaviour of humans and other animals, and by lumping very different kinds of human interaction together without sensitivity to the particular social contexts of those interactions or to their dynamic nature. Of the authors whom I have surveyed in this section, Wrangham and Peterson and de Waal depend most heavily on detailed comparisons between humans and other animals, particularly apes. They argue that notwithstanding the obvious differences between human cultures and the social systems of other apes, their shared evolutionary history gives reason to think that there are certain emotional dispositions and patterns of behaviour that are genuinely homologous between humans and other species. Wrangham and Peterson do also take a certain amount of time and trouble to characterize, with reference to a range of anthropological studies, the human behaviours and interactions which they claim are paralleled by aspects of ape social life. While these arguments might not satisfy trenchant critics such as Rose, it is clear that neither the parallels between human and ape behaviour nor the characteristics of human behaviour discussed by these authors are presented anything like as simplistically as the examples that Rose chooses as his chief targets (many of which, in any case, are taken from behavioural genetics rather than sociobiology).[32]

5 *They obscure the distinction between proximal and distal causes of social problems,* thereby also diverting attention from the most promising opportunities for intervention to address those problems. Of the sources that I have surveyed, the two that most directly discuss social problems are those by Mann (infant neglect) and Wrangham and Peterson (male violence). Neither of these seems committed to dissenting from the point being made in this critique. As I shall observe later in this chapter, even hard-line evolutionary psychologists can readily agree that social conditions *interact* with genetic predispositions to bring about certain kinds of behaviour, and that the social conditions may prove a more promising point of intervention to address problematic

---

32 See Steven Rose, *Lifelines: Life beyond the Gene,* 2nd edn, London: Vintage, 2005, pp. 278–95.

behaviour.[33] Wrangham and Peterson, too, conclude their exploration of male violence by proposing political means to empower women and so curb such violence; their claim, in effect, is that an evolutionary perspective can actually help *clarify* the social and political interventions needed to address problems.

A related danger, noted in Chapter 1, is that such findings could be used to support social stereotypes and the stigmatization of particular individuals or groups – socially excluded young males, vulnerable mothers or children with severe disabilities, for instance. It is clear that there is nothing in the accounts that I have surveyed to condone such stereotyping or stigmatization, but, in discussions of such sensitive matters, alertness to the risk that one's proposals or conclusions could be co-opted by others for such purposes is certainly in order.

In addition to these general critiques of evolutionary psychology and reductive forms of sociobiology, various particular criticisms have been levelled at Williams's exercise in debunking natural morality.[34] In particular, Williams displays some confusion as to which kinds of phenomenon are, and which are not, properly subject to moral evaluation. Lacking an account of the distinction between moral and non-moral evil, he attributes 'gross immorality' to a natural process which he believes to be devoid of any conscious agency. Within his materialist frame of reference, this attribution appears incoherent. Moreover, whatever practical problems they pose for moral action in the world, the discouraging features that he attributes to the evolutionary process should not be a problem for him at the theoretical level (so to say), since he regards morality proper as a phenomenon peculiar to human culture, to be adopted and followed in defiance of the evolutionary process. His negative evaluation of the evolutionary process, if true, would pose more of a problem to those working within the frame of a Christian doctrine of creation, committed as they are to the affirmation that the universe is the work of a good Creator who has pronounced the creation 'very good'. One aspect of this difficulty is the issue of theodicy, which has arisen at various points in this book and will be briefly discussed in Chapter 8. However, I shall also suggest in Chapter 7 that if there is any truth in Williams's and others' debunking of natural human 'morality', this could turn out to be less problematic for Christian theology than might initially be supposed.

---

33 John Tooby and Leda Cosmides, 'The Psychological Foundations of Culture', in Barkow *et al.*, *The Adapted Mind*, pp. 19–136 (pp. 38–40); see below, pp. 147–9.

34 See, especially, Michael Ruse, 'Response to Williams: Selfishness Is Not Enough,' *Zygon*, 23.4 (1988), pp. 413–16.

To sum up the discussion of this section: having summarized a variety of claims that our evolutionary inheritance sometimes predisposes us to morally problematic forms of behaviour, I have assessed those claims against a range of criticisms sometimes levelled at sociobiology and evolutionary psychology. I have suggested that one can acknowledge the criticisms without denying the possibility that our evolutionary history has left us with predispositions for or against certain kinds of behaviour, and that these predispositions might in some cases hinder us from behaving as we ought. If that possibility is allowed, two further questions arise: first, to the extent that we act under the influence of such predispositions, must we be considered not to be acting freely? Secondly, to the extent that our actions are not truly free, must we conclude that we cannot be held morally responsible for them? These questions will be explored further in the next section.

2 Determinism, freedom and responsibility

a *Determinisms: genetic, biological, environmental, social*

The challenge of evolutionary biology to commonsense notions of free-will and responsibility was put with particular force by E. O. Wilson in his early sociobiological book *On Human Nature*:

> [I]f our genes are inherited and our environment is a train of physical events set in motion before we were born, how can there be a truly independent agent within the brain? The agent itself is created by the interaction of the genes and the environment. It would appear that our freedom is only a self-delusion.[35]

This aspect of Wilson's sociobiology drew the fire of his critics from the outset. For example, Steven Rose wrote in a review of *On Human Nature* that

---

35 Edward O. Wilson, *On Human Nature*, Cambridge, MA: Harvard University Press, 1978, p. 71; note, however, that this apparently hardline determinism was qualified by a recognition of the immense complexity of mental processes (p. 77). This view is restated in Wilson's more recent writing: he still believes that mental processes are deterministic and infers from this that free will should, strictly speaking, be considered an illusion; however, the vast complexity and chaotic dynamics of mental processes allow us to proceed for all practical purposes as if we had free will: *Consilience: The Unity of Knowledge*, London: Abacus, 1999, pp. 130–2.

for Wilson human males have a constant tendency towards polygyny, females towards constancy (don't blame your mates for sleeping around, ladies, it's not their fault they are genetically programmed). Genetic determinism constantly creeps in at the back door.[36]

And Stephen Jay Gould expressed the concern that '[I]f we are programmed to be what we are, then these traits are ineluctable. We may, at best, channel them, but we cannot change them either by will, education or culture.'[37]

A famous piece of neurobiological research from the 1980s might seem to lend some support to Wilson's claim that our free will is 'only an illusion'. Benjamin Libet and his colleagues studied the timing of the 'readiness potential', a pattern of brain activity associated with the initiation of voluntary actions (in Libet's experiments, flicking an electric switch). They found that the readiness potential in their experimental subjects occurred approximately 350–400 milliseconds *before* the subjects' reported time of decision, which itself was about 200 milliseconds before the action.[38] A number of neuroscientists have interpreted this result as meaning that apparently voluntary actions are not in fact freely willed by the conscious mind; at most, the latter can only exercise a last-minute (or last-tenth-of-a-second) veto on 'decisions' that are really taken unconsciously. As Daniel Dennett puts it, it appears to show that '[w]hen you *think* you're deciding, you're actually just passively watching a sort of delayed internal videotape . . . of the *real* deciding that happened *unconsciously* in your brain quite a while before "it occurred to you" to flick'.[39]

What is at stake in these arguments about biological determinism and free will, and why do they generate so much heat? The criticisms levelled at Wilson by Rose and Gould raise a number of concerns about sociobiological versions of determinism. First, Rose and Gould read the sociobiologists as claiming that *biology is destiny*: that some behaviours are 'in our genes' or 'genetically programmed', in a way that means *both* that we cannot avoid performing those behaviours *and* that there is nothing

36 Steven Rose, 'Pre-Copernican Sociobiology?', *New Scientist* 80 (1978), pp. 45–6, quoted by Richards, *Human Nature*, p. 102.

37 Stephen Jay Gould, *Ever Since Darwin*, London: Burnett, 1978, p. 238, quoted by Richards, *Human Nature*, p. 103.

38 For a recent account and discussion of this research, see Benjamin Libet, 'Do We Have Free Will?', *Journal of Consciousness Studies*, 6 (1999), pp. 47–57, reprinted in Robert Kane (ed.), *The Oxford Handbook of Free Will*, Oxford: Oxford University Press, 2002, pp. 551–64.

39 Daniel C. Dennett, *Freedom Evolves*, London: Allen Lane, 2003, p. 229.

we can do to change them. If biology is destiny, then both freedom of choice and the possibility of moral improvement are placed in doubt. Second, if free will is called into question, so, it would seem, is the possibility of moral responsibility: 'don't blame your mates for sleeping around, ladies, it's not their fault they're genetically programmed'. Legal as well as moral responsibility might also be rendered problematic if the concept of free will is eroded. Third, the possibility of moral responsibility might be called into question in another, more fundamental, way. It would seem to be a condition of moral responsibility that we can give reasons, of the sort that can be morally evaluated, for our actions. But if all our thoughts and actions are the products of deterministic physical processes, then it is open to question whether reasons can truly be said to give rise to actions. As Dawkins and others have recognized, this problem is not peculiar to sociobiology, but would be posed by any sort of physical determinism.[40] However, it certainly is posed by sociobiology and other forms of 'gene-machine' Darwinism insofar as they presuppose a deterministic understanding of human action. Finally, there is the vague worry that all of this somehow erodes human dignity by undermining our image of ourselves as autonomous moral agents, a worry that will be addressed only indirectly in what follows.

It is often pointed out that any form of determinism, be it genetic, environmental, social or anything else, is equally problematic for common-sense notions of free will. There is nothing special about biological determinism, sociobiology or evolutionary psychology in this respect.[41] While this is perfectly true, there may be at least two worries particularly associated with biological forms of determinism. First, it may be thought that biologically determined traits would be harder to alter than socially determined ones: this is the thought behind Gould's critique, quoted above. Second, there may be a worry that altering biologically determined traits would require more morally problematic methods, such as eugenics or genetic engineering, than altering socially determined traits. As we shall see, though, these assumptions are open to question.

b   Is biology destiny?

One of the errors of which 'gene-machine' Darwinists are sometimes held to be guilty is a simplistic and misleading form of genetic determin-

---

40 Richard Dawkins, *The Extended Phenotype*, Oxford: Oxford University Press, 1982, pp. 9–13, quoted by Richards, *Human Nature*, pp. 102–4.

41 E.g. Dennett, *Freedom Evolves*, pp. 156–62; Richards, *Human Nature*, pp. 100–23.

ism in which there are 'genes for' behavioural traits, and there is a simple causal relationship between the genes and the traits. One possible source of this accusation is the theoretical work of Hamilton, Trivers and others, on which sociobiology and evolutionary psychology are partly based. Theoretical biologists do, perforce, sometimes deal in theoretical abstractions such as 'genes for' altruism, cheating, retaliation and so on in order to construct manageable mathematical models of how such characteristics could be subject to natural selection. There is no reason to suppose that theorists make the mistake of forgetting that such constructs are abstractions, though when their work is popularized this language does lend itself to careless talk about genes for this or that.[42] Whatever their origins, however, such simplistic forms of genetic determinism are easily and routinely repudiated by 'gene-machine' Darwinists, who have no difficulty in agreeing that any phenotype is the product of an interaction between genetic and environmental determinants, and that most of the phenotypes in view in these discussions are generated by the highly complex interactions of large numbers of genetic and environmental factors acting together by way of intricate developmental pathways.[43] That is why the term 'biological determinism', which entails the claim that all human behaviour is the outcome of deterministic processes involving both genetic and environmental factors, is preferable to talk of 'genetic determinism', which gives the impression that behaviours are caused by genes alone.

This also means that the contrast I summarized at the end of the last sub-section, between the implications of biological and social determinisms, is not one to which even evolutionary psychologists are committed. It is not necessarily true to say that biologically determined traits would be hard or impossible to change, or that socially determined traits would be easier to alter. Nor would morally problematic methods necessarily be required to alter biologically determined traits. Because any biologically determined trait involves an interaction between genes and environment, it is often possible to change the trait (or its conse-

---

42 See, e.g., Robert Wright, *The Moral Animal: Evolutionary Psychology and Everyday Life*, London: Abacus, 1996, pp. 162–5, for evidence of such careless talk. There is a parallel, and perhaps greater, problem in the field of behavioural genetics: for a helpful critical treatment, see Erik Parens, 'Genetic Differences and Human Identities: On Why Talking about Behavioral Genetics Is Important and Difficult', *Hastings Center Report Special Supplement*, 34.1 (2004), pp. S1–S36.

43 E.g. Dennett, *Freedom Evolves*, pp. 156–62; Wright, *Moral Animal*, pp. 346–50. It should be noted that even this might over-simplify matters, since 'the environment' is not static, but is constantly changing as a result of new interactions; my thanks to Jacqui Stewart for pointing this out.

quences) by manipulating the environment. As Dennett points out, the effects of a genetic tendency to myopia can be reversed by wearing spectacles, and even in the case of a single-gene metabolic disorder such as phenylketonuria the symptoms can be avoided by keeping one's diet free of phenylalanine.[44] (Of course, many genetic disorders cannot be treated so simply and effectively, which is why there is such great interest in gene therapy, as will be discussed in Chapter 9.) Evolutionary psychologists make the same point about complex behavioural traits:

> Neither 'biology,' 'evolution,' 'society,' or 'the environment' directly impose behavioural outcomes, without an immensely long and intricate intervening chain of causation involving interactions with an entire configuration of other causal elements. Each link of such a chain offers a possible point of intervention to change the final outcome.[45]

'Gene-machine' Darwinists, then, can hold that genes influence behaviour while easily dissociating themselves from the simplistic view that genes (alone) cause behaviour. They can equally easily dissociate themselves from the fatalistic view that there is nothing we can do about behavioural traits that are 'in our genes'. But none of this amounts to a denial of determinism *per se*, and the questions about free will and responsibility remain.

Earlier I observed that Libet's work appears to many to provide evidence for Wilson's claim that free will is an illusion. But it is far from clear that it does so. The phenomenon observed by Libet was that the readiness potential associated with an action occurred significantly before the subject's conscious awareness of the decision to act, and the inference frequently drawn from this is that 'before you are aware that you're thinking about moving your arm, your brain is at work preparing to make that movement!'[46] The conscious 'you' only has a 100-millisecond window in which to veto the decision that has already been made. But, as Dennett argues, it is distinctly odd (for those who are not Cartesian dualists, at any rate) to drive a wedge in this way between *you* and *your brain*.[47] The assumption underlying such an interpretation seems to be that the real 'you' inhabits some kind of command-and-control centre – what Dennett calls a 'Cartesian theater' – where it can simultaneously issue commands and be aware of issuing them. But if the

44 Dennett, *Freedom Evolves*, p. 156.

45 Tooby and Cosmides, 'The Psychological Foundations of Culture', p. 39.

46 Michael Gazzaniga, *The Mind's Past*, Berkeley: University of California Press, 1998, p. 73, quoted by Dennett, *Freedom Evolves*, p. 230.

47 Dennett, *Freedom Evolves*, pp. 227–42.

self is not isolated from the workings of the brain (and, we might add, the body) in this way, the puzzling implications of Libet's result seem to become less problematic:

> When we remove the Cartesian bottleneck, and with it the commitment to the ideal of the mythic time *t*, the instant when the conscious decision happens, Libet's discovery of a 100-millisecond veto window evaporates. Then we can see that our free will, like all our other mental powers, has to be smeared out over time, not measured at instants ... You are not out of the loop; you *are* the loop.[48]

Libet's work, then, does not show that commonsense notions of free will are illusory. But it could still be the case that the biological determinism espoused by many Darwinians leaves no room for truly free and responsible decision-making. In his response to the charges of genetic determinism, quoted earlier, Dawkins is somewhat non-committal about this question but, in a famous rhetorical flourish that I quoted in Chapter 2, he expresses confidence that '[w]e, alone on earth, can rebel against the tyranny of the selfish replicators'.[49] But can we, really? Some popular writers, such as Robert Wright, seem to doubt it: according to Wright, the 'metaphysical doctrine' of free will is part of an 'outmoded worldview'. It has in the past been a 'useful fiction' in both law and morality, indispensable for promoting social cohesion, but it is now rapidly on the wane, and with it the retributive notion that wrongdoers deserve blame or punishment. In the legal arena, its demise will have to pave the way for a utilitarian theory of punishment: 'we must get used to the idea of holding robots responsible for their malfunctions – so long, at least, as this accountability will do some good'. In morality, Wright worries that the loss of belief in free will might have a self-fulfilling effect, eroding social pressures and sanctions that have in the past acted as effective restraints on seriously harmful behaviour.[50] This

---

48 *Freedom Evolves*, pp. 241–2.

49 Richard Dawkins, *The Selfish Gene*, 2nd edn, Oxford: Oxford University Press, 1989, p. 201.

50 Wright, *Moral Animal*, pp. 349–58; quotations at pp. 358 and 355. Other aspects of Wright's account, however, such as the moral inspiration he draws from Charles Darwin's own life (pp. 375–9), might invite the question how consistently he follows through this line of thought. One disturbing implication of Wright's robustly utilitarian doctrine of punishment, not addressed in his account, would be to remove any possibility of setting limits in principle to what may be done by way of judicial punishment. On Wright's view, if the gain in utility were sufficiently great, presumably society would be justified in doing whatever was necessary to restrain, re-programme or destroy the 'malfunctioning robot'.

question – are we truly capable of rebelling against the tyranny of the selfish replicators? – calls for a slightly closer look at determinism and freedom.

c   Is determinism compatible with freedom?

Can we rebel against the tyranny of the selfish replicators? Our response to that question will depend on our conclusions about determinism and its compatibility with free will. A full survey of the philosophical arguments around this issue is beyond the scope of the present work; what I shall attempt to do in what follows is to suggest a route through these debates that I believe is both plausible and consistent with the conclusions reached elsewhere in the book, without attempting to offer a detailed defence of the route that I choose.

First, I shall assume that brain processes are, at least to a first approximation, deterministic. What I mean by this is that any brain event is the result of a chain of physical causes that, could they all be traced by an observer, would furnish a complete explanation of the event. The phrase 'to a first approximation' allows me to neglect quantum indeterminacy in the states of subatomic particles in the brain, on the assumption that quantum events are likely to be cancelled out rather than amplified as we move from microscopic to macroscopic descriptions of the brain's state. However, my account does not depend on a conclusion about quantum indeterminacy: as I shall observe, there are reasons to think that even if quantum fluctuations did have significant effects on the macroscopic state of the brain they could not contribute what is needed for freedom.

My deterministic assumption is strictly limited in scope: all I am assuming is that in the brain, as in other biological systems, there is no need to invoke non-physical causes in order to account for physical effects. I am not making the bigger claim that the world is an entirely deterministic system, and therefore my deterministic assumption does not commit me to a naturalistic or reductionist position. Nor does it entail any claims about the possibility, scope or manner of divine action in the world at large. Furthermore, it is entirely consistent with the view that the brain is a highly complex chaotic system, and therefore that no practically conceivable amount of computing power would be sufficient to predict the future state of the brain from a complete description of its present state.

This assumption coheres with the relational understanding of human persons that I sketched in Chapter 4, in which a person's identity develops in its particular ways as a product of the history of his or her communication and relationships with God and with other humans. An additional reason for maintaining this non-dualistic assumption in the present discussion is what I take to be the majority view among neuroscientists, that, while nothing in neuroscience strictly disproves Cartesian dualism, the problem of giving a scientific account of how a non-material soul could be the cause of physical events is dauntingly difficult.[51]

Is free will compatible with such a determinist picture of human thought and action? To answer that question, we must be clearer what we mean by freedom. David Hume famously distinguished between *liberty of spontaneity*, 'that which is oppos'd to violence', and *liberty of indifference*, 'that which means a negation of necessity and causes'.[52] Liberty of spontaneity is the freedom from force, coercion or constraint on our actions, while liberty of indifference denotes a radical unpredictability. Many libertarians regard the liberty of indifference as a necessary part of the free will that they wish to defend.[53] Alan Torrance, for example, argues that 'a genuine indeterminacy in human agency' is needed to allow space for responsibility, accountability and even rationality.[54]

The perceived need to maintain the liberty of indifference presumably accounts for the attractiveness of quantum indeterminacy to some libertarians. For example, Robert Kane holds that quantum indeterminacy is necessary for our most pivotal decisions (those leading to 'self-forming

51 For a contrasting view, however, see Keith Ward, *Defending the Soul*, Oxford: Oneworld, 1992, pp. 134–52.

52 David Hume, *A Treatise of Human Nature*, ed. L. A. Selby-Bigge, rev. P. H. Nidditch, Oxford: Clarendon Press, 1978 (1739–40), p. 407.

53 I am using 'libertarian' not in the sense in which it is used by political theorists, but in the sense in which it appears in the commonly used classification of positions on determinism and free will: *compatibilists* hold that determinism and free will are compatible, *incompatibilists* that they are not; incompatibilists are further subdivided into *hard determinists*, who hold that determinism is true and rule out free will, and *libertarians*, who hold that since we have free will, determinism must be false. See Dennett, *Freedom Evolves*, pp. 97–8. A further possible position, adopted for example by Galen Strawson, is that, regardless of whether determinism is true or false, libertarian free will is impossible: see, e.g., Strawson, 'The Bounds of Freedom', in Kane, *The Oxford Handbook of Free Will*, pp. 441–60.

54 Alan Torrance, 'Developments in Neuroscience and Human Freedom: Some Theological and Philosophical Questions', *Science and Christian Belief*, 16.2 (2004), pp. 123–37 (p. 127). Torrance, like many authors, conflates the discussion of free will and responsibility – as, indeed, I have done up to this point. However, while the two are obviously closely linked, there is heuristic value in maintaining some distinction between them; accordingly, the rest of the present subsection will concentrate mainly on free will, and discussion of responsibility will be largely reserved for the end of this subsection and the next.

actions'), in order to guarantee that these decisions really could have gone either way and were truly 'up to us'.[55] These decisions occur when the agent has good reasons for either course of action, so, whichever way the decision goes, it is genuinely hers, not a mere fluke. An agent's moral character can be developed over the years by a lifetime of these hard and finely balanced decisions. However, Dennett argues that this account of character-building self-forming actions, cogent and convincing as it is, can be supported equally well by determinism, and 'can't harness inde-terminism in any way that distinguishes it from determinism'.[56] If Dennett is right, the liberty of indifference is not, as some libertarians think, necessary for truly free actions. Furthermore, as Torrance acknowledges, the danger with emphasizing the liberty of indifference is that we can find ourselves insisting that, to be truly free, a decision must have a random, unpredictable or even arbitrary character. This seems distinctly odd, since commonsense notions of human agency suggest that if we saw someone, most of whose decisions were unpredictable and arbitrary, we would be more likely to question her mental health than to think her truly free. Intuitively, we regard a person's actions as most truly free (and certainly most responsible) not when they are arbitrary, but when they flow from her most deep-seated commitments and desires. This, of course, is the point of Kane's stipulation that a self-forming action must be the outcome of a decision between two or more alterna-tives each of which is directed to a goal that the agent wants to achieve.[57]

Compatibilists, in contrast, are more likely to stress the liberty of spontaneity: to hold that what makes an action free is that it is not forced or coerced, but done for reasons that we can own. One question that arises immediately about this view, of course, is in what sense an action can be said to be done for a reason if it is the outcome of a deter-ministic chain of physical cause and effect. One popular answer has been offered by non-reductive physicalists such as Nancey Murphy.[58] Murphy points out that the operations of an electronic calculator obey the laws of physics but also conform to the rationality of arithmetic

---

55 See, e.g., Robert Kane, 'Some Neglected Pathways in the Free Will Labyrinth', in Kane, *Free Will*, pp. 407–37.

56 Dennett, *Freedom Evolves*, pp. 97–139; quotation at p. 126.

57 E.g. Kane, 'Some Neglected Pathways', pp. 417–18.

58 For a presentation and critical discussion of Murphy's non-reductive physical-ism, see Nancey Murphy, 'Physicalism without Reductionism: Toward a Scientifically, Philosophically and Theologically Sound Portrait of Human Nature', Philip Clayton, 'Shaping the Field of Theology and Science: A Critique of Nancey Murphy' and Dennis Bielfeldt, 'Nancey Murphy's Nonreductive Physicalism', *Zygon*, 34 (1999), pp. 551–71, 609–18 and 619–28 respectively.

because it has been so constructed that 'its causal processes model arithmetic transformations'.[59] She proposes a model whereby the brain, by responding to feedback from the environment, could become structured in such a way that its causal processes also correspond to rational operations, so that reason can 'get its grip on the causal transitions between brain states'.[60]

Non-reductive physicalism has attracted its fair share of critics, notably Jaegwon Kim, who argues that physicalism is inevitably reductive. He attacks the use that Murphy and others have made of the notion that mental events 'supervene' on physical events:[61] if one physical event is a sufficient cause of another, there seems to be no causal work left for 'supervenient' mental events to do, so one mental event cannot be said to be the cause of another in any significant sense.[62] Murphy's recent account of mental causation is partly an attempt to respond to Kim's challenge by 'reframing' it. Whereas Kim frames the question in terms of physical and mental states or properties, and asks what work is left for mental properties to do if physical properties are causally sufficient, Murphy argues that '[t]he crucial issue is whether the sequence [of mental states] is a *reasoned* sequence or merely a *causal* sequence'.[63] In the same article, and elsewhere, she also takes issue with Kim's understanding of supervenience both because it fails to express the original meaning of the term and because it seems to ensure the reductionist conclusion for which Kim wishes to argue.[64] If Murphy is right, then it does seem possible to give an account of a decision in which it is at one and the same time both the outcome of deterministic neural processes and freely made by the agent for her own reasons.

---

59 Nancey Murphy, 'The Problem of Mental Causation: How Does Reason Get Its Grip on the Brain?', *Science and Christian Belief*, 14.2 (2002), pp. 143–57 (p. 146).

60 Murphy, 'The Problem of Mental Causation', p. 146.

61 For Murphy's use of supervenience, see 'Physicalism without Reductionism', esp. pp. 556–61.

62 E.g. Jaegwon Kim, 'The Myth of Nonreductive Materialism', in Richard Warren and Tadeusz Szubka (eds.), *The Mind–Body Problem*, Oxford: Blackwell, 1994, pp. 242–60; also Kim, *Supervenience and the Mind*, Cambridge: Cambridge University Press, 1993.

63 Murphy, 'The Problem of Mental Causation', p. 145.

64 According to Murphy, Kim's understanding of supervenience 'in terms of co-variation of properties: there can be no mental difference without a physical difference' is faulty both because it fails to express the dependence of supervenient on subvenient properties, and because it ensures the reducibility of the former to the latter: Murphy, 'The Problem of Mental Causation', p. 144 n. 4; see also id., 'Response to Cullen', *Science and Christian Belief*, 13.2 (2001), pp. 161–3. The latter is a response to Lindsay Cullen, 'Nancey Murphy, Supervenience and Causality', *Science and Christian Belief*, 13.1 (2001), pp. 39–50.

However, Torrance poses two further problems for such a compatibilist account, with its emphasis on the liberty of spontaneity. The first is that the liberty of spontaneity can easily become a drastically cut-down version of freedom amounting to no more than 'the uninterrupted outworkings of . . . brain states with respect to which no external constraints are registered'; he suggests that this view would be corrosive of moral responsibility, since it could lead us to regard the whole range of human behaviour from the deepest atrocity to the highest sanctity as expressions of 'brain states with respect to which the relevant agents *have* no responsibility'.[65] Secondly, from the standpoint of Christian faith, this view of human action poses a problem of theodicy, since '[e]very act of murder, rape and child abuse, not to mention the holocaust *in toto*, requires to be seen as concretely and specifically willed, decreed and determined by God'.[66] I shall have a little more to say about theodicy in Chapter 8: for now I simply reiterate that I have only assumed a deterministic view of the workings of the brain, not a comprehensively deterministic view of the universe. I think it is possible to say so much without being committed to the view that every individual act of 'murder, rape and child abuse' is directly willed by God. Torrance's other objection to compatibilism, that it offers only a diminished account of freedom that cannot support moral responsibility, seems to rest on the truth of the oft-repeated Kantian slogan '"Ought" implies "Can"'. To a brief discussion of that slogan I now turn.[67]

---

65 Torrance, 'Developments in Neuroscience and Human Freedom', p. 129, emphasis in original.

66 'Developments in Neuroscience and Human Freedom', p. 129.

.67 Having rejected Cartesian dualism and physicalism, Torrance follows Teed Rockwell in proposing a 'pluralistic' or, in Nancy Cartwright's phrase, 'dappled', world in which a variety of emergent phenomena at the macroscopic level 'have a causal impact on the shape of things': 'Developments in Neuroscience and Human Freedom', p. 135, citing Teed Rockwell, 'Physicalism, Non-reductive', in Chris Eliasmith (ed.), *Dictionary of Philosophy of Mind*, online at http://philosophy. uwaterloo.ca/MindDict/ (accessed 21 August 2006) and Nancy Cartwright, *The Dappled World: A Study of the Boundaries of Science*, Cambridge: Cambridge University Press, 1999. This proposal is no more than briefly sketched out either by Rockwell or by Torrance, but it is difficult to see how the picture of emergent properties exercising top-down causation is so very different from the understanding of supervenience articulated by Murphy against Kim and others. If pluralism is a viable alternative to dualism, then, it may be because it turns out to be a more sophisticated version of compatibilist physicalism. If, in contrast, it really is distinct from physicalism, it is not immediately clear that it can avoid the difficulties of Cartesian dualism: perhaps Rockwell gives the game away with his comment, 'One could flippantly say that when one asks a pluralist "are you a dualist" the correct answer is "yes, at the very least".'

d Does 'ought' imply 'can'?

The slogan '"ought" implies "can"' has been the subject of a detailed study by Roger White, who observes that, although the phrase seems not to appear in Kant's writings, the claim that it expresses 'has central structural significance in [his] whole moral thought'.[68] Most famously, it forms a crucial part of his argument for freedom in the second *Critique*.[69] But although the claim that 'ought' implies 'can' seems intuitively plausible, it is by no means self-evident, and Kant does not offer a fully worked-out defence of it. White surveys the various justifications that can be found at different points in Kant's ethical writings, showing that they are very diverse, somewhat inconclusive and imply a range of different interpretations of the slogan. He argues that Kant's most basic reason for insisting that 'ought' implies 'can' is that to deny it

> threatens to undermine . . . the ultimate significance of the practices of praise and blame. It is *these* notions which had fundamental importance for Kant's whole ethical outlook and which were put in jeopardy if 'ought' did not imply 'can'.[70]

In other words, the crucial point Kant seems to be making is that it is inappropriate for me to reproach myself or be blamed for my failure to keep the moral law, or to be praised for keeping it, unless my keeping it is in some sense 'under my ultimate control';[71] unless, in other words, I am free. White suggests that Kant's view is a secularized version of the position articulated by Erasmus against Luther's thesis that '[i]t is dangerous to believe that the existence of a law implies that it can be obeyed, for the law is fulfilled by the grace of God'.[72] Erasmus' objection to this claim was a matter of theodicy: a Creator who demanded obedience to laws that human creatures were incapable of obeying, and then punished humans for their disobedience, would be an unjust

---

68 Roger M. White, '"Ought" Implies "Can": Kant and Luther, a Contrast', in George MacDonald Ross and Tony McWalter (eds.), *Kant and His Influence*, Bristol: Thoemmes, 1990, pp. 1–72 (p. 1).

69 See, e.g., Immanuel Kant, *Critique of Practical Reason and Other Works on the Theory of Ethics*, trans. Thomas Kingsmill Abbott, 5th edn, London: Longmans, Green and Co., 1898, pp. 117–19.

70 White, '"Ought" Implies "Can"', p. 42; emphasis in original.

71 '"Ought" Implies "Can"', p. 42.

72 Martin Luther, *Disputation against Scholastic Theology*, in *Luther: Early Theological Works* (Library of Christian Classics, 16), ed. and trans. James Atkinson, London: SCM Press, 1962, pp. 266–73 (p. 270).

God.[73] Kant's argument is clearly very different from Erasmus', in that it is our reason, not God, that promulgates the moral law. But according to White, Kant's notions of praiseworthiness and blameworthiness are the 'secular analogues' of Erasmus' notions of divine reward and punishment.[74] The contrast drawn by White, then, is between two opposing moral visions. The vision espoused by Kant, and in a very different way by Erasmus before him, is based on *merit*. In Kant's version, the notions of praiseworthiness and blameworthiness lie at its heart. Accordingly, in mapping the moral life, he has to start

> by considering what Man can do [and allowing] *that* to define the scope of what could count as a legitimate account of the good life. It is because *'Ought' implies 'Can'* that 'nothing is good without qualification, save only a good will'.[75]

White briefly sketches the contrasting moral vision exemplified by Luther thus:

> One may . . . think . . . of God's commandments [not as a kind of moral obstacle race, but] as simply the Law of life: that living according to the Law of love will be the life for which God has created Man, and according to which man [*sic*] will find life and fulfilment. If Man through his own perversity rejects that life, turns his heart in upon itself, he may radically cut himself off from the possibility of the good life so that, thereafter, if freedom, love and even happiness are to be available to him it will only be by an act of divine grace, which is based entirely on a divine initiative.[76]

Within the frame of this moral vision, notions of praise and blame, or guilt and worthiness, will have their place, but they will not be central. White argues that this vision is preferable to the more circumscribed one exemplified by Kant's thought, because the latter omits many of the most important things that we might wish to say about the good life.

This contrast of moral visions is echoed by Alistair McFadyen's complaint that modern talk of the pathological in human affairs operates

---

73 Erasmus, *On the Freedom of the Will*, trans. E. Gordon Rupp and A. N. Marlow, in *Luther and Erasmus* (Library of Christian Classics, 17), London: SCM Press, 1969, pp. 35–97 (pp. 87–9, 93–4).

74 White, '"Ought" Implies "Can"', p. 70.

75 '"Ought" Implies "Can"', p. 68; emphasis original.

76 '"Ought" Implies "Can"', p. 70.

within a 'moral' frame of reference (in a fairly narrow sense of the word 'moral') designed to track moral accountability for situations and actions so that praise, blame, reward and punishment may be fairly apportioned.[77] This way of speaking about the pathological tends to lead us to utilize frameworks of understanding that are 'pragmatically atheist': that is to say, even if we believe in God, we employ conceptual frameworks for interpreting the world, and guiding our action in it, in which reference to God makes no difference to our understanding and practice; God-talk is practically excluded from those frameworks. In Chapter 7 I shall argue, following McFadyen, that some modern Christian discussions of sin are unduly constrained by such narrow moral frameworks, but that a theological understanding of sin, more broadly conceived, offers a richer and more fruitful way to think about the problems of evolution, freedom and wickedness. For the present, however, it is time to draw together some of the threads of the discussion thus far.

3 Responding to moral failure

In the first part of this chapter, I surveyed claims that some morally problematic aspects of human behaviour and character are in some measure the product of our evolutionary history: that either specific problematic behaviours or (more plausibly) general inclinations and psychological traits disposing us to problematic ways of behaving proved adaptive for our ancestors during some part of our evolutionary history, and were accordingly favoured by natural selection. When such a suggestion is made, it immediately raises concerns about biological determinism, free will and responsibility for our actions. As I observed earlier in this chapter, part of the dispute between 'gene-machine'

---

77 Alistair I. McFadyen, *Bound to Sin: Abuse, Holocaust and the Christian Doctrine of Sin*, Cambridge: Cambridge University Press, 2000, pp. 19–22. While McFadyen is careful not to suggest that this tracking of moral accountability is the only function of moral frameworks, his understanding of what constitutes a moral frame of reference does seem a narrower one than at least some moral philosophers and moral theologians would wish to own. As we shall see in Chapter 7, McFadyen rightly wishes to liberate sin-talk from the confines of this narrowly conceived moral frame of reference; but much, perhaps all, of what he is advocating could be accommodated within the kind of *moral* vision, more expansively understood, that is illustrated by White's thumbnail sketch. In one sense this may be merely a dispute about words, but it does seem worth emphasizing that a theological study of the human good in the light of evolutionary biology can encompass the sorts of concerns expressed by McFadyen without ceasing to be a study in Christian *ethics*.

Darwinists, such as Richard Dawkins and Robert Wright, and 'blank-paper' Darwinists, such as Steven Rose, is about the extent to which our actions are determined or controlled by our genes (interacting with each other and with the environment, as everyone agrees), whether such determination leaves us free to change our behaviour and whether we can properly be held morally or legally accountable for our actions.

These concerns are intensified if we hold that, from a scientific point of view, the brain, like other parts of the body, is most plausibly regarded (to a first approximation, at least) as a deterministic biological system. I argued that if this is so, and if we reject dualistic understandings of the human person, it is still possible to give an account of free will in which our actions can be understood as done for reasons that we can own, and can be subject to moral evaluation. Incompatibilist critics doubt whether such a view allows for a concept of freedom that can sustain moral accountability, understood in terms of praiseworthiness and blameworthiness. Hard determinists conclude that the notions of free will and moral responsibility (in any ultimate sense) are untenable; in the legal sphere this could mean, as Robert Wright thinks, that people should be regarded as automata who do not *deserve* punishment for offences they commit, but that punishment should nonetheless be used according to utilitarian criteria. Libertarians, on the other hand, argue that an adequate notion of free will and responsibility requires an indeterminist account of mental causation, such as the pluralism advocated by Alan Torrance.

When the debate is set up along these lines, however, it makes certain assumptions: in particular, the Kantian assumption that 'ought' implies 'can'. Though this claim is intuitively plausible to modern readers, it is far from self-evident and, as White has argued, it presupposes a rather narrowly bounded moral vision based on merit, in which the notions of praise and blame are central. In a more widely drawn moral vision it is not axiomatic that 'ought' implies 'can'. Reframing the debate in these broader terms should save us from over-preoccupation with conundrums about the extent of the influence exercised over our behaviour by our genes and environmental circumstances beyond our control, and how much moral or legal elbow-room this influence leaves us.

This wider vision suggests instead a picture of human agency in which we have choices and act for reasons that we can call our own, but in which our thinking, feeling and acting are influenced, perhaps sometimes radically constrained, by factors out of our control; among those factors may be aspects of our evolutionary inheritance. These influences and constraints may obscure and distort our moral insight and may limit the possibilities for action that are open to us. In the extreme, it is not inconceivable that some courses of action that can be coherently thought of as human possibilities may be rendered effectively unrealizable for us by the factors that constrain us. But these constraints, however extreme, do not exempt our thinking, feeling and acting from moral evaluation, though they may well mitigate judgements about our praiseworthiness or blameworthiness. Indeed, judgements about praise and blame will assume less importance within such a moral vision, and in some cases may become more or less irrelevant.[78] This is not to say that questions of moral accountability in the narrower sense of praise and blame should be excluded from this wider moral vision: they are still part of the picture, and the related questions of *legal* accountability and the just use of judicial punishment must still be faced. But as White says, '[q]uestions of praise, blame and guilt . . . [should only] be raised after other questions have been raised'.[79]

Two further issues then arise. One is the question of theodicy, the fifth of the issues that in Chapter 2 I identified as arising from Huxley's Romanes Lecture. I shall return to this question in Chapter 8. The other is the sixth and last of Huxley's questions: if we accept a view of moral agency in which biological and other factors sometimes make it difficult or even impossible, things being as they are, for us to be the kind of people and live the kind of lives that we ought, what if anything can be done about such moral incapacity?

Even 'gene-machine' Darwinists, in attempting to answer this question, can coherently give considerable weight to familiar, everyday means of moral and social influence, since the social, cultural and moral context in which we live is part of the environment with which our genes interact. As I observed earlier, Tooby and Cosmides hold that each link in the long and complex causal chain leading to an action is a possible site for intervention aimed at influencing behaviour. For example, Janet Mann's proposal, that scarcity of resources is one of the factors that activates a psychological mechanism leading mothers to neglect very

---

78 White draws this point out with reference to Shakespeare's Othello, who is subjected by Iago to a devastatingly effective manipulation of his thinking and feeling, with the result that his moral reason becomes so distorted as to persuade him that he should kill Desdemona. It is clear, as White says, that Shakespeare 'is engaged in a profound *ethical* exploration of Othello and his relationships', and the moral judgement that Othello went terribly astray in his treatment of Desdemona is very much to the point; but 'the question whether we blame Othello or not is of hardly any interest whatever' ('"Ought" Implies "Can"', p. 71; emphasis original).
79 '"Ought" Implies "Can"', p. 71.

sick infants, implies that alleviating the poverty of these mothers should help keep the mechanism switched off.[80]

But one does not have to be a fully paid-up 'gene-machine' Darwinist to think that social and political action may only go so far in influencing behaviour: it is possible that some of our problematic traits and tendencies are so deeply rooted in us that changing our physical environment or social context at best moderates or redirects, but does not suppress or remove, them. Wrangham and Peterson argue that male violence is deeply embedded in human nature, a legacy from our chimpanzee-like ancestors of five million years ago. On this view, it is improbable in the extreme that this legacy could be jettisoned, though Wrangham and Peterson do think that it can be ameliorated in various ways.[81] Both Mann and Hrdy argue that, under some circumstances, neglect of infants and even infanticide are remarkably persistent in human societies even when there are strong social and legal sanctions against such things; though again, neither Mann nor Hrdy suggests that such behaviour *cannot* be changed.[82]

If there are morally problematic aspects of human character and behaviour that are difficult to change by social and political means, then T. H. Huxley's speculations about changing human nature itself reappear on the agenda. As I observed in Chapter 2, he appears to have had some form of eugenics in mind in the closing sentences of the Romanes Lecture, though in his further reflections on the subject in the 'Prolegomena' he expressed grave reservations about such programmes.[83] Dissociated from the racist and colonialist character of Victorian eugenics – indeed, explicitly directed *against* xenophobia, among other things – the idea that we may be able to change the genetic determinants of human behaviour has received attention from more recent writers. Selective breeding makes a brief appearance in Wrangham and Peterson's discussion, only to be swiftly dismissed as unworkable: they pin their hopes instead on democratic politics, together with political and cultural changes such as the growth in global communications, that can support the empowerment of women.[84] The burgeoning of both neurobiology and molecular biology in recent decades has also led to speculations about manipulating the roots of human behaviour by

---

80 Mann, 'Nurturance or Negligence', p. 385.
81 Wrangham and Peterson, *Demonic Males*, pp. 231–51.
82 Hrdy, *Mother Nature*, pp. 288–350; Mann, 'Nurturance or Negligence', p. 385.
83 Huxley, 'Prolegomena', in *Collected Essays*, vol. 9, pp. 1–45 (pp. 22–3, 36–7); see further Goslee, 'Evolution, Ethics and Equivocation', pp. 147–55.
84 Wrangham and Peterson, *Demonic Males*, pp. 239–51.

means of genetic engineering, drugs or both.[85] Professional scientists express extreme scepticism about some of these forms of manipulation, but, as I shall note in Chapter 9, it is possible that others are more feasible. Such speculations raise the question as I formulated it in Chapter 2: in what ways (if any) and with what limits (if any) is it right to try and redesign ourselves in an attempt to ameliorate some of our moral problems? To address this question satisfactorily from a theological standpoint, it must be located within the wider moral-theological vision towards which I have been pointing in the later parts of this chapter. That vision will be elaborated in the next two chapters, after which I shall return in Chapter 9 to a discussion of the rights and wrongs of using technology to try and solve human problems.

---

85 See, e.g., Jonathan Glover, *What Sort of People Should There Be? Genetic Engineering, Brain Control and Their Impact on Our Future World*, Harmondsworth: Pelican, 1984.

7

Salvation and Sin (1):
Holy Love and Original Sin

One of the first moves that Mary Midgley makes in her treatment of wickedness is to bracket talk of God out of the discussion.[1] She does so for quite understandable and even laudable reasons: she observes that we seem to find it very difficult to focus our minds on a serious enquiry about what wickedness is and how it works, and wishes to resist any strategy that could serve as an evasion of this serious intellectual work. One such evasive strategy, she believes, is the notion that 'once we got rid of religion, all problems of this kind would vanish'; though implausible, this strategy 'is often used by those who do not want to think seriously on this subject, and who prefer a ritual warfare about the existence of God to an atrociously difficult psychological enquiry'.[2] In resisting this kind of evasive strategy, she says, she does not deny that questions of religion are important, nor even that they will make a difference to the way we think about the problem of evil: her target is, rather, a kind of intellectual and psychological laziness that finds it easier to fight old and well-rehearsed intellectual battles than to do new work.

Understandable though Midgley's strategy is, however, there is a sense in which – for practical purposes, at any rate – it prejudges the question of the existence of God. This can be seen in her discussion of determinism and free will, where she observes that the tension in orthodox Christianity between divine foreknowledge and human responsibility has great imaginative force and tends to dominate our thinking about free will: '[a]ccordingly, when the focus shifted from God's foreknowledge to science, the supernatural figure in the background was not properly exorcised and removed from the controversy as he ought to

---

1 Mary Midgley, *Wickedness: A Philosophical Essay*, London: Routledge, 2001 (1984), pp. 6–7.
2 *Wickedness*, p. 7.

have been'.[3] It seems that Midgley treats claims about both divine and scientific foreknowledge of human actions as formally equivalent, and believes that such claims do no useful work in thinking about free will and responsibility, serving rather to muddy the waters. Notwithstanding her earlier disclaimer, this strategy appears, more or less, to be a form of what Alistair McFadyen calls 'pragmatic atheism', in which 'reference to God is taken in practice to make no difference to the interpretation, explanation and understanding of the world; no difference to acting and living in it'.[4] One sign that this is going on is that Midgley reflects popular usage in treating the word 'sin' simply as a synonym for 'wrongdoing', thereby obscuring the possibility that 'sin' may be something distinct from, though related to, moral transgression.[5] This is not merely a semantic quibble: if it is true, as I shall seek to show in this chapter and the next, that a theological account can enrich, extend and sometimes challenge the things that scientists and philosophers say about these questions, thinking about moral transgression in isolation from a more complete theological notion of sin may distort, not clarify, the picture.

My claim in this chapter and the next, then, is that a Christian theological account of our moral and spiritual problem, and the solution which God offers to that problem, can enrich, extend and challenge the evolutionary discussion of our moral limitations presented in Chapter 6. The area of Christian theology which bears on our moral and spiritual problem, of course, is that known as the doctrine of sin, while God's answer to the problem is variously described as salvation, redemption, reconciliation and atonement.[6] It might seem logical to take these two

---

3 *Wickedness*, p. 103.

4 Alistair McFadyen, *Bound to Sin: Abuse, Holocaust and the Christian Doctrine of Sin*, Cambridge: Cambridge University Press, 2000, p. 8.

5 Midgley, *Wickedness*, pp. 10–13; the context is her reflection on a popular journalistic discussion of the subject. She remarks that this discussion does not seem to understand sin 'in a restrictive way as an offence against God' (p. 11); but in this and the next chapter I shall argue, as does McFadyen, that to use the language of sin in an overtly theological way actually places the concept in a more *expansive*, not 'restrictive', frame of reference than treating it as identical with moral transgression. The contrast can be further drawn out by comparing Midgley's difficulty with the language of original sin ('On the face of it, this phrase is contradictory. Sin must, by definition, be deliberate' (p. 12)) with the account in section 3 below, in which 'deliberate' is exactly what original sin is *not*.

6 There is some variation within the theological literature in the way in which this language is used: Karl Barth, for example, uses 'reconciliation' for his exposition of what is frequently called the doctrine of redemption – the saving work of God in Christ (*Church Dogmatics* (hereafter *CD*), IV.1–3) – while reserving the word 'redemption' for the future saving work of the Holy Spirit, which was to have been the subject of the

themes in that order: first, a theological description of our problem as sin, then an account of the saving work by which God addresses our problem. However, I shall instead follow the precedent set in some of the chief sources of my own account, and integrate the accounts of salvation and sin more closely together in such a way that it is the doctrine of salvation, rather than of sin, that shapes the contours of the account. My reason for doing this is that, as Colin Gunton and others have said, the doctrine of sin is, as it were, the shadow of the doctrine of salvation.[7] If it is true that God's self-revelation in Jesus Christ is at the heart of our knowledge of God, ourselves and the world, then it is surely unwise to think that we could work out antecedently what our moral and spiritual need is, independently and in advance of our knowledge of what God has done in Christ to meet that need. The point is put particularly trenchantly by Barth, who argues that such an attempt would itself be a form of sinful human pride:

> [T]his conception of sin, which is so acceptable in its basic perversion, is the fatal fruit of that arbitrary act as such in which man himself undertakes to set up a criterion for the knowledge of sin, in which this knowledge is simply a matter of self-communing, and man becomes his own law-giver and accuser and judge . . . In opposition to [this view] we maintain the simple thesis that only when we know Jesus Christ do we really know that man is the man of sin, and what sin is, and what it means for man.[8]

Accordingly, in the following account I shall outline a number of aspects of God's saving activity, as they are attested in various ways by the Bible and articulated by the strands of Christian theological tradition with which I am engaging. I shall draw out the implications of these aspects of God's saving work for our understanding of human sin – that is to say, of the moral and spiritual predicament which God addresses in his saving work on our behalf in Christ.[9] I shall also seek to show how these

---

projected fifth volume of *CD*. In what follows I shall mostly (though not exclusively) use 'salvation' and its cognates, as having the widest and most inclusive field of reference.

7 E.g. Colin Gunton, *The Actuality of Atonement: A Study of Metaphor, Rationality and the Christian Tradition*, Edinburgh: T&T Clark, 1988, p. 119.

8 *CD* IV.1, pp. 388–9.

9 At the end of the last chapter, I drew attention to McFadyen's critique of what he calls moral frames of reference for addressing the 'pathological' in human affairs: *Bound to Sin*, pp. 19–22 and *passim*. The phrase 'moral and spiritual predicament' here is intended to suggest the broadening and reshaping of that frame of reference, along similar lines to those advocated by McFadyen, which will be argued for in this chapter.

insights into our need and God's response can engage with the issue of our moral limitations and failures, as that issue is raised by evolutionary biology.

1   Holy love and the 'cruciality of the cross'

I begin with that great Congregationalist theologian of the late nineteenth and early twentieth centuries, Peter Taylor Forsyth.[10] One of his abiding concerns was to reassert, against the nineteenth-century liberalism in which he had been trained, 'the cruciality of the cross':[11] the centrality for Christian faith, preaching and theology of the one act by which God in Christ reconciled the world to himself. From this vantage point, Forsyth learns a number of things. First, the universe we inhabit is inescapably a *moral* universe. Indeed, the objective moral structure of the universe is in a sense the ultimate reality that confronts us in creation, a moral ordering of things that reflects the holiness of God himself. This moral ordering of things confronts us in our conscience, in which '[m]an ... even finds the voice of God'[12] – though, as we shall see, this does not mean that Forsyth is at all optimistic about our natural capacity to know, let alone to do, the good. For the next thing that Forsyth is able to see clearly from the vantage point of the 'cruciality of the cross' is that the situation of the human race is *tragic*.[13] Our sin has breached the moral ordering of the universe; moreover, this is not a matter of an impersonal law that has been broken, or a cosmic account out of balance, but the rupturing of the relationship between a holy God and the human race, and of ourselves we are quite unable to heal that broken relationship.[14]

Because human sin breaches the objective moral order of the universe, which is the reflection of God's own holiness, it is a great mistake to imagine that a loving God could simply forgive our sin in the easy sense of overlooking it or passing it over. In a passage that strikingly fore-

---

10 On what follows, see further Trevor A. Hart, 'Morality, Atonement and the Death of Jesus: The Crucial Focus of Forsyth's Theology', in Trevor Hart (ed.), *Justice the True and Only Mercy: Essays on the Life and Theology of Peter Taylor Forsyth*, Edinburgh: T&T Clark, 1995, pp. 16–36.

11 P. T. Forsyth, *The Cruciality of the Cross*, 2nd edn, London: Independent Press, 1948 (1909).

12 Forsyth, *Positive Preaching and the Modern Mind*, London: Hodder and Stoughton, 1907, p. 351.

13 *Positive Preaching*, pp. 341–2.

14 Forsyth, *The Work of Christ*, London: Hodder and Stoughton, 1910, pp. 123–4.

shadows Bonhoeffer's contrast of cheap with costly grace,[15] Forsyth attacks this notion forthrightly:

> There is no doubt that it is a very popular notion. 'How natural for God to forgive. It is just like Him.' Whereas the real truth is that it is only like the God familiar to us from the Cross, and not from our natural expectation . . . We should realize how far from a matter of course forgiveness [is] for a holy, and justly angry, God, for all His love. A free forgiveness flows from moral strength, but an easy forgiveness only means moral weakness. How natural for God to forgive! Nay, if there be one thing in the world for ever supernatural it is real forgiveness – especially on the scale of redemption. It is natural only to the Supernatural.[16]

God's love cannot be an easy indulgence which leniently passes over human sin, 'reducing the holy law of His nature to a bye-law that He can suspend'.[17] To use one of Forsyth's most characteristic phrases, the love of God revealed in the cross of Christ is *holy love*, and the forgiveness of our sins calls for a 'satisfaction' of God's holiness.

In giving an account of the atonement, Forsyth uses Anselmian language and indeed expresses appreciation for Anselm; at the same time, he criticizes Anselm for '[putting] theology on a false track' by focusing too much on the satisfaction of God's offended *honour* by Christ's voluntary *suffering*.[18] It is God's holiness rather than honour which must be satisfied, says Forsyth, and this can only be done by perfect holiness. Forsyth repeatedly insists, furthermore, that the cross was not a matter of God's punishment of Christ for human sin,[19] and that it was not suffering and death *per se* that brought about our reconciliation with God. Rather, as Trevor Hart puts it, '[i]t was the voluntary *submission* to suffering [and] death, and the acknowledgment of them as the righteous judgement of God upon human sin which was the holy, and therefore the satisfying, thing'.[20] While aspects of Forsyth's account of the atonement remain perhaps obscure, it is clear enough that our reconciliation with God is not an impersonal transaction, but the restoration of a personal relationship breached by human sin.

---

15 Dietrich Bonhoeffer, *The Cost of Discipleship*, trans. R. H. Fuller, rev. Irmgard Booth, London: SCM Press, 1959, pp. 35–47.
16 Forsyth, *Positive Preaching*, p. 295.
17 *Positive Preaching*, pp. 353–4.
18 *Work*, p. 223.
19 *Work*, pp. 156–7.
20 Hart, 'Morality, Atonement and the Death of Jesus', p. 33 (emphasis original).

Another thing that stands out in Forsyth's account is the solidarity of the human race.[21] What Christ has achieved through the cross is not the reconciliation of a series of isolated individuals with God; rather, '[w]e are each one of us saved in the salvation of the [human] race, in a collectivist redemption'.[22] As individuals, we receive this reconciliation with God through the work of Christ in us, making us 'a new creation in Jesus Christ'.[23] It is this regenerative work of Christ in each of us that creates in us a 'repentance and . . . sanctity [that] are of saving value before God'.[24] Again, aspects of this remain obscure, and Forsyth himself remarks that '[w]e need not get lost in discussing the metaphysic of it'.[25] But it is clear enough that, for any individual, the changes associated with her reconciliation with God are the work of Christ in her (as distinct, say, from a merely 'exemplarist' understanding of what the death of Christ accomplishes in and for the individual) and involve her in a new kind of solidarity with Christ and with the new humanity that he has brought into being.

Forsyth, as I noted earlier, is a robust critic of the liberal theology of his contemporaries and an advocate of what he calls a 'positive', 'evangelical' theology.[26] However, he believes that theology must be not only 'positive' but also 'modern'.[27] One aspect of this is that, unlike some of his contemporaries, he welcomes and builds upon the biblical criticism of his day; another is that his theology is the product of an extraordinary range of intellectual engagement not only with historical and contemporary theology but also with philosophy, literature and other disciplines.[28] A third is, as he puts it, to 'ethicize' Christianity and the message of the Cross:[29] the holiness of God is equated with the *moral* order of the universe, and sin with a mutiny against that moral order. The atonement, likewise, is God's action to set right this breach of the moral order of things. As McFadyen argues, this tendency to express the doctrines of sin and redemption within the confines of moral frames of reference, for all its strength, is a highly problematic strategy.[30] While Forsyth's notion of

---

21 Forsyth, *Work*, pp. 119–23.

22 *Work*, p. 114.

23 *Work*, p. 215.

24 *Work*, p. 213.

25 *Work*, p. 216.

26 E.g. *Positive Preaching*, pp. 199–243.

27 *Positive Preaching*, pp. 247–90.

28 See, further, Alan P. F. Sell, 'P. T. Forsyth as Unsystematic Systematician', in Hart, *Justice the True and Only Mercy*, pp. 110–45 (pp. 111–19).

29 Forsyth, *Positive Preaching*, pp. 293–333.

30 See above, n. 9, and Chapter 6, section 2d. It should be said that for Forsyth, the strategy of 'ethicizing' the Gospel was part of his reaction against nineteenth-century

what is meant by the ethical and the moral is wider-ranging than that criticized by McFadyen, and he expressly seeks to resist 'the reduction of religion to ethics, and faith to cold morality',[31] his conception of God's holiness does at times appear unhelpfully bound to moral categories. In later sections of this chapter, I shall seek ways of expressing an understanding of our predicament and God's response within broader frames of reference than Forsyth's predominantly moral ones.

More positively, though, we can learn from Forsyth of the 'cruciality of the cross': the holy love of God at work in the death of Jesus Christ to heal the disastrous damage caused by human sin. We can also learn that the damage that needs to be healed is not the transgression of some impersonal law, or an imbalance in a set of cosmic accounts, but a fundamental distortion of *relationships*: a practical denial of the holiness of God, a refusal of the proper response to God's holiness and derivatively, we might add, a distortion of right relationships with one another and with the rest of the created order. Next, I shall explore in more detail the nature of these distortions and of the action that God has taken to heal them.

2 Pride, sloth and falsehood

In his massive treatment of the doctrine of reconciliation,[32] Karl Barth weaves together accounts of the person of Christ, the work of Christ and human sin. In the threefold structure of his exposition, the three Christological foci – Jesus as divine, as human and as divine–human – disclose three different aspects of God's reconciling work and three aspects of human sin.

a Humility and pride

In the first part, Barth expounds the life, death and resurrection of Jesus Christ as the humility and obedience of the eternal Son of God. The

---

liberalism, a way of supporting his renewed emphasis on the holiness of God and his stress on the 'cruciality of the cross'. But in this respect, perhaps, the weakness of his strategy was that it shared too much common ground with the liberalism which it was intended to oppose. An 'ethicized' Christianity might look very different from a 'liberal' Christianity (in the way in which Forsyth understood that term), but in the long run the former, as well as the latter, risks speaking of sin in insufficiently theological terms and so lending support to the 'pragmatic atheism' diagnosed by McFadyen.

31 Forsyth, *Positive Preaching*, p. 301.
32 Barth, *CD* IV.1–3.

incarnation was 'the way of the Son of God into the far country': Jesus Christ, the Son of God, has identified himself with sinful humanity symbolized by the prodigal son in the parable who travelled into a far country and squandered his inheritance in dissolute living (Luke 15.11–32). In his death, 'the Judge [has been] judged in our place': the Son of God, who had no sin, both pronounced his judgement on our sin and took that judgement upon himself. The resurrection of Jesus is 'the great verdict of God, the fulfilment and proclamation of God's decision concerning the event of the cross . . . its acceptance as the act of [Jesus Christ's] obedience which judges the world, but judges it with the aim of saving it'.[33] As God's 'Yes' to Jesus Christ it is therefore also '[his] Yes to man and the world, even in the No of the cross which it includes' (p. 347). From this Christological standpoint, Barth learns that 'the sin of man is the pride of man' (p. 413). By contrast with the Son of God who became human for our sakes, 'we want to be God' (p. 418); by contrast with the Lord who became a servant, we '[want] to be lord' (p. 432); by contrast with the divine Judge who 'fulfilled the divine judgement in such a way that He caused Himself to be judged, so that we should not suffer what we deserved', we 'set [ourselves] in the wrong by wanting to be [our] own judge instead of allowing that God is in the right against [us]' (p. 445); and finally, our pride means that we '[live] in the meaningless idea' of being our own helpers, by contrast with Jesus Christ, who 'on [our] behalf . . . cried on the cross, the helpless One taking the place of all those who gaily help themselves: "My God, my God, why hast thou forsaken me?"' (p. 467).

Barth acknowledges that the definition of sin as pride does not exhaust the meaning of sin: as we shall see, his other two christological perspectives offer complementary understandings. But even so, he says, this definition 'denotes more than just a part of the content. Sin in its unity and totality is always pride.'[34] He is by no means alone in placing this emphasis on sin as pride: as McFadyen comments, the mainstream of Christian tradition has regarded it as the paradigmatic sin.[35] One of the best-known twentieth-century expositions of sin as pride comes from Reinhold Niebuhr,[36] who argues that the two basic forms of sin, pride and sensuality, both stem from different kinds of anxiety: on the one hand, anxiety about our finitude and the contingency of our exist-

---

33 *CD* IV.1, p. 309. Page numbers in brackets in this paragraph refer to this work.
34 *CD* IV.1, p. 413.
35 McFadyen, *Bound to Sin*, pp. 134–8.
36 Reinhold Niebuhr, *The Nature and Destiny of Man: A Christian Interpretation*, vol. 1: *Human Nature*, London: Nisbet, 1941, pp. 190–220.

ence; on the other, the anxiety of being unable to be satisfied with what we have achieved, because we 'stand under seemingly limitless possibilities'.[37] Pride, the attempt 'to deny the contingent character of [our] existence', Niebuhr regards as more basic than sensuality, the 'effort to escape from the freedom and the infinite possibilities of spirit by becoming lost in the detailed processes, activities and interests of existence'.[38]

In his description of sin as pride, Niebuhr adopts a traditional distinction between pride of power, pride of knowledge and pride of virtue. Pride of power may be manifested in a false sense of security or in a sense of insecurity in which the ego seeks to secure its position by arrogating more influence or control to itself. It may be assisted by intellectual pride (the error of taking finite and partial knowledge to be ultimate and certain) in the form of ideological legitimation of the powerful. Moral pride is essentially self-righteousness: Niebuhr quotes Luther to the effect that 'the unwillingness of the sinner to be regarded as a sinner [is] the final form of sin'.[39] And moral pride can finally give rise to spiritual pride, religious intolerance and self-righteousness.

Connections could obviously be made between these analyses of sin as pride and the evolutionary insights into human wickedness surveyed earlier. First, and most obviously, Niebuhr's description of the pride of power illuminates the many and various ways by which human beings seek control, authority and influence over one another, whether by brute force, cunning or in other ways. As I described in Chapter 6, some evolutionary writers, such as Richard Wrangham and Dale Peterson, claim that the tendency to seek such power goes back a long way in our evolutionary history.[40] However, I wish to suggest a different kind of connection which points beyond this kind of correlation and shows that a theological analysis of sin as pride offers a much richer and fuller picture than can be supplied simply by reflection on our evolutionary history. In Chapter 6, I noted that some writers attempt to use claims about human evolution to debunk our impression of ourselves as moral beings, suggesting that natural selection could have favoured tendencies both to apply our moral beliefs selectively, when it is to our advantage to do so, and to hold an over-generous estimate of our own moral qualities. In other words, it is sometimes proposed that natural selection has favoured both hypocrisy and self-deception.[41] Even leaving aside the

---

37 *Nature and Destiny*, vol. 1, p. 196.
38 *Nature and Destiny*, vol. 1, p. 197.
39 *Nature and Destiny*, vol. 1, p. 212.
40 See above, Chapter 6, section 1a (i).
41 See above, Chapter 6, section 1a (iii).

obviously unwholesome aspects of our putative evolutionary inheritance, such as violence and parental neglect, it is sometimes said that those aspects of our nature of which we are most inclined to be proud might not be in very good shape. Now as I have emphasized in previous chapters, these claims are controversial and in some cases highly speculative. But if there is even a grain of truth in them – if what T. H. Huxley called our 'ethical nature', viewed in the light of our evolutionary history, looks less magnificent than we like to think – they might turn out to resonate, in surprising ways, with the theological analysis of pride offered here.

As I observed towards the end of Chapter 4, Barth famously equated the serpent's promise in Genesis 3.5 with the 'establishment of ethics', a point echoed by Bonhoeffer's claim that the first task of Christian ethics is to 'invalidate' the knowledge of good and evil.[42] The point is elaborated by Barth, who argues that one aspect of the sin of pride is to want to be our own judge, to know good and evil.[43] He holds that our belief that we can, like God, distinguish between good and evil is sheer self-deception, 'and in this self-deception, in the delusion that we are doing good and avoiding evil, we actually eschew the good and do evil'.[44] If knowledge of our evolutionary history calls into question our confidence in our 'ethical nature', or our capacity to know good and evil, then Darwin and some of his recent intellectual heirs may be performing the valuable role of 'masters of suspicion', unmasking some of our human pretensions in a way that can make possible a theological account of a more trustworthy foundation on which our moral life may be built.[45]

But if it is true that an evolutionary debunking of human ethical nature lends support to a theological analysis of sin as pride, then this particular version of evolutionary suspicion points beyond itself to a much broader moral picture than evolutionary thought itself can supply. For the theological analysis of sin as pride shows that its most

42 Barth, *CD* IV.1, p. 448; Dietrich Bonhoeffer, *Ethics* (*Dietrich Bonhoeffer Works*, vol. 6), ET ed. by Clifford J. Green, Minneapolis: Fortress, 2005, p. 299.

43 *CD* IV.1, pp. 445–53.

44 *CD* IV.1, p. 453.

45 There are obvious parallels with Barth's use of Feuerbach's dictum that theology is anthropology: e.g., *CD* I.2, pp. 4–7, and II.1, pp. 287–97; see Trevor Hart, 'Revelation', in John Webster (ed.), *The Cambridge Companion to Karl Barth*, Cambridge: Cambridge University Press, 2000, pp. 37–56 (pp. 40–1). Barth's appropriation of Feuerbach, of course, was in order to critique *theological* approaches which he considered inadequate and, if evolutionary insights are to play an analogous role in the critique of approaches to ethics, it will be at least as much in the critique of unsatisfactory theological approaches to ethics as of secular approaches.

fundamental aspect is a deep distortion of our relationship with God. Rather than accepting as gift our creaturely nature and calling to be in covenant with God, we become turned in on ourselves, attempting to live for ourselves, thinking that we 'can be [our] own source and standard, the first and the last . . .'.[46] In Barth's terms, rather than accepting our true fulfilment as servants of God, we try to be our own lords; rather than acknowledging the justice of God we try to be our own judges of good and evil; rather than relying on God as our true helper, we try to be our own helpers. Barth argues that in all these aspects the God whom we try to be like is a distorted image, a projection of our own imaginations, to which the self-revelation of God in Jesus Christ is completely opposed.[47] By striving to be like this God of our own devising, we alienate ourselves from a truly fulfilling and life-giving relationship with the God who is made known in Jesus Christ.

There are, of course, real and terrible 'horizontal' dimensions of this distortion of relationships. We become alienated from one another: trying to be our own lords means lording it over others, making ourselves the judges of good and evil results in our unleashing real evil on the world in the mistaken confidence that we are doing good, and so on. We also become alienated from ourselves, distorting and harming ourselves. But these horizontal distortions, important though they are, are derivative of the basic 'vertical' distortion in our relationship with God. By pointing beyond itself in this way, an evolution-inspired critique of human ethical nature already begins to place our talk of sin in a more expansive theological frame of reference than the one with which we began.

At this point it is worth briefly noting two other contributions that an evolutionary account makes to the discussion. First, it helps to keep our attention focused on the fact that we are embodied beings. As I suggested in Chapter 4 when discussing relational Christian anthropologies, talk of sin as distortion of our relationships with God, one another and ourselves, and of salvation as the healing and transformation of those relationships, could be at risk of becoming somewhat disembodied. An evolutionary perspective prompts us to table the questions whether our propensity towards sin is to some extent rooted in our biological nature and, if so, how we can speak of God's saving activity in ways which address the biological as well as other dimensions of our sin. Secondly, an evolutionary perspective would appear to raise the question of theodicy in a particular way: if evolution is in some sense the

---

46 CD IV.1, p. 421.
47 CD IV.1, pp. 422, 436–7, 452–3, 466–7.

means by which God has created us, the discovery that there are evolutionary causes of some aspects of human sin might appear to mean that God is the author of those aspects of sin. I shall return to both of these issues in later sections of this chapter.

b   Exaltation and sloth

In the first part of Barth's doctrine of reconciliation, as we have seen, he expounds the work of Christ as the humble obedience of the Son of God; from this he learns that the basic form of human sin, from which the Son of God in his humility saves us, is pride. In the second part, he describes the same subject-matter as 'the exaltation of the Son of Man'.[48] Jesus is not only the eternal Son of God, who willingly humbled himself for our sakes and, as our Judge, allowed himself to be judged in our place. He is also the Son of Man, the 'royal man', the true and perfect human being who alone fulfils our human destiny and calling. The 'journey of the Son of God into the far country' is also 'the homecoming of the Son of Man'; the 'abasement' (*exinanitio*) of God is also the 'exaltation' (*exaltatio*) of the human being.[49] And his exaltation reaches its climax in the Cross:

> It is only then – not before – that there did and does take place the realisation of the final depth of humiliation, the descent into hell of Jesus Christ the Son of God, but also His supreme exaltation, the triumphant coronation of the Son of Man. And after this event the revelation of Jesus Christ could be and necessarily was the revelation of His completed Messianic work . . . The resurrection and ascension of Jesus Christ are the completed revelation of Jesus Christ which corresponds to His completed work.[50]

As George Hunsinger puts it,

> [a]s he died the death of the sinner, the Son of God entered the nadir of his humiliation for our sakes, even as his exaltation as the Son of man attained its zenith in that sinless obedience which, having freely embraced the cross, would be crowned by eternal life.[51]

---

48 *CD* IV.2, §64.
49 *CD* IV.2, p. 21.
50 *CD* IV.2, p. 141.
51 George Hunsinger, 'Karl Barth's Christology: Its Basic Chalcedonian Character', in Webster, *The Cambridge Companion to Karl Barth*, pp. 127–42 (pp. 135–6).

From this Barth learns that sin not only takes the heroic and Promethean form of pride, 'but also, in complete antithesis yet profound correspondence, the quite unheroic and trivial form of *sloth* . . . the countermovement to the elevation which has come to man from God Himself in Jesus Christ'.[52] Sloth, says Barth, is a tardiness, failure or inaction that is just as reprehensible as the active sin of pride. But although sloth has an essentially negative or inactive character, he insists that it is not 'a milder or weaker or less potent type of sin'[53] than pride, and, indeed, it is a kind of action: 'The idler or loafer does something . . . He turns his back on God, rolling himself into a ball like a hedgehog with prickly spikes. At every point . . . this is the *strange inactive action* of the slothful man.'[54] As with pride, then, so with sloth: the basic distortion of sin is a distortion of our relationship with God.

In the case of sloth, this distortion takes the form of a refusal of the freedom to receive the wisdom and enlightenment of the Word made flesh: we prefer instead to remain in darkness, stupidity and folly.[55] But again, as with pride, this basic distortion of our relationship with God is also associated with distortions of our relationships with one another, of the unity and order of our own being and of the temporal and limited character of our own existence.[56] (It should be noted in passing that neither here nor in his analysis of sin as pride does he explicitly consider the distortion of our relationship with the non-human creation, though he could very well do so.)[57]

This understanding of sin as sloth is an important corrective to a one-sided conceptualization of sin as pride. In this vein, some feminist theologians have sought to challenge and correct an over-emphasis on sin as pride with a recovery of the language of sloth.[58] They argue that the account offered by Niebuhr and others, in which pride, or inordinate self-assertion, is the paradigmatic sin, names male experience accurately. Under the conditions of patriarchy, men do indeed tend to

---

52 *CD* IV.2, p. 403, emphasis added.
53 *CD* IV.2, p. 405.
54 *CD* IV.2, pp. 404–5, emphasis added.
55 *CD* IV.2, pp. 409–32.
56 *CD* IV.2, pp. 432–83.
57 Cf. *CD* III.4, pp. 348–56.
58 E.g. Judith Plaskow, *Sex, Sin and Grace: Women's Experience and the Theologies of Reinhold Niebuhr and Paul Tillich*, Lanham, MD: University Press of America, 1980; Daphne Hampson, 'Reinhold Niebuhr on Sin: A Critique', in Richard Harries (ed.), *Reinhold Niebuhr and the Issues of our Time*, Oxford: Mowbray, 1986, pp. 46–60; and (albeit with reservations about some versions of the argument) Mary Grey, *Redeeming the Dream: Feminism, Redemption and Christian Tradition*, London: SPCK, 1989, pp. 15–19; see McFadyen, *Bound to Sin*, pp. 131–66.

be socialized in ways that encourage a high degree of autonomy, independence from others, self-centredness and powerful assertion of one's own interests over against others – socialization conducive to the sin of pride. But women tend to be socialized in quite the opposite way: to be so oriented towards others and so consumed in nurturing and self-giving (which, in patriarchal contexts, is often not reciprocated) that the integrity and identity of the self are dissipated. This experience of 'self-loss' is what some feminist theologians mean by retrieving the language of sin as sloth, a form of sin that involves both a failure to realize oneself and make use of one's freedom and an acquiescence in the oppressive structures of patriarchy.[59]

McFadyen argues that this feminist naming of sin as sloth is in fact quite different from the more traditional accounts given by Barth and others, in which sloth remains a form of action for which one is morally culpable, and may indeed turn out to be a disguised form of self-centredness and therefore of pride.[60] So far as Barth is concerned, the contrast is perhaps over-drawn: much of the feminist picture of loss and dissipation of the self is recognizable in Barth's characterization of 'the strange inactive action' of the slothful human being. But it is true to say that Barth does wish to retain the notion that sloth is a freely willed action for which we are accountable. (This perhaps reflects his desire, in common with other modern theologians, to retain what McFadyen calls moral frames of reference for thinking about sin, and his corresponding unease with traditional concepts of original sin[61] – an issue which will be taken up in a later section.) According to McFadyen, the more radical feminist reappropriation of the term shows how women's self-direction and self-determination are not obliterated under the conditions of patriarchy, but are radically distorted, redirected and co-opted into collusion with the oppressive dynamics of a situation. Women under the conditions of patriarchy do not cease to make choices; rather, their choices operate within the limits defined by the patriarchal dynamic within which they, as well as men, have been socialized. Thus, for McFadyen, this language meets the need for a way of speaking of 'victims' willing and choosing', of 'victims' sin', without falling into the oppressors' trap of blaming the victim, a need demonstrated by his analysis of the 'concrete pathologies' of child sexual abuse and the holocaust.[62]

---

59 McFadyen, *Bound to Sin*, pp. 141–2.
60 *Bound to Sin*, pp. 139–40.
61 *CD* IV.1, pp. 499–501.
62 McFadyen, *Bound to Sin*, pp. 145–50; cf. pp. 57–104. The question might still be pressed whether there are those who suffer such extreme forms of oppression that

There might seem to be an obvious correlation to be made between a feminist theological analysis of pride and sloth and evolutionary claims about sexual roles and relationships, the latter backed up by studies of our primate relatives. In mammals, so the argument goes, the minimum investment of resources needed for a male to generate offspring is far lower than for a female: the female incurs the cost of pregnancy and lactation, while all that the male need contribute is 'a few minutes of sex and a teaspoon of semen', as Steven Pinker crudely, if graphically, puts it.[63] On this view, natural selection could be expected to have given rise to males who are eager for as much sex, with as many different partners, as possible, and to females who are more 'coy' – to use Darwin's loaded term, still frequently repeated in the popular literature.[64] Such an argument also predicts that males will compete with one another for access to females, and that, in species with social hierarchies, the highest-status males will enjoy by far the greatest access. But humans, for whatever evolutionary reason, are also a species with unusually high male parental investment by primate standards: human males, unlike most other primates, help to provide food and care for their offspring. This, it is argued, creates a selection pressure for males to tend to monopolize their long-term mates, while also taking any available opportunity for brief liaisons with other partners. The picture sometimes painted is of males who have evolved to be inordinately competitive, self-assertive, aggressive towards other males and proprietary towards females (in fact, to display many of the characteristics of pride) while females are the more passive partners, their energies largely consumed in the gestation and nurture of their young.

---

they are effectively deprived of moral agency, as Katie Geneva Cannon has argued of African-American women during and after the time of slavery in the United States: *Black Womanist Ethics*, Atlanta, GA: Scholars Press, 1988. Yet even then, what is in view does not seem to be a *complete* obliteration of willing, but rather its radical constraint and distortion by extreme oppression, since Cannon's project is precisely to recover the stories of women who, under such conditions, manifested an 'invisible dignity', a 'quiet grace' and an 'unshouted courage'.

63 Steven Pinker, *How the Mind Works*, London: Penguin, 1998, p. 468. The foundational theoretical articulation of parental investment is Robert L. Trivers, 'Parental Investment and Sexual Selection', in Bernard Campbell (ed.), *Sexual Selection and the Descent of Man 1871–1971*, Chicago, IL: Aldine, 1972, pp. 136–79, also online at http://orion.oac.uci.edu/~dbell/Trivers.pdf (accessed 21 August 2006).

64 Charles Darwin, *The Descent of Man, and Selection in Relation to Sex*, London: John Murray, 1871, repr. with introduction by John Tyler Bonner and Robert M. May, Princeton, NJ: Princeton University Press, 1981, vol. 1, p. 273; Robert Wright, *The Moral Animal: The Evolutionary Psychology of Everyday Life*, London: Abacus, 1996, e.g. p. 33.

But this correlation should be treated with great suspicion. The picture sketched here has been subjected to withering criticism from feminist biologists such as Sarah Blaffer Hrdy, who argue that evolutionary research since Darwin's day has been distorted by gender stereotypes of active, aggressive males and passive, nurturing females. These stereotypes have conditioned the questions asked by (mostly male) biologists, who have looked for, and found, aggressive, competitive male behaviour, and have simply assumed that females play a passive role; their results have also sometimes been used to legitimate the gender stereotypes which informed the choice of research questions in the first place.[65] When the number of women making careers in biology rose, and biologists began to study the behaviour of female primates, their results called the dominant assumptions seriously into question. Female langurs, for instance, 'were anything but [sexually passive and "coy"]', sometimes actively soliciting sex from roving males that approached their troop, and successful mother chimpanzees 'were not simply doting nurturers but entrepreneurial dynasts as well',[66] both of these behaviours being, in different species and circumstances, strategies for ensuring the survival and reproductive success of their offspring. But even if it should turn out, once the distorting effect of gender stereotypes was corrected, that there were a grain of truth in the notion of aggressive, competitive males and more passive females (and Hrdy, for one, certainly does not wish to deny *all* differences between male and female reproductive strategies), the ethic of 'the command of God the Creator' articulated in previous chapters would support the analysis of this chapter in naming both pride and sloth as *sins*. A patriarchal social dynamic in which men tended to be socialized as proud and women as slothful should be judged sinful, any alleged biological origins notwithstanding.

c   The victor and the true witness

Probably the most difficult New Testament metaphors of salvation for modern readers to accept are those that speak of Jesus Christ as the victor in a cosmic conflict of good and evil, particularly when the forces of evil are personified as the devil and demons. Yet this language, if not ubiquitous, is widespread in the New Testament. To give a few examples: in the wilderness, Jesus is tempted by the devil but resists (Matt. 4.1–11 = Luke 4.1–13); the synoptic Gospels portray his healing work

---

65 Sarah Blaffer Hrdy, *Mother Nature: A History of Mothers, Infants, and Natural Selection*, New York: Pantheon, 1999, pp. 3–54.

66 Hrdy, *Mother Nature*, pp. 34, 52.

as involving the defeat of unclean spirits, the 'binding of the strong man' (Mark 3.22–7); in his death, 'the ruler of this world [is] driven out' (John 12.31); the Pauline literature speaks of Christ's triumph over the 'rulers and authorities', which therefore have no power to threaten us (Col. 2.15; Rom. 8.38); the Son of God 'was revealed . . . to destroy the works of the devil' (1 John 3.8); and the book of Revelation proclaims the victory of the slain Lamb over the devil and his angels. Notoriously, in the early Church, these metaphors inspired atonement theories 'of dubious rationality and morality', as Colin Gunton puts it,[67] such as the idea that Jesus' humanity was the bait hiding the fishhook of his divinity, on which the devil, deceived by the bait, was impaled.[68] It was in reaction to such excesses that Anselm proposed his theory of satisfaction, a development welcomed by P. T. Forsyth as an advance (albeit one that brought its own problems), but famously regretted by Gustaf Aulén as a descent from the classic 'dramatic' view of the atonement into rationalism and legalism.[69]

There seem to be two main problems with this language of Christ's victory over cosmic forces of evil. One is that, as sometimes expressed, it is, in Gunton's words, so 'naïvely supernaturalist' and anthropomorphic as to '[appear] ridiculously primitive'.[70] The other is that it seems to be a mythological account of a battle fought in some cosmic realm remote from human life on planet earth, and it is unclear how the outcome of such a battle could be decisive for human destiny.[71] However, Gunton shows persuasively how these problems might be addressed. The over-mythologized character of the language results from a tendency in the early Church to use it in a less restrained way than the New Testament authors did, and to take the latter's metaphors too literally.[72] When the more restrained character of the New Testament's language is taken seriously, the principalities and powers are best understood as 'earthly realities',[73] forces that affect human affairs in this

---

67 Gunton, *Actuality*, p. 63.

68 Gregory of Nyssa, *Great Catechism*, XXIV, in Philip Schaff and Henry Wace (eds.), *Nicene and Post-Nicene Fathers*, 2nd ser., vol. 5, Edinburgh: T&T Clark, 1892, p. 494.

69 Forsyth, *Work*, p. 232; Gustaf Aulén, *Christus Victor: An Historical Study of the Three Main Types of the Idea of the Atonement*, trans. A. G. Herbert, London: SPCK, 1931.

70 Gunton, *Actuality*, pp. 66, 69.

71 *Actuality*, p. 63.

72 *Actuality*, pp. 63–4.

73 George B. Caird, *The Language and Imagery of the Bible*, London: Duckworth, 1980, p. 232, cited by Gunton, *Actuality*, p. 65.

world, but are resistant to description in purely empirical or rationalistic terms. 'The texts present us not with superhuman hypostases trotting about the world, but with *the metaphorical characterisation of moral and cosmic realities which would otherwise defy expression*.'[74]

But is such language serviceable today? As Gunton observes, while there is little talk of demons, the language of the *demonic* has been reappropriated in philosophy and literature as well as theology.[75] Some recent authors, however, are sceptical about the value of such language. Adam Morton, for example, believes that this language makes it easier for us to label others as evil, which in turn encourages us to regard their motives as alien and incomprehensible and makes us readier to contemplate doing atrocious things to *them*: thus evil can have a 'dangerous self-fulfilling quality', and the language of the demonic is 'worryingly well-suited for this role'.[76] Furthermore, the demonic image might seem attractive and fascinating to some people, and lead them to try and emulate it, precisely because it is inscrutable: 'One can worship the devil, or admire Hitler. And the less real the psychological insight that comes with the image the better it can serve this role . . . Though there are no devils, people's beliefs in devils can be a powerful force for evil.'[77]

There is certainly a worthwhile caution here against over-dramatic or lazy use of the language of the demonic, which could indeed do damage. But Morton's description of the 'demonic image' which he wishes to reject conflates a number of different themes, including evil beings with unintelligible motives (such as zombies and vampires), the desire for autonomy over against God, and temptation which gets its power from a combination of repressed sexual desire and rebelliousness.[78] This amalgam, which perhaps contains elements of caricature, is not exactly what Gunton and others have in mind in arguing for the value of the language of the demonic; in refusing to use this language, Morton risks rejecting a concept with real and much-needed explanatory power. Other philosophers, such as Dorothy Emmet, have found the concept of the demonic necessary, as Gunton puts it, 'to express the helplessness of human agents in the face of psychological, social and cosmic forces in various

---

74 Gunton, *Actuality*, p. 66, emphasis original. For a more extensive treatment along somewhat similar lines, see Walter Wink, *Naming the Powers: The Language of Power in the New Testament*, Philadelphia, PA: Fortress, 1984.

75 *Actuality*, p. 67. It is even to be found in popular scientific literature, e.g. Richard Wrangham and Dale Peterson, *Demonic Males: Apes and the Origins of Human Violence*, London: Bloomsbury, 1997.

76 Adam Morton, *On Evil*, London: Routledge, 2004, pp. 4–6, 31–2.

77 Morton, *On Evil*, pp. 32–3.

78 *On Evil*, pp. 22–9.

combinations', a helplessness which, he says, must be understood theologically as originating in the worship of that which is not God: 'If the created order, or part of it, is treated as god, then it behaves like god for those who so treat it, but for destructive rather than creative ends.'[79]

Idolatry, the worship of that which is not God, can be understood as the ultimate lie; so the victory of Jesus – won in the totality of his life, death and resurrection – can be understood from this perspective as his refusal to submit to the ultimate falsehood. This is seen with particular clarity in the temptation narratives when he refuses Satan's bargain of power in return for worship (Matt. 4.8–10 = Luke 4.5–8). Gunton remarks that '[i]t was therefore a sure instinct . . . that led Barth to expand the slogan "Jesus is the Victor" in terms of his witnessing to the truth'.[80] Having treated the priestly and kingly offices of Christ in the first and second parts of his doctrine of reconciliation, Barth turns in the third part to the prophetic office. Jesus Christ the Mediator is the Prophet and true Witness who makes known the reconciling work of God; his prophetic work is the true light which shines in the darkness and overcomes its opposition.[81]

The shadow of this aspect of Christ's work is the understanding of sin as falsehood, by which we defend ourselves from the threat and offence of the good news of Jesus Christ:

> God confronts [the man of sin] as the One who is incomparably free, and it is his own liberation by and for the free God, in which he himself is to be the one who in his own way is incomparably free, which is at issue and which he is required to accept. God makes Himself known as his God, as his loving Father and Lord, Friend and Helper, who opens up to him the fullness of His treasures . . .
>
> The man of sin starts back from this free God and his own liberation by and for Him. Like a tornado, this God sweeps away all the assurances, props and supports which he seeks in relation both to God and himself, and therefore all his reservations and excuses, all his attempts to hold aloof from God, to maintain himself against Him, to secure a place of his own.[82]

Therefore we devise various stratagems to protect ourselves against the truth with which the true Witness confronts us. Barth describes

---

79 Gunton, *Actuality*, pp. 70, 72, citing Dorothy Emmet, *The Moral Prism*, London: Macmillan, 1979.

80 *Actuality*, p. 78.

81 Barth, *CD* IV.3, §§ 69.3, 70.1.

82 *CD* IV.3, pp. 446–7.

falsehood as the 'specifically Christian form of sin',[83] characteristic of the 'Christian age' between Christ's resurrection and final return. He comments that falsehood is at its most mature and effective when it can assimilate as much of the truth as possible, giving itself an appearance of earnestness, respectability and devoutness;[84] one is reminded of the advice, attributed to Sam Goldwyn, that 'sincerity's the main thing, and once you learn to fake that, everything else is easy'.

As with the other aspects of sin discussed in this section, it is possible to propose connections with theories and speculations about human evolution. In Chapter 6 I noted the idea, canvassed by some evolutionary writers, that natural selection in our highly complex social species could have favoured tendencies both to hypocrisy and to self-deception – the latter because we are most effective at deceiving others when we are convinced of the deception ourselves, since (unfortunately for Sam Goldwyn) fake sincerity is rarely as convincing as the genuine article.[85] As I have repeatedly emphasized, these claims are highly speculative; whatever their merits, a theological analysis in any case broadens the picture far beyond evolutionary biology, emphasizing that sin as falsehood is fundamentally a distortion of our relationship with God and, derivatively, of our relationships with one another and ourselves. Furthermore, should the evolutionary process by which we have been brought into being have left us with any kind of propensity to falsehood, that might once again raise the question of theodicy (to which I shall return in due course), but it ought not to alter our assessment of falsehood as sin.

According to Barth, it is our sin in the form of falsehood that brings us under the threat of condemnation, for God's Word of truth brings us the good news of our deliverance from the guilt of our pride and slavery to our sloth; therefore, 'in refusing the Word of truth [we refuse our] pardon'.[86] There is an element of this self-deceiving falsehood in our pride and our sloth: for example, in the pride that makes us want to be our own helpers, we deceive ourselves into thinking that we can help ourselves, and thereby alienate ourselves from the true source of our help.[87] When I come in Chapter 9 to discuss the proper scope and limits

---

83 *CD* IV.3, pp. 434–5.

84 *CD* IV.3, pp. 436–9.

85 Dennis Krebs *et al.*, 'On the Evolution of Self-Knowledge and Self-Deception', in Kevin MacDonald (ed.), *Sociobiological Perspectives on Human Development*, New York: Springer-Verlag, 1988, cited by Wright, *Moral Animal*, p. 268.

86 Barth, *CD* IV.3, p. 463.

87 *CD* IV.1, pp. 458–78.

of human action in the world, these warnings about falsehood, and self-deception in particular, will be germane. I shall suggest there that a characteristic temptation of well-meaning people in technological societies is to think that every human predicament can be solved by technical skill and cleverness, thereby obscuring the knowledge of where our true help is to be found.

My focus in this subsection has been largely on the origins of the 'demonic' in the idolatry which is the ultimate lie, and that has led me to a more general consideration of that kind of distortion in our relations with God, one another and ourselves which can be characterized as falsehood. But what of the more spectacular forms of behaviour which may immediately come to mind when the word 'demonic' is used: extreme violence, for example, of a kind which seems arbitrary and unintelligible? Can evolutionary insights shed any light on such forms of the 'demonic', and make any contribution to the theological picture that has been sketched here? There are many reports of behaviour among our primate relatives that appears to answer to the description of 'demonic' in this sense: infanticide, attacks on rivals in which they are not only killed but mutilated, and even behaviour that is interpreted by observers as cruelty and *Schadenfreude*.[88] In some cases, examples of such behaviour were initially written off, somewhat anthropomorphic-ally, as aberrant and insane, but it has later been argued that they offer identifiable advantages in terms of reproductive fitness. So it is some-times proposed that our evolutionary history has included selection pressures that have favoured some predisposition to such behaviours, at least under some circumstances. Perhaps also, more indirectly, more general traits (such as aggression) that proved adaptive during our evo-lutionary history could, under circumstances when normal restraints are removed, lead to acts of extreme and egregious wickedness.[89] But while we need to understand such behaviour, and while a theological analysis of the 'demonic' which critically appropriates evolutionary insights could conceivably help us to do so, we should be wary of too great a fascination with extreme and spectacular wickedness. The emphasis of Gunton's account, on which I have drawn heavily in this sub-section, is to use the extreme to shed light on the condition of all of us – an emphasis he shares with Morton, for all their differences about the proper source of that light. 'In the great literary depictions, the very

---

88 See above, Chapter 6, section 1a.

89 This is proposed by Adam Morton in his 'barrier theory' of evil: *On Evil*, pp. 34–68.

difference of the characters from the ordinary enables us to see the horror of demonic moral behaviour. But the characters are great also because they cast light on the plight of the rest of us, at least as we are apart from grace.'[90] If we are to understand sin as demonic falsehood, it is falsehood in which we all participate in our various ways, and the victory won by Jesus Christ is won on behalf of us all.

3   Original sin

In Chapter 6 I remarked, following Roger White, that Luther's moral vision is antithetical to Kant's in part because Luther has a doctrine of sin which is far more radical than Kant's notion of 'radical evil':

> [Luther] argues in a number of ways that the nature of sin was such that man had rendered himself incapable of fulfilling the Law, and hence that it could only be by divine grace liberating Man that such a thing as obeying the Law of God could ever occur.[91]

This observation brings us to the heart of the understanding of sin that I have been developing in this chapter. Sin is far more than a series of wrong deeds or even reprehensible motives or intentions; it is a radical distortion of our relationship with God, and derivatively of our relationship with one another, ourselves and the rest of the created order, that renders us incapable of living the good life for which we have been created.

The classic formulation of this view in Western Christianity has been the doctrine of original sin, succinctly summarized by Alistair McFadyen, who draws out four key features of original sin from the tradition.[92] First, it is a *contingent*, not necessary, result of human freedom: sin entered the world by means of the freely chosen acts of the first human couple, described in the Fall narrative of Genesis 3. Secondly, it is *radical*, in the sense that it goes to the root of our human condition. We have inherited from Adam and Eve both the incapacity to avoid sin and reliably to choose the good, and the accountability for their original sin: 'we stand before God guilty for Adam's sin even before we get

---

90 Gunton, *Actuality*, p. 74.

91 Roger M. White, '"Ought" Implies "Can": Kant and Luther, a Contrast', in George MacDonald Ross and Tony McWalter (eds.), *Kant and His Influence* (Bristol: Thoemmes, 1990), pp. 1–72 (pp. 67–8).

92 McFadyen, *Bound to Sin*, pp. 16–18.

around to doing any sinning of our own'.[93] Thirdly, it is *communicable*: we all inherit it *'prior* to our achievement of personhood';[94] in the Augustinian version, it is passed on through the biological process of procreation, which since the Fall is always tainted with wrongly ordered sexual desire. Finally, it is *universal*: we are all the heirs of our first parents' sin, and we are all unable to avoid sinning ourselves.

There are various difficulties which must be addressed in one way or another if the doctrine of original sin is to shed any light on the questions being explored in this chapter. Probably the most familiar are those highlighted by feminist critiques that charge the Augustinian tradition with demonizing women, sexuality and the material creation, and legitimating patriarchy by means of a transcendent, authoritarian God who is a projection of human male authority. While these critiques are undoubtedly justified in many respects, I believe it is possible to reappropriate the doctrine of original sin in a manner that goes a long way towards addressing the concerns expressed therein. Constraints of space preclude an extended discussion of feminist critiques at this point, but I have attempted earlier in this chapter to incorporate insights from feminist discussions, and McFadyen, on whom my account of original sin draws heavily, has offered a more extended response to feminist critiques of the doctrine of original sin.[95]

Another obvious difficulty which must be cleared out of the way is the apparent impossibility of reading Genesis 3 as literal history if we also accept an evolutionary account of human origins.[96] Creationists such as E. H. Andrews make much of this difficulty, arguing for example that Paul's parallelism between Adam and Christ (Rom. 5.12–21) depends on there having been an historical Adam. If there was no historical Adam, so the argument goes, Paul's account of the atoning work of Christ collapses, so the theological cost to Christians of holding to the theory of evolution is unacceptably high.[97] No doubt this line of argument would also be congenial to scientifically minded atheists who wish to show that Christian belief is untenable after Darwin.

---

93 *Bound to Sin*, p. 16.
94 *Bound to Sin*, p. 17, emphasis original.
95 See, e.g., *Bound to Sin*, pp. 202–12.
96 See, e.g., Karl Rahner, 'Theology and Monogenism', in *Theological Investigations*, vol. 1, London: Darton, Longman and Todd, 1961, pp. 229–96, and 'Evolution and Original Sin', *Concilium*, 26 (1967), pp. 61–73, both cited by McFadyen, *Bound to Sin*, p. 18.
97 E. H. Andrews, 'The Biblical and Philosophical Case for Special Creation', in Derek Burke (ed.), *Creation and Evolution*, Leicester: Inter-Varsity Press, 1985, pp. 226–52 (p. 232).

Some Christian biologists, in an effort to do justice both to their science and to the biblical roots of their faith, attempt to reconcile human evolution with the historicity of the Fall narrative. For example, R. J. Berry, who like Andrews accepts the logic that Romans 5 and other New Testament texts require the existence of an historical Adam, infers from details in Genesis 2–4 that Adam, Eve and their immediate descendants lived approximately 10–15,000 years ago on the edge of the Anatolian Plateau.[98] They obviously could not have been the *genetic* ancestors of all living humans, but Berry conjectures that they became the *spiritual* ancestors of us all by virtue of being the first humans into whom God breathed the divine image, which all other members of the species were also subsequently given. In addition to being an ordinary member of the species *Homo sapiens*, Adam thus became the first member and 'federal head' of *Homo divinus*.[99] Before this spiritual inbreathing, no human would have had a personal relationship with God, and sin (as a distortion of that relationship) would therefore have been impossible; '[o]nce we became *Homo divinus*, our rebellion necessarily disrupted the newly-established relationship'.[100]

Berry's account, as I have said, is clearly motivated by a desire to do justice both to the overwhelming evidence for an evolutionary account of human origins and to the biblical roots of Christian faith, a motivation which, as should be clear by now, I fully share. But his way of holding these things together is problematic in important respects. In particular, the somewhat obscure account of federal headship that he derives from Kidner does not make it at all clear why, if each of Adam's contemporaries had God's image individually breathed into him or her, Adam's original sin had to go on to infect all members of the species. In other words, Berry's account can certainly do justice to the contingency of original sin (Adam's and Eve's first sin was a freely willed choice), but it is far less clear that it can give a satisfactory account of its radicality, communicability or universality.

To insist on the historicity of Adam and Eve and of the Fall in this way is to allow oneself to be painted unnecessarily into a corner. As Barth comments,

---

98 R. J. Berry, 'This Cursed Earth: Is "the Fall" Credible?', *Science and Christian Belief*, 11.1 (1999), pp. 29–49 (pp. 35–41); *God's Book of Works: The Nature and Theology of Nature*, London: Continuum, 2003, pp. 227–32.

99 Berry, 'This Cursed Earth', p. 39, quoting Derek Kidner, *Tyndale Commentary on Genesis*, London: Tyndale Press, 1967, pp. 30, 29, on 'federal headship'.

100 Berry, 'This Cursed Earth', p. 41.

We miss the unprecedented and incomparable thing which the Genesis passages tell us of the coming into being and existence of Adam if we try to read and understand it as history, relating it either favourably or unfavourably to scientific palaeontology, or to what we know with some historical certainty concerning the oldest and most primitive forms of human life.[101]

We would be better advised to treat the early chapters of Genesis as 'biblical saga', the genre

in which intuition and imagination are used but in order to give prophetic witness to what has taken place by virtue of the Word of God in the (historical or pre-historical) sphere where there can be no historical proof. It was in this sphere of biblical saga that Adam came into being and existed. And it was in this sphere . . . that there took place the fall, the fall of the first man. The biblical saga tells us that world-history began with the pride and fall of the first man.[102]

Furthermore, it is quite mistaken to think that the Pauline parallel between Adam and Christ requires an historical Adam as the prototype, as it were, of which Christ is the fulfilment. Barth re-emphasizes here that we only know about human sin in the mirror of the work of Christ, as that which was 'set aside in His death'.[103] Therefore the parallel between Adam and Christ must be understood the other way round, as

the parallel between Christ and Adam . . . [Paul] knew Jesus Christ first and then Adam. But that means that in Adam, in his existence and act and function, in his relationship to the race which derived from him, he saw again, as it were, the negative side of Jesus Christ. . . . It is in relation to the last Adam that this first Adam, the unknown of the Genesis story, has for Paul existence and consistence, and that in what is said of him he hears what is true and necessarily true of himself and all men.[104]

This first Adam is of interest simply in the sense that he 'did in the insignificant form of the beginner that which all men have done after

---

101 *CD* IV.1, p. 508.
102 *CD* IV.1, p. 508; Barth pointedly avoids using the slippery word 'myth', which he has earlier sharply differentiated from 'saga' (p. 336). See also *CD* III.1, pp. 76–94.
103 *CD* IV.1, p. 502.
104 *CD* IV.1, pp. 512–13.

him'.[105] The point of the parallel between Christ and Adam is that our history, apart from the saving work of Christ, is a history of sin, 'Adamic history'. The significance of the Fall narrative is that '[t]here never was a golden age. There is no point in looking back to one. The first man was immediately the first sinner.'[106]

This reading of the Fall narrative enables us to make theological sense of the claims by some primatologists that the rudiments of both good and bad behaviour can be discerned in our primate relatives, and of the inference that both good and bad in human nature are, at least in part, products of an evolutionary history older than *Homo sapiens*.[107] It is sometimes even conjectured that the knowledge of right and wrong was favoured by natural selection precisely because of its evolutionary utility in controlling behaviours that threatened the reproductive fitness of our ancestors. In a social species, so the argument goes, reciprocal altruism would be favoured by natural selection, but the reproductive fitness of those who practised it could be threatened by free-riders; so the capacity to detect cheating, and the disposition to name it as wrong and to operate social sanctions against it, could also be favoured by natural selection.[108] On this view, then, the knowledge of right and wrong could have arisen as a way of naming and controlling behaviours which were already part of the behavioural repertoire of the species. If this is true, then certainly in this sense 'there never was a golden age': for as long as our species has known of right and wrong, we have been capable of both, and perhaps biased in some ways towards certain kinds of wrongdoing.

But there might be more to be said than this. It is sometimes assumed that the emergence of the knowledge of right and wrong during our evolutionary history is a positive development, associated in some way with our being made in God's image.[109] But the fragment of Bonhoeffer's *Ethics* cited earlier might suggest a very different assessment: 'The knowledge of good and evil appears to be the goal of all ethical

---

105 *CD* IV.1, p. 509.
106 *CD* IV.1, p. 508.
107 E.g. Frans B. M. de Waal, *Good Natured: The Origins of Right and Wrong in Humans and Other Animals*, Cambridge, MA: Harvard University Press, 1996; Wrangham and Peterson, *Demonic Males*.
108 See, e.g., Robert L. Trivers, 'The Evolution of Reciprocal Altruism', *Quarterly Review of Biology*, 46 (1971), pp. 35–56; Leda Cosmides and John Tooby, 'Cognitive Adaptations for Social Exchange', in Jerome H. Barkow *et al.*, *The Adapted Mind: Evolutionary Psychology and the Generation of Culture*, Oxford: Oxford University Press, 1992, pp. 163–228; de Waal, *Good Natured*, pp. 154–62.
109 E.g. Berry, *God's Book of Works*, pp. 74–6, 228.

reflection. The first task of Christian ethics is to [invalidate] that knowledge.'[110] In his exposition of Genesis 2 and 3, Bonhoeffer describes the knowledge of good and evil as a fundamental division in the human being, which comes with the Fall. Before the Fall, '[a]s one who lives in the unity of obedience Adam does not comprehend that which is two-sided; as one who lives in the unity of the knowledge of God as the center and boundary of human life Adam cannot conceive of the breaking apart of that knowledge into good and evil'.[111] But when the human beings take the fruit and eat it, they really do become 'like God' (*sicut deus*), knowing good and evil. The serpent's promise, though, is both true and false: 'for humankind to become sicut deus as the serpent promises can be nothing but what the Creator calls death';[112] death not in the sense of 'the abolition of one's being as a creature [but of] no longer being able to live before God, and yet having to live before God . . . standing before God as an outlaw, as one who is lost and damned, but not as one who no longer exists'.[113] Bonhoeffer powerfully contrasts the image of God (*imago dei*) with the serpent's promise of being *sicut deus*, like God:

> Imago dei – bound to the word of the Creator and deriving life from the Creator; sicut deus – bound to the depths of its own knowledge of God, of good and evil. Imago dei – the creature living in the unity of obedience; sicut deus – the creator-human-being who lives on the basis of the divide between good and evil. Imago dei, sicut deus, agnus dei [the Lamb of God] – the human being who is God incarnate, who was sacrificed for humankind sicut deus, in true divinity slaying its false divinity and restoring the imago dei.[114]

In Bonhoeffer's perspective, then, if there was a natural 'knowledge' of right and wrong, or of good and evil, which emerged during our evolutionary history, it should most likely be understood as part of the problem rather than part of the solution: knowledge that encourages us to be

---

110 Bonhoeffer, *Ethics*, p. 299.

111 Bonhoeffer, *Creation and Fall: A Theological Exposition of Genesis 1–3* (*Dietrich Bonhoeffer Works*, vol. 3), ET ed. by John W. de Gruchy, trans. Douglas Stephen Bax, Minneapolis: Fortress, 1997, p. 87. Note that for Bonhoeffer, as for Barth, this is obviously not to be taken as a literal historical narrative: see pp. 31–3. These ideas about the knowledge of good and evil are reprised in *Ethics*, pp. 299–309.

112 *Creation and Fall*, p. 112.

113 *Creation and Fall*, p. 90.

114 *Creation and Fall*, p. 113.

like God, knowing about God, good and evil for ourselves, rather than relating to God in love and faith. In this respect, too, if Bonhoeffer is right, there never was a golden age: the first hominids to know good and evil were already, by virtue of that knowledge, alienated from God, from one another, from themselves and from the rest of the created order.[115]

I noted earlier Barth's unease with the language of original sin. It is possible that one reason for this unease is his unswerving determination to continue affirming the goodness of God's creation, including the human creation, even in the face of our corruption:

> [Man] has not lost – even in part – the good nature which was created by God, to acquire instead another and evil nature. . . . The seriousness of his situation is much greater than can be expressed by the idea of a setting aside or damaging of his nature which is good. It consists in the crying contradiction that he sets himself – his being in the integrity of his human nature and his being in covenant with God – in the service of evil, and that he now has to exist in that service.[116]

Certainly this commitment must serve as a plumbline for any doctrine of sin that is developed in dialogue with evolutionary biology: if it calls into question the affirmation that human beings, in common with the rest of creation, are created 'very good' by God, then something has gone badly wrong with it.[117] However, a second reason for Barth's

---

115 Cf. Bonhoeffer, *Ethics*, p. 303: 'Their life is now divided, estranged from God, other human beings, material things, and themselves.' To refer as I have done to the 'first hominids to know good and evil' is to write, somewhat artificially, as if there had been a sharp transition between ignorance and knowledge, whereas what is in view, of course, is the gradual emergence of this knowledge during our evolutionary history.

116 Barth, *CD* IV.1, pp. 492–3.

117 If we say too simplistically that evolution was the means that God used to create humans, and that our evolutionary history has left us with some kind of propensity to sin, then we do indeed risk calling into question the goodness of God's creation. The danger can, I think, be avoided by recalling the point made in Chapter 4, that a distinction must be maintained (however hard it is to specify) between the *nature* (and natural history) that is disclosed by scientific investigation and the *creation* that we know in and through Christ. It is through Christ, not by studying our evolutionary origins, that we know what it is to have been created 'very good'. Furthermore, if, with Barth and Bonhoeffer, we decline to read the Creation and Fall narratives as historical accounts, then there is no particular difficulty in saying that we are God's good creatures, that God's good purposes in and for us have been subverted by sin, and that both these things have been true of us since the beginnings of our history. God's saving work in Christ, begun in the life, death and resurrection of Jesus and to be fulfilled at the eschaton, as Bonhoeffer affirms (above, n. 113), is the promise that this division within us will be healed.

unease with the notion of original sin is his continuing commitment to what McFadyen calls a moral frame of reference for thinking about sin. This commitment is not unequivocal: Barth warns against trying to lessen the force of the questions with which the doctrine of sin faces us by giving them 'a moralistic turn in order to be able to return an optimistic answer'.[118] And, true to his theological method, it is from the universal and radical scope of God's saving work in Christ that Barth learns of the universal and radical nature of human corruption; 'The fact that Jesus Christ died totally for the reconciliation of every man as such . . . means decisively that this corruption is both radical and total.'[119] However, it is striking that, in order to describe our corruption, he borrows, with explicit acknowledgement of Kant, the latter's language of 'an evil principle', a 'bias towards evil' and 'radical evil'.[120] If Roger White is right to suggest that this language emerges from a moral vision opposed in central respects to that of the Reformers,[121] we might expect to find some significant internal tensions in Barth's account of original sin. And indeed there does appear to be some tension between, on the one hand, his emphasis on the depth and radicality of our own corruption, and our complete inability to extricate ourselves from our own predicament, and, on the other, his insistence (in the context of a discussion of the sinlessness of Jesus) that '[i]t is not really of necessity, but only in fact, that human nature wills to sin, and does sin, and therefore can sin'.[122] This ongoing commitment to a moral frame of reference is what lies behind his rejection of any notion of inherited sin (*Erbsünde*):

> It is not surprising that when an effort is made to take the word 'heir' seriously, as has occasionally happened, the term 'sin' is necessarily dissolved. Conversely, when the term 'sin' is taken seriously, the term 'heir' is necessarily explained in a way which makes it quite unrecognisable . . . 'Hereditary sin' has a hopelessly naturalistic, deterministic and even fatalistic ring.[123]

118 *CD* IV.1, p. 498.

119 *CD* IV.1, p. 492. According to Stanley Hauerwas, this is in sharp contrast to Reinhold Niebuhr, who, though he reaches apparently similar conclusions about human sin, arrives at them from the other direction, beginning with anthropology: *With the Grain of the Universe: The Church's Witness and Natural Theology*, Grand Rapids, MI: Brazos, 2001, pp. 117–20.

120 *CD* IV.1, p. 495; cf. Immanuel Kant, *Religion Within the Limits of Reason Alone*, trans. Theodore M. Green and Hoyt H. Hudson, New York: Harper, 1960, pp. 15–39.

121 White, '"Ought" Implies "Can"', pp. 45–6.

122 Barth, *CD* IV.2, p. 93.

123 *CD* IV.1, pp. 500–1.

Yet this opposition between the concepts of 'sin' and 'heir' becomes unnecessary if we broaden our frame of reference for thinking about sin beyond the moral. McFadyen, for example, draws on descriptions of concrete 'pathologies' (child abuse and the holocaust), feminist accounts of sloth and Augustine's account of original sin to give an account of sin which is not reducible to the sum of our individual decisions and acts. The willing and choosing of victims, perpetrators and bystanders has to be understood in the context of a deeply distorted dynamic that co-opts and redirects their 'whole life-intentionality (drives, desires, rationality, etc.)', distorts their perceptions of reality – good and bad, right and wrong, healthy and unhealthy, etc. – and 'blocks access to transcendent criteria of meaning and value'.[124] On this understanding, willing is not the exercise of arbitrary, unconstrained choice – as if, at every point of decision, we stood at a crossroads and could take either way[125] – but rather a 'situated and relational' process by which 'we incorporate ourselves into, internalise and redouble, dynamics which are generally supra-personal and not of our own making, whilst adding our own personal power to them'.[126] Neither is freedom to be understood as a lack of constraint on our choice, but as 'being pulled in an orientation towards what is genuinely good', towards that which supports the integrity of our being and our relations with others; to orient our willing in other directions would undermine, not support, our personal integrity and relations, and would be a diminution, not an exercise, of our freedom.[127] The orientation of our willing which is the *conditio sine qua non* of our personal integrity and right relations is an orientation in joy, faith and worship towards the triune God whose being is revealed in the death and resurrection of Jesus Christ to be characterized by 'abundant goodness and plenitude'.[128]

From this it becomes clear that sin is to be understood as, at root, idolatry: the orientation of one's 'life-intentionality' onto some other end or goal than the abundant, life-giving God revealed in Jesus. Such misplaced orientation distorts every aspect of life, so that, as we have seen, a fundamental distortion in our relationship with God also results in distorted relations with others, ourselves and the created order.

---

124 McFadyen, *Bound to Sin*, pp. 194–9; quotations at p. 195.
125 White's metaphor for Kant's understanding of the moral life: '"Ought" Implies "Can"', p. 45.
126 McFadyen, *Bound to Sin*, p. 203.
127 *Bound to Sin*, p. 204.
128 *Bound to Sin*, pp. 205–16; quotation at p. 210.

'Whereas true worship energises the loving dynamics of genuine community, idolatry undermines them (Babel).'[129] Pride (as the misconceived and self-deluding attempt to direct one's life in isolation from God), sloth (as the disorientation and dissipation of one's energies and personal integrity) and falsehood (which misrepresents the structure of reality, the nature of good and evil, right and wrong, and the nature of God and God's relations to us) can all be conceived as aspects of idolatry. When the fundamental dynamics of our lives, relationships and social structures are so misdirected, they can only be reoriented from outside (as it were) by God's grace and the work of the Spirit. The nature of the triune God's being, characterized by a relational dynamic of overflowing love and joy, means that this redirection of our lives by God's grace could not be further from an alien, heteronomous imposition that disempowers us or subverts the integrity of our lives. Rather, to be reoriented towards the triune God is to be caught up into the divine dynamics of love and praise in such a way that our living is energized and transformed.[130]

I have already suggested ways in which an evolutionary perspective might be correlated with an account of original sin so understood.[131] First, and more trivially, it is conceivable (though, as I have said before, such speculations are at best under-determined by the evidence) that we have inherited dispositions, favoured by natural selection in some

---

129 *Bound to Sin*, p. 226.

130 *Bound to Sin*, pp. 212–16; the theme of transformation will be taken up in the next chapter.

131 For a notable recent attempt to make these connections that contrasts sharply with my own, see Patricia A. Williams, *Doing without Adam and Eve: Sociobiology and Original Sin*, Minneapolis, MN: Fortress, 2001. One point of contact between our accounts is that Williams too recognizes that the Christian doctrine of sin arises from reflection on the death of Jesus: if our atonement required the death of the Son of God, our predicament must have been truly terrible. However, unlike me, she regards this inference as false, both because she does not read Genesis 3 as the story of a fall into sin and because evolutionary biology tells us that Adam and Eve never existed (like Andrews and Berry, but unlike me, she assumes that the traditional doctrine of original sin requires there to have been an historical Adam and Eve). In her sociobiologically inspired revision of the doctrine of original sin, the propensity to sin is an inevitable by-product of our human freedom and creativity; this leads to an exemplarist doctrine of the atonement and a theodicy which seems to require that we live in the best of all possible worlds. The contrasts between our accounts stem in part from particular disagreements (such as the necessity or otherwise, for the traditional doctrine of original sin, of the historicity of Adam and Eve), but more importantly and fundamentally from methodological differences. Williams essentially allows the natural sciences and their methods to determine the shape of the enquiry, to which Christian doctrine is then required to accommodate itself. In Chapter 3, I explained my reasons for not adopting such a methodology.

period of our evolutionary history, towards at least some of the distortions of relationship named earlier in this chapter: inordinate self-assertion (in the form of aggression, status-seeking and the like), perhaps some forms of 'self-loss', and certain forms of falsehood. In other words, it is conceivable that we have inherited from our earliest human ancestors ('from our first parents', as it were) a *tendency* to sin – though, as everyone agrees, such a tendency would be far from deterministic. This is of course a biological inheritance, though hardly in the way Augustine thought.

More significantly, I have suggested, following Bonhoeffer, that we should perhaps understand our natural 'knowledge' of right and wrong as part of our problem rather than part of its solution: an aspect of human being *sicut deus* ('like God', in the serpent's sense) rather than of the *imago dei*. If this is so, and this knowledge of right and wrong is also in some way a product of our evolutionary history, then it would appear that a more profound aspect of original sin – guilt in the sense of a basic distortion in our standing before God (and derivatively, before one another, ourselves and the created order) – could be inherited (in part, perhaps, biologically) from our earliest human ancestors.

On the assumption that our picture of original sin includes these two evolutionary elements, it will certainly do justice to three of the classic aspects of the doctrine of original sin identified by McFadyen: its radicality, communicability and universality. Its contingency, though, would appear to be rendered problematic on this view. Certainly I have argued that the contingency of original sin cannot be understood in terms of a first human couple having had a free choice whether or not to sin, and having, as a matter of fact, chosen wrongly. It seems to me, *pace* Berry, that an evolutionary account of human origins must rule out any notion of the literal historical fall of a first couple. In a more general sense, of course, the course of evolution is always contingent, and the details of our evolutionary history could have turned out differently. Whether any evolutionary history could have omitted all of the problematic characteristics that I have discussed and still produced anything like us (whether, in other words, it could still have been in any meaningful sense 'our' history) is a moot point, though in Chapter 6 I noted Wrangham and Peterson's suggestion, made with reference to the differences between bonobos and chimpanzees, that it could.

But this issue of contingency might suggest that a modification is in order to the more fundamental of the correlations that I have made

---

132 Barth, *CD* IV.2, pp. 415–16.

between human evolution and original sin: the identification of our natural knowledge of right and wrong with human being *sicut deus*, as Bonhoeffer puts it. Rather than saying that our evolved, natural knowledge of right and wrong was *necessarily* a manifestation of humanity *sicut deus*, it might be better to say that, *as it happens*, it became such. Perhaps we ought to say that it could have been different: our natural knowledge of right and wrong could have been oriented to our relationship with God, and could have become an aspect of the *imago dei*. Putting the matter this way seems to offer less by way of explanation of the origin and cause of sin, but even my earlier, less nuanced formulation probably offered less than it appeared to in this respect: since original sin is not, on any reasonable account, *reducible* to evolved biological traits, dispositions or conditions, a biological account of the origins of the human characteristics which contribute to it could at best be a partial explanation.

In any event, it is probably wise to acknowledge that the origins of human sin are inevitably to some extent a mystery, that sin is a brute fact for which, in a sense, no reason can be given.[132] The most pressing question with which the doctrine of original sin faces us does not have to do with curiosity as to how this all began, but with our standing in relation to God, one another, ourselves and the created order. Accordingly, my purpose in bringing an account of original sin into contact with evolutionists' questions about our moral weakness and failure was not so much to try and explain the origins of sin as to explore whether insights from biology could inform a Christian doctrine of salvation and sin, and to argue that the Christian doctrine, by broadening the frame of reference beyond the narrowly moral, can offer a more satisfactory picture of our human situation than secular accounts that become caught up in tensions about freedom, determinism, responsibility and so forth.

However, I have already acknowledged that the account of original sin I have proposed, with its critical appropriation of insights about human evolution, does appear to create an important difficulty about the goodness of a God who causes or permits an evolutionary process that has this outcome. Accordingly, in the next chapter I shall turn first to the question of theodicy.

8

Salvation and Sin (2):
Theodicy and Hope

1 The justification of God

In the last chapter I canvassed the possibility that there could be an evolutionary component to original sin in two senses. First, our evolutionary history might have left us with a disposition towards some or all of the essential forms of sin characterized by Barth: pride, sloth and falsehood. Secondly, and more fundamentally, that history could have left us in a situation of sin, in that our natural knowledge of right and wrong can be described as an aspect of fallen human being, *sicut deus* ('like God'). I commented at the end of the chapter that this would appear to raise a question of theodicy, or the justice of God, since it might appear to make God responsible for original sin. This is obviously not a new problem for Christian theology – older accounts of original sin had trouble with the serpent, who was after all the subtlest of God's *creatures* (Gen. 3.1) – but in the present discussion the old problem at any rate appears in a new and powerful guise. The problem of God's apparent responsibility for human sin, of course, is by no means the only problem of evolutionary theodicy: many have echoed T. H. Huxley[1] in thinking that the pain, suffering, death and enormous waste that seem to be essential features of the evolutionary process raise profoundly perplexing questions about the goodness, or perhaps even the existence, of God. A full discussion of these wider questions of evolutionary theodicy is beyond the scope of this book, but something must be said about the narrower question of God's apparent responsibility for human sin.[2]

---

1 See above, Chapter 2, section 3 (v).

2 The wider questions have been discussed, and a variety of answers proposed, by many authors, including: Ruth Page, *God and the Web of Creation*, London: SCM Press, 1996; Thomas F. Tracy, 'Evolution, Divine Action and the Problem of Evil', in Robert J. Russell, William R. Stoeger, SJ, and Francisco J. Ayala (eds.), *Evolutionary and Molecular Biology: Scientific Perspectives on Divine Action*, Notre Dame:

To many, the so-called 'free-will defence' in respect of the 'moral evil' done by humans (the good of there being creatures able freely to love God and choose good justifies the risk that those creatures will abuse their freedom by doing evil), together with John Polkinghorne's so-called 'free-process defence' in respect of 'natural evils' such as earth-quakes (a world capable of producing complex, conscious life must be complex and causally open-ended, which entails the possibility of things going wrong),[3] seem particularly appealing solutions to the problems of theodicy. It might appear that the free-will defence was the appropriate one to deploy in response to our present question about the origins of human sin. But, quite apart from the well-known difficulties of that defence,[4] it does not seem to meet our present case for two particular reasons. First, it seems to assume a concept of free will that, following McFadyen, I have argued is problematic: what he calls 'the underlying notion of the will as a neutral organ of arbitrary choice (*liberum arbitrium indifferentiae*)'.[5] Secondly, as Patricia Williams observes, since humans are the products of a natural process, the distinction between natural and moral evil collapses, at least to some extent.[6] To put the point more concretely, since we are here concerned precisely with the question of the Creator's responsibility for those aspects of human sin which can be understood as products of a natural evolutionary process, it would seem to be some version of the free-process defence that is required. There is no other way in which God's good purposes for the creation could be achieved, so the argument goes, than by means of an open-ended evolutionary process with all its risk and pain. For example, if one of God's chief goals for the creation is to bring forth conscious, loving creatures who freely choose relationships with God and with one another, this could only be achieved (it is said) by such a process: living

University of Notre Dame Press, 1998, pp. 511–30; Arthur Peacocke, 'The Cost of New Life', in John Polkinghorne (ed.), *The Work of Love: Creation as Kenosis*, London: SPCK, 2001, pp. 21–42; Holmes Rolston III, 'Kenosis and Nature', in Polkinghorne, *The Work of Love*, pp. 43–65; Patricia A. Williams, *Doing without Adam and Eve: Sociobiology and Original Sin*, Minneapolis: Fortress, 2001, pp. 159–76. For a helpful critical survey of this literature, as well as some constructive proposals, see Christopher Southgate, 'God and Evolutionary Evil: Theodicy in the Light of Darwinism', *Zygon*, 37.4 (2002), pp. 803–24.

3 John Polkinghorne, *Science and Providence: God's Interaction with the World*, London: SPCK, 1989, pp. 59–68.

4 Briefly rehearsed by Southgate, 'God and Evolutionary Evil', p. 812.

5 Alistair McFadyen, *Bound to Sin: Abuse, Holocaust and the Christian Doctrine of Sin*, Cambridge: Cambridge University Press, 2000, p. 126. I am not suggesting that this is a necessary connection, only that this notion of the will very often seems to be in the background in accounts of the free-will defence.

6 Williams, *Doing without Adam and Eve*, p. 169.

organisms complex enough for free choice and loving relationship could only come into being through a process like Darwinian evolution with its subtle interplay of chance and necessity. Such a process is inevitably risky and messy, but the good of the goal is so great as to justify the risk of things going wrong – in particular, for our present purposes, of those complex organisms evolving to be sinners.[7]

The two main kinds of difficulty with this line of argument can be stated in fairly general terms as questions: first, could God's purposes for creation *really* not have been achieved in some other way? Secondly, even if they could not, do they *really* justify all that suffering? Both these questions seem to me quite likely to be unanswerable. With regard to the first, a Darwinian evolutionary process is the only way we know of in which complex, conscious life *has* come into being, and there may be very good reasons for thinking that in our universe this kind of process is the only kind by which such life *could* come into being. But it is hard to imagine how we could settle the question whether God could, in principle, have created some kind of universe in which complex, conscious life could come into being without the costs of an evolutionary process.

The second question expresses the challenge which Dostoevsky famously put into the mouth of Ivan Karamazov in a passage frequently quoted in these discussions. After recounting terrible stories of tortured children, Ivan says that no future good, however great, could justify such evil: 'too high a price is asked for such harmony; it's beyond our means to pay so much to enter on it. And so I hasten to give back my entrance ticket . . . It's not God that I don't accept, Aloysha, only I most respectfully return Him the ticket.'[8] Others might wish to argue that Dostoevsky's Ivan is wrong – that he seems 'more concerned that his cynicism be vindicated than that the innocent be redeemed'[9] – but it is difficult to know how we, with our limited, biased and distorted scales of value, could even begin to answer that question. Perhaps only an all-knowing God, who loves every part of the creation as 'very good', can. Most writers who wish to claim that the good of creation is ultimately

---

7 For versions of the free-process defence, see, e.g., Peacocke, 'The Cost of New Life', esp. pp. 36–7, and Michael Ruse, *Can a Darwinian Be a Christian? The Relationship between Science and Religion*, Cambridge: Cambridge University Press, 2001, pp. 134–8. For a critical appraisal of such arguments, see Southgate, ' God and Evolutionary Evil', pp. 811–15.

8 Fyodor Dostoevsky, *The Brothers Karamazov* (trans. Constance Garnett, London: Heinemann, 1912), p. 251.

9 R. E. Creel, *Divine Impassibility*, Cambridge: Cambridge University Press, 1986, p. 151, quoted by Polkinghorne, *Science and Providence*, p. 64.

worth the suffering do indeed acknowledge the mystery and the impossibility of human beings making such a calculation with any confidence;
they also tend to argue in various ways that God chooses to be vulnerable to creation's suffering, that God suffers and struggles with the suffering creation, and that it is this suffering companionship of God with
the creation which will ultimately redeem the suffering.[10]

There is no denying the seriousness of the issue: the horrors not only
of the twentieth century, but also already of the twenty-first, present
repeated reminders of the evil of which human beings are capable; if that
evil is in part a product of our evolutionary history, no-one can be insen-
sitive to questions about the goodness, perhaps even the existence, of a
God who brought us to being by means of such a process. These questions represent for many perhaps the greatest stumbling block to faith.
And there is much to be welcomed in the answers that have been
proposed, particularly when they discern in the cross of Christ the revelation of God's solidarity with, and costly love for, the creation, and
the ultimate sign of hope that creation's suffering will be redeemed.

However, there is also a real danger in the way in which the question
is frequently put and addressed. The language of free-will and free-
process *defences* takes us straight to the law-court, with God as the
prisoner in the dock. It would be tempting for those on either side of the
argument to understand themselves either as prosecuting counsel, trying
to secure a conviction on charges of incompetence, impotence, indifference or malevolence, or as defence counsel trying to exonerate God of
those charges. But to set up the argument in this way, whichever side we
place ourselves on, would be an exercise in distancing ourselves from
God, judging God's goodness or badness in the abstract, in isolation
from a relationship of love and praise. As such it would perpetuate what
I have argued, following McFadyen, is a radically distorted dynamic,
one in which we withhold our personal energies from a relation of joy,
faith and worship to God, and direct them instead onto some other
object. The question of theodicy must be faced, but we must be very
careful about the manner in which we face it. Rather than imagining
ourselves to be either prosecuting or defending God, we might be better
advised to do our theodicy in something like the way in which it is done
by both Barth and P. T. Forsyth.

It might appear that Barth wants nothing to do with theodicy,
because to prevail upon God to justify Godself to us would be a par-

---

10 So, e.g., Polkinghorne, *Science and Providence*, pp. 63–8; Peacocke, 'The Cost of
New Life', pp. 35–42; Southgate, 'God and Evolutionary Evil', pp. 816–21.

ticularly egregious example of pride. Accordingly, those who have received the freedom of faith, even though they sin, suffer and experience the power of evil in the world, 'have no further need to study demonology, or to set up an independent doctrine *De peccato*, or to work out a theodicy'.[11] Certainly Barth has no time for an abstract discussion of theodicy, in isolation from God's self-revelation in Christ, but this does not mean that he must remain silent on the question of God's justice and justification. In the first part of his doctrine of reconciliation he argues with some care that 'in [the] work of the justification of unrighteous man God also and in the first instance justifies Himself'.[12] This is not, of course, because of any obligation – 'God does not owe anyone anything – least of all an account of the righteousness of what He does or does not do'[13] – but is God's free choice for our sakes. We need to know that the judgement of God and our justification in the death and resurrection of Jesus Christ have a 'meaning' for God as well as for us: 'if this relationship is only external for God, and does not mean anything to Him, or anything more than any other relationship . . . do I have an answer at all . . . to the question how am I to find a gracious God?'[14] And the meaning that we can discern in God's work is simply a vindication of what Barth calls the right of God. God's right as Creator is vindicated over against the invasion of the creation by evil and chaos; God's right as the one who has elected humanity to be God's covenant-partners is vindicated over against our transgression which seeks to refuse this election; and, in the resurrection, Jesus Christ is shown to be truly the Son of God whose death on the cross accomplished the reconciling work of

> the One who has loved and elected man from all eternity . . . [Christ's suffering and death] is revealed [by the resurrection] as the right of the One who in His grace does not will the death of a sinner, but that he should be converted and live; as the right of the One who in His wisdom knows the sickness of man but also the means to heal him; as the right of the One who in His omnipotence can give power to death, but in order to set for it a positive goal, in order to limit and overcome it and to take away its power from it.[15]

---

11 Barth, *Church Dogmatics* (hereafter *CD*), IV.2, p. 245.
12 *CD* IV.1, pp. 559–68; quotation at p. 561.
13 *CD* IV.1, p. 567.
14 *CD* IV.1, p. 560.
15 *CD* IV.1, p. 566.

In the light of this freely willed self-justification of God in and through Christ's reconciling work, Barth concludes that 'we are well advised to let drop this anxious questioning of Him and instead to ask ourselves what use we are going to make of the freedom which He obviously willed to give us'[16] – a conclusion that, in the light of the foregoing discussion, is not to be read as an authoritarian closing down of the question of God's goodness, but as pointing us towards the place where we can receive the best possible assurance of God's goodness.

Like Barth, P. T. Forsyth, working out a theodicy in response to the catastrophe of the First World War,[17] refuses to engage in abstract speculations. Instead, as Colin Gunton puts it, he 'argues for the justice of God . . . by showing how God deals with evil historically and in practice'.[18] This means that Forsyth's account of the justice of God, like Barth's, is centred resolutely on the cross of Christ. Intriguingly, Forsyth also directly addresses the question of evolutionary suffering (in the broader sense characterized by Southgate), strikingly anticipating some of the themes that are to be found in more recent evolutionary theodicies:

There is an Eye, a Mind, a Heart, before Whom the whole bloody and tortured stream of evolutionary growth has flowed . . . And in the full view of it He has spoken. As it might be thus: 'Do you stumble at the cost? It has cost Me more than you – Me who see and feel it all more than you who feel it but as atoms might . . . For it cost Me My only and beloved Son to justify My name of righteousness, and to realise the destiny of My creature in holy love. And all mankind is not so great and dear as He. Nor is its suffering the enormity in a moral world that His Cross is. I am no spectator of the course of things, and no speculator on the result. I spared not My own Son. We carried the load that crushes you. It bowed Him into the ground. On the third day He rose with a new creation in His hand, and a regenerate world, and all things working together for good to love and the holy purpose in love. And what He did I did. How I did it? How I do it? This you know not now, and could not, but you shall know hereafter . . . In that day the anguish will be forgotten for joy that a New Humanity is born into the world.[19]

---

16 *CD* IV.1, p. 568.
17 P. T. Forsyth, *The Justification of God: Lectures for War-time on a Christian Theodicy*, 2nd edn, London: Latimer House, 1948 (1916).
18 Colin E. Gunton, *The Actuality of Atonement: A Study of Metaphor, Rationality and the Christian Tradition*, Edinburgh: T&T Clark, p. 106.
19 Forsyth, *Justification*, pp. 164–5.

In this remarkable passage, Forsyth shows himself sensitive to the pain and cost of evolution for the whole creation, not just for humankind, though he does seem to make the suggestion, criticized by Southgate and others, that the justification of the whole creation's suffering will be found in the fulfilment of humankind's destiny. That criticism notwithstanding, he appears to anticipate three, if not four, of Southgate's proposals for an evolutionary theodicy: the latter's ontological claim 'that it was God who created and continues to sustain both the matter and the natural processes of the universe', his teleological claim 'that human beings' freely chosen response to the grace of God is a principal goal of God in creation', his kenotic claim 'that God suffers with God's creation through self-emptying love, of which Christ's Cross is indicative',[20] and the first of his soteriological claims, that 'God does not abandon the victims of evolution'.[21] Forsyth shows that if we begin, not from abstract metaphysical speculation, but from God's concrete action in the world in the life, death and resurrection of Jesus Christ, there is every reason to make claims along these lines about the justice and goodness of God. Accordingly, I am also sympathetic to the second of Southgate's soteriological claims, that 'humans have a calling, stemming from the transformative power of Christ's action on the Cross, to participate in the healing of the world'.[22] I shall return to this claim in the next chapter.

In respect of the narrower question about the goodness of God in the light of the apparent evolutionary contribution to human sinfulness, I remarked earlier that while it seems plausible that there was no other way to create beings like us than by means of a risky process of evolution, we cannot know this for certain. To affirm belief in God as Creator of 'all that is, seen and unseen' is to say at any rate that the kind of world that God has in fact created, and called 'very good', is a world that has given rise to humans by such a process. If we wish to know about the goodness of God, however, we must look to the life, death and resurrection of Jesus Christ, in which God has acted decisively to deal with human sinfulness, and in which God promises the hope of our ultimate healing and transformation, together with that of the whole created order.

---

20 Forsyth would, though, say much more than 'indicative'. In this connection, his strongly 'kenotic' Christology should be noted: see, e.g., *The Person and Place of Jesus Christ*, London: Hodder and Stoughton, 1909, pp. 293–320.

21 Southgate, 'God and Evolutionary Evil', p. 817.

22 'God and Evolutionary Evil', p. 817.

2 Transformed relationships and the redemption of our bodies

Hitherto in this chapter and the last, while I have sought to keep the discussions of salvation and sin integrated, and to let the understanding of sin that I have been developing be consistently shaped by an understanding of salvation, the accent has at times been more on sin than on salvation. In the final two sections, I shall attempt to redress that balance somewhat by giving a more explicit account of the effect of God's saving work, and by glancing in the direction of the future hope promised by this work.

If sin is understood as fundamentally a distortion of our relationship with God, and derivatively of our relations with one another, ourselves and the created order, that implies what I have already suggested at various points: that God's saving work, in the light of which we understand sin, must be understood as a fundamental reshaping of those relationships. This is not, of course, to be understood merely as a restoration to the way they were 'in the beginning', 'before' everything went wrong. It has already become clear, both through Barth's reading of the Fall narrative and from an evolutionary understanding of human origins, that there is no past golden age to which we can look back with longing, and to which we could be restored. Rather, the healing of our distorted relations must be understood as a *transformation*, directed not to a restoration of the past, but to the future and to the ultimate fulfilment of God's good purposes for humans and the whole created order.

In his study of salvation, David Ford depicts various aspects of this salvific transformation of selves and their relations through the key metaphor of 'facing'.[23] To take just one of his examples: the letter to the Ephesians describes the 'transformative communication' made possible by God's saving work in Christ;[24] indeed, it not only describes that communication but exemplifies it, being itself an act of transformative communication characterized by an extraordinary richness and extravagance of language. The saving work of Christ creates a community of new selves, new because of their new location 'in Christ'. 'In Christ', old boundaries are radically transformed, and barriers such as that between Jews and Gentiles broken down (Eph. 2.11–22). The selves reconstituted in this new community are 'singing selves' who, being 'filled with

---

23 David F. Ford, *Self and Salvation: Being Transformed*, Cambridge: Cambridge University Press, 1999.

24 Ford, *Self and Salvation*, pp. 107–36; on 'transformative communication', see esp. pp. 108–10.

the Spirit', are to '[address] one another in psalms, hymns and spiritual songs, singing and making melody to the Lord in [their] hearts' (5.18–19).[25] This transformation, worked by the Spirit, has the potential to heal the idolatry which McFadyen identifies as the distortion at the heart of sin, by orienting us toward God in true worship. But the Ephesians are also enjoined to address *one another* in their singing, and Ford shows how this music-making has the power to transfigure everyday human relationships within the community. For example, it can foster a kind of 'being subject to one another' (5.21) without domination that, if seriously practised, could completely transform all kinds of social relationships.[26]

This transformation has the potential to affect not only face-to-face relationships and communities but also political structures and institutions. The picture of the renewed community painted in Ephesians is of one in which the irreducibly necessary minimum standard of justice for all can be discerned and practised, while also being supplemented, stretched and challenged by the 'superabundance' of love.[27] Furthermore, the virtues that can be collectively described under the heading of 'gentleness' have the potential to transfigure our understandings of power, authority and strength, and to call into question the assumption that coercive force is essential for the survival of just institutions: 'The challenge of Ephesians . . . is not just to strive for Ricoeur's supplementary compassion and generosity but to try and make them constitutive.'[28]

Elsewhere in his essay, Ford draws attention to Bonhoeffer's remarks about the 'view from below': during the years of Nazi rule, Bonhoeffer says,

> We have for once learnt to see the great events of world history from below, from the perspective of the outcast, the suspects, the maltreated, the powerless, the oppressed, the reviled – in short, from the

---

25 *Self and Salvation*, pp. 120–9.

26 *Self and Salvation*, pp. 122–5. In the Ephesian context, the implications of this for relations between husbands and wives, parents and children and masters and slaves are spelled out in 5.22–6.9.

27 *Self and Salvation*, pp. 133–5, drawing on Paul Ricoeur's concept of 'the "good life", with and for others, in just institutions': *Oneself as Another*, Chicago, IL: University of Chicago Press, 1992, p. 172.

28 *Self and Salvation*, pp. 132–3, 135–6; quotation at p. 136. Ford develops these thoughts in response to the suspicion that the dynamics of the community might lend themselves to abuse, particularly in the form of triumphalism, domination and the suppression of difference; I shall briefly return to this question in the next section.

perspective of those who suffer . . . We have to learn that personal suffering is a more effective key, a more rewarding principle for exploring the world in thought and action than personal good fortune.[29]

There are strong and obvious resonances between this and the hermeneutical claim of liberation theology that the perspective of the oppressed, not that of the powerful, is the one from which the Scriptures should be interpreted, the world understood and action directed. The transformation that God works in human lives, relationships and communities includes a radical inversion of hierarchies, power structures and status, with equally radical implications both for the way in which we interpret the world and for the way in which we order our life within it. Thus, for example, if McFadyen is right about the pervasive structural distortions highlighted by feminist theologies of sin, what is called for is a radical reorientation that transforms our perceptions of reality, our place in it, the interpersonal relations, the social structures and the cultural dynamics all of which contribute to our socialization as men and women. The Church, for all that it has too often been part of the problem rather than part of the solution, is called to live as a community that embodies and bears witness to this transformation, in ways that also have the potential to challenge and change the wider society within which it is located.[30]

In drawing this thumbnail sketch of what salvation might mean in terms of transformed relationships, I have borrowed heavily from David Ford. Ford himself, though, expresses significant reservations about this language of relationship, describing it as 'perhaps the main contemporary over-emphasis'; reflecting on the dead face of Jesus on the cross, he remarks that

It is only in a peculiar sense that one can talk of a dead face being 'in relationship' with others. If this dead face of Jesus is intrinsic to salvation, then there is needed a radical critique of concepts of salvation which major on ideas of mutuality, reciprocity, interpersonal

---

29 Dietrich Bonhoeffer, *Letters and Papers from Prison*, enlarged edn, ed. Eberhard Bethge, trans. Reginald Fuller *et al.*, London: SCM Press, 1971, p. 17. Ford uses this passage as an interpretative key to understanding Bonhoeffer's prison writings, particularly his reflections on the Christian vocation to live responsibly before God in a world come of age: *Self and Salvation*, pp. 253–9.

30 See, further, e.g., Amy Laura Hall, 'Naming the Risen Lord: Embodied Discipleship and Masculinity', in Stanley Hauerwas and Samuel Wells, eds., *The Blackwell Companion to Christian Ethics*, Oxford: Blackwell, 2004, pp. 82–94.

consciousness or communication, including 'facing' [his own key metaphor].[31]

If it is possible once again to be in relationship with this Jesus who died on the cross, it is only because of God's astonishing act of raising him from the dead, a 'God-sized event . . . than which none better or greater could be conceived'.[32] Crucially, Jesus' resurrection does not set aside or make light of his death: the heavenly worship in the book of Revelation, for example, is of 'the Lamb that was slaughtered' (e.g. Rev. 5.11), who was dead and is alive for ever and ever (1.18). It is to him, the one who both died and has been raised, that the true, anti-idolatrous worship of the transformed community is directed.

There might be a point of contact here with the critical appropriation of evolutionary insights that I have attempted in this chapter and the last. Perhaps part of the difficulty with describing both fallenness and salvation purely in 'relational' terms is that such talk lends itself too easily to domestication: part of its appeal, to those who have been formed by a modern scientific culture, is that it seems to offer an understandable, comfortably non-miraculous way of thinking about sin and salvation. It is much harder to find comfortably non-miraculous ways of speaking about the hope of the redemption of our bodies and the liberation of the creation from its bondage to decay (Rom. 8.18–24). Yet I have already canvassed the suggestion that there might be a biological aspect to our fallenness: that our evolutionary history might have bequeathed to us both a tendency to certain forms of distorted relationship and part of the condition of original sin, understood as human nature *sicut deus* ('like God' in the sense promised by the serpent in Genesis 3). Furthermore, the evolutionary theodicies to which I referred briefly in the last section draw attention to the suffering and struggle of the non-human creation, and many of them appeal explicitly to the promise of creation's liberation in Romans 8. In short, if our talk of salvation does not include the hope that the material creation (including our own bodies) will be transformed in ways most likely beyond our scientific imagination, then we run the risk that our theological and ethical vision will become disembodied and thereby distorted. This hope of ultimate transformation is, of course, an eschatological promise, and in the final section of this chapter I shall make a few suggestions as to the relevance of this eschatological hope to our living here and now in response to God's saving activity.

31 Ford, *Self and Salvation*, p. 205.
32 *Self and Salvation*, pp. 210–11.

3   Ultimate hope and penultimate responsibility

a   The ultimate and the penultimate

God's saving activity in the world is utterly and startlingly *new*, yet also related in complex ways to everyday human existence. The newness is at least in part a consequence of the seriousness of our need and the radical nature of God's way of meeting that need. P. T. Forsyth brings this out strikingly when he says that God's reconciling work 'does not come in to grout the gaps in nature, not simply to bless nature, but to change it, to make a new earth from a foundation in a new heaven'.[33] Bonhoeffer, in another fragment of his *Ethics*,[34] describes God's saving work as the 'ultimate': God's final word to us in Christ, which brings us justification and new life. The ultimate 'involves a complete break with all that has gone before'; it is God's 'judgement on the penultimate ways and things' by which we seek to save ourselves and justify ourselves before God.[35]

Yet for Bonhoeffer, that is not all there is to say. The ultimate also 'holds open a certain space for the penultimate',[36] because the latter is the realm through which people must pass before they can hear God's justifying word. This means that 'the penultimate must be preserved for the sake of the ultimate'.[37] Penultimate activities like feeding the hungry, housing the homeless and building just and ordered social structures are not ultimate activities – they do not themselves bring God's justifying word to people – but they can serve to *prepare the way* for the coming of that word. The ultimate and the penultimate are thus held together in a subtle and complex relation. Bonhoeffer rejects two 'extreme' ways of relating them: the 'radical solution', which would utterly do away with everything penultimate in the face of Christ's coming, and the 'compromise', in which the penultimate 'retains its inherent rights' while the ultimate 'stays completely beyond daily life and in the end serves only as the eternal justification of all that exists'.[38] The radical 'cannot forgive God for having created what is' and consciously or unconsciously hates the creation; compromise springs from 'animosity against the justifica-

---

33 Forsyth, *Justification*, p. 79.

34 Dietrich Bonhoeffer, *Ethics* (*Dietrich Bonhoeffer Works*, vol. 6), ET ed. Clifford J. Green, Minneapolis, MN: Fortress, 2005, pp. 146–70.

35 *Ethics*, pp. 149, 150.

36 *Ethics*, p. 159.

37 *Ethics*, p. 160.

38 *Ethics*, pp. 153, 154.

tion of the sinner by grace alone' and seeks to protect 'the world, and life in it . . . from this invasion into its domain'.[39] Both are 'opposed to Christ . . . [the] relationship between the ultimate and the penultimate is resolved only in [him]' – a resolution summed up thus:

> In Jesus Christ we believe in the God who became human, was crucified, and is risen. In the becoming human we recognize God's love towards God's creation, in the crucifixion God's judgment on all flesh, and in the resurrection God's purpose for a new world. Nothing could be more perverse than to tear these three apart, because the whole is contained in each of them . . . A Christian ethic built only on the incarnation would lead easily to the compromise solution; an ethic built only on the crucifixion or only on the resurrection of Jesus Christ would fall into radicalism and enthusiasm. The conflict is resolved only in their unity.[40]

In connection with the penultimate, Bonhoeffer is prepared to pay serious attention to the 'natural', which he understands as 'that form of life preserved by God for the fallen world that is directed towards justification, salvation and renewal through Christ'.[41] As such, the notion of the natural must be differentiated from talk both of the creaturely (which does not take account of the Fall) and of the sinful (which does not take account of the creaturely). It is a penultimate category, validated by its relation to the coming of Christ, and as such is opposed to the 'unnatural': 'that which, after the Fall, closes itself off from the coming of Jesus Christ'.[42] This allows an important place for human reason: while formally the natural 'can only be recognized by looking at Jesus Christ', in terms of content, 'human "reason" is the organ for recognizing the natural'.[43] On this basis, Bonhoeffer sets up an account of natural rights, which he uses as a framework for the discussion of a number of concrete ethical issues, particularly those to do with the right to life, the protection of the body, marriage and reproduction.[44]

---

39 *Ethics*, pp. 155, 156.

40 *Ethics*, p. 157.

41 *Ethics*, p. 174.

42 *Ethics*, p. 173. Bonhoeffer is critical of his own Lutheran tradition for focusing so much on the 'ultimate' of justification by faith in Christ that it neglected the this-worldly task of discriminating between the natural and the unnatural, a task which, as Ford comments, was made urgent for Bonhoeffer by 'the Nazi assault on ordinary goodness': Ford, *Self and Salvation*, pp. 246–7.

43 Bonhoeffer, *Ethics*, p. 174.

44 *Ethics*, pp. 178–218. The concrete issues discussed include suicide, euthanasia, capital punishment, torture, legal restrictions on marriage, sterilization and contracep-

All of this might seem to be in some tension with his bold statement, quoted earlier, that the first task of Christian ethics is to invalidate the knowledge of good and evil.[45] However, it seems clear from the discussion as a whole that Bonhoeffer is not conceding *autonomy* to reason in any simple way: he emphasizes, in opposition to the Catholic theologian Josef Pieper, that 'the full scope of reason is understood as entangled in the fall',[46] and in his discussion of substantive issues it seems that the deliverances of reason are always subject to correction in the light of Christ.[47] Within these limits, though, reason receives a new validity as part of the penultimate. And this thought extends and qualifies the comments I made in the last chapter about the natural knowledge of right and wrong. There I suggested that (though it could have turned out differently) our natural knowledge of right and wrong has in fact turned out to be an aspect of human nature *sicut deus* and, as such, part of the condition of original sin. The role of Christian ethics, as Bonhoeffer says, is to invalidate such knowledge. But fallen human reason and knowledge are not only *invalidated* by the coming of Christ; they are also *re-validated* as part of the penultimate, existing now for the sake of the ultimate. Our natural knowledge of right and wrong, then, can be '[taken] captive to obey Christ' (2 Cor. 10.5), and can serve to prepare the way for his coming. In the next chapter I shall also suggest that at least some uses of science, technology and medicine can also be regarded as having penultimate roles, and that Bonhoeffer's category of the penultimate can help us to develop criteria for discriminating between right and wrong uses of these products of human reason.

b 'Already' and 'Not yet'

The tension between the ultimate and the penultimate, to which Bonhoeffer draws attention, is related to the familiar tension between the 'already' and the 'not yet' of the Christian eschatological hope. Barth explicates this in terms of the *parousia*, the coming of Christ: in his account, it is one event with three forms which, like the persons of

---

tion; as the editorial notes to these passages in *Ethics* 6 make clear, much of this discussion contains very thinly veiled criticism of the laws and practices of the Third Reich.

45 *Ethics*, p. 299.
46 *Ethics*, p. 175, n. 1.
47 E.g. in the discussion of euthanasia, where explicitly biblical and theological objections are deployed against 'the false presupposition that life consists only in its social utility', *Ethics*, p. 193.

the Trinity, must be distinguished but not separated.[48] The first is the resurrection of Jesus Christ; the second is the outpouring of the Spirit on his disciples and the third is his promised final return and the fulfilment of all things in him. Barth thus affirms that we are already, since Easter, living in the last days, and '[i]f we could see with God's eyes, we should realise that . . . everything is already very different, all things being made new and set aright'; but he is well aware that this reality is hidden from us: '[t]he only thing is that we cannot see in this way'.[49] Barth is acutely aware of the tension between the 'already' and the 'not yet', and thoroughly realistic about the present struggle and suffering of humans and the creation as a whole. He returns repeatedly to the question why there should be this interval between Christ's resurrection and his final return. Part of the answer is that this interval gives the creation the time and space to share actively in the fruits of God's reconciling work. To have brought this work to fulfilment without allowing such space and time would, as it were, have contradicted the internal logic of election, reconciliation and covenant by making the world's free response to God impossible: in Barth's striking metaphor, 'showing to the world and men only the kind of lop-sided favour which European nations used to exercise without consulting them to the peoples of their colonies'.[50] Another part of the answer is, without forgetting the 'provoking and even dreadful riddle' of the world's struggle and suffering, to draw attention to the 'bright and luminous side' of the riddle: that, in the second form of the *parousia*, the outpouring of the Spirit, no less than in Christ's resurrection or final return, God's glory is made known.[51]

The promise of Christ's final return and the fulfilment of all things relativizes, yet also mandates, human action in the world to exercise responsible care for one another, ourselves and those parts of the non-human creation that are within our reach. The eschatological hope frees us, as Allen Verhey put it, from 'the crushing burden of messianic pretensions'.[52] We cannot and need not perfect or save the world by our

---

48 Barth, *CD* IV.3, pp. 290–367.

49 *CD* IV.3, p. 317.

50 *CD* IV.3, pp. 331–3; quotation at p. 333.

51 *CD* IV.3, pp. 360–2; quotations at p. 360. The manner in which Barth puts this point, '*Supposing* that the great regime of the transition which characterises the "still" and "not yet" . . . is not at all negative as His regime . . . but a specific form of the pitying love of God . . .?' (pp. 360–1, emphasis added) suggests that what he believes is needed in response to the question is, in effect, a transformation of our Christian and theological imagination.

52 Allen Verhey, *Reading the Bible in the Strange World of Medicine*, Grand Rapids: Eerdmans, 2003, p. 140.

own efforts; this 'ultimate' work is God's, not ours. But it leaves us the 'penultimate' responsibility of acting in the world so as to 'shape the future',[53] or to improve the world and the conditions of human life in it. Not to do so would be a refusal of our vocation and a betrayal of our responsibility that would perpetuate the distortion of our relations with God, one another and the world. Moral and theological discernment, however, is required between different kinds of action in the world. Truly 'responsible' action (to borrow one of Bonhoeffer's key terms) will not only be satisfied with penultimate, rather than ultimate, tasks, but will also, within this penultimate sphere, be characterized by its conformity to the shape of God's saving activity.[54]

c   A cosmic and universal hope

These reflections about the human responsibility to act in the world in the light of God's promised future lead to my final point about the saving work of God: that this work is cosmic and universal in its scope. The closing vision of the book of Revelation is of 'a new heaven and a new earth' (21.1); Paul looks forward to the liberation of the creation 'from its bondage to decay' (Rom. 8.21); and I am working on the assumption, shared by the authors on whom I have drawn,[55] that Christ's atoning death was for all people.

But the affirmation that God's saving work in and through Christ is cosmic and universal in its scope can seem a scandalous thing to say in a pluralist world, as David Ford is keenly aware: 'Of contemporary issues of exclusion, one of the most sensitive for Christians is that of other religions ... What does it mean to realise that those of other faiths (and none) are before the face of Christ?'[56] Though, as he acknowledges, Ford does not address this question comprehensively in his essay on salvation, there are at various points in that essay indications of how Christians might speak of Christ's universal significance in ways that are not triumphalist, coercive or totalitarian. For example, in his discussion of Ephesians, he acknowledges that the letter could be read as supporting Christian triumphalism and imperialism, particularly with reference

---

53 The phrase is that of James H. Burtness, *Shaping the Future: The Ethics of Dietrich Bonhoeffer*, Philadelphia, PA: Fortress, 1985.

54 Cf. the fragment 'Ethics as Formation', in Bonhoeffer, *Ethics*, pp. 76–102, esp. pp. 92–9.

55 Though it has not, of course, been shared by all strands of my own Reformed tradition.

56 Ford, *Self and Salvation*, p. 270.

to the relations of Christians and Jews. Yet, he argues, the whole tenor of its ethics, Christology and ecclesiology is against such readings. The community's ethic is to be fundamentally non-coercive in character; a communal identity shaped by the letter's Christology will be character-ized by suffering, not coercive, witness, openness to 'radical reconcep-tions of [its] boundaries' and the awareness that it has no 'overview' of the extent or character of Christ's love; and the letter's 'high' eccle-siology implies that judgement (particularly in respect of its use of power and its manner of communication) begins, not with the world, but with the household of God.[57] There is here more than might initially be thought in common with Barth, who demonstrates that it is possible to combine even a robust insistence that 'Jesus Christ is the one and only Word of God, that He alone is the light of God and the revelation of God' with the ready acknowledgement that there may be all kinds of other true 'words, lights, revelations, prophecies and apostolates' in the world 'outside the circle of the Bible and the Church'.[58] The point is that for Barth it is *Jesus Christ* who is the one Word of God, and the Church has no monopoly (or, as Ford would say, 'overview') of the ways in which this Word is made known in the world.[59]

Another implication of the cosmic scope of God's saving work is that there cannot be some area of human life which has its own autonomous existence, independent of the life, death and resurrection of Christ. Opposing forms of Christian thought which divide 'the whole of reality into sacred and profane', Bonhoeffer puts it like this:

> There are not two realities, but *only one reality*, and that is God's reality revealed in Christ in the reality of the world . . . The world has no reality of its own independent of God's revelation in Christ. It is a denial of God's revelation in Jesus Christ to wish to be 'Christian' without being 'worldly' or [to] wish to be worldly without seeing and recognizing the world in Christ.[60]

---

57 *Self and Salvation*, pp. 130–3; quotation at p. 133.

58 Barth, *CD* IV.3, pp. 86–165; quotations at p. 97.

59 See, further, J. Augustine Di Noia, OP, 'Religion and the Religions', in John Webster (ed.), *The Cambridge Companion to Karl Barth*, Cambridge: Cambridge University Press, 2000, pp. 243–57. Di Noia argues that a careful reading of the relevant sections of the *Dogmatics* refutes the charge of simple exclusivism frequently levelled at Barth. He also points out that Barth's writing on religion and the religions predates the emergence of the theology of religions as a sub-discipline. This means, first, that Barth's treatment of 'religion' is in some ways still shaped by his nineteenth-century liberal Protestant antecedents, and, secondly, that he nowhere offers a compre-hensive 'theology of religions', for all that he has important and suggestive things to say.

60 Bonhoeffer, *Ethics*, pp. 57–8.

In other words, there is no aspect of the world or of human life that is in principle untouched by God's saving activity in Christ; Christians are committed to the attempt to re-envision every aspect of the world and human existence through the lens of Christ. In the next chapter I shall argue that this claim commits Christians in principle to the attempt to evaluate every form of human action in the world (including scientific, technological and medical activity) in terms of its conformity to the shape of God's saving work: genuinely 'penultimate' activity is that which is oriented towards the 'ultimate'.

To affirm the cosmic and universal scope of God's saving work in Christ, though, would appear to invite two further related objections that we might call the 'Alpha Centauri question' and the 'Triassic question'. By the first of these I mean that almost all of the universe as we know it is unimaginably remote from human life on planet earth, and would seem to be entirely untouched by human sin. In what sense, if any, can it be described either as fallen or as redeemed by the divine–human life, death and resurrection of Jesus Christ? The 'Triassic question' is the temporal counterpart of the 'Alpha Centauri question': on the timescale of biological evolution, the whole of human history, including the appearance of Jesus Christ, is the merest twinkling of an eye. In what sense, if any, can we speak of the saving work of Christ as having any relevance to the vast tracts of evolutionary time that passed and the myriads of species that appeared and vanished before humans ever made their entrance? Of course, it is hardly a new insight that there is much more to creation than that with which humans, and human salvation history, have to do (cf. Job 38–41), but the questions are posed particularly sharply by modern cosmology and evolutionary biology.

There is a danger that an attempt to answer these questions might become an exercise in sheer speculation, more or less free of anchorage in any reliable source of knowledge. It seems to me that one should be very modest in what one attempts to say about such questions; but with due modesty, there are a few things which can and should be said. First, we have no warrant to think that God's care is in any way limited, spatially or temporally, to part of the creation. To say that God is the Creator (which, of course, also means the sustainer) of 'all that is, seen and unseen', and to take seriously the text 'God saw everything that he had made, and it was very good' (Gen. 1.31), is to be committed to affirming God's creative and sustaining love for all the created universe. Furthermore, the God of whom we affirm this is 'the *triune* Creator', as biblical texts and strands of tradition emphasizing the roles of the Son (e.g. John 1.3; Col. 1.15–20) and the Spirit (e.g. Gen. 1.2; Ps. 104.29,

30; and, if the Spirit is to be identified with Wisdom, Prov. 8.22–31) remind us.[61] So we can say that God, in Christ and by the Spirit, shows continual love and care for the whole created universe, though the ways in which the love of God is expressed and practised in respect of almost all of it are bound to be quite beyond our imagining.

Secondly, within the sphere that we can know about through Jesus Christ, it would seem that the scope of God's saving work extends beyond the salvation of humankind to the non-human creation. From this we can infer that in some sense the non-human creation needs saving, whether because it is directly affected by human sin (as the bio-sphere of planet earth is, in obvious and serious ways) or because in some other way it is 'fallen', flawed or diverted from God's good purposes for it. Thus Paul can write that the creation is 'subjected to futility' and that the saving work of God centred in Christ extends to the liberation of creation from its 'bondage to decay' (Rom. 8.18–24). Again, consider-able reticence is in order as to the nature of this futility and the manner of this liberation: there is a great deal that we do not, and perhaps cannot, know, and that may be God's concern but none of ours.

Thirdly, however, we certainly have a responsibility to God in respect of those parts of the creation – non-human as well as human – that are within our reach, expressed for example by the commands to 'have dominion' over the created world and to 'till it and keep it' (Gen. 1.28; 2.15). The nature, scope and detailed shape of this responsibility in respect of the non-human creation is, of course, debated at length.[62] In the next chapter I shall propose some theological criteria by which to judge human action in the world, and these may suggest some of the outlines of our responsibility. One general suggestion that is often canvassed, however, is that humans are called to have some kind of 'priestly' role in respect of the creation, '[offering] up to God in articu-lated form that creaturely praise which our self-centred acquisitiveness makes it so hard for us to hear . . . [and also offering] up to God the creaturely pain that goes with the praise'.[63] With the caveat, suggested by my earlier reference to Job 38–41, that there seem to be large parts of

---

61 Colin E. Gunton, *The Triune Creator: A Historical and Systematic Study*, Grand Rapids, MI: Eerdmans, 1998, pp. 14–24, who argues for a trinitarian reading of Old Testament texts such as Gen. 1.2 in the light of later, Christian, tradition. On the identification of Wisdom and the Spirit, see Celia Deane-Drummond, *Creation through Wisdom: Theology and the New Biology*, Edinburgh: T&T Clark, 2000, pp. 121–4.

62 For a valuable recent survey, see Celia Deane-Drummond, *The Ethics of Nature*, Oxford: Blackwell, 2004.

63 Southgate, 'God and Evolutionary Evil', p. 817.

the creation that do a good job of praising God without any help from humans, there is every reason to agree with this description of the human vocation in respect of creation. In the context of his evolutionary theodicy, Southgate goes on to sketch out some implications of this priestly role in relation to human action in the world, and, again, I shall revisit some of his proposals in the next chapter.

In this chapter and the last, I have sought to show how a theological account of salvation and sin can offer a broader and more helpful framework for thinking about human wickedness than the frameworks within which the latter is commonly considered. Thus the rather tangled question, 'Does our biological inheritance inhibit us from living as we should?', can be addressed by an account of original sin which includes the darker side of our evolutionary inheritance, but places it within a much broader framework in which sin is understood as the distortion of our relationships with God, one another, ourselves and the created order. Within this account, the problem of biological determinism and free will can be reframed by holding that true freedom does not consist in the exercise of unconstrained choice, but in the orientation of our willing and desiring onto its proper object, God, and that, under the conditions of sin, our willing, whether we have much power or little, is not obliterated, but co-opted and diverted to pathological ends. The problem of moral responsibility for behaviours that may be partly biologically determined is also helpfully reshaped by recalling that this account does not restrict sin-talk to a moral frame of reference, narrowly understood, but uses a much broader frame; thus it is possible to speak of a shared, even inherited, solidarity in sin for which we cannot be held to blame. But all this talk of sin is only the shadow of our understanding of God's saving work, centred on the life, death and resurrection of Christ, which decisively reshapes our distorted relationship with God, makes possible the transformation of our human and this-worldly relationships and places before us the hope of the redemption of our bodies and the liberation of the creation. At various points in the chapter, the question has arisen of the implications of this saving work of God and our promised future hope for human action in the world here and now. It is to that question that I shall turn in the next chapter.

9

Working Out Our Own Salvation?

1 Medicine, technology and the Baconian project

In previous chapters, I have tried to articulate a Christian doctrine of salvation and sin that places talk of sin in a far broader frame of reference than the narrowly moral, and have discussed the possible relevance of insights about our evolutionary history to that account of sin. The pervasively destructive consequences of human sin for both human and non-human life on earth hardly need spelling out. To point to a few examples relevant in various ways to the argument of this chapter: individuals bring ill-health upon themselves in many ways by their actions and life-orientations;[1] far more widespread ill-health is the consequence of what liberation theologians call 'structural sin' – economic, social and political injustice, both within wealthy nations and across the world;[2] the human exploitation of non-human animals – for instance, in intensive forms of farming, transportation and slaughter for meat – is responsible for a great deal of animal pain and suffering; in the coming

---

1 As I write these words, there is news of a campaign by the British Government to try and stem the massive increase in obesity in the UK, which brings many attendant health problems with it. The message that is being promoted is hardly startling: many people could reduce their weight by eating less, particularly less sugary and fatty food, and exercising more. See Anon., '"Minister for Fitness" Appointed', BBC News, 23 August 2006, online at http://news.bbc.co.uk/go/pr/fr/-/1/hi/health/5277350.stm (accessed 24 August 2006).

2 For a recent report on health inequalities in Europe, see Johan P. Mackenbach, *Health Inequalities: Europe in Profile* (an independent, expert report commissioned by the UK Presidency of the EU, February 2006), online at http://ec.europa.eu/health/ph_determinants/socio_economics/documents/ev_060302_rd06_en.pdf (accessed 24 August 2006). For the international picture, see the annual *World Health Reports* of the World Health Organization, beginning with *The World Health Report 1995: Bridging the Gaps*, Geneva: World Health Organization, 1995; all the reports are online at http://www.who.int/whr/en/ (accessed 24 August 2006). It is also true that individuals' choices and actions damaging to their own health may be determined, at least in part, by various kinds of wrong or harm that those individuals have suffered, either from other individuals or from oppressive social structures. There are points of contact here with Alistair McFadyen's analysis of victims' willing and choosing, discussed in Chapter 7.

century, ecological damage attributable to human activity threatens to cause an enormous amount of suffering and death, which is likely to affect the world's poorest populations disproportionately.[3] And much more human and non-human suffering seems to come into the category of 'natural evil': disease that is apparently not in any direct way a product of patients' or others' behaviour, natural disasters that do not appear to have a human cause, and, as writers on evolutionary theodicy observe, pain, death and extinction that seem to be intrinsic to the evolution of life on earth.

In the face of this picture, various questions arise about human action in the world in an attempt to avert or ameliorate the damage done by these various forms of sin and evil. There are questions about what is possible: what kinds of change for the better are we, or are we not, capable of achieving, either in principle or in practice? There are also questions about what is morally acceptable. Are there any limits to the extent of the change we ought to try to achieve? Are there any kinds of change that we should not attempt? What means, if any, should we not use even in order to bring about good ends? There are, of course, countless ways in which humans try to change the world that they live in. In this chapter, I shall concentrate on the use of science and technology – in particular, technologies arising from the biological and medical sciences – to try and address the various forms of sin and evil sketched out in the last paragraph. I shall focus on three areas of technology in particular, either that are used in an effort to improve the world and the conditions of human life in it or whose use to those ends has been the subject of speculation. One caveat is in order: some of the uses of technology that I shall outline are already technically possible, and in some cases almost routine. Others are not yet technically possible, but there is good reason to think that sooner or later they will be. Still others are much more remote possibilities, and in some cases there may be good reasons to think that they will never be feasible (though, of course, it can be hazardous to say 'never' with complete confidence). I shall try to make clear which is which, and I hope that I shall not be responsible for sowing any confusion or alarm about 'what the scientists are about to do to us'. But it is worth thinking about even the more remote possibilities by way of thought-experiments, since they might help clarify theological and ethical insights which can also shed light on more proximate possibilities.

---

3 See, e.g., John McGhie *et al.*, *The Climate of Poverty: Facts, Fears and Hope. A Christian Aid Report*, London: Christian Aid, 2006, online at http://www. christian-aid.org.uk/indepth/605caweek/index.htm (accessed 24 August 2006).

a Human genetic modification

The array of techniques now available for manipulating DNA, coupled with the understanding of human genetics offered by the sequencing of the human genome, opens up the prospect of both somatic cell and germ line genetic manipulation of human beings for a variety of purposes.[4] At the modest end are somatic cell therapies for disorders caused by lesions in single genes, such as cystic fibrosis, Duchenne muscular dystrophy, beta-thalassaemia and so on. There have been experimental attempts at such therapies since the beginning of the 1990s, though so far with relatively little success. It is sometimes suggested that the rational design of drug therapies for these diseases, based on the understanding of their genetic mechanisms, will prove a more effective therapeutic approach than gene therapy *per se*.[5] With the sequencing of the human genome, there is increasing interest in the genetic factors contributing to other, more common disorders such as various forms of cancer and heart disease; again, though, therapeutic benefits may come more from an improved understanding of the disease mechanisms, allowing better-tailored approaches to prevention and drug therapy, than from gene therapy *per se*. A more ambitious and distant prospect is germ line therapy (also known as inheritable genetic modification, or IGM), which would have the aim not only of treating genetic diseases in individual patients, but also of ensuring that they were not at risk of passing those diseases on to their children. In Britain, experimental somatic cell therapies are permitted under the oversight of a regulatory body,[6] but germ line therapy is illegal. British legislation is based on the recommendations of the Clothier Committee, which argued that the risk–benefit balance was acceptable for somatic cell therapy, but not for germ line therapy, whose potential effects would be much further-reaching,

---

4 Germ line cells are those directly involved in the production of gametes (eggs and sperm); those cells that are not (the vast majority of cells in the body) are collectively known as 'somatic' cells. Genetic modifications made only to somatic cells (for example, to the cells lining the lungs of a patient with cystic fibrosis) could not be passed on to that individual's children, whereas genetic changes made to his or her germ line cells could be. For helpful brief surveys of human genetic manipulation and related areas, see John Bryant and Peter Turnpenny, 'Genetics and Genetic Modification of Humans: Principles, Practice and Possibilities', and Mary J. Sellar, 'Genes, Genetics and the Human Genome: Some Personal Reflections', in Celia Deane-Drummond (ed.), *Brave New World? Theology, Ethics and the Human Genome*, London: T&T Clark, 2003, pp. 5–26 and 27–43 respectively.

5 Bryant and Turnpenny, 'Genetics and Genetic Modification of Humans', p. 19.

6 The Gene Therapy Advisory Committee: see http://www.advisorybodies.doh. gov.uk/genetics/gtac/ (accessed 24 August 2006).

and whose risks were correspondingly greater, less well understood and harder to manage.[7]

A more distant prospect still, and also illegal in Britain and many other countries, is the genetic *enhancement* of traits that are not associated with disease. Speculations about genetic enhancement range from modifying hair and eye colour to raising intelligence and musical ability.[8] At one end of the scale would be relatively simple modifications to bring about desired changes. For example, the World Anti-Doping Agency, which monitors illicit performance enhancement by athletes, has begun to fund research into tests for so-called 'gene doping'.[9] The concern is that attempts might be made to introduce genes for proteins such as insulin-like growth factor (IGF-1) into athletes' muscle tissues in an attempt to enhance muscle growth. At the other end of the scale is speculation that it might one day be possible to use genetic manipulation, possibly in combination with other technological means such as drugs, to modify complex behavioural and personality traits in order (for example) to give ourselves a greater capacity for sympathy and altruism, less of a tendency to violence and intolerance, and so on. Jonathan Glover, for example, wrote in the 1980s that

> we have a tribal psychology well adapted to survival in the Stone Age ... These aspects of our nature are not all entirely bad ... But, taken together, they have contributed to the catastrophes we all know. And now they threaten the survival of our species. If either environmental or genetic methods are available, we may be wise to change ourselves if we can.[10]

This strikingly echoes T. H. Huxley's hope that 'the intelligence which has converted the brother of the wolf into the faithful guardian of the flock ought to be able to do something towards curbing the instincts of savagery in civilized man'.[11] Professional biologists tend to express

---

7 Sir Cecil Clothier (chairman), *Report of the Committee on the Ethics of Human Genetic Manipulation*, London: Her Majesty's Stationery Office, 1992.

8 Typical speculations are summarized by Bryant and Turnpenny, 'Genetics and Genetic Modification of Humans', p. 21.

9 Anon., 'Tests to Find Gene Cheats', *New Scientist*, 11 December 2004, p. 4. See, further, the pages on gene doping on the World Anti-Doping Agency's website, at http://www.wada-ama.org/en/dynamic.ch2?pageCategory.id=526 (accessed 28 August 2006).

10 Jonathan Glover, *What Sort of People Should There Be? Genetic Engineering, Brain Control and Their Impact on Our Future World*, Harmondsworth: Pelican, 1984, pp. 183–4.

11 T. H. Huxley, 'Evolution and Ethics', in *Evolution and Ethics and Other Essays* (*Collected Essays*, vol. 9), London: Macmillan, 1894, pp. 46–116 (p. 85).

extreme scepticism about the feasibility of ever doing this kind of thing by genetic means, since the traits in question are multifactorial (influenced by many genetic and environmental factors). Even if all the relevant genetic factors could be identified, the task of introducing them into a fertilized egg, making them function properly and controlling the environmental influences with which they would interact may be too complex ever to be feasible.[12] Erik Parens remarks in this connection that

> it is difficult for those of us who think and speak about bioethical matters to strike a balance between responsibly contemplating theoretical possibilities like 'genetic enhancement' and responsibly conveying how little is currently understood about how such enhancements might be achieved.[13]

However, if genetic enhancement of behavioural and personality traits is a remote possibility, it might be the case that other areas of biomedical science, such as neuropharmacology, offer us a more immediate prospect of wide-ranging technological means to modify our own and other people's behaviour and personalities.[14] If nothing else, genetic enhancement might serve as a useful thought-experiment on which to test theological insights that could shed light on more complex and ambiguous technological developments closer to our own present reality.

b Human cloning and embryonic stem cell technology[15]

Ever since Ian Wilmut and his co-workers first succeeded in cloning an adult mammal (Dolly the sheep) by somatic cell nuclear transfer (SCNT) in 1997,[16] there has been fevered speculation about human reproduc-

---

12 So, e.g., Sellar, 'Genes, Genetics and the Human Genome', pp. 41–2. Note, however, that her final comment in this connection, 'Quite apart from all this, current legislation does not permit such a thing!', begs the question, since part of what is at issue is whether the legislation should ever be changed *in order* to permit it. For a very helpful brief survey of the relevant science, as well as its social and ethical implications, see also Erik Parens, 'Genetic Differences and Human Identities: On Why Talking about Behavioral Genetics Is Important and Difficult', *Hastings Center Report*, 34.1 (2004), pp. S1–S36.

13 Parens, 'Genetic Differences and Human Identities', p. S29.

14 See, e.g., Steven P. R. Rose, 'Neurogenetic Determinism and the New Euphenics', *British Medical Journal*, 317 (1998), pp. 1707–8.

15 This subsection is taken, with modifications, from Neil G. Messer, *The Ethics of Human Cloning*, Cambridge: Grove, 2001, pp. 6–8.

16 Ian Wilmut et al., 'Viable Offspring Derived from Foetal and Adult Mammalian Cells', *Nature*, 385 (1997), pp. 810–13.

tive cloning – that is, the use of the cloning technique to produce a new human individual genetically identical to an existing human being.[17] In conjunction with human embryonic stem cell (HESC) technology, it has also raised the possibility of a range of therapeutic and research applications, sometimes collectively referred to as 'therapeutic cloning'. These include the following:[18]

- If a patient needed a supply of cells or tissues for grafting (for example, to replace heart muscle, brain tissue or skin that has been damaged by accident or disease), a nucleus from one of her cells could be implanted into a donated egg cell to produce an embryo that could then be used as a source of stem cells. Animal research suggests that if stem cells are injected into a tissue or organ, they can become incorporated into it and function as a normal part of it.
- In a women carrying a mitochondrial disease, nuclear transfer technology could be used to create a hybrid egg cell containing a nucleus from one of her eggs but mitochondria from an unaffected donor, which could then be fertilized *in vitro*. This should be distinguished from the use of reproductive cloning to avoid mitochondrial disease (a possibility that has also been canvassed),[19] since, in the scenario considered here, the embryo would result from the fertilization of an egg by a sperm cell, as in normal conception.
- Cloning could be used to create human embryos for research into fertility and reproduction, the mechanisms underlying cancer, ageing and other areas; currently research on human embryos up to 14 days after fertilization is permissible in the UK under the terms of the Human Fertilisation and Embryology Act (1990).

Many of these applications would involve the creation of a human embryo to be used in research or as a source of cells. The end result of

---

17 Strictly speaking, the new individual would not be quite identical, since the small quantity of DNA located, not in the nuclei, but in the mitochondria of the clone's cells would not come from the donor of the nucleus (the 'original' of whom the clone would be a genetic copy) but from the egg cell into which the donated nucleus was transferred: see further Messer, *The Ethics of Human Cloning*, pp. 3–6.

18 See Human Genetics Advisory Commission / Human Fertilisation and Embryology Authority, *Cloning Issues in Reproduction, Science and Medicine*, London: HGAC, 1998; Nuffield Council on Bioethics, *Stem Cell Therapy: The Ethical Issues*, London: Nuffield Council, 2000; and Liam Donaldson (chair), *Stem Cell Research: Medical Progress with Responsibility*, London: Department of Health, 2000. Applications such as these depend on the fact that embryonic stem cells are *pluripotent*: that is, they have the potential to differentiate into any of the different types of cell found in the adult's body.

19 Messer, *The Ethics of Human Cloning*, pp. 5–6.

either would be the destruction of the embryo. It has been suggested that it may be possible to make pluripotent human stem cells directly from adult somatic cells without having to create embryos *en route*, drawing on the lessons learned from cloning. There is controversy as to how likely this is, and whether it could be done without some initial research on embryonic stem cells. The UK Chief Medical Officer's Expert Group took the view that research on embryonic stem cells would be necessary first, and recommended that this should be permitted by law.[20] Accordingly, early in 2001, the UK Parliament extended the provisions of the Human Fertilisation and Embryology Act to make such research possible.[21] At the time of writing, no scientists have succeeded in making human embryonic stem-cell lines by SCNT. Reports of success by a South Korean research group in 2004 and 2005 were subsequently retracted when they were found to be fraudulent, but the goal of producing stem cells by SCNT is still energetically pursued by many stem-cell biologists.[22]

c Genetically modified crops

In recent years there has been massive research and development investment in the genetic modification of plants for agricultural and other uses. Researchers in the field list a wide range of actual or potential applications of plant genetic manipulation, including the following:[23]

- Plants could be genetically modified to make them more tolerant of 'abiotic stresses' such as soil acidity, the presence of toxins such as aluminium in the soil, frost, drought and high salinity. Some of these forms of stress tolerance could make the crops more profitable to

---

20 Donaldson, *Stem Cell Research*, paras. 2.11–2.14, 5.10. There are also more recent reports suggesting that parthenogenetic blastocysts, made by treating unfertilized egg cells in a way that causes them to divide as if they have been fertilized, could also offer a source of pluripotent stem cells without the need to create and destroy embryos: see N. T. Rogers *et al.*, 'Phospholipase Cζ Causes Ca²⁺ Oscillations and Parthenogenetic Activation of Human Oocytes', *Reproduction*, 128 (2004), pp. 697–702.

21 *Hansard (House of Commons Daily Debates)*, 19 December 2000, col. 266; *Hansard (House of Lords Debates)*, 22 January 2001, col. 124. Human reproductive cloning remains illegal in the UK.

22 See Evan Y. Snyder and Jeanne F. Loring, 'Beyond Fraud – Stem-Cell Research Continues', *New England Journal of Medicine*, 354.4 (2006), pp. 321–4.

23 For what follows, see Donald Bruce and Anne Bruce (eds.), *Engineering Genesis: The Ethics of Genetic Engineering in Non-Human Species*, London: Earthscan, 1998, pp. 33–55, and references therein.

grow in industrialized countries. Others might make it possible to cultivate currently unusable or marginal land in developing countries, and to counteract some of the effects of global climate change on agriculture.

- Genes coding for a wide variety of proteins for medical and veterinary applications, such as vaccines, hormones, antibodies and other pharmaceutical products, could be introduced into plants by means of genetically modified plant viruses. The plants' own cells would produce the desired proteins. In some cases, the proteins would have to be extracted and purified from the host plant tissues; in other cases, the same techniques might be used to make 'edible vaccines' by introducing the gene for an immunity-inducing peptide[24] into an appropriate crop plant. Some authors speculate that this technique could make it much easier than at present to immunize developing country populations against serious diseases. Crops could also be nutritionally enhanced with a view to combating deficiency diseases affecting some developing country populations, as in the well-known example of 'golden rice', which was modified to contain raised levels of vitamin A.

- Insect viruses are sometimes already used as an alternative to chemical insecticides against insect pests, such as certain species of caterpillar, that attack crops. However, the wild-type viruses may be somewhat ineffective as pesticides (for example, because their life cycle is slow enough to allow the caterpillars to do a great deal of damage to the crop before being destroyed), and some research has focused on modifying insect viruses in various ways to make them more effective as pesticides: for example, by increasing their virulence or broadening the range of insect species that they will infect.

- Crops could be modified to have properties that make them easier for growers, shippers and retailers to handle, and/or more attractive to consumers. A famous example was the first GM crop to be sold in the shops, the Flavr Savr™ tomato marketed between 1994 and 1997, which was modified to slow down its ripening process, so that it could be left to develop more flavour on the vine before being picked and shipped.

- Crops could also be designed to secure the profits of plant breeding corporations by incorporating 'terminator' and 'traitor' technologies

---

24 A peptide is a short sequence of amino acids, the building-blocks of proteins. In some cases, a short sequence of amino acids can stimulate the body's immune system to mount an immune response against a protein, for example found in an invading micro-organism, that contains the same sequence.

that force farmers to buy new seed each growing season. In the late 1990s, public pressure forced Monsanto to distance itself from these technologies.[25]

Human genetic modification, cloning and embryonic stem cell research and plant genetic modification suggest ways in which biological and medical technologies might conceivably be deployed to address a range of problems of sin and evil in the areas alluded to at the beginning of this chapter. To speculate about modifying human nature to make ourselves more sympathetic and altruistic, less violent and so on – if such things could ever be achieved by genetic, pharmacological or other techno-logical means – is, in effect, to contemplate using technology to amelior-ate aspects of human sinfulness. The medical problems addressed by gene therapy and stem cell technology would appear to be instances of 'natural evil', though in such areas it can be difficult to disentangle natural evil from the consequences of human sin in various forms. Some of the applications of plant genetic modification appear to address agri-cultural and health problems in developing countries that, again, would seem to be attributable to a complex mix of natural evil and human sin. Other applications of these technologies, of course, are directed towards ends – such as maximizing corporate profits or enhancing athletic per-formance – that do not seem to have the amelioration of such human problems directly in view.

Standard public discourse about the use of biotechnology to alleviate human problems reflects what Gerald McKenny and others have called the 'Baconian project'.[26] By this is meant a set of attitudes, aspirations and practices that have their beginnings in the work of Francis Bacon and some of his seventeenth-century contemporaries and that underpin the modern practice of technology, particularly in medicine. The Puritan valuing of ordinary life and the imperative to meet the needs of one's neighbours, combined with the replacement of teleological by mechan-istic understandings of nature, encouraged the human control of nature with the aims of glorifying God and meeting human needs. Bacon

---

25 Donald Bruce and Don Horrocks (eds.), *Modifying Creation? GM Crops and Food: A Christian Perspective*, Carlisle: Paternoster, 2001, pp. 132–4.

26 Gerald P. McKenny, *To Relieve the Human Condition: Bioethics, Technology and the Body*, Albany, NY: State University of New York Press, 1997, pp. 17–21; Robert Song, 'The Human Genome Project as Soteriological Project', in Deane-Drummond, *Brave New World?*, pp. 164–84. Song emphasizes that Francis Bacon himself is not to be held responsible for all the developments described under the heading of the 'Baconian project': p. 173 n. 13.

valued the practical sciences for making such control possible, and disparaged the 'speculative sciences' of mediaeval scholasticism because they did nothing 'to relieve and benefit the condition of man'.[27] At their beginnings, these aspirations were rooted firmly in Puritan soil, and this fact set boundaries on what may be done in their pursuit. However, the project became increasingly secularized during subsequent centuries, as belief in divine providence waned, human benefit became identified by the early Utilitarians with pleasure and the absence of pain, and Romanticism developed a new emphasis on 'inwardness' and self-determination. Thus, as Robert Song puts it, the legacy of the Baconian project to modern medicine is the 'twin ideals' of 'the elimination of suffering and the maximisation of individual choice', ideals that are not limited to the cure of particular pains or diseases, but extend to the hope for freedom from human finitude and mortality.[28]

None of the critics of the Baconian project wishes to deny the genuine benefits gained from technological medicine, to retreat to some pre-technological golden age or to seek a publicly enforced consensus about the goods to be pursued in technological medicine. But they do point out that some central moral commitments of older medical and religious traditions are marginalized by the modern project, and that this gives rise to important problems. As McKenny puts it,

> In the modern discourse, moral convictions about the place of illness and health in a morally worthy life are replaced by moral convictions about the relief of suffering and the expansion of choice, concepts of nature as ordered by a telos or governed by providence are replaced by concepts of nature as a neutral instrument that is brought into the realm of human ends by technology, and the body as object of spiritual and moral practices is replaced by the body as object of practices of technological control.[29]

A number of related consequences follow from this. One is that, within this framework, the moral language is no longer available for expressing certain kinds of concern, and some questions become difficult or impossible to ask. In particular, any attempt to place limits on the use of technology to relieve suffering is apt to appear arbitrary, idiosyncratic and callous, and it becomes difficult to ask whether the pursuit of this

---

27 Francis Bacon, *The New Organon and Related Writings*, ed. Fulton H. Anderson, New York: Liberal Arts Press, 1960, pp. 71–2, quoted by McKenny, *To Relieve the Human Condition*, p. 18.

28 Song, 'The Human Genome Project', p. 174.

29 McKenny, *To Relieve the Human Condition*, p. 21.

human good might ever be in conflict with other, perhaps more important, human goods. Another consequence is that to make the body the object of technological control with the aim of relieving suffering can, paradoxically, contribute to the alienation and suffering of embodied persons.[30] A third, as Allen Verhey has argued, is that Bacon's disparagement of the 'speculative sciences' has had the effect of cutting his successors off from the sources of wisdom that might enable them to know how to use technology rightly.[31] Science and technology do not have within themselves the intellectual and moral resources to guide their wise use.

2   Technological projects and the Christian narrative

From a Christian theological perspective, a more satisfactory moral analysis of technological projects such as those in the three areas surveyed in the previous section must locate them within the Christian narrative and the understanding of humans and nature that it suggests. Within the framework of that narrative, humans and nature are to be understood as *created*, *fallen* and *being saved*. Such an understanding has been worked out in detail in previous chapters, and is recapitulated here as a basis for a theological assessment of technological projects.

1   *Created*. As I suggested, following Gunton and others, in Chapter 4, the distinctive Christian doctrine of creation *ex nihilo* by a triune Creator has enabled Christian theology to say a number of important and distinctive things about the universe. Among these are: that the universe is created by God's sovereign will and with a purpose; that it is 'very good', not merely instrumentally, but in and for itself; that God is continually and intimately involved with the creation, but in such a way as to leave it free to be itself; that the created order has a destiny 'which is something more than a return to its beginnings'; that humanity has a distinctive calling 'to be and to act in such a way as to offer the whole created order as a response of praise to its maker', and that this responsibility 'takes shape through [Jesus Christ]'.[32]

---

30 Allen Verhey, *Reading the Bible in the Strange World of Medicine*, Grand Rapids: Eerdmans, 2003, pp. 285–6.

31 Verhey, *Reading the Bible*, pp. 151–2.

32 Colin E. Gunton, 'The Doctrine of Creation', in Colin E. Gunton (ed.), *The Cambridge Companion to Christian Doctrine*, Cambridge: Cambridge University Press, 1997, pp. 141–57; quotations at pp. 143 and 144.

2   *Fallen*. However, God's loving purposes for humanity and for the creation are subverted by human sin. Sin is best understood as a radical distortion of our relationship with God and, derivatively, the distortion of our relations with one another, ourselves and the rest of the created order. This distortion of relationships can be mapped in various ways – for Barth, for example, it takes the forms of pride, sloth and falsehood – but fundamentally it must be described as idolatry: a refusal to orient our personal being and energies towards God in love, joy and praise. The Western Christian tradition's language of 'original sin' articulates the claim that this condition of sin is not merely incidental, but is something in which we are all entangled and from which, of ourselves, we are powerless to break free. The doctrine of original sin does not depend on the literal, historical fall of a first human couple: it is better understood as an indication that for as long as there have been humans, we have been in this condition. Original sin can be described in various ways as 'inherited'. We are all, to a greater or lesser extent, born into distorted relationships and social structures, so we are formed and socialized as persons in distorted ways and pass on these forms of distortion in our turn. It could also be that we have inherited from our evolutionary history a disposition to various forms of distortion: thus our 'inheritance' of predisposition to sin could turn out to be a complex mix of the biological and the social. But, more fundamentally, the language of original sin, if understood in a broader frame of reference than the moral, points to a kind of inherited 'guilt' which is difficult to articulate in a narrowly moral frame of reference: we are born into a condition of corporate human alienation from God which can best be described as idolatry. Again, it is conceivable that this inherited condition of alienation from God has a component that is a product of our evolutionary history.

It is often said that not only humankind but also the non-human creation is in some way 'fallen'. Some aspects of this claim are easy to understand: the damaging consequences of human sin for those parts of the creation that are within our reach are evident. But the claim is sometimes stated in ways that go beyond merely saying that humans, in their sin, inflict damage on the non-human creation; the creation as a whole is said to be 'subjected to futility' and in 'bondage to decay', in the language of Romans 8. This idea is sometimes linked to the suffering and waste that has characterized the evolutionary history of life on earth. When we think about ages, or parts of the creation, remote from human existence, it is hard to speak with any confidence. We can, however, say two things: first, that human action has inflicted great damage on the biosphere of planet earth; secondly, that the evolutionary history of life on earth has been characterized by a great amount of destruction and what appears from our perspective to be pain and waste, quite independently of the activity of *Homo sapiens*, who is a very late arrival on the evolutionary scene. These two observations help to fill out somewhat the Pauline language of the creation's subjection to futility, and suggest that the non-human, as well as the human, creation stands in need of divine transformation.

3   *Being saved.* As Colin Gunton puts it, the existence of sin and evil in the world 'means that creation's purpose can be achieved only by its redirection from within by the creator himself'.[33] In the Christian tradition, this redirecting or saving work is centred on the divine–human person of Jesus Christ: his life and ministry in first-century Palestine, his death by crucifixion and his resurrection from the dead. His death on the cross is at the very heart of God's saving work, but should not be understood in isolation from his life or from his resurrection. The saving work of God in and through Jesus Christ can be articulated in many ways: that Jesus renders the proper acknowledgement of God's justice that humanity refuses to render, thereby healing the breach in relationship between God and humanity; that Jesus the Son of God refuses the form of human pride that wants to be its own judge, freely taking the divine judgement upon himself and becoming 'the Judge judged in our place'; that Jesus the true and representative human is exalted to the rightful relationship with God that we in our sloth refused, and that, in solidarity with him, all of humanity is exalted; that Jesus resists to the end the 'demonic' power of idolatrous falsehood, so that the Cross becomes, paradoxically, the decisive victory over evil; and many more besides. This language is to be understood as metaphorical, not to be mythologized by being taken over-literally; but such metaphorical language (and, furthermore, the wide variety of metaphors to be found in the New Testament and in Christian reflection thereon) is indispensable in articulating the reality of God's saving work.

The saving work of God makes possible the transformation of human lives, relationships and social structures, enabling the creation of renewed forms of human community oriented to the triune God in a dynamic of love, joy and praise. Human relationships are also to be transformed so as to embody 'good news to the poor': to be characterized by the absence of coercion and domination and by the radical revi-

---

33 Gunton, 'The Doctrine of Creation', p. 143.

sion of social structures and hierarchies. God's saving work offers the eschatological hope, not only of the completion of this renewal of human relations but also of the 'redemption of our bodies' and the liberation of the material creation from its current 'subjection to futility'. This 'ultimate' saving work of God radically judges and invalidates all our this-worldly efforts to transform the world, but at the same time offers them a new validity and divine mandate as forms of 'penultimate' activity that can prepare the way for the ultimate.

At the end of the last chapter I remarked that the cosmic and universal scope of God's saving work in Christ means that there is no aspect of the world or of human life in the world that is in principle untouched by this work, and that Christians are committed to the attempt to re-envision every aspect of the world and human existence through the lens of Christ. If this is so, then in order to make a moral appraisal of any human project, including any of the technological projects with which I began this chapter, we must ask whether or not it goes with the grain of God's saving activity in and through the life, death and resurrection of Jesus Christ. Careful discernment may be required to answer that question, for there are subtle as well as blatant ways of going against the grain of God's work. It is possible to do so, not only by overtly serving the ends of chaos and destruction but also by setting up would-be substitutes for God's saving activity. The latter is perhaps a characteristic temptation of well-intentioned people in the modern world: not to use technologies for overtly selfish or destructive ends, but to imagine that any human predicament can be solved by human cleverness and skill.

3   Diagnostic questions

In the light of what has been said about God's saving activity, it is possible to suggest some diagnostic questions that may help us to discern whether any particular technological project goes with or against the grain of God's saving work.

a   Is the project good news to the poor?

Who stands to gain from it, and at whose expense? Does it embody or point towards the transformed forms of relationship and social structure alluded to in Chapter 6, or does it work against those forms of transformation? Does it unsettle or reinforce relationships of coercion and domination? Does it empower, or further disempower, those who are relatively powerless; does it tend to bring the marginalized towards the centre, or to marginalize them further?

This question is relatively easily stated, but may be complex to answer, since it requires us to attend to the complex web of interconnecting political, social, economic and environmental effects which may follow from a technological project.[34] Furthermore, what could be called a Niebuhrian caution might be in order: within a fallen world, a certain toughness, perhaps even coercive force and violence, may sometimes be needed precisely to protect the innocent and the vulnerable. To assume that it is possible to set up transformed ways of going about our public business in a world that is far from transformed may be not only naive but dangerous.[35] Yet even if we acknowledge the need to be realistic about the world as it is, there is always the danger that such 'realism' will be co-opted as a rationalization of the interests of the powerful.[36] Perhaps something like David Ford's challenge – to try and make gentleness, compassion and generosity not merely supplementary to justice but 'constitutive' of human community – is needed in order to keep us true to our proper commitments.[37] It may also follow from this that transformed communities which are prepared to witness to this different way of living, even when that means that they suffer violence at the hands of the powerful, can be indispensable irritants and goads provoking others to be open to the transformation made possible by God's grace. And even in arenas of public and corporate decision-making which may not appear to show many signs of the transformation of human community mapped in Chapter 6, it is still worth drawing attention to the question whether a particular technological project will be good or bad news for the poor, the powerless and the marginalized.[38]

---

34 For an example of such attention, see Márcio Fabri dos Anjos, 'Power, Ethics and the Poor in Human Genetics Research', in Maureen Junker-Kenny and Lisa Sowle Cahill (eds.), *The Ethics of Genetic Engineering* (*Concilium*, 1998/2), pp. 73–82.

35 Cf. Reinhold Niebuhr's famous dichotomy between love and justice, e.g. in *Moral Man and Immoral Society*, New York: Scribners, 1932, pp. 257–77.

36 Duncan B. Forrester, *Christian Justice and Public Policy*, Cambridge: Cambridge University Press, 1997, p. 219.

37 David F. Ford, *Self and Salvation: Being Transformed*, Cambridge: Cambridge University Press, 1999, p. 136.

38 There have been examples in medicine and biotechnology where corporate policy and practice have changed, apparently in response to public pressure motivated by a concern for the poor and marginalized. One is the back-pedalling by agrochemical companies on the development of terminator and traitor technologies in plant biotechnology, noted earlier. Another is the increased availability in developing countries of

b   Is the project an attempt to be 'like God', or does it conform to the image of God?

This question alludes to the contrast drawn by Bonhoeffer, in his reflection on the Fall narrative in Genesis 3, between human attempts to be 'like God' (*sicut deus*), in the tempting but ultimately destructive way promised by the serpent, and creaturely human existence in the 'image of God' (*imago dei*).[39] What I mean by an attempt to be like God is a form of action in the world which embodies a forgetfulness of our finitude, an assumption that given enough time, effort and investment, we can achieve virtually anything we wish to, and a tendency to think that every human problem is susceptible to a technological fix. Such attitudes constitute one of the forms of pride characterized by Barth, wanting to be our own helper and thereby turning away from the source of our greatest and truest help.[40] By contrast, by activity that conforms to the image of God, I mean responsible action that both respects human finitude and honours our divine mandate to make something of the world. It is important to stress that these descriptions are sketches of the internal logic, as it were, of the different forms of activity, not necessarily of the conscious motivations or intentions of the agents. It would be foolish to imagine that only Christian scientists and technologists, self-consciously acting as God's stewards, were capable of activity that conformed to the image of God: Bonhoeffer regards the 'penultimate' and the 'natural' as spheres of 'secular' at least as much as churchly activity.[41] Conversely, a self-consciously Christian motivation is no guarantee against the temptation to act 'like God'. One could cite Joseph Fletcher as an example of a Christian theologian insufficiently aware of this danger in the context of biotechnology and medicine:

> The future is not to be sought in the stars but in us, in human beings. We don't pray for rain, we irrigate and seed clouds; we don't pray for

---

affordable anti-retroviral drugs to combat HIV and AIDS, though on this front there is still much to be done: for detailed information, see the website of the Campaign for Access to Essential Medicines, sponsored by the NGO *Médecins sans Frontières*, http://www.accessmed-msf.org/ (accessed 24 August 2006).

39 Dietrich Bonhoeffer, *Creation and Fall: A Theological Exposition of Genesis 1–3* (*Dietrich Bonhoeffer Works*, vol. 3), ET ed. by John W. de Gruchy, trans. Douglas Stephen Bax, Minneapolis: Fortress, 1997, p. 113. See above, Chapter 7, section 3.

40 Karl Barth, *Church Dogmatics*, ET ed. by G. W. Bromiley and T. F. Torrance, 13 vols, Edinburgh: T&T Clark, 1956–75 (hereafer *CD*), vol. IV.1, pp. 458–78.

41 Cf. Dietrich Bonhoeffer, *Ethics* (*Dietrich Bonhoeffer Works*, vol. 6), ET ed. Clifford J. Green, Minneapolis: Fortress, 2005, pp. 171–218.

cures, we rely on medicine . . . This is the direction of the biological revolution – that we turn more and more from creatures to creators.[42]

In connection with this question, it is worth returning briefly to the final proposal of Christopher Southgate's evolutionary theodicy, discussed in Chapter 8: that 'humans have a calling, stemming from the transformative power of Christ's action on the Cross, to participate in the healing of the world'.[43] Southgate extends Philip Hefner's concept of human beings as created co-creators to propose that the healing of our relationships with God and one another might enable us also 'to take up [our] place . . . as co-redeemers with Christ of the whole evolutionary process'.[44] He speculates, for example, that 'wise humans, living simply but ingeniously, might *end the pattern of mass extinction* that has been a necessary feature of teleological creation but that loses its necessity in a fulfilled creation'.[45]

I am uneasy about the language both of created co-creators and of co-redeemers, because I am not convinced that this language strikes the right balance between a properly humble acknowledgement of our finitude and a properly bold acceptance of the divine mandate to make something of the world. I would prefer simply to speak of humans as redeemed creatures with a divine mandate to act responsibly in the world so as to 'prepare the way of the Lord'. But, with that caveat, I am highly sympathetic to Southgate's suggestion that human action in the world in response to God's saving work in Christ could have far-reaching significance for the non-human as well as the human creation. So, for example, the notion that we might be able to end the evolutionary pattern of mass extinctions altogether strikes me as over-ambitious (are we ever likely to be able to protect the planet from the various kinds of natural catastrophe that are supposed to have precipitated previous mass extinctions?), but it is much more persuasive to suggest that humans both can and should seek ways to address the present, largely human-caused, phase of mass extinction.[46]

---

42 Joseph Fletcher, *The Ethics of Genetic Control: Ending Reproductive Roulette*, Garden City, NY: Doubleday, 1974, p. 200, quoted in Ronald Cole-Turner (ed.), *Human Cloning: Religious Responses*, Louisville, KY: Westminster John Knox, 1997, p. xii.

43 Christopher Southgate, 'God and Evolutionary Evil: Theodicy in the Light of Darwinism', *Zygon*, 37.4 (2002), pp. 803–24 (p. 817).

44 Southgate, 'God and Evolutionary Evil', p. 818.

45 'God and Evolutionary Evil', pp. 819–20, emphasis original.

46 See, further, Richard Leakey and Roger Lewin, *The Sixth Extinction: Biodiversity and Its Survival*, London: Weidenfeld and Nicolson, 1996.

c   What attitude does the project embody towards the material world (including our own bodies)?

Like the second question, the third is about the internal logic embodied in different kinds of practice, not only or necessarily about the conscious attitude or understanding of the participants. Two errors must be avoided: one is a *hatred* of the material world that is expressed in either a flight from it or a violent subjection of it. The technological control over the natural world that is sought by the Baconian project is one expression of this error, but there are others. The second error is a *reduction* of everything to the material and a denial that there is any more to human existence than can be expressed in some scientific 'theory of everything'. One example of this is the reductionism of authors like Dennett who wish to make Darwinian descent with modification into a theory of everything;[47] another is the reductionist 'biomedical model' of health and disease that underpins some of the more extravagant hopes invested in the Human Genome Project.[48] These errors, it will be noticed, have striking similarities to Bonhoeffer's two rejected 'extreme' accounts of the relationship of the ultimate to the penultimate. The various forms of the hatred of the material world, which locate our hope either in a flight from the material or in its subjugation, correspond to Bonhoeffer's 'radicalism' which 'cannot forgive God for having created what is'.[49] The various ways of reducing everything to the material, either denying the existence of any realm beyond the here and now or bracketing out its relevance to our action in this world, are versions of Bonhoeffer's 'compromise' which allows the ultimate 'no say in the formation of life in the world'.[50] More satisfactory technological projects will embody and express a proper respect for the material world, valuing it as good in and for itself, not merely instrumentally; they will refuse to make an idol of the material or invest all human hope in it; they will display an honesty about the finitude of the material world, and of our embodied existence in it, that points beyond the material world to the hope of its ultimate transformation.

---

47 Daniel C. Dennett, *Darwin's Dangerous Idea: Evolution and the Meanings of Life*, London: Penguin, 1996.

48 For a critique of the biomedical model with reference to the Human Genome Project, see Neil G. Messer, 'The Human Genome Project, Health and the "Tyranny of Normality"', in Deane-Drummond, *Brave New World?*, pp. 91–115.

49 Bonhoeffer, *Ethics*, p. 155.

50 *Ethics*, p. 156.

d   What attitude does the project embody towards past failures?

Many of the problems enumerated at the beginning of this chapter are attributable, at least in part, to human failures of one sort or another: the ill-health that results from individuals' failure to take responsibility for their health; the much greater amount of ill-health that results from economic inequality; the ecological damage that results from individuals and communities pursuing their own interests while taking too little thoughts for the consequences of their actions; and so on. In other words, in a theological perspective, many of the human problems that are in view in this chapter are in one way or another, at least in part, consequences of human sin.

In the language of Christian tradition, the appropriate response to sin is repentance (*metanoia*, a change of heart or mind): an honest acknowledgement before God and one another of our sins and our sinfulness, and a desire for our lives to be different, with God's help, in the future. To try and extricate ourselves from the consequences of our sins without the honesty of repentance would be to replicate, not to solve, our problems, because – once again – it would be an instance of pride in the form of self-help that entailed turning away from the true source of our help.

Accordingly, technological projects intended to ameliorate the effects of past human failures (sins) ought to embody an attitude that could be described as repentant. Once again, this is a claim about the internal logic embodied in a project, not necessarily about the conscious attitudes of the participants therein. I am not claiming that the only valid kind of technological project to ameliorate human and ecological problems is one accompanied by overt acts of repentance, faith and prayer – welcome though these would undoubtedly be. Rather, I mean that such projects should be characterized by an acknowledgement (implicit or explicit) of past failures and mistakes, an awareness that things must be different in the future, and an openness to the help that will be needed if things are to be different.[51] To take an illustrative example from another area of ecological concern, these considerations might make us far less impressed by a strategy of CO_2 'emissions trading', if that were to be used as a way of relieving a wealthy population of any responsibility for altering its patterns of consumption, than by a strategy that also sought

---

51   Cf. Stephen Clark's remark that '[s]omething like a religious experience may be necessary' to awaken us from our shared addiction to the way of life that has precipitated our ecological crisis: *How to Think about the Earth: Philosophical and Theological Models for Ecology*, London: Mowbray, 1993, p. 6.

to reduce CO_2 emissions by seeking alternative energy sources and reducing energy use.

4   Assessing the projects

I end this chapter by returning, in reverse order, to the three areas of technology with which I began – genetically modified crops, human cloning and stem cell technology, and human genetic manipulation – and drawing some conclusions about each, tentatively and in outline, in the light of the diagnostic questions I have just suggested.

a   Genetically modified crops

In my comments on GM crops, I shall bracket out the detailed questions about their effects on human health, indigenous forms of agriculture, biodiversity and so forth, since it is beyond the scope of this book to assess the evidence on these matters fully. But answers to such questions would have to be incorporated into the outlines of my response in order to arrive at a fully adequate ethical analysis of any concrete use of this technology. In this of all areas, one cannot make a tidy separation between principles and pragmatic considerations.

One of the things that should concern us most about plant genetic modification as currently practised is that it seems to proceed on the assumption that nature is unproblematically manipulable in the service of human expediency, preference or profit. In other words, it is a clear example of what I referred to earlier as the Baconian project: the technological control of nature so as to meet human needs and extend individual choice. I suggested earlier that this attitude embodies a kind of hatred of the material world that regards it as indifferent or hostile to human interests and seeks its subjugation. Yet in this way of regarding genetically modified crops, there can also sometimes be a tendency to reduce everything to the material, for example by seeking technological solutions to complex human problems such as hunger and malnutrition.[52] Paradoxically, therefore, there may be elements of both the

---

52 Michael Northcott takes advocates of GM crops to task for doing this in a way that ignores the social-scientific literature on the causes of hunger and malnutrition: '"Behold, I have set the land before you" (Deut. 1.8): Christian Ethics, GM Foods and the Culture of Modern Farming', in Celia Deane-Drummond and Bronislaw Szerszynski with Robin Grove-White (eds.), *Re-Ordering Nature: Theology, Society and the New Genetics*, London: T&T Clark, 2003, pp. 85–106 (p. 97). Robert Song,

'radicalism' and the 'compromise' identified and criticized by Bonhoeffer as inadequate ways of relating the ultimate to the penultimate.

These critical comments should not be construed as a blanket dis-approval of all attempts to 'improve upon nature': a theological under-standing of the material world as God's creation means that we are not committed to regarding 'nature' or 'the way things are' as sacrosanct. All agriculture is in a sense an improvement upon nature, and it would be a strange theological analysis indeed which concluded that all forms of agriculture were to be rejected. Indeed, farming has for a very long time been close to the heart of Jewish and Christian understandings of humanity's place in nature, and one of the earliest sources of the notion that humans have a divine mandate to make something of the world uses agricultural imagery (Gen. 2.15). My worries about the attitudes embodied in the current practice of plant genetic modification are more specific. Within the frame of a 'Baconian' attitude, we might come to assume that our relation to the rest of the creation is one of mastery without limits; furthermore, certain questions (for example, about the appropriateness of *these* means to *this* good end) become difficult or impossible to ask.

All this, though, might seem a rather self-indulgent sort of scrupu-losity in the face of a massive, and growing, problem of world hunger. In such a context, are genetically modified crops not urgently needed to increase global food production and meet the needs of the poor for food security? Are they not therefore, in the most direct way possible, good news to the poor?

As the technology is currently practised, there appears to be good reason to doubt that they are. Commentators express concern that research and development is largely directed to the priorities of Western markets rather than the needs of farmers and communities in develop-ing countries, that multinational corporations may exploit the genetic resources and indigenous knowledge of developing countries without making adequate recompense and that terminator and traitor tech-nologies, should they be deployed by plant breeding and agrochemical corporations, would have a massively disproportionate detrimental effect on farmers in developing countries.[53] Yet these are contingent, not

---

in the context of human genetics, has argued that the Baconian project is not neces-sarily reductionist, but does have a 'natural affinity for reductive approaches': Song, 'The Human Genome Project', p. 182.

53 Northcott, '"Behold, I have set the land before you"', pp. 99–101; Bruce and Bruce, *Engineering Genesis*, pp. 245–53; Bruce and Horrocks, *Modifying Creation?*, pp. 129–36.

necessary, features of the way the technology is practised. There are examples of its being used to benefit the health of poor communities, such as 'golden rice'. It is possible to conceive of other applications that would genuinely be 'good news to the poor'. Even so trenchant a critic such as Michael Northcott allows that

> It is possible to imagine a world where biotechnology is utilised to promote sustainable, low-energy, low-waste, low-pollution, labour-intensive, traditional mixed farming . . . [in which] genetic engineering would be used to enhance the sustainability and lower intensity of agriculture, to reduce soil erosion, enhance biodiversity, increase tree cover in arable farming regions, reduce water usage and eliminate chemical dependence.[54]

This is not so very different from the vision of some advocates of GM, but unlike them, Northcott believes that it is 'more fantasy than reality [because of] the control exercised over global agriculture by seed corporations and chemical companies'.[55] Those more positive about the technology hope to find ways of shifting the balance of power in its development and redirecting its priorities to the advantage of developing countries.[56]

On the whole, these considerations do not add up to a blanket rejection of all genetically modified crops, but they do suggest that there is a great deal wrong with the way the technology of plant genetic modification is currently being used and developed, and that much of this is attributable to the global economic and political context in which it is located. A radical reordering of priorities and control would be required for the technology to measure up to the diagnostic questions I have suggested. To a large extent, a Christian ethical appraisal of GM crops will turn on the likelihood of such a reordering being achieved.

b Health

Before discussing human cloning and stem cell technology and human genetic manipulation, some preliminary remarks about health and

---

54 Northcott, '"Behold, I have set the land before you"', p. 99.

55 '"Behold, I have set the land before you"', pp. 99–100.

56 Gordon Conway, 'Crop Biotechnology: Benefits, Risks and Ownership', paper presented to the OECD Conference on the Scientific and Health Aspects of Genetically Modified Foods, Edinburgh, February–March 2000; quoted in Bruce and Horrocks, *Modifying Creation?*, p. 137.

disease are in order, since both these areas of technology are more or less located in the sphere of health care. It is easy to assume that we understand what we mean by health and disease, but they turn out on closer inspection to be very elusive concepts.[57] Elsewhere I have argued that two highly influential accounts of health and disease, the reductionist 'biomedical model' that understands health as species-typical biological functioning and the World Health Organization definition of health as 'a state of complete physical, mental and social well-being',[58] are unsatisfactory in various ways. I have advocated, with reference to the healing miracles of the Gospels and to St Paul's 'thorn in the flesh' (2 Cor. 12.1–10), an alternative model in which health is understood theologically as a real and precious good, but not the only or the ultimate good; in which sickness and physical suffering are recognized as real and sometimes terrible torments, signs that the created order is badly astray from God's loving purposes, yet sometimes also occasions for people to discover the goodness and love of God; in which the relationship between power and weakness, suffering and success, is so complex as to defy easy description.[59] Such an understanding of health and disease will enable us to see health care and medical research as in principle a legitimate part of responsible action in the world, part of our God-given mandate. Yet at the same time it will caution us against making an idol of health or investing all our human hopes therein. It will thus enable us to say that we *may* not necessarily do everything we *can* do, and that other human goods than health also have a claim on our resources.

c   Human cloning and stem cell technology

I have argued elsewhere that reproductive cloning would, in the terms I have adopted from Bonhoeffer, amount to a human attempt to be 'like God' rather than activity that conforms to the image of God.[60] Therapeutic cloning, however, could be directed towards human health understood in the way outlined here. The aims and goals of the thera-

---

57 Kenneth M. Boyd, 'Disease, Illness, Sickness, Health, Healing and Wholeness: Exploring Some Elusive Concepts', *Journal of Medical Ethics: Medical Humanities*, 26 (2000), pp. 9–17.

58 *Constitution of the World Health Organization*, Geneva: World Health Organization, 1948 (updated 1977, 1984 and 1994), Preamble; available on the WHO website at http://www.who.int/about/en/ (accessed 24 August 2006).

59 Messer, 'The Human Genome Project'. The last few lines are drawn, with modifications, from p. 107. My account is heavily indebted to Barth, *CD* III.4, pp. 356–74.

60 Messer, *The Ethics of Human Cloning*.

peutic cloning projects currently being undertaken or envisaged – the understanding and ultimately treatment of devastating diseases and injuries – can quite plausibly be understood as being in line with God's saving work. However, most therapeutic cloning projects that are currently envisaged (certainly any involving embryonic stem cells) would entail the creation and destructive use of human embryos. Some Christians would hold that even if the ends of such a project were in line with God's redemptive work, its means would include the destruction of nascent and innocent human beings, and would therefore be in opposition to God's purposes in creation and redemption. In the language made famous by Pope John Paul II, such projects would be expressions of a 'culture of death', not the 'Gospel of life'.[61] They would therefore deny that Christian ethics could ever approve such a project. Others would argue that not all destructive use of human embryos should be prohibited, and therefore that HESC research might be justified if the end is sufficiently important.[62]

Much of this debate, as it is commonly set up, turns on the moral status of the embryo: is the embryo a person (where 'person' is philosophical shorthand for a being with the moral status that we normally accord to adult humans), a potential person, or a bundle of cells with little moral significance in and of itself? If it is the first, so the argument often goes, then the destructive use of embryos cannot be justified, any more than it would be to dissect a healthy baby in order to obtain spare parts for surgery. If it is no more than a bundle of cells, then its destructive use seems much less morally problematic. If it is regarded as a 'potential person', or in some other way accorded a moral status intermediate between that of a person and that of a lump of tissue, then it is likely also to be accorded an intermediate level of protection: for example, restrictions but not an outright ban on embryo research, as in current British legislation. An 'agnostic' position on the status of the embryo is often held to justify a permissive view about its use, but Robert Song, borrowing a phrase from Germain Grisez, argues that such justifications are inconsistent, since 'to be willing to kill what for all one knows is a person is to be willing to kill a person'.[63] However, a difficulty

---

61 John Paul II, *Evangelium Vitae*, Dublin: Veritas, 1995; see esp. §63 (pp. 113–15).

62 E.g. Gene Outka, 'The Ethics of Human Stem Cell Research', in Brent Waters and Ronald Cole-Turner (eds.), *God and the Embryo: Religious Voices on Stem Cells and Cloning*, Washington, DC: Georgetown University Press, 2003, pp. 29–64.

63 Robert Song, 'To Be Willing to Kill What for All One Knows Is a Person Is to be Willing to Kill a Person', in Waters and Cole-Turner, *God and the Embryo*, pp. 98–107.

with framing the question in terms of the personhood of the embryo is that, as Maureen Junker-Kenny puts it, '[a]ny definition of the beginning . . . of human personhood is caught in a practical hermeneutical circle. We define its starting point because we want to act in a certain way, and we act according to how we have defined it.'[64] A related danger is that, like the lawyer's question to Jesus, 'Who is my neighbour?' (Luke 10.29), the question 'Who, or what, counts as a person?' can be used as a self-interested way of limiting our moral concern.[65]

A possible way through these difficulties is suggested by Karl Barth, who in his treatment of abortion frames the issue as a question of how we are to understand and interpret the biblical command 'Thou shalt not kill'.[66] Admittedly, Barth begins his discussion with what looks very much like an ontological claim about the foetus, not using the terminology of personhood, but using language with much the same import: 'the unborn child is . . . a man and not a thing, nor a mere part of the mother's body'.[67] To kill a foetus is therefore to take on oneself the terrible responsibility for taking the life of a fellow human being whose life is God's gift and is owned by God. Furthermore, this human being is already one for whom Christ has died; '[t]he true light of the world shines already in the mother's womb'.[68] All this means that 'a definite No must be the presupposition of any further discussion'.[69] The command to protect human life generates a strong prohibition of abortion, and Barth regards a situation in which it is widely practised as unquestionably wicked. Barth's treatment, however, differs from the discussions of personhood criticized by Hays and others in that he does not need to make an ontological claim about personhood or humanhood do the ethical work that is required of it by others. The rightness or wrongness of abortion ultimately turns, not on the status of the foetus, but on the command of God. This allows Barth to say that the prohibition of abortion is not absolute, and there could be exceptional cases (*Grenzfälle* of the sort discussed in Chapter 5) where it 'does not consti-

---

64 Maureen Junker-Kenny, 'Embryos *in vitro*, Personhood, and Rights', in Maureen Junker-Kenny (ed.), *Designing Life? Genetics, Procreation and Ethics*, Aldershot: Ashgate, 1999, pp. 130–58 (p. 133).

65 Richard B. Hays, *The Moral Vision of the New Testament*, Edinburgh: T&T Clark, 1997, p. 451; see also Ian A. Mcfarland, 'Who Is my Neighbor?: the Good Samaritan as a Source for Theological Anthropology', *Modern Theology*, 17.1 (2001) pp. 57–66.

66 Barth, *CD* III.4, pp. 415–23.

67 *CD* III.4, p. 415.

68 *CD* III.4, p. 416.

69 *CD* III.4, p. 417.

tute murder but is in fact commanded'.[70] These are the most serious of cases where the life or health of the mother is at stake, and abortion might not be commanded even in such boundary situations; we cannot know in advance.

By the same token, it could be argued that the command to protect human life generates a strong, but not absolute, presumption against the destructive use of human embryos. There could be exceptional situations where such use for research or therapy is not prohibited, but commanded. These would almost certainly be the most serious of situations, where the life or health of patients was at stake and the therapeutic or research goals could not be achieved in any other way. Such a line of thought might, for example, require that research on alternative sources of pluripotent stem cells (such as adult tissues or parthenogenetic blastocysts) be pursued as energetically as possible, even if embryonic stem cells seemed to offer an easier and shorter route to the same results.

The question then arises how such moral conclusions should be translated into a legislative or regulatory framework. As Barth recognizes in the case of abortion, legislation is ill-adapted for responsiveness to the command of God in particular situations.[71] Perhaps the best that it could do in the case of embryonic stem cell research would be to establish a regulatory framework that encouraged the priorities for which I have argued (for example, by requiring researchers to show both that the aims and goals of their proposed project were of the first importance and that they could not realistically be met by any other approach) and that created the space within which individual researchers and clinicians could take responsibility before God for their response to the sixth commandment.[72]

---

70 *CD* III.4, p. 421.

71 *CD* III.4, p. 422.

72 One difficulty with the argument I have developed here, as David Clough has pointed out to me, is that it could set a dangerous precedent of permitting, and legislating for, the taking of a human life for the sake of other lives, simply on the basis that God *might* conceivably command such an action. Could the same kind of argument not be mounted in favour of euthanasia, which Barth rules out without qualification (*CD* III.4, pp. 423–7) or infanticide, which no plausible Christian ethics can support (I am not referring to the difficult dilemmas that must be faced in neonatal medicine about the giving or withholding of treatment in particular hard cases)? One way of supporting my argument would be to show that for abortion and HESC research, but not euthanasia or infanticide, exceptional cases can be envisaged which would not be transgressions of the rule that life should be protected, 'but rather . . . unusual mode[s] of keeping it' (Nigel Biggar, *The Hastening That Waits: Karl Barth's Ethics*, Oxford: Clarendon Press, 1993, p. 34). If this kind of discrimination turned out to be impossible, my argument would be seriously called into question.

d Human genetic manipulation[73]

It seems to me that one of the chief moral and spiritual hazards of human genetic manipulation (in common with other ambitious technological interventions on the human body) is a version of what Bonhoeffer calls the radicalism that cannot forgive God the creation.[74] In other words, human genetic manipulation seems to involve attempts to overcome, or escape from, the limitations of some or all human bodies. It would be all too easy for the internal logic of such projects (remember that I am not necessarily talking about the conscious motivation of particular participants) to include a frustration with, and an attempt to deny, the finitude associated with our embodied existence. There is a danger that such projects would both embody and encourage a falling-out, as Bonhoeffer puts it, with the material creation, and a refusal to accept the particular contingencies, limitations and opportunities that it presents.

However, not all limitations are the same. The distinction between those limitations imposed on bodily existence by disease or injury and those that are a function of human embodiment as such, however difficult it is to describe or map that distinction precisely, would seem to be both real and crucially important. If something, such as a genetic mutation that causes cystic fibrosis, has gone wrong with my body, then to use technology in an attempt to put right what has gone wrong need not be expressive of a hatred of my finite creaturely existence. On the contrary, it could be understood as a proper aspect of Bonhoeffer's 'penultimate': a piece of responsible human action that goes with the grain of the ultimate healing of creation promised by God in and through Christ. As such it would represent a proper valuing, not the hatred or rejection, of the material creation. This could be said in principle of either somatic cell or germ line gene therapy; there is no morally or theologically fundamental distinction between them, though at present there are good pragmatic reasons, such as the balance of risks and benefits, for being much more cautious about permitting the latter than the former.

It is much more doubtful, though, that the same could be said of a project such as 'gene-doping' with the aim of increasing muscle growth and enhancing athletic performance. This would appear to be a techno-

---

73 See further Neil G. Messer, 'Human Cloning and Genetic Manipulation: Some Theological and Ethical Issues', *Studies in Christian Ethics*, 12.2 (1999), pp. 1–16; 'Human Genetics and the Image of the Triune God', *Science and Christian Belief*, 13.2 (2001), pp. 99–111.

74 See above, n. 50.

logical attempt to circumvent a limitation that is not pathological, but simply a feature of embodied human existence. Such an attempt at 'cosmetic' genetic enhancement, unlike therapeutic projects such as the treatment of cystic fibrosis, would appear to express a kind of rejection of the material creation.[75]

But what of genetic enhancement for more morally serious purposes? Let us imagine, by way of a thought-experiment, that T. H. Huxley's hopes were realized, and it became feasible to improve the moral character of human beings, either by genetic manipulation or by other technological means such as neuropharmacology. The seriousness of this project could hardly be denied: as Jonathan Glover puts it,

> Preserving the human race as it is will seem an acceptable option to all those who can watch the news on television and feel satisfied with the world. It will appeal to those who can talk to their children about the history of the twentieth century without wishing they could leave some things out.[76]

It is obvious enough that human beings are in serious need of help to become better people and to build better communities. Unlike the gene-doping of athletes, such a project would not be an attempt to circumvent human limitations that we ought to learn to live with. It would be an attempt to put right something that is seriously and dangerously wrong with us, however that wrong has come about. However, within a Christian ethical frame of reference, it would be a seriously mistaken attempt. The mistake lies in the belief that this is the kind of human problem that can and should be addressed by human ingenuity and technique. In Chapter 7, I canvassed the possibility that some aspects of human sin might be in part products of our evolutionary history, and, if that is so, then it is not inconceivable that manipulation of human biological nature might make a difference to those aspects of sin.[77]

---

75 It could be asked whether this line of argument does not require me to object to all kinds of inventions, such as bicycles, cars and aeroplanes, that humans use to overcome non-pathological limitations. However, I think a distinction can be maintained between, on the one hand, inventing artefacts that extend the possibilities of life in the world and, on the other, wanting to make ourselves into a *different kind of creature*. My thanks to David Clough for raising this question with me.

76 Glover, *What Sort of People Should There Be?*, p. 56.

77 The caveat expressed by Mary Sellar and others must be remembered at this point, however: even if aspects of behaviour and character were shaped in part by genetic determinants, it would not necessarily follow that it would ever be feasible to alter those aspects of behaviour and character by genetic manipulation; see above, n. 12.

However, I also argued that sin is fundamentally to be understood as a radical distortion of our relationship with God, and derivatively of our relations with one another, ourselves and the rest of the created order. If, as Barth says, one aspect of that distortion is the pride that makes us want to be our own helpers rather than turning to God as the true source of our help, then to try and mend our broken relations with God, one another, ourselves and the creation by means of our technical skill would perpetuate, not heal, the problem. Therefore to use technology in an attempt to make ourselves good would be better understood as a substitute for the salvation offered by God than as responsible human action oriented to God's saving work.

The discussion thus far has distinguished between gene *therapy* and genetic *enhancement*, but it should be noted that the borderline between the two is notoriously vague, depending as it does on the elusive concepts of health and disease. Elsewhere I have argued that it is probably impossible to render this distinction entirely clear-cut or to devise a neat procedure for assigning particular cases to one or other category. Rather, a form of 'practical wisdom' (*phronēsis*) is needed to discern the appropriate way to think about, and respond to, particular conditions and cases. This practical wisdom is formed by participation in the life, worship and witness of the Christian community.[78] The approach suggested in the present chapter extends that proposal: by offering a set of diagnostic questions by which to assess any particular project on its theological merits, it saves us from placing too much weight on a potentially ambiguous assignment to one or other category. In general, however, I suspect that the use of these questions would lead us to respond positively to at least some of what is thought of as 'therapy', and to reject most or all of what is envisaged under the heading of 'enhancement'. If these theological and moral conclusions were to be translated into public policy, which necessarily deals in generalizations, the safest way of doing so would be to permit only those genetic manipulation projects which could unambiguously be called therapeutic. There would not be much difficulty, for example, in assigning attempts to treat serious single-gene disorders like cystic fibrosis to this category, and with caveats about safety, efficacy, the appropriate use of resources and so forth, such attempts should be welcomed.

The caveat about the appropriate use of resources is a reminder that one question to be asked of any concrete project, in the area either of human genetic manipulation or of stem cell research, would be: is it

---

78 See, further, Messer, 'The Human Genome Project', pp. 109–13.

good news to the poor, the vulnerable, the marginalized, the oppressed? For a project directed towards the treatment of a serious disease, of course, the suffering and vulnerability of patients would give a powerful *prima facie* reason for answering 'Yes'. But the question would prompt us to ask, for example, who would have access to the treatment, who would benefit financially and in other ways from making it available and to whose, if anyone's, detriment.[79] It would also prompt us to ask whether there are other health-related goods, or goods other than health, which could be better pursued with the limited resources of money, time and skill that the project would demand. Such questions become easier to ask when we learn to value the material creation (including our bodily life and health) properly, to hope and pray for its transformation, and to avoid making it into an idol or burdening it with our ultimate hopes.

79 For example, see Fabri dos Anjos, 'Power, Ethics and the Poor', for concerns about the exploitation of the genetic material of people in developing countries.

10

Conclusion

In Chapter 3, I indicated that the remainder of the book would be, among other things, a test of the merits of the theological account that I proposed to develop as an alternative to the reductionism exemplified by Dennett. If it could meet three tests, I suggested, it would thereby show itself to be more satisfactory than the latter. First, it should be able to incorporate whatever is well-founded in the evolutionary accounts on which reductionists draw. Secondly, it should be able to address issues and take account of evidence that reductionist views have difficulty in handling convincingly. Thirdly, it should be able to clarify, challenge and reshape the moral concepts and experience discussed in the evolution-and-ethics literature, where those concepts and that experience display incoherence or confusion.

In articulating one particular theological account of the doctrines of creation, sin and salvation and bringing that account into engagement with the issues in play in the evolution-and-ethics literature, I have tried to show that there are good reasons to think that it can meet these tests. A few examples, illustrative rather than exhaustive, follow.

1 Incorporating whatever is well-founded in the accounts on which reductionists draw

Developing this part of the argument, as I have observed at various points, calls for due caution about the speculative and contested nature of many of the evolutionary claims about human morality that have been discussed in this book. With that caveat, I have argued that an account of human being as moral being, developed on the basis of a theological understanding that the world and humans have been created 'very good' by God, is well able to assimilate the proposal that aspects of moral experience emerged as a result of the evolutionary process that gave rise to our species. Such a theological account can also take from human evolutionary history a useful reminder that human persons,

whose personal identities are constituted by the history of their relationships with God and one another in the world, are also physically
embodied beings to whom some possibilities are open and others not.
Likewise, a Christian doctrine of sin can make sense of evolutionary
claims and speculations that aspects of our evolutionary inheritance
give rise to morally problematic ways of being and acting in the world:
the doctrine of sin articulates the insight that God's good creation has
become disastrously diverted from its proper ends and goals, so that, as
Colin Gunton puts it, only its 'redirection from within' by its Creator
can restore it to its proper direction.[1] Christians are thereby able to say
both that the material world is 'very good' and that all is by no means as
it should be. Specific correlations can be made between evolutionary
proposals and this theological account – for example between evolutionary and theological accounts of pride – though in the nature of the
case, these correlations are highly provisional, and I have suggested that
in many cases they must be treated with considerable caution.

2   Handling issues evidence with which reductionist views have difficulty

Reductionist views in which every aspect of human nature is *merely* the
product of some kind of evolutionary process manifest a certain amount
of difficulty giving an account of genuine altruism that extends beyond
kin altruism, reciprocity and manipulation. The difficulty is hinted at in
T. H. Huxley's acknowledgement of the 'seeming paradox' that 'ethical
nature, while born of cosmic nature, is necessarily at enmity with its
parent',[2] a paradox that George Williams also acknowledged a century
later.[3] This is not to say that it is impossible to give an account of
genuine altruism within a reductionist frame of reference: one could say,
for example, as Williams does, that it is an accidental by-product of a
boundlessly stupid evolutionary process, though the further questions
also noted in earlier chapters, about why an accidental by-product of a
boundlessly stupid process should have any claim on us, also then arise.

---

1 Colin Gunton, 'The Doctrine of Creation', in Colin E. Gunton (ed.), *The
Cambridge Companion to Christian Doctrine*, Cambridge: Cambridge University
Press, pp. 141–57 (p. 143).

2 Thomas Henry Huxley, *Evolution and Ethics and Other Essays* (*Collected
Essays*, vol. 9), London: Macmillan, 1894, p. viii.

3 George C. Williams, 'Huxley's Evolution and Ethics in Sociobiological Perspective', *Zygon*, 23.4 (1988), pp. 383–407.

Be that as it may, I suggested in Chapters 4 and 5 that a Christian account of humans and the world as parts of God's good creation, and right action as going 'with the grain' of God's good purposes in creation, can give an account, both of *how* moral claims that call for a genuine regard of the other arise, and of *why* we should take notice of them. This does not, of course, amount to an exclusive claim for the particular kind of theological ethic that I have been developing: numerous non-reductionist answers to these questions have been canvassed, including (for example) those of Mary Midgley and Anthony O'Hear, to which I referred briefly in Chapter 4. But it is to suggest that this is one case in which, by the second of my three tests, this theological ethic performs better than the reductionism of Dennett and others.

3   Clarifying, challenging and reshaping moral concepts and experience

I have argued that a Christian understanding of human being as moral being can incorporate evolutionary accounts of the origins of morality without having to regard the latter as nothing but the product of evolution. I have also suggested that genuine altruism causes a problem for reductionist accounts, but that this Christian understanding can give a coherent account of it. However, I also argued in Chapters 4 and 5 that the Christian tradition on which I have drawn should not be content simply to accept, as given, the notions of 'morality' and 'altruism' in view in the evolution-and-ethics literature. I claimed, following Bonhoeffer, that such a theological ethic must regard 'morality', *qua* merely human project to know and do the good, as invalidated in the light of Christ's coming. I later argued that the ongoing difficulties that have been associated with the concept of altruism become easy to understand when we realize that it is a secularized, and thereby truncated and distorted, version of the Christian concept of *agapē*. A Christian theological engagement with discussions of evolutionary ethics, therefore, can both clarify and enrich those discussions by reframing arguments about altruism in terms of the biblical command to love our neighbour.

In similar vein, much of Part 3 was occupied with an attempt to enrich and extend evolutionary discussions about the problem of human moral failure and its possible solutions by reframing them as discussions of sin and salvation (or, following the order that I advocated, salvation and sin). In the final chapter of that part, I attempted a related piece of reshaping by criticizing customary ways of thinking ethically about technological projects to improve ourselves and the world, and suggesting a more comprehensive and theologically satisfactory framework within which such projects may be morally assessed.

In Chapter 3 I borrowed a well-known phrase of Darwin's, describing the main part of this book as 'one long argument' building a cumulative case that the Christian moral tradition it articulates has more to offer than reductionism has in responding to evolutionary issues and insights. The examples I have given here are, I think, indications that some kind of case has indeed been built, though there is plenty of scope for further development and strengthening of it. In one sense, the book has been an attempt at a critical and constructive engagement on an external front (so to say), with a series of questions and challenges put to Christian ethics on the basis of (certain readings of) evolutionary biology. But at the same time, it has been an argument intended for my theological colleagues about the most appropriate manner in which to conduct such an engagement. In contradistinction to modes of Christian apologetic engagement that tend to proceed by trimming the claims of Christian faith to fit the confines of a scientific world-view, I have attempted to show that a full-blooded articulation of a particular Christian tradition, sharp corners intact and rough edges un-smoothed, can offer rich resources for a coherent and fruitful engagement with issues raised by the natural sciences.

There are loose ends and items of unfinished business a-plenty. I draw attention to three; readers will doubtless be able to suggest more. The first arises from my appeal in Chapter 5 to John Hare's Scotist divine command ethic. More could usefully be done to show that, as I hinted,[4] that appeal is not inconsistent with the natural law-like features that I have wished to attribute to Barth's ethics of creation. My appeal through Hare to Duns Scotus also sets up a tension with my critique in Chapter 3 of problematic assumptions about the univocity of language in materialists such as Dawkins and Dennett, since such assumptions are commonly traced in part to Duns Scotus.[5] My suspicion is that this tension can be resolved, but a fuller account is needed to show how. Secondly, having argued in Chapter 4 that a scientific account of 'nature' is not the same kind of thing as a theological doctrine of 'creation', and having thereby raised the question of how they are related, I have not properly answered that question. The mere reminder

---

4 See above, Chapter 5, n. 88.

5 See, e.g., Simon Oliver, 'What Can Theology Offer to Religious Studies?', in M. Warrier and S. Oliver (eds.), *Theology and Religious Studies: An Exploration of Disciplinary Boundaries*, forthcoming, 2007.

that they are not the same thing has done useful work at various points in my argument, but my failure to specify their relationship precisely has led to certain lingering ambiguities at various points, for example in my discussion of evolutionary theodicies in Chapter 8. An answer could be developed drawing on Eugene Rogers's account of nature and grace in Aquinas and Barth, cited in Chapter 5, and Bonhoeffer's account of natural life, discussed in Chapter 8, but, again, further work is required. Thirdly and finally, my account ended with some practical ethical conclusions about technological projects. The conclusions were drawn from the theological analysis developed in Chapter 9 and earlier chapters; however, they were not presented only as instructions about the conduct of Christian people and communities, but as moral claims that hold good in the public arena beyond the walls of the Church. I did not, though, say very much about how such distinctively Christian moral claims and arguments might be advanced in that public arena. Elsewhere I have suggested in outline a variety of modes of Christian engagement with public ethical debates, including the problematizing of dominant approaches, the affirmation and support of whatever is consonant with a Christian moral vision, and – perhaps most importantly – the embodiment in the community of the Church of a form of communal life that renders distinctively Christian moral convictions intelligible.[6] A fuller elaboration is needed, though, of the lines of communication that could be established between my Christian ethical analysis and public decision-making about the practical questions that I have discussed. There remain, then, a good many blank spaces on the map that I have attempted to draw. However, if the theological tradition articulated here is as rich as I have claimed in resources for engagement with contemporary questions, there is every reason to be confident that those spaces need not remain blank for long.

---

6 See Neil G. Messer, 'Healthcare Resource Allocation and the "Recovery of Virtue"', *Studies in Christian Ethics*, 18.1 (2005), pp. 89–108 (pp. 105–7), and, further, Michael Banner, *Christian Ethics and Contemporary Moral Problems*, Cambridge: Cambridge University Press, 1999; and Duncan Forrester, *Christian Justice and Public Policy*, Cambridge: Cambridge University Press, 1997.

Bibliography

Allen, Joseph L., *Love and Conflict: A Covenantal Model of Christian Ethics*, Lanham, MD: University Press of America, 1995 (1984).

Andrews, E. H., 'The Biblical and Philosophical Case for Special Creation', in Derek Burke (ed.), *Creation and Evolution*, Leicester: Inter-Varsity Press, 1985, pp. 226–52.

Anon., 'The Romanes Lecture', *The Oxford Magazine*, 11 (24 May 1893), pp. 380–1, online at http://alepho.clarku.edu/huxley/bib2.html (accessed 16 December 2005).

—— 'Tests to Find Gene Cheats', *New Scientist*, 11 December 2004, p. 4.

—— 'Did Humans and Chimps Once Merge?', *New Scientist*, 20 May 2006, p. 14.

—— 'Hobbit Brain "Too Small" to Be New Species', *New Scientist*, 27 May 2006, p. 15.

—— '"Minister for Fitness" Appointed', BBC News, 23 August 2006, online at http://news.bbc.co.uk/go/pr/fr/-/1/hi/health/5277350.stm (accessed 24 August 2006).

Arnhart, Larry, *Darwinian Natural Right: The Biological Ethics of Human Nature*, Albany, NY: State University of New York Press, 1998.

—— 'The Darwinian Moral Sense and Biblical Religion', in Philip Clayton and Jeffrey Schloss (eds.), *Evolution and Ethics: Human Morality in Biological and Religious Perspective*, Grand Rapids: Eerdmans, 2004, pp. 204–20.

Augustine of Hippo, *Confessions*, in Whitney J. Oates (ed.), *Basic Writings of St Augustine*, vol. 1, New York: Random House, 1948, pp. 3–256.

Aulén, Gustaf, *Christus Victor: An Historical Study of the Three Main Types of the Idea of the Atonement*, trans. A. G. Herbert, London: SPCK, 1931.

Ayala, Francisco J., 'The Evolution of Life: An Overview', in Robert John Russell, William R. Stoeger, SJ, and Francisco J. Ayala (eds.), *Evolutionary and Molecular Biology: Scientific Perspectives on Divine Action*, Vatican City State: Vatican Observatory / Berkeley, CA: Center for Theology and the Natural Sciences, 1998, pp. 21–57.

Bacon, Francis, *The New Organon and Related Writings*, ed. Fulton H. Anderson, New York: Liberal Arts Press, 1960.

Banner, Michael, *Christian Ethics and Contemporary Moral Problems*, Cambridge: Cambridge University Press, 1999.

Barbour, Ian G., *Nature, Human Nature and God*, London: SPCK, 2002.

—— 'On Typologies for Relating Science and Religion', *Zygon*, 37.2 (2002), pp. 345–59.

Barkow, Jerome H., Leda Cosmides and John Tooby (eds.), *The Adapted Mind:*

Evolutionary Psychology and the Generation of Culture, New York: Oxford University Press, 1992.

Barth, Karl, *Church Dogmatics*, ET ed. by G. W. Bromiley and T. F. Torrance, 13 vols., Edinburgh: T&T Clark, 1956–75.

—— *The Christian Life*, trans. Geoffrey Bromiley, new edn, London: T&T Clark, 2004 (1981).

Berry, R. J., 'This Cursed Earth: Is "the Fall" Credible?', *Science and Christian Belief*, 11.1 (1999), pp. 29–49.

—— *God's Book of Works: The Nature and Theology of Nature*, London: T&T Clark (Continuum), 2003.

Bielfeldt, Dennis, 'Nancey Murphy's Nonreductive Physicalism', *Zygon*, 34 (1999), pp. 619–28.

Biggar, Nigel, *The Hastening That Waits: Karl Barth's Ethics*, Oxford: Oxford University Press, 1993.

Blackmore, Susan, *The Meme Machine*, Oxford: Oxford University Press, 1999.

Boehm, Christopher, 'Explaining the Prosocial Side of Moral Communities', in Philip Clayton and Jeffrey Schloss (eds.), *Evolution and Ethics: Human Morality in Biological and Religious Perspective*, Grand Rapids: Eerdmans, 2004, pp. 78–100.

Bonhoeffer, Dietrich, *The Cost of Discipleship*, trans. R. H. Fuller, rev. Irmgard Booth, London: SCM Press, 1959, pp. 35–47.

—— *Letters and Papers from Prison*, enlarged edn, ed. Eberhard Bethge, trans. Reginald Fuller *et al.*, London: SCM Press, 1971.

—— *Creation and Fall: A Theological Exposition of Genesis 1–3* (*Dietrich Bonhoeffer Works*, vol. 3), ET ed. John W. de Gruchy, trans. Douglas Stephen Bax, Minneapolis: Fortress, 1997.

—— *Ethics* (*Dietrich Bonhoeffer Works*, vol. 6), ET ed. Clifford J. Green, Minneapolis: Fortress, 2005.

Boyd, Kenneth M., 'Disease, Illness, Sickness, Health, Healing and Wholeness: Exploring Some Elusive Concepts', *Journal of Medical Ethics: Medical Humanities*, 26 (2000), pp. 9–17.

Broad, C. D., 'Critical Notice of Julian Huxley's *Evolutionary Ethics*', *Mind*, 53 (1944), pp. 344–67, also online at http://www.ditext.com/broad/huxley.html (accessed 16 August 2006).

Brooke, John Hedley, 'The Huxley–Wilberforce Debate: Why Did It Happen?', *Science and Christian Belief*, 13.2 (2001), pp. 127–41, also online with a discussion at http://www.st-edmunds.cam.ac.uk/cis/brooke/index.html (accessed 14 December 2005).

Brown, Andrew, 'The Human Factor', *The Guardian*, 29 July 2006.

Bruce, Donald, and Anne Bruce (eds.), *Engineering Genesis: The Ethics of Genetic Engineering in Non-Human Species*, London: Earthscan, 1998.

Bruce, Donald, and Don Horrocks (eds.), *Modifying Creation? GM Crops and Food: A Christian Perspective*, Carlisle: Paternoster, 2001.

Brunner, Emil, *Man in Revolt: A Christian Anthropology*, trans. Olive Wyon, London: Lutterworth, 1939.

Brunner H. G., *et al.*, 'Abnormal Behavior Associated with a Point Mutation in the Structural Gene for Monoamine Oxidase A', *Science*, 262 (1993), pp. 578–80.

Bryant, John, and Peter Turnpenny, 'Genetics and Genetic Modification of

Humans: Principles, Practice and Possibilities', in Celia Deane-Drummond (ed.), *Brave New World? Theology, Ethics and the Human Genome*, London: T&T Clark, 2003, pp. 5–26.

Burhoe, Ralph Wendell, 'On "Huxley's Evolution and Ethics in Sociobiological Perspective"', *Zygon*, 23.4 (1988), pp. 417–30.

Burtness, James H., *Shaping the Future: The Ethics of Dietrich Bonhoeffer*, Philadelphia, PA: Fortress, 1985.

Caird, George B., *The Language and Imagery of the Bible*, London: Duckworth, 1980.

Calvin, John, *Institutes of the Christian Religion*, trans. Henry Beveridge, 2 vols., repr. Grand Rapids: Eerdmans, 1983.

Campaign for Access to Essential Medicines website, http://www.accessmed-msf.org/ (accessed 24 August 2006).

Cantor, Geoffrey, and Chris Kenny, 'Barbour's Fourfold Way: Problems with His Taxonomy of Science–Religion Relationships', *Zygon*, 36.4 (2001), pp. 765–81.

Cartwright, Nancy, *The Dappled World: A Study of the Boundaries of Science*, Cambridge: Cambridge University Press, 1999.

Cela-Conde, Camilo J., 'The Hominid Evolutionary Journey: A Summary', in Robert John Russell, William R. Stoeger, SJ, and Francisco J. Ayala (eds.), *Evolutionary and Molecular Biology: Scientific Perspectives on Divine Action*, Vatican City State: Vatican Observatory / Berkeley, CA: Center for Theology and the Natural Sciences, 1998, pp. 59–78.

Churchill, Robert Paul, and Erin Street, 'Is There a Paradox of Altruism?', in Jonathan Seglow (ed.), *The Ethics of Altruism*, London: Frank Cass, 2004, pp. 87–105.

Clark, Stephen R. L., *How to Think about the Earth: Philosophical and Theological Models for Ecology*, London: Mowbray, 1993.

—— *Biology and Christian Ethics*, Cambridge: Cambridge University Press, 2000.

Clayton, Philip, *God and Contemporary Science*, Edinburgh: Edinburgh University Press, 1997.

—— 'Shaping the Field of Theology and Science: A Critique of Nancey Murphy', *Zygon*, 34 (1999), pp. 609–18.

—— 'Biology and Purpose', in Philip Clayton and Jeffrey Schloss (eds.), *Evolution and Ethics: Human Morality in Biological and Religious Perspective*, Grand Rapids: Eerdmans, 2004, pp. 318–36.

Clayton, Philip, and S. Knapp, 'Rationality and Christian Self-Conceptions', in W. M. Richardson and W. J. Wildman (eds.), *Religion and Science: History, Method, Dialogue*, London and New York: Routledge, 1996.

Clayton, Philip, and Jeffrey Schloss (eds.), *Evolution and Ethics: Human Morality in Biological and Religious Perspective*, Grand Rapids: Eerdmans, 2004.

Clothier, Sir Cecil (chairman), *Report of the Committee on the Ethics of Human Genetic Manipulation*, London: Her Majesty's Stationery Office, 1992.

Clough, David, *Ethics in Crisis: Interpreting Barth's Ethics*, Aldershot: Ashgate, 2005.

Cobb, John B., Jr, 'Befriending an Amoral Nature', *Zygon*, 23.4 (1988), pp. 431–6.

Cole-Turner, Ronald (ed.), *Human Cloning: Religious Responses*, Louisville, KY: Westminster John Knox, 1997.

Bibliography

Comte, Auguste, *Système de Politique Positive* (1851–4), in G. Lenzer (ed.), *Auguste Comte and Positivism: The Essential Writings*, Chicago, IL: University of Chicago Press, 1983.

Cosmides Leda, and John Tooby, 'Cognitive Adaptations for Social Exchange', in Jerome H. Barkow *et al.*, *The Adapted Mind: Evolutionary Psychology and the Generation of Culture*, Oxford: Oxford University Press, 1992, pp. 163–228.

Creel, R. E., *Divine Impassibility*, Cambridge: Cambridge University Press, 1986.

Cronin, Helena, *The Ant and the Peacock: Altruism and Sexual Selection from Darwin to Today*, Cambridge: Cambridge University Press, 1991.

Cronk, Lee, 'Evolutionary Theories of Morality and the Manipulative Use of Signals', *Zygon*, 29.1 (1994), pp. 81–101.

Cullen, Lindsay, 'Nancey Murphy, Supervenience and Causality', *Science and Christian Belief*, 13.1 (2001), pp. 39–50.

Darwin, Charles, *The Origin of Species by Means of Natural Selection; or, The Preservation of Favoured Races in the Struggle for Life*, ed. J. W. Burrow, London: Penguin, 1968; repr. 1985 (orig. pub. London: John Murray, 1859).

—— *The Descent of Man, and Selection in Relation to Sex*, London: John Murray, 1871, repr. with introduction by John Tyler Bonner and Robert M. May, Princeton, NJ: Princeton University Press, 1981.

Darwin, Francis (ed.), *The Life and Letters of Charles Darwin*, 2 vols., New York: Appleton, 1905, online at http://pages.britishlibrary.net/charles.darwin/texts/letters/letters1_fm.html (accessed 13 October 2006).

Dawkins, Richard, 'In Defence of Selfish Genes', *Philosophy*, 56 (1979), pp. 556–73. Also online at http://www.royalinstitutephilosophy.org/articles/ (accessed 13 August 2006).

—— *The Extended Phenotype: The Gene as the Unit of Natural Selection*, Oxford: W. H. Freeman, 1982.

—— *The Blind Watchmaker*, Harlow: Longman, 1986.

—— *The Selfish Gene*, 2nd edn, Oxford: Oxford University Press, 1989 (1976).

Deane-Drummond, Celia, *Creation through Wisdom: Theology and the New Biology*, Edinburgh: T&T Clark, 2000.

—— *Biology and Theology Today*, London: SCM Press, 2001.

—— *The Ethics of Nature*, Oxford: Blackwell, 2004.

Dembski, William A., *Intelligent Design: The Bridge between Science and Theology*, Downers Grove, IL: InterVarsity Press, 1999.

Dennett, Daniel C., *Darwin's Dangerous Idea: Evolution and the Meanings of Life*, London: Penguin, 1996.

—— *Freedom Evolves*, London: Allen Lane, 2003.

Desmond, Adrian, *Huxley: From Devil's Disciple to Evolution's High Priest*, London: Penguin, 1998.

Desmond, Adrian, and James Moore, *Darwin*, London: Penguin, 1992.

Dobzhansky, Theodosius, 'Nothing in Biology Makes Sense Except in the Light of Evolution', *American Biology Teacher*, 35 (1973), pp. 125–9; reprinted in Mark Ridley (ed.), *Evolution* (Oxford Readers), Oxford: Oxford University Press, 1997, pp. 378–87.

Donaldson, Liam (chair), *Stem Cell Research: Medical Progress with Responsibility*, London: Department of Health, 2000.

Bibliography

Dostoevsky, Fyodor, *The Brothers Karamazov*, trans. Constance Garnett, London: Heinemann, 1912.

Eldredge, Niles, *Reinventing Darwin: The Great Evolutionary Debate*, London: Phoenix, 1996.
Emmet, Dorothy, *The Moral Prism*, London: Macmillan, 1979.
Erasmus, Desiderius, *On the Freedom of the Will*, trans. E. Gordon Rupp and A. N. Marlow, in *Luther and Erasmus* (Library of Christian Classics, 17), London: SCM Press, 1969, pp. 35–97.

Fabri dos Anjos, Márcio, 'Power, Ethics and the Poor in Human Genetics Research', in Maureen Junker-Kenny and Lisa Sowle Cahill (eds.), *The Ethics of Genetic Engineering* (*Concilium*, 1998/2), pp. 73–82.
Farber, Paul Lawrence, 'French Evolutionary Ethics during the Third Republic: Jean de Lanessan', in Jane Maienschein and Michael Ruse (eds.), *Biology and the Foundations of Ethics*, Cambridge: Cambridge University Press, 1999, pp. 84–97.
Fiddes, Paul, *The Creative Suffering of God*, Oxford: Oxford University Press, 1989.
Fisher, R. A., 'The Nature of Inheritance', from *The Genetical Theory of Natural Selection*, Oxford: Oxford University Press, 1930, reprinted in Mark Ridley (ed.), *Evolution* (Oxford Readers), Oxford: Oxford University Press, 1997, pp. 22–32.
Fletcher, Joseph, *The Ethics of Genetic Control: Ending Reproductive Roulette*, Garden City, NY: Doubleday, 1974.
Flint, James, 'Don't Worry, Be Happy' (review of Jonathan Haight, *The Happiness Hypothesis*), *The Guardian*, 22 July 2006.
Ford, David, 'On Being Theologically Hospitable to Jesus Christ: Hans Frei's Achievement', *Journal of Theological Studies*, NS, 46.2 (1995), pp. 532–46.
—— *Self and Salvation: Being Transformed*, Cambridge: Cambridge University Press, 1999.
Forrester, Duncan B., *Christian Justice and Public Policy*, Cambridge: Cambridge University Press, 1997.
Forsyth, P. T., *Positive Preaching and the Modern Mind*, London: Hodder and Stoughton, 1907.
—— *The Person and Place of Jesus Christ*, London: Hodder and Stoughton, 1909.
—— *The Work of Christ*, London: Hodder and Stoughton, 1910.
—— *The Cruciality of the Cross*, 2nd edn, London: Independent Press, 1948 (1909).
—— *The Justification of God: Lectures for War-time on a Christian Theodicy*, 2nd edn, London: Latimer House, 1948 (1916).
Frei, Hans W., *Types of Christian Theology*, ed. George Hunsinger and William H. Placher, New Haven, CT: Yale University Press, 1992.

Galton, Francis, 'Hereditary Talent and Character', *Macmillan's Magazine*, 12 (1865), pp. 157–66, 318–27, online at http://galton.org/essays/1860-1869/galton-1865-hereditary-talent.pdf (accessed 14 December 2005).
Gazzaniga, Michael, *The Mind's Past*, Berkeley: University of California Press, 1998.

Bibliography

Gene Therapy Advisory Committee website, http://www.advisorybodies.doh. gov.uk/genetics/gtac/ (accessed 24 August 2006).

Gill, Robin, *Churchgoing and Christian Ethics*, Cambridge: Cambridge University Press, 1999.

Glover, Jonathan, *What Sort of People Should There Be? Genetic Engineering, Brain Control and Their Impact on Our Future World*, Harmondsworth: Pelican, 1984.

Goslee, David, 'Evolution, Ethics and Equivocation: T. H. Huxley's Conflicted Legacy', *Zygon*, 39.1 (2004), pp. 137–60.

Gould, Stephen Jay, *Ever since Darwin*, London: Burnett, 1978.

—— 'Evolution: The Pleasures of Pluralism', *New York Review of Books*, 26 June 1997, pp. 47–52, online at http://www.stephenjaygould.org/reviews/gould_pluralism.html (accessed 10 August 2006).

—— *Rocks of Ages: Science and Religion in the Fullness of Life*, London: Vintage, 2002.

—— *The Structure of Evolutionary Theory*, Cambridge, MA: Harvard University Press, 2002.

Gould, S. J., and R. C. Lewontin, 'The Spandrels of San Marco and the Panglossian Paradigm: A Critique of the Adaptationist Programme', *Proceedings of the Royal Society of London*, series B, 205 (1979), pp. 581–98, reprinted in Mark Ridley (ed.), *Evolution* (Oxford Readers), Oxford: Oxford University Press, 1997, pp. 139–54.

Graham, Keith, 'Altruism, Self-Interest and the Indistinctness of Persons', in Jonathan Seglow (ed.), *The Ethics of Altruism*, London: Frank Cass, 2004, pp. 49–67.

Grant, Colin, *Altruism and Christian Ethics*, Cambridge: Cambridge University Press, 2001.

Gregory of Nyssa, *Great Catechism*, XXIV, in Philip Schaff and Henry Wace (eds.), *Nicene and Post-Nicene Fathers*, 2nd ser., vol. V, Edinburgh: T&T Clark, 1892.

Grey, Mary, *Redeeming the Dream: Feminism, Redemption and Christian Tradition*, London: SPCK, 1989.

Gunton, Colin E., *The Actuality of Atonement: A Study of Metaphor, Rationality and the Christian Tradition*, Edinburgh: T&T Clark, 1988.

—— 'The Doctrine of Creation', in Colin E. Gunton (ed.), *The Cambridge Companion to Christian Doctrine*, Cambridge: Cambridge University Press, 1997, pp. 141–57.

—— *The Triune Creator: A Historical and Systematic Study*, Grand Rapids: Eerdmans, 1998.

—— *Act and Being: Towards a Theology of the Divine Attributes*, London: SCM Press, 2002.

Haarsma, Loren, 'Evolution and Divine Revelation', in Philip Clayton and Jeffrey Schloss (eds.), *Evolution and Ethics: Human Morality in Biological and Religious Perspective*, Grand Rapids: Eerdmans, 2004, pp. 153–70.

Habgood, John, *The Concept of Nature*, London: Darton, Longman and Todd, 2002.

Haldane, J. B. S., 'Disease and Evolution', *La Richercha Scientifica*, 19, suppl. (1949), pp. 68–76, reprinted in Mark Ridley (ed.), *Evolution* (Oxford Readers),

Oxford: Oxford University Press, 1997, pp. 41–7.

Hall, Amy Laura, 'Naming the Risen Lord: Embodied Discipleship and Masculinity', in Stanley Hauerwas and Samuel Wells (eds.), *The Blackwell Companion to Christian Ethics*, Oxford: Blackwell, 2004, pp. 82–94.

Hamilton, William D., 'The Evolution of Altruistic Behaviour', *American Naturalist*, 97 (1963), pp. 354–6, reprinted with commentary in id., *The Narrow Roads of Gene Land: The Collected Papers of W. D. Hamilton*, vol. 1, Oxford: W. H. Freeman, 1996.

—— 'The Genetical Evolution of Social Behaviour', parts I and II, *Journal of Theoretical Biology*, 7 (1964), pp. 1–52, reprinted with commentary in id., *The Narrow Roads of Gene Land*, vol. 1.

Hampson, Daphne, 'Reinhold Niebuhr on Sin: A Critique', in Richard Harries (ed.), *Reinhold Niebuhr and the Issues of Our Time*, Oxford: Mowbray, 1986, pp. 46–60.

Hansard (House of Commons Daily Debates), 19 December 2000, col. 266.

Hansard (House of Lords Debates), 22 January 2001, col. 124.

Hare, John E., *God's Call: Moral Realism, God's Commands, and Human Autonomy*, Grand Rapids: Eerdmans, 2001.

—— 'Is There an Evolutionary Foundation for Human Morality?', in Philip Clayton and Jeffrey Schloss (eds.), *Evolution and Ethics: Human Morality in Biological and Religious Perspective*, Grand Rapids: Eerdmans, 2004, pp. 187–203.

Hart, Trevor A., 'Morality, Atonement and the Death of Jesus: The Crucial Focus of Forsyth's Theology', in Trevor Hart (ed.), *Justice the True and Only Mercy: Essays on the Life and Theology of Peter Taylor Forsyth*, Edinburgh: T&T Clark, 1995, pp. 16–36.

—— *Regarding Karl Barth: Essays toward a Reading of His Theology*, Carlisle: Paternoster, 1999.

—— 'Revelation', in John Webster (ed.), *The Cambridge Companion to Karl Barth*, Cambridge: Cambridge University Press, 2000, pp. 37–56.

Hauerwas, Stanley, *A Community of Character: Toward a Constructive Christian Social Ethic*, Notre Dame, IN: University of Notre Dame Press, 1981.

—— *With the Grain of the Universe: The Church's Witness and Natural Theology*, Grand Rapids, MI: Brazos, 2001.

Haught, John F., *God after Darwin: A Theology of Evolution*, Boulder, CO: Westview, 2000.

Hayek, F. A., *The Fatal Conceit*, London: Routledge, 1988.

Hays, Richard B., *The Moral Vision of the New Testament: Community, Cross, New Creation*, Edinburgh: T&T Clark, 1997.

Hrdy, Sarah Blaffer, 'Comments on George Williams's Essay on Morality and Nature', *Zygon*, 23.4 (1988), pp. 409–11.

—— *Mother Nature: A History of Mothers, Infants, and Natural Selection*, New York: Pantheon, 1999.

Hull, David L., 'God of the Galapagos', *Nature*, 352 (1991), pp. 485–6.

Human Genetics Advisory Commission / Human Fertilisation and Embryology Authority, *Cloning Issues in Reproduction, Science and Medicine*, London: HGAC, 1998.

Hume, David, *A Treatise of Human Nature*, ed. L. A. Selby-Bigge, rev. P. H. Nidditch, Oxford: Clarendon Press, 1978 (1739–40).

—— *Dialogues Concerning Natural Religion*, ed. Stanley Tweyman, London: Routledge, 1991.

Hunsinger, George, 'Karl Barth's Christology: Its Basic Chalcedonian Character', in John Webster (ed.), *The Cambridge Companion to Karl Barth*, Cambridge: Cambridge University Press, 2000, pp. 127–42.

Huxley, Thomas Henry, 'On the Reception of the Origin of Species' (1887), online at http://alepho.clarku.edu/huxley/Book/Recep.html (accessed 14 July 2006).

—— *Hume: With Helps to the Study of Berkeley* (*Collected Essays*, vol. VI), London: Macmillan, 1894 (1878), online at http://alepho.clarku.edu/huxley/CE6/index.html (accessed 14 December 2005).

—— *Man's Place in Nature* (*Collected Essays*, vol. VII), London: Macmillan, 1894, pp. vi–ix, online at http://alepho.clarku.edu/huxley/CE7/ (accessed 14 December 2005).

—— 'Prolegomena', in *Evolution and Ethics and Other Essays* (*Collected Essays*, vol. IX), London: Macmillan, 1894, pp. 1–45, also online at http://alepho.clarku.edu/huxley/CE9/ (accessed 14 December 2005).

—— 'Evolution and Ethics' (The Romanes Lecture, 1893), in *Collected Essays*, vol. IX, pp. 46–116.

—— 'Science and Morals', in *Collected Essays*, vol. IX, pp. 117–46.

—— 'The Struggle for Existence in Human Society', in *Collected Essays*, vol. IX, pp. 195–236.

Huxley, Julian, 'Evolutionary Ethics' (The Romanes Lecture, 1943), in T. H. Huxley and Julian Huxley, *Evolution and Ethics: 1893–1943*, London: Pilot Press, 1947, pp. 103–51.

John Paul II, *Evangelium Vitae*, Dublin: Veritas, 1995.

Junker-Kenny, Maureen, 'Embryos *in vitro*, Personhood, and Rights', in Maureen Junker-Kenny (ed.), *Designing Life? Genetics, Procreation and Ethics*, Aldershot: Ashgate, 1999, pp. 130–58.

Kane, Robert, 'Some Neglected Pathways in the Free Will Labyrinth', in Robert Kane (ed.), *The Oxford Handbook of Free Will*, Oxford: Oxford University Press, 2002, pp. 407–37.

Kant, Immanuel, *Critique of Practical Reason and Other Works on the Theory of Ethics*, trans. Thomas Kingsmill Abbott, 5th edn, London: Longmans, Green and Co., 1898.

—— *Religion within the Limits of Reason Alone*, trans. Theodore M. Green and Hoyt H. Hudson, New York: Harper, 1960.

Karmiloff-Smith, Annette, 'Why Babies' Brains Are Not Swiss Army Knives', in Hilary Rose and Steven Rose (eds.), *Alas Poor Darwin: Arguments against Evolutionary Psychology*, London: Jonathan Cape, 2000, pp. 144–56.

Kidner, Derek, *Tyndale Commentary on Genesis*, London: Tyndale Press, 1967.

Kim, Jaegwon, *Supervenience and the Mind*, Cambridge: Cambridge University Press, 1993.

—— 'The Myth of Nonreductive Materialism', in Richard Warren and Tadeusz Szubka (eds.), *The Mind–Body Problem*, Oxford: Blackwell, 1994, pp. 242–60.

Kimura, Motoo, 'Recent Development of the Neutral Theory Viewed from the Wrightian Tradition of Population Genetics', *Proceedings of the National*

Academy of Sciences of the USA, 88 (1991), pp. 69–73, reprinted in Mark Ridley (ed.), *Evolution* (Oxford Readers), Oxford: Oxford University Press, 1997, pp. 88–94.

Krebs, Dennis, *et al.*, 'On the Evolution of Self-Knowledge and Self-Deception', in Kevin MacDonald (ed.), *Sociobiological Perspectives on Human Development*, New York: Springer-Verlag, 1988.

Kreitman, Martin, 'The Neutral Theory Is Dead. Long Live the Neutral Theory', *BioEssays*, 18 (1996), pp. 678–82; reprinted in Mark Ridley (ed.), *Evolution* (Oxford Readers), Oxford: Oxford University Press, 1997, pp. 100–8.

Kropotkin, Petr, *Mutual Aid: A Factor of Evolution*, London: Heinemann, 1902, online at http://socserv2.socsci.mcmaster.ca/~econ/ugcm/3113/kropotkin/mutaid.txt (accessed 15 December 2005).

Krötke, Wolf, 'The Humanity of the Human Person in Karl Barth's Anthropology', trans. Philip G. Ziegler, in John Webster (ed.), *The Cambridge Companion to Karl Barth*, Cambridge: Cambridge University Press, 2000, pp. 159–76.

Leakey, Richard, and Roger Lewin, *The Sixth Extinction: Biodiversity and Its Survival*, London: Weidenfeld and Nicolson, 1996.

Libet, Benjamin, 'Do We Have Free Will?', *Journal of Consciousness Studies*, 6 (1999), pp. 47–57, reprinted in Robert Kane (ed.), *The Oxford Handbook of Free Will*, Oxford: Oxford University Press, 2002, pp. 551–64.

Long, D. Stephen, *Tragedy, Tradition, Transformism: The Ethics of Paul Ramsey*, Boulder, CO: Westview, 1995.

Lucas J. R., and Janet Browne, 'The Huxley–Wilberforce Debate Revisited', 6 November 2003, online at http://users.ox.ac.uk/~jrlucas/revisit.html (accessed 4 August 2006).

Lumsden, Charles J., and Edward O. Wilson, *Genes, Mind and Culture*, Cambridge, MA: Harvard University Press, 1981.

Luther, Martin, *Disputation against Scholastic Theology*, in *Luther: Early Theological Works* (Library of Christian Classics, 16), ed. and trans. James Atkinson, London: SCM Press, 1962, pp. 266–73.

McFadyen, Alistair I., *The Call to Personhood: A Christian Theory of the Individual in Social Relationships*, Cambridge: Cambridge University Press, 1990.

—— *Bound to Sin: Abuse, Holocaust and the Christian Doctrine of Sin*, Cambridge: Cambridge University Press, 2000.

Mcfarland, Ian A., 'Who Is My Neighbor?: The Good Samaritan as a Source for Theological Anthropology', *Modern Theology*, 17.1 (2001), pp. 57–66.

McGhie, John, *et al.*, *The Climate of Poverty: Facts, Fears and Hope. A Christian Aid Report*, London: Christian Aid, 2006, online at http://www.christian-aid.org.uk/indepth/605caweek/index.htm (accessed 24 August 2006).

McGrath, Alister, *Dawkins' God: Genes, Memes and the Meaning of Life*, Oxford: Blackwell, 2005.

MacIntyre, Alasdair, *After Virtue: A Study in Moral Theory*, 2nd edn, London: Duckworth, 1985 (1981).

—— *Whose Justice? Which Rationality?* London: Duckworth, 1988.

Mackenbach, Johan P., *Health Inequalities: Europe in Profile* (an independent, expert report commissioned by the UK Presidency of the EU, February 2006), online at http://ec.europa.eu/health/ph_determinants/socio_economics/ documents/ev_060302_rdo6_en.pdf (accessed 24 August 2006).

McKenny, Gerald P., *To Relieve the Human Condition: Bioethics, Technology and the Body*, Albany, NY: State University of New York Press, 1997.

Maddox, John, *et al.*, 'Discussion: Genes, Mind and Culture', *Zygon*, 19.2 (1984), pp. 213–32.

Mann, Janet, 'Nurturance or Negligence: Maternal Psychology and Behavioral Preference among Preterm Twins', in Jerome H. Barkow, Leda Cosmides and John Tooby (eds.), *The Adapted Mind: Evolutionary Psychology and the Generation of Culture*, New York: Oxford University Press, 1992, pp. 367–90.

May, William F., 'The Medical Covenant: An Ethics of Obligation or Virtue?', in Gerald P. McKenny and Jonathan R. Sande (eds.), *Theological Analyses of the Clinical Encounter*, Dordrecht: Kluwer, 1994, pp. 29–44.

MedLine Plus Medical Dictionary, online at http://www.nlm.nih.gov/medlineplus/mplusdictionary.html (accessed 18 July 2006).

Messer, Neil G., 'Human Cloning and Genetic Manipulation: Some Theological and Ethical Issues', *Studies in Christian Ethics*, 12.2 (1999), pp. 1–16.

—— *The Ethics of Human Cloning*, Cambridge: Grove, 2001.

—— 'Human Genetics and the Image of the Triune God', *Science and Christian Belief*, 13.2 (2001), pp. 99–111.

—— 'The Human Genome Project, Health and the "Tyranny of Normality"', in Celia Deane-Drummond (ed.), *Brave New World? Theology, Ethics and the Human Genome*, London: T&T Clark, 2003, pp. 91–115.

—— 'Healthcare Resource Allocation and the "Recovery of Virtue"', *Studies in Christian Ethics*, 18.1 (2005), pp. 89–108.

Midgley, Mary, 'Gene-juggling', *Philosophy*, 54 (1979), pp. 439–58. Also online at http://www.royalinstitutephilosophy.org/articles/ (accessed 13 August 2006).

—— 'Selfish Genes and Social Darwinism', *Philosophy*, 58 (1983), pp. 365–77. Also online at http://www.royalinstitutephilosophy.org/articles/ (accessed 13 August 2006).

—— *The Ethical Primate: Humans, Freedom and Morality*, London: Routledge, 1994.

—— *Beast and Man*, rev. edn, London: Routledge, 1995 (1978).

—— 'Why Memes?', in Hilary Rose and Steven Rose (eds.), *Alas, Poor Darwin: Arguments against Evolutionary Psychology*, London: Jonathan Cape, 2000, pp. 67–84.

—— *Wickedness: A Philosophical Essay*, London: Routledge, 2001 (1984).

Miller, Kenneth R., *Finding Darwin's God: A Scientist's Search for Common Ground between God and Evolution*, New York: Perennial (HarperCollins), 2002.

Moore, G. E., *Principia Ethica*, Cambridge: Cambridge University Press, 1959 (1903).

Morris, Henry M. (ed.), *Scientific Creationism*, San Diego, CA: Creation-Life, 1974.

Morton, Adam, *On Evil*, London: Routledge, 2004.

Murphy, Nancey, 'Physicalism without Reductionism: Toward a Scientifically, Philosophically and Theologically Sound Portrait of Human Nature', *Zygon*, 34 (1999), pp. 551–71.

—— 'Response to Cullen', *Science and Christian Belief*, 13.2 (2001), pp. 161–3.
—— 'The Problem of Mental Causation: How Does Reason Get Its Grip on the Brain?', *Science and Christian Belief*, 14.2 (2002), pp. 143–57.

Niebuhr, Reinhold, *Moral Man and Immoral Society*, New York: Scribners, 1932.
—— *The Nature and Destiny of Man: A Christian Interpretation*, vol. 1: *Human Nature*, London: Nisbet, 1941, pp. 190–220.
di Noia, J. Augustine, OP, 'Religion and the Religions', in John Webster (ed.), *The Cambridge Companion to Karl Barth*, Cambridge: Cambridge University Press, 2000, pp. 243–57.
Northcott, Michael, '"Behold, I have set the land before you" (Deut. 1.8): Christian Ethics, GM Foods and the Culture of Modern Farming', in Celia Deane-Drummond and Bronislaw Szerszynski with Robin Grove-White (eds.), *Re-Ordering Nature: Theology, Society and the New Genetics*, London: T&T Clark, 2003, pp. 85–106.
Nuffield Council on Bioethics, *Stem Cell Therapy: The Ethical Issues*, London: Nuffield Council, 2000.

O'Donovan, Oliver, *Resurrection and Moral Order: An Outline for Evangelical Ethics*, 2nd edn, Leicester, Apollos, 1994.
O'Hear, Anthony, *Beyond Evolution: The Limits of Evolutionary Explanation*, Oxford: Oxford University Press, 1997.
Ohta, Tomoko, 'The Current Significance and Standing of Neutral and Nearly Neutral Theories', *BioEssays*, 18 (1996), pp. 673–7, reprinted Mark Ridley (ed.), *Evolution* (Oxford Readers), Oxford: Oxford University Press, 1997, pp. 94–100.
Oliver, Simon, 'What Can Theology Offer to Religious Studies?', in M. Warrier and S. Oliver (eds.), *Theology and Religious Studies: An Exploration of Disciplinary Boundaries*, forthcoming, 2007.
Outka, Gene, 'The Ethics of Human Stem Cell Research', in Brent Waters and Ronald Cole-Turner (eds.), *God and the Embryo: Religious Voices on Stem Cells and Cloning*, Washington, DC: Georgetown University Press, 2003, pp. 29–64.

Page, Ruth, *God and the Web of Creation*, London: SCM Press, 1996.
Pannenberg, Wolfhart, 'Eternity, Time and the Trinitarian God', *CTI Reflections*, 3 (1999), pp. 49–61.
Parens, Erik, 'Genetic Differences and Human Identities: On Why Talking about Behavioral Genetics Is Important and Difficult', *Hastings Center Report Special Supplement*, 34.1 (2004), pp. S1–S36.
Paul, Diane B., 'Darwin, Social Darwinism and Eugenics', in Jonathan Hodge and Gregory Radick (eds.), *The Cambridge Companion to Darwin*, Cambridge: Cambridge University Press, 2003, pp. 214–39.
Peacocke, Arthur, *Theology for a Scientific Age*, 2nd enlarged edn, London: SCM Press, 1993.
—— 'Science and the Future of Theology: Critical Issues', *Zygon*, 35.1 (2000), pp. 119–40.
—— 'The Cost of New Life', in John Polkinghorne (ed.), *The Work of Love: Creation as Kenosis*, London: SPCK, 2001, pp. 21–42.

——*Paths from Science towards God: The End of All Our Exploring*, Oxford: Oneworld, 2001.

Pinker, Steven, *How the Mind Works*, London: Penguin, 1998.

Plaskow, Judith, *Sex, Sin and Grace: Women's Experience and the Theologies of Reinhold Niebuhr and Paul Tillich*, Lanham, MD: University Press of America, 1980.

Polkinghorne, John, *Science and Providence: God's Interaction with the World*, London: SPCK, 1989.

——*Science and Christian Belief: Theological Reflections of a Bottom-Up Thinker*, London: SPCK, 1994.

——*Faith, Science and Understanding*, London: SPCK, 2000.

——*Science and the Trinity: The Christian Encounter with Reality*, London: SPCK 2004.

Pope, Stephen J., *The Evolution of Altruism and the Ordering of Love*, Washington, DC: Georgetown University Press, 1994.

Rachels, James, *Created from Animals: The Moral Implications of Darwinism*, Oxford: Oxford University Press, 1990.

Rahner, Karl, 'Theology and Monogenism', in *Theological Investigations*, vol. 1, London: Darton, Longman and Todd, 1961, pp. 229–96.

——'Evolution and Original Sin', *Concilium*, 26 (1967), pp. 61–73.

Ramsey, Paul, *War and the Christian Conscience: How Shall Modern War Be Conducted Justly?* Durham, NC: Duke University Press, 1961.

——*The Patient as Person: Explorations in Medical Ethics*, New Haven, CT: Yale University Press, 1970.

——*Basic Christian Ethics*, new edn with foreword by Stanley Hauerwas and D. Stephen Long (Library of Theological Ethics), Louisville: Westminster/John Knox, 1993 (1950).

Richards, Janet Radcliffe, *Human Nature after Darwin: A Philosophical Introduction*, London: Routledge, 2000.

Richards, Robert J., 'A Defense of Evolutionary Ethics', *Biology and Philosophy*, 1 (1986), pp. 265–93, reprinted as Appendix 2 of id., *Darwin and the Emergence of Evolutionary Theories of Mind and Behavior*, Chicago: University of Chicago Press, 1987.

Richerson, Peter J., and Robert Boyd, 'Darwinian Evolutionary Ethics: Between Patriotism and Sympathy', in Philip Clayton and Jeffrey Schloss (eds.), *Evolution and Ethics: Human Morality in Biological and Religious Perspective*, Grand Rapids: Eerdmans, 2004, pp. 50–77.

Ricoeur, Paul, *Oneself as Another*, Chicago, IL: University of Chicago Press, 1992.

Ridley, Mark, *Evolution*, 3rd edn, Oxford: Blackwell, 2003.

Rincon, Paul, 'Fossils Fill Gaps in Human Lineage', BBC News, 12 April 2006, online at http://news.bbc.co.uk/go/pr/fr/-/1/hi/sci/tech/4900946.stm (accessed 2 August 2006).

Rockwell, Teed, 'Physicalism, Non-reductive', in Chris Eliasmith (ed.), *Dictionary of Philosophy of Mind*, online at http://philosophy.uwaterloo.ca/MindDict/ (accessed 21 August 2006).

Rogers, Eugene F., *Thomas Aquinas and Karl Barth: Sacred Doctrine and the Natural Knowledge of God*, Notre Dame, IN: University of Notre Dame Press, 1999.

Rogers, N. T., *et al.*, 'Phospholipase Cζ Causes Ca²⁺ Oscillations and Partheno-genetic Activation of Human Oocytes', *Reproduction*, 128 (2004), pp. 697–702.

Rolston, Holmes, III, *Genes, Genesis and God: Values and Their Origins in Natural and Human History*, Cambridge: Cambridge University Press, 1999.

—— 'Kenosis and Nature', in John Polkinghorne (ed.), *The Work of Love: Creation as Kenosis*, London: SPCK, 2001, pp. 43–65.

Rose, Hilary, and Steven Rose (eds.), *Alas Poor Darwin: Arguments against Evolutionary Psychology*, London: Jonathan Cape, 2000.

Rose, Steven, 'Pre-Copernican Sociobiology?', *New Scientist*, 80 (1978), pp. 45–6.

—— 'Neurogenetic Determinism and the New Euphenics', *British Medical Journal*, 317 (1998), pp. 1707–8.

—— *Lifelines: Life beyond the Gene*, 2nd edn, London: Vintage, 2005.

Ruse, Michael, *Taking Darwin Seriously: A Naturalistic Approach to Philosophy*, Oxford: Blackwell, 1986.

—— 'Response to Williams: Selfishness Is Not Enough', *Zygon*, 23.4 (1988), pp. 413–16.

—— 'The Significance of Evolution', in Peter Singer (ed.), *A Companion to Ethics*, Oxford: Blackwell, 1991, pp. 500–10.

—— 'Evolutionary Ethics in the Twentieth Century: Julian Sorrell Huxley and George Gaylord Simpson', in Jane Maienschein and Michael Ruse (eds.), *Biology and the Foundations of Ethics*, Cambridge: Cambridge University Press, 1999, pp. 198–224.

—— *Can a Darwinian Be a Christian? The Relationship between Science and Religion*, Cambridge: Cambridge University Press, 2001.

Russell, Colin A., 'Where Science and History Meet: Some Fresh Challenges to the Christian Faith?', *Science and Christian Belief*, 13.2 (2001), pp. 113–25.

Schwöbel, Christoph, 'Human Being as Relational Being: Twelve Theses for a Christian Anthropology', in Christoph Schwöbel and Colin E. Gunton (eds.), *Persons, Divine and Human: King's College Essays in Theological Anthropology*, Edinburgh: T&T Clark, 1991, pp. 141–65.

Scott, Peter, *A Political Theology of Nature*, Cambridge: Cambridge University Press, 2003.

Sell, Alan P. F., 'P. T. Forsyth as Unsystematic Systematician', in Trevor Hart (ed.), *Justice the True and Only Mercy: Essays on the Life and Theology of Peter Taylor Forsyth*, Edinburgh: T&T Clark, 1995, pp. 110–45.

Sellar, Mary J., 'Genes, Genetics and the Human Genome: Some Personal Reflections', in Celia Deane-Drummond (ed.), *Brave New World? Theology, Ethics and the Human Genome*, London: T&T Clark, 2003, pp. 27–43.

Seth, Andrew, 'Man's Place in the Cosmos', *Blackwood's Edinburgh Magazine*, 154 (December 1893), pp. 823–34, online at http://alepho.clarku.edu/huxley/bib2.html (accessed 16 December 2005).

Singer, Peter, 'Ethics and Sociobiology', *Zygon*, 19.2 (1984), pp. 141–58.

Smith, Barbara Herrnstein, 'Sewing Up the Mind: The Claims of Evolutionary Psychology', in Hilary Rose and Steven Rose (eds.), *Alas Poor Darwin: Arguments against Evolutionary Psychology*, London: Jonathan Cape, 2000, pp. 129–43.

Smith, John Maynard, 'Weismann and Modern Biology', *Oxford Surveys in*

Evolutionary Biology, 6 (1989), pp. 1–12, reprinted in Mark Ridley (ed.), *Evolution* (Oxford Readers), Oxford: Oxford University Press, 1997, pp. 17–22.

Snyder, Evan Y., and Jeanne F. Loring, 'Beyond Fraud – Stem-Cell Research Continues', *New England Journal of Medicine*, 354.4 (2006), pp. 321–4.

Sober, Elliott, and David Sloan Wilson, *Unto Others: The Evolution and Psychology of Unselfish Behavior*, Cambridge, MA: Harvard University Press, 1998.

Song, Robert, 'The Human Genome Project as Soteriological Project', in Celia Deane-Drummond (ed.), *Brave New World? Theology, Ethics and the Human Genome*, London: T&T Clark, 2003, pp. 164–84.

—— 'To Be Willing to Kill What for All One Knows Is a Person Is to Be Willing to Kill a Person', in Brent Waters and Ronald Cole-Turner (eds.), *God and the Embryo: Religious Voices on Stem Cells and Cloning*, Washington, DC: Georgetown University Press, 2003, pp. 98–107.

Southgate, Christopher, 'God and Evolutionary Evil: Theodicy in the Light of Darwinism', *Zygon*, 37.4 (2002), pp. 803–22.

Spencer, Herbert, *Social Statics; or the Conditions Essential to Human Happiness Specified and the First of Them Developed*, London: Chapman, 1851.

—— 'Progress: Its Law and Causes', *The Westminster Review*, 67 (April 1857), abridged version online at http://www.fordham.edu/halsall/mod/spencer-darwin.html (accessed 14 December 2005).

—— *The System of Synthetic Philosophy*, 10 vols, London and Edinburgh: Williams and Norgate, 1860–93.

—— *The Data of Ethics*, London: Williams and Norgate, 1884 (1879).

Stannard, Russell, 'God in and beyond Space and Time', in Philip Clayton and Arthur Peacocke (eds.), *In Whom We Live and Move and Have Our Being: Panentheistic Reflections on God's Presence in a Scientific World*, Grand Rapids: Eerdmans, 2004, pp. 109–20.

Stephen, Leslie, 'Ethics and the Struggle for Existence', *Contemporary Review* 64 (August 1893), pp. 157–70, online at http://alepho.clarku.edu/huxley/bib2.html (accessed 16 December 2005).

Stewart, Jacqui A., *Reconstructing Science and Theology in Postmodernity: Pannenberg, Ethics and the Human Sciences*, Aldershot: Ashgate, 2000.

Strawson, Galen, 'The Bounds of Freedom', in Robert Kane (ed.), *The Oxford Handbook of Free Will*, Oxford: Oxford University Press, 2002, pp. 441–60.

Tanner, Kathryn, 'Creation and Providence', in John Webster (ed.), *The Cambridge Companion to Karl Barth*, Cambridge: Cambridge University Press, 2000, pp. 111–26.

Thomas Aquinas, *Summa Theologiae*, ET ed. Thomas Gilby, OP, 60 vols, London: Eyre and Spottiswode, 1964–76.

van Till, Howard J., 'Are Bacterial Flagella Intelligently Designed? Reflections on the Rhetoric of the Modern ID Movement', *Science and Christian Belief*, 15.2 (2003), pp. 117–40.

Tooby, John, and Leda Cosmides, 'The Psychological Foundations of Culture', in Jerome H. Barkow, Leda Cosmides and John Tooby (eds.), *The Adapted Mind: Evolutionary Psychology and the Generation of Culture*, New York: Oxford University Press, 1992, pp. 19–136.

Torrance, Alan, 'Developments in Neuroscience and Human Freedom: Some

Theological and Philosophical Questions', *Science and Christian Belief*, 16.2 (2004), pp. 123–37.

Torrance, Thomas F., *Theological Science*, London: Oxford University Press, 1969.

Tracy, Thomas F., 'Evolution, Divine Action and the Problem of Evil', in Robert J. Russell, William R. Stoeger, SJ, and Francisco J. Ayala (eds.), *Evolutionary and Molecular Biology: Scientific Perspectives on Divine Action*, Notre Dame: University of Notre Dame Press, 1998.

Trivers, Robert L., 'The Evolution of Reciprocal Altruism', *Quarterly Review of Biology*, 46 (1971), pp. 35–56.

—— 'Parental Investment and Sexual Selection', in Bernard Campbell (ed.), *Sexual Selection and the Descent of Man 1871–1971*, Chicago, IL: Aldine, 1972, pp. 136–79, also online at http://orion.oac.uci.edu/~dbell/Trivers.pdf (accessed 21 August 2006).

Vanhoozer, Kevin, 'Human Being, Individual and Social', in Colin E. Gunton (ed.), *The Cambridge Companion to Christian Doctrine*, Cambridge: Cambridge University Press, 1997, pp. 158–88.

Verhey, Allen, *Reading the Bible in the Strange World of Medicine*, Grand Rapids: Eerdmans, 2003.

de Waal, Frans B. M., *Chimpanzee Politics: Power and Sex among the Apes*, New York: Harper and Row, 1982.

—— *Good Natured: The Origins of Right and Wrong in Humans and Other Animals*, Cambridge, MA: Harvard University Press, 1996.

Wallace, Alfred Russel, 'The Origin of Human Races and the Antiquity of Man Deduced From the Theory of "Natural Selection"', *Journal of the Anthropological Society of London*, 2 (1864), pp. clviii–clxxxvii, online at http://www.wku.edu/~smithch/wallace/S093.htm (accessed 14 December 2005).

Ward, Keith, *The Concept of God*, Oxford: Blackwell, 1974.

—— *Defending the Soul*, Oxford: Oneworld, 1992.

—— *God, Chance and Necessity*, Oxford: Oneworld, 1996.

Wells, Samuel, 'How Common Worship Forms Local Character', *Studies in Christian Ethics*, 15.1 (2002), pp. 66–74.

Wenham, Gordon J., *Genesis 1–15* (Word Biblical Commentary, 1), Waco, TX: Word, 1987.

White, Lynn, Jr, 'The Historical Roots of Our Ecologic Crisis', *Science*, 155 (1967), pp. 1203–7.

White, Roger M., '"Ought" Implies "Can": Kant and Luther, a Contrast', in George MacDonald Ross and Tony McWalter (eds.), *Kant and His Influence*, Bristol: Thoemmes, 1990, pp. 1–72.

Williams, George C., *Adaptation and Natural Selection*, Oxford: Oxford University Press, 1966.

—— 'Huxley's Evolution and Ethics in Sociobiological Perspective', *Zygon*, 23.4 (1988), pp. 383–407.

—— 'Reply to Comments on "Huxley's Evolution and Ethics in Sociobiological Perspective"', *Zygon*, 23.4 (1988), pp. 437–8.

Williams, Patricia A., *Doing without Adam and Eve: Sociobiology and Original Sin*, Minneapolis, MN: Fortress, 2001.

Bibliography

Wilmut, Ian, *et al.*, 'Viable Offspring Derived from Foetal and Adult Mammalian Cells', *Nature*, 385 (1997), pp. 810–13.

Wilson, David Sloan, *Darwin's Cathedral: Evolution, Religion, and the Nature of Society*, Chicago, IL: University of Chicago Press, 2002.

Wilson, Edward O., *The Insect Societies*, Cambridge, MA: Harvard University Press, 1971.

—— *Sociobiology: The New Synthesis*, abridged edn, Cambridge, MA: Harvard University Press, 1980 (1975).

—— *On Human Nature*, Cambridge, MA: Harvard University Press, 1978.

—— *Consilience: The Unity of Knowledge*, London: Abacus, 1999.

Wink, Walter, *Naming the Powers: The Language of Power in the New Testament*, Philadelphia, PA: Fortress, 1984.

Wispelaere, Jurgen de, 'Altruism, Impartiality and Moral Demands', in Jonathan Seglow (ed.), *The Ethics of Altruism*, London: Frank Cass, 2004, pp. 9–33.

Woolcock, Peter G., 'The Case against Evolutionary Ethics Today', in Jane Maienschein and Michael Ruse (eds.), *Biology and the Foundations of Ethics*, Cambridge: Cambridge University Press, 1999, pp. 276–306.

World Anti-Doping Agency website, at http://www.wada-ama.org/en/dynamic. ch2?pageCategory.id=526 (accessed 28 August 2006).

World Health Organization, *Constitution of the World Health Organization*, Geneva: World Health Organization, 1948 (updated 1977, 1984 and 1994), Preamble, available online at http://www.who.int/about/en/ (accessed 24 August 2006).

—— *The World Health Report 1995: Bridging the Gaps*, Geneva: World Health Organization, 1995, online at http://www.who.int/whr/en/ (accessed 24 August 2006).

Wrangham, Richard, and Dale Peterson, *Demonic Males: Apes and the Origins of Human Violence*, London: Bloomsbury, 1997.

Wright, Robert, *The Moral Animal: Evolutionary Psychology and Everyday Life*, London: Abacus, 1996.

Wright, Sewall, 'The Roles of Mutation, Inbreeding, Crossbreeding, and Selection in Evolution', *Proceedings of the VI International Congress of Genetics*, 1 (1932), pp. 356–66, reprinted in Mark Ridley (ed.), *Evolution* (Oxford Readers), Oxford: Oxford University Press, 1997, pp. 32–40.

Zizioulas, John D., 'Preserving God's Creation. Three Lectures on Theology and Ecology. I', *King's Theological Review*, 12 (1989), pp. 1–5.

Index of Names and Subjects

abortion 240–1
Adam
  historicity 185–6, 193 n. 131
  and Jesus Christ 187–8
  knowledge of good and evil 189
adaptationism 15–16, 142
affections 120
agapē 111–12, 113, 248
  see also love
agriculture 236
Allen, Joseph L., on the Church as
  covenant community 94 n. 99
altruism 5, 13, 33, 45, 84, 116–17, 247,
  248
  among human beings 67–72
  among insects 65–6
  'gene for' 11, 14–15
  genetic basis 68–71
  and kin selection 66–7
  and moral objectivity, Richards's views
    102
  and moral obligation 109–10
  reciprocal altruism 33, 67, 69
  see also neighbour-love
Andrews, E. H., on Adam's historicity 185
animals, behaviour, compared with
  human behaviour 16–17
Anselm of Canterbury 167
  satisfaction theory 179
anthropology *see* human beings;
  reductionist view of human nature
anti-retroviral drugs 231 n. 38
Aristotle 46, 116
Arnhart, Larry
  on Darwin as intellectual heir of Thomas
    Aquinas 118
  on nature and the good 119, 120
Athanasius 75
atonement 167, 179–80, 191
  see also reconciliation; redemption;
    salvation
Augustine of Hippo 75, 76–7, 78
  on original sin 185

Aulén, Gustaf, criticizes Anselm's
  satisfaction theory 179
Axelrod, Robert, on reciprocal altruism
  67

Bacon, Francis 224–5, 226
Baconian project 84 n. 71, 224–5, 226,
  233
  in relation to genetically modified crops
    235, 236
'bad' (in Spencer's evolutionary ethic)
  98–9
Bagehot, Walter 25
Barbour, Ian G., typology for interaction
  between science and religion 49 n. 19
Barth, Karl
  on abortion 240–1
  on biblical creation narratives as 'saga'
    77
  Christology 212
  and consideration of the engagement of
    theology with biology 60–1
  on covenant and creation 117 n. 78,
    121–2
  on divine command ethics 106–8, 120,
    120 n. 89, 122–5, 127–8
  on euthanasia 241 n. 72
  on freedom in fellowship 123–6, 127–8
  on God as 'timeless' 76
  on the goodness of creation 190
  on the historicity of the Creation and
    Fall narratives 186–8
  on the human project of ethics as pride
    93
  on Jesus' exaltation 174–5
  on Jesus' prophetic role 181
  on original sin 190–1
  on the *parousia* 209–10
  on reconciliation 164 n. 6, 169–70,
    172–3
  on salvation and sin 92 n. 92
  on sin 165, 228
    as falsehood 180–1, 182

as pride 169–70, 172–3, 175, 231
as sloth 175, 176
and theodicy 199–201
Basil of Caesarea 75
relationships within creation 90
behaviour
comparisons between human and animal behaviour 16–17
genetic modification 219–20
relationship between genes and 14–15
Behe, Michael 4
belief, Polkinghorne's views 58
Berry, R. J., on the historicity of the Fall narrative 186
Big Bang 51, 77
Biggar, Nigel
on Barth's divine command ethic 107, 108, 120
on Barth's theological anthropology 125–6
biology
engagement with theology 48–55, 60–1
influence on ethics 5
see also natural science
Boehm, Christopher, on group selectionism 69–70, 71
Bonhoeffer, Dietrich 236
on attitudes toward the material world 233
on ethics 5, 93–4, 172, 188–90
on the Fall narrative 231
human history viewed 'from below' 204–5
on Jesus Christ's universal significance 212
on 'radicalism' and 'compromise' 242
on the 'ultimate' and the 'penultimate' 207–9, 211
bonobos, non-violence 135–6
Boyd, Robert, on cultural group selectionism 70, 74
brain processes, deterministic nature 151, 153
British Association, Oxford debate (1860) 22
Broad, C. D., criticisms of Julian Huxley 100
Brunner, Emil, on gender roles 124
Buddhism, Huxley's account of 28, 29, 31

Calvin, John 120 n. 89
on sin and moral understanding 119 n. 83
'can', and 'ought' 156–7, 159

Cannon, Katie Geneva 177 n. 62
Cartesian dualism 149, 150, 152, 155 n. 67
Cela-Conde, Camilo, on genetic relationships between hominids 12
cells
germ line 218, 242
human embryonic stem cell (HESC) technology 221, 239, 241 n. 72
somatic 218, 242
somatic cell nuclear transfer (SCNT) 220, 222
'chance', and 'necessity' 56
character, understood in terms of human response to God's call 107–8
child–parent relationships 124
chimpanzees
and humans 12
male violence 134–6, 161
sexual behaviour 178
see also non-human primates
Christian doctrine 49 n. 18
Christian ethics *see* ethics
Christian life, and communicative action 81
Christian moral tradition, comparison with reductionist anthropology 47–8
Christian worship 82
Christianity
'liberal' *versus* 'ethicized', in Forsyth's thought 168–9
relations with evolutionary biology 2–3
Christology
Barth's Christology 212
Polkinghorne on 59
Church
as 'community of character' (Hauerwas) 95
as community constituted by the new covenant 94–5
as embodiment of and witness to God's transformative work 205
civilization, and ethics, T. H. Huxley's view 31
Clark, Stephen R. L.
critique of 'stewardship' and 'priesthood' as models of human relationship with the non-human world 91
on Darwinism and eugenics 25 n. 22
on repentant attitudes towards the ecological crisis 234 n. 51
Clayton, Philip, on altruism and neighbour-love 110
cloning, human *see* human cloning
Clothier Committee 218–19

Clough, David, on Biggar's understanding of Barth's ethics 120 n. 89
CO_2 emissions 234–5
command of God, ethics as 106–8, 119–20, 122–5, 127–8
communicative action, and the Christian life 81
communities, moral communities 88–9
community welfare, as 'highest moral good' (Richards) 101–2
companionship 91 n. 87
compatibilism 152 n. 53, 153–5
'compromise', as unsatisfactory way of relating the 'ultimate' and the 'penultimate' (Bonhoeffer) 207–8
Comte, Auguste 111, 112
conduct 98
contingency, within the doctrine of original sin 194–5
Cosmides, Leda 160
cosmogony 51
covenant relationship, God with human beings 94–5
creatio ex nihilo 75–6, 78
creation
  and covenant 117 n. 78, 121–3
  doctrine of 74–9, 82, 85–8, 91–2, 228, 247
  God's creative activity 114
  goodness of 77–8, 85–6, 88, 96, 106, 122
  and the doctrine of sin 190
  human beings within 83–8, 90–2, 106, 248
  moral relationships with the non-human creation 90–2
  and nature 121–2, 249–50
  Polkinghorne's account 59
  see also Barth, Karl; human beings; salvation
creationism 54
  and evolution 185–7
  and reductionism 3–4
the 'creaturely', Bonhoeffer's understanding 208
Cronin, Helena, on manipulation 67–8, 68 n. 14, 71
Cronk, Lee, on the genetic basis of altruism and morality 68 n. 14
cross, 'cruciality of' (Forsyth) 166–9
cuckoos, and manipulation 67–8
cultural group selectionism 70
culture 86
  as affected by Darwinism (Dennett) 46–7, 51

and ethics, T. H. Huxley's view 31, 36
and the evolution of morality (Richerson and Boyd) 70
and genetic development 71–3
human cultures and animals cultures 143
origins 14

Darwin, Charles
  on the evolution of morality 118
  on group selectionism 70
  natural selection 6–9
    and ethics 25
    and selection levels 10
  The Origin of Species 1, 22
  theodicy 39
Darwin, Erasmus 6
Darwinian fundamentalism 51
Darwinism 6–9
  as challenge to Christianity 3
  Dennett's understanding of 4, 50–3, 57
  and the doctrine of creation 82
  influence 1
  and reductionist views of human nature 46–7
  social Darwinism 24
  see also evolution; evolutionary ethics
Dawkins, Richard 139
  argues against God's existence 52–3
  on genes as the fundamental level of selection 10–11
  on genetic determinism 150
  notion of 'memes' 33
  The Selfish Gene, ethical implications 37, 43
Dembski, William 4
democratic politics 161
demonic 180–1, 183–4
  see also evil
Dennett, Daniel C.
  biological reductionism 50–3, 54, 57
  on Darwinism 4, 46–7
  on determinism 149–50, 153
  on evolutionary epistemology 57
  human nature and evolutionary ethics 43–4
  on moral development 33, 42
  and the naturalistic fallacy 101
  neo-Darwinism and memology 71–2, 74
  on the readiness potential and free will 146
  reductionism 233, 246
  on the 'sacredness' of the world 86
deoxyribonucleic acid (DNA), effects on evolutionary theories 9–10, 221 n. 17

Desmond, Adrian, on the
  Huxley–Wilberforce debate (1860)
  22 n. 6
determinism 141, 145–7
  biological determinism 147–51
  compatibility with free will 151–5
  Midgley's views 163–4
  and moral failure 158–9
divine command ethics 106–8, 119–20,
  122–5, 127–8
DNA (deoxyribonucleic acid) structure,
  significance for evolutionary biology
  9–10
Dobzhansky, Theodosius 1
Dolly the sheep 220
dominion 90, 91–2
Dostoevsky, Fyodor, on theodicy 198
drugs, modification of human behaviour
  by 162
dualism, Cartesian dualism 149, 150,
  152, 155 n. 67
Duns Scotus, John 120 n. 89, 249
  divine command ethic 119–20
  doctrine of univocity 53 n. 32

ecological damage, as a consequence of
  sin 216–17
Eldredge, Niles 142
embryos *see* human embryos
Emmet, Dorothy 180
Enlightenment project 46, 47 n. 13, 105
environment, and biological determinism
  148–9
Ephesians
  God's saving work in Christ 203–4
  universal significance of Christ 211–12
epistemology, Polkinghorne on 58–9
Erasmus, criticisms of Luther in respect of
  moral accountability 156–7
eros 113
eschatology
  and the doctrine of creation 75
  Polkinghorne's views 59
ethics
  'biology of ethics' 5, 99–100
  'ethics' and 'morality' 18 n. 51, 32 n. 38
  and evolution 1–2, 21, 97
    and morality 32–4, 42
    T. H. Huxley's account 27–32
    see also Huxley, Thomas Henry,
      'Evolution and Ethics'
  and human origins 12–13
  theological critique of 93–4, 188–90
  see also evolutionary ethics; evolutionary
    psychology; morality

Eucharist 82, 94, 95
eugenics 25, 40, 161
euthanasia 241 n. 72
Eve, historicity 193 n. 131
evil 85
  and the doctrine of creation 75
  moral evil 164, 197
  natural evil 217, 224
evolution
  'adaptationist' views of 15–16
  and the concept of sin 173–4
  and creationism 185–7
  and the doctrine of creation 74–9
  ethical implications 1–2
  and ethics 21
    and morality 32–4, 42
    T. H. Huxley's account 27–32
    see also Huxley, Thomas Henry,
      'Evolution and Ethics'
  and the Fall narrative 186–8
  implications for understanding of
    'ethical nature' 172
  and moral failure 158–62
  and morality 5–6, 32–4, 42, 246–7, 248
  Morris's rejection 54 n. 36
  and original sin 188, 193–5, 215
    theodicy 196–202
  relations with Christianity 2–3
  and salvation 206
  sexual roles and relationships 177–8
  and sin 243–4
  and sociality 83
  see also Darwinism; human evolution
'Evolution and Ethics' (the Romanes
  Lecture, 1893)(T. H. Huxley) 4, 21–2,
  41
  argument 27–32
  attack on Spencer 35
  on the changing of human nature
    through technology 40, 43
  consideration of evolutionary ethics and
    morality 36–7, 43
  on the content of evolutionary ethics
    35–6, 42–3
  intellectual context 22–7
  invitation to deliver 27
  justification of evolutionary ethics 34–5,
    42
  moral development 32–3, 42
  negative evaluation of evolution 133,
    138
  questions arising from 32–41, 42–6
  theodicy 38–40, 43
  see also Huxley, Thomas Henry
evolutionary biology

Darwinism 6–9
genetic drift and the neutral theory of
molecular evolution 9–10
human origins 12–14
levels of selection 10–12
and molecular genetics 9–10
neo-Darwinism (the 'modern synthesis')
71–2
see also natural selection
evolutionary epistemology 57 n. 51
evolutionary ethics
and Christian ethics 249
content 35–6, 42–3
Herbert Spencer's account 97–8
justification 34–5, 42
and moral failure *see* Chapter 6
and morality 36–8, 43, 95–6
nineteenth century views 97–9
and technological manipulation of
human nature 40–1, 43
and theodicy 38–40, 43
twentieth century 99–104
see also Darwinism; determinism; ethics;
neighbour-love
evolutionary 'naturalists' 99
evolutionary psychology 2, 13–14
criticisms 14–18, 140–5
and human origins 13–18
exaptation 16
explanation 55–6

fact, separation from value 105
Fall narrative 93, 172, 189, 190 n. 117,
193 n. 131, 194, 196, 206, 208, 231
and evolution 186–8
see also sin
falsehood
as idolatry 193, 228
and sin 181–4
the family, Barth on 124, 127
Farber, Paul Lawrence, on circularity of
some accounts of evolutionary ethics
45–6
farming 236
female–male relationships 123–4
females
male violence towards 134 n. 4
see also male violence
sexual roles and relationships 177–8
feminism
critiques of original sin 185, 192
critiques of sociobiology and
evolutionary psychology 118–19, 178
on sin as sloth 175–7
Feuerbach, Ludwig Andreas, on theology

as anthropology 172 n. 45
Fisher, R. A. 8
'fittest', concept, T. H. Huxley's views
30–1
Flavr Savr™ tomatoes 223
Fletcher, Joseph 115
on turning from creatures into creators
231–2
Ford, David
on human community 230
on salvation 203–6, 211–12
forgiveness 167
Forsyth, Peter Taylor
on Anselm's satisfaction theory 179
on the 'cruciality of the cross' 166–9
on the newness of God's salvific work
207
and theodicy 201
free will 192
and determinism 145 n. 35, 146–7,
149–50, 151–5
free-will defence, in relation to theodicy
197, 199
Midgley's discussion 163–4
free-process defence, in relation to natural
evil 197–8, 199
freedom
freedom in fellowship (Barth) 123–6,
127–8
Hume's account 152
and moral accountability 156–8, 159
as proper orientation of human will and
desire to God 215
Frei, Hans W., typology of Christian
theology 49–50

Galton, Francis 133
on natural selection and heredity 24, 25,
25 n. 20
gender roles, Brunner's view 124
gene doping 219, 242–3
see also genetic modification, human
gene-culture co-evolution 71
genes
alleles 8
as basis for altruism and morality 68–71
effects
on behaviour 15
on selection 10–11
'genes for' behavioural traits 11, 14–15,
33, 67
and kin selection 66
Genesis, book of
as cosmogony (Dennett) 51
creation narratives 84–5, 90

genetic determinism 148–50
genetic drift 9, 16
genetic engineering 162
  see also cells; genetic modification
genetic modification
  human
    germ line (inheritable) 218, 242
    non-therapeutic (enhancement) 219
    somatic cell 218, 220, 222, 242
    therapeutic 220–2, 238–41
    plant (GM crops) 222–4, 230 n. 38,
      235–7
genetic predispositions, and social
    problems 143–5
genetics
  and human origins 12
  molecular genetics 9–10
genotypes 15
gentleness 204
germ-plasm 8
Gladstone, William 27
Glover, Jonathan, on genetic modification
    of human behaviour 41, 219, 243
Gnosticism, understanding of creation 78
God
  belief in 73
  bracketed out of Midgley's treatment of
    wickedness 163–4
  call of
    and human morality 89–90, 92
    through Jesus Christ 94–5
  command of
    ethics as 106–8, 122–5, 127–8
      Biggar's account 120
      Hare's account 119–20
  creative activity 75–6, 77–8, 84–6, 114,
    213–14, 226, 248
  eternal life with as the *telos* of human
    existence 127
  existence 55–7
  'God of the gaps' 51
  Kingdom of 115
  knowledge about 122
  love of 111–15
  relationship with 173, 175
  response to sin 164–6, 166–9
  saving work of 214, 218, 228–9
    as salvation from falsehood 181–4,
      194
    as salvation from pride 93, 165,
      170–1, 174–5, 182, 234
    as salvation from sloth 182, 227
  technological projects as attempts to be
    'like God' 231–2
  and theodicy 196–202

  transcendence of, and theological
    language 52–3
  see also Holy Spirit; *imago Dei*; Jesus
    Christ; Trinity
Goldwyn, Sam 181
good 85, 98–9, 102
  dependence upon nature 119
  Macintyre's consideration of 112
Goslee, David, criticisms of T. H. Huxley
    21
Gould, Stephen Jay
  criticisms of adaptationism 16
  on Dennett's Darwinian fundamentalism
    51
  on E. O. Wilson's determinism 146
  on selection levels in evolution 12
  theodicy 39
grace, perfection of nature 117–18
Grant, Colin
  on altruism and neighbour-love 111–14
  criticisms of Stephen Pope's discussion of
    altruism 116–17
Gray, Asa, theodicy 39
great apes, human evolutionary
    relationships with 22–3
Greg, William 25
Grenzfälle 108
group selectionism 10–12, 69–70, 71
Gunton, Colin E.
  on atonement theories 179–81
  on the demonic 183–4
  on the doctrine of creation 85, 91–2,
    228, 247
  and evolution 74–9
  on Forsyth's theodicy 201–2
  on humanity's relationship with non-
    human creation 91–2
  on salvation 228
  on sin and salvation 165
  on the Trinity 114

Haarsma, Loren, on the genetic basis of
    altruism and morality 68–9
Haldane, J. B. S. 8, 109
Hamilton, William D.
  on altruism 11, 13
  on kin selection 66–7, 70
Hare, John E. 249
  divine command ethic 119–20
Hart, Trevor
  on analogical language in theology 53
  on atonement 167
Hauerwas, Stanley, concept of the Church
    95 n. 101
Hays, Richard, on neighbour-love 127

health, theological understanding of
237–8

Hefner, Philip, on human beings as
created co-creators 232

heredity, and natural selection 24

HESC (human embryonic stem cell)
technology 221, 239, 241 n. 72

Hinduism, Huxley's account of 28, 29

holiness 125 n. 108

Holy Spirit
outpouring, at the *parousia* 210
presence within the Church 95
see also God

hominids, genetic relationships 12

Homo divinus 186

Homo erectus 12

Homo sapiens 12, 96, 186, 188, 228

Hooker, Joseph 1 n. 1
on the Huxley–Wilberforce debate
(1860) 22 n. 6

Hrdy, Sarah Blaffer 161
on gender stereotyping in evolutionary
research 105, 118–19, 178

Hull, David, on the character of God as
inferred from the evolutionary process
39

human beings 79–83
altruism 67–72
communication between 81–2
as created co-creators 232
embodiment 82–3
evolutionary relationships with great
apes 22–3
fallen state 226, 227–8
sicut deus 189, 194, 195, 196, 206,
209, 231
and the *imago Dei* 79–80
and morality
and creation 83–8
and God's call 89–90, 92
and personal identity 88–9, 92–3
in relationship with non-human
creation 90–2
salvation and sin 92–5
teleological understanding of (with
reference to Thomas Aquinas) 105–6
see also creation; salvation

human brain 15

human cloning
reproductive 220–1, 238
therapeutic 220–2, 238–41

human communities, transformation 230

human creatures *see* human beings

human embryonic stem cell (HESC)
technology 221, 239, 241 n. 72

human embryos, research on 221–2,
239–41

human evolution 1, 12–18
relationships with the great apes 22–3
see also evolution

human existence, teleology 127

Human Fertilization and Embryology Act
(1990) 221, 222

human gene pool, survival of, as core
moral value (Wilson) 100

human genetic modification 218–20,
242–5

Human Genome Project 233

human life
protection 239, 240, 241
Barth's account 108 n. 41

human nature, technological modification
of 40–1, 43, 224

human origins
and ethical behaviour 12–13
evolutionary psychology 13–18
genetics 12

human race
solidarity, with regard to salvation 168
tragic situation 166

human reason, importance of,
Bonhoeffer's account 208

human relationships, contingency 124–5

human reproductive cloning 220–2,
238–41

human rights 47 n. 13

human sinfulness, God's apparent
responsibility for 196

humanity
responsibility for creation 214–15
salvation 5
sicut deus 189, 194, 195, 196, 206, 209,
231

humans *see* human beings

Hume, David 34, 62
on freedom 152
influence on T. H. Huxley 30 n. 33
on 'is' and 'ought' 98, 104
theodicy 38

Hunsinger, George, on Jesus' exaltation
(in Barth's thought) 174

Huxley, Julian
evolutionary ethics 35–6, 42, 45, 100
modern synthesis 9
and the naturalistic fallacy 34

Huxley, Thomas Henry
on biology and theology 61–2
on changing human nature 161
critique of evolutionary ethics 97, 98
on Darwinism 7

on 'ethical nature' 172
  conflict with 'cosmic nature' 32, 33,
    38, 62, 247
Man's Place in Nature 23
'Prolegomena' 27 n. 31, 30 n. 33, 40,
  161
'The Struggle for Existence in Human
  Society' 25–6, 30, 31, 38
on use of technology to modify human
  behaviour 31, 219
see also 'Evolution and Ethics' (the
  Romanes Lecture, 1893)(T. H. Huxley)
Hymenoptera, altruism 65–6

I–Thou encounters 116
IBE (inference to the best explanation)
  55, 56
idolatry 181
  and falsehood 193, 228
  healing of 204
  sin understood as 192–3, 228
ill-health, as a consequence of sin 216
imago Dei 189, 194, 195, 231
  and the call of the neighbour 90
  doctrine 79–80
  in the New Testament 92, 94
  see also God
in vitro fertilization 221
Incarnation
  doctrine of 76, 92, 170, 208
  see also Jesus Christ
incompatibilism 152 n. 53, 159
individual selection 10
infanticide 241 n. 72
infants
  male violence towards 134 n. 4
  neglect of high-risk infants 136–7,
    160–1
inference to the best explanation (IBE)
  55, 56
inheritance 8–9
insect viruses, use in genetically modified
  crops 223
insects, altruistic behaviour in 65–6
intelligent design 3, 4
Irenaeus of Lyons, on creation 75, 78
'is'
  and 'ought' 5, 98, 100–2, 104, 117, 128
  T. H. Huxley's view 30
Israel, ancient Israel (Huxley's account)
  28

Jesus Christ 6
  and Adam 187–8
  and the atonement 191

call 80–1
creative role 226
death, as reconciliation 200–1
and the doctrine of reconciliation,
  Barth's account 169–70
exaltation 174–5
humanity 122–3, 126–7
as *imago Dei* 92, 94
as key to knowledge of the divine
  ordering of the world 125 n. 108
and knowledge of human sinfulness 165
parousia 209–11
'penultimate' and 'ultimate' resolved in
  208
prophetic role 181
as revelation of God's goodness 202
saving work 203–6, 228
and the sense of personal identity 92–4
solidarity with humanity in the cross
  168
universal significance 211–13
as victor 178–81
see also God; Incarnation, doctrine of;
  Trinity
John Paul II 239
judicial punishment 150, 159, 160
Junker-Kenny, Maureen, on personhood
  340
justice 62
  T. H. Huxley's account 28–9

Kane, Robert
  on quantum indeterminacy 152–3
  on self-forming actions 153
Kant, Immanuel
  language of 'radical evil', used by Barth
    191
  moral vision 184
  use of '"ought" implies "can"' 156–7,
    159
Kidner, Derek 186 n. 99
Kim, Jaegwon, criticisms of non-reductive
  physicalism 154
Kimura, Motoo, neutral theory of
  molecular evolution 9–10
kin selection 33, 45, 66–7, 70, 101, 109
  contribution to Christian accounts of
    neighbour-love (Pope) 116
knowledge of good and evil 5, 85, 93, 96
  Barth's view 172–3
  Bonhoeffer's account 172, 188–90,
    208–9
  Moore's view 98–9
  Rachels's view 99
  Spencer's view 98

T. H. Huxley's view 29–32, 98
Thomas Aquinas' view 105
Kropotkin, Prince Petr, on mutual aid
    26–7, 37–8
Krötke, Wolf, on male–female
    relationships in Barth's thought 123

Lamarck, Jean-Baptiste 6, 7
Lamarckianism 23 n. 11
Lanessan, Jean de, evolutionary ethics 45
language, univocity of 53
langurs, sexual behaviour 178
liberation theology 205
libertarianism 152 n. 53
    and judicial punishment 159
'liberty of indifference' (Hume) 152–3
'liberty of spontaneity' (Hume) 152–3
Libet, Benjamin, on neurobiology and free
    will 146, 149, 150
Linnaean Society 1 n. 1
living for oneself 81 n. 61
Lorenz, Konrad, ethology 74 n. 44
love
    agapē 111–12, 113, 248
    God's love 111–15
    see also neighbour-love
Luther, Martin
    on moral accountability, contrasted with
        Erasmus and Kant 156–7
    moral vision 184
    on sin 171
Lyell, Sir Charles 1 n. 1

McFadyen, Alistair 205
    concepts of free will 164, 197
    critique of moral frame of reference for
        talking about sin 168–9, 191, 192
    on the healing of idolatry 204
    on the *imago Dei* 79–81
    on moral accountability 157–8
    on original sin 93 n. 93, 184–5, 194
    on the 'pathological' in human affairs
        165 n. 9
    on personal identity 88, 92
    on 'pragmatic atheism' 164
        and moral accountability 158
    on sin as pride 170
    on sin as sloth 176
MacIntyre, Alasdair
    on altruism and egoism 112
    on the Enlightenment project 46,
        47 n. 13
    on moral communities and character
        formation 88
    on the separation of fact from value
        105, 106

McKenny, Gerald P.
    on the 'Baconian project' 224, 225
    on subjugation of nature 84
male violence 133–6, 143, 161
    curbing of 144
    and evolutionary adaptations 142
male–female relationships 123–4
males, sexual roles and relationships
    177–8
manipulation 67–8, 71
Mann, Janet
    adaptationism 142
    on determinism 141
    on genetic predispositions and social
        problems 143
    on maternal care and neglect of high-risk
        infants 136–7, 160–1
marriage, and male–female relationships
    123–4
mass extinction, attempts to influence
    232
material world, attitudes towards 233
maternal care, and neglect of high-risk
    infants 136–7, 160–1
memes 33, 42, 43, 72
memology 72
Mendel, Gregor
    on inheritance 8–9
    T. H. Huxley's ignorance of 21
'mental modules' 13
'mental organs' 13
Midgley, Mary
    on determinism 141
    on embodiment 83
    on humans as animals 82
    rejection of memology 72
    rejection of the notion of memes 33–4,
        42
    on social instincts as the basis for
        morality 72–3
    on wickedness 163–4
minds, product of genes 15
modern synthesis 9
'molecular clock' 10
molecular evolution, neutral theory of
    (Kimura) 9–10
Moltmann, Jürgen, Trinitarian theology
    of 80
Monod, Jacques 56–7
Monsanto 224
Moore, George Edward, on the
    naturalistic fallacy 34, 98–9, 102, 104
moral accountability, and freedom
    156–8, 159
moral incapacity 160

moral obligation, and altruism 109–10
moral responsibility, arising from the
  parousia 210–11
morality
  and ethics 18 n. 51, 32 n. 38, 65
  and evolution 36–8, 43, 95–6, 246–7,
    248
  evolutionary biological understandings
    of 5–6, 32–4, 42, 158–62
  evolutionary effects on culture 70
  genetic basis 68–71
  and human beings
    and creation 83–8, 90–2, 106, 248
    and God's call 89–90, 92
    and personal identity 88–9, 92–3
    in relationship with non-human
      creation 90–2
    salvation and sin 92–5
  as merely human project, invalidated by
    Jesus Christ's coming (Bonhoeffer)
    188–9, 209, 248
  natural morality, Williams's negative
    evaluation of 144
  and nature 104–5, 106
  objectivity of, Woolcock's account
    103–4
  Ruse's ethical scepticism 101, 102–3
  and social instincts 72–4
  see also ethics
Morris, Henry M., rejection of evolution
  54 n. 36
Morton, Adam, on the demonic 180
Murphy, Nancey, non-reductive
  physicalism 153–4
mutual aid 26–7

the 'natural', Bonhoeffer's understanding
  of 208
natural law theory 5, 105, 107, 109, 120
natural rights, Bonhoeffer's account
  208–9
natural science
  Barth's attitude towards 125 n. 109
  P. A. Williams's attitude towards 193
  and theology 55–60
  Torrance's attitude towards 87–8
  see also biology; science
natural selection 1, 6–9, 23, 39
  and altruism 67–8, 188
  evolutionary effects 70, 75, 142, 148,
    177
  levels of 10
  and parental investment 136–7
  possibly favours tendencies to sin 193–4
  and sin as falsehood 181–2

and sin as pride 171–2
and social and political life 24–6
see also evolutionary biology
natural theology 86–8
naturalistic fallacy 34, 98–9, 102, 104–5
  Dennett's view 101
  and evolutionary ethics 34, 42
nature
  as the basis of an understanding of the
    good 119
  and creation 121–2, 249–50
  interference with 41
  and morality 38–9, 61–2, 87, 104–5,
    106, 138
  perfection through grace 116–18
  Rolston's account 87
  subjugation in the modern era 235–6
    McKenny's account 84, 225
  understood as created, fallen and being
    saved 190 n. 117, 207, 226–9
Nazi Germany 74 n. 44
Nazi ideology 125 n. 108
Neanderthals, relationship to modern
  humans 12
'necessity', and 'chance' 56
neighbour, call of, and the moral life
  89–90
neighbour-love
  and altruism 110–15, 127–8
  and evolutionary ethics 115–21, 122–8
neo-Darwinism (the 'modern synthesis')
  71–2
Nicene Creed, Polkinghorne's use of
  58–60
Niebuhr, Reinhold, on sin 170–1
Nietzsche, Friedrich Wilhelm 46
di Noia, J. Augustine, on Barth's account
  of religion and the religions 212 n. 59
NOMA (non-overlapping
  magisteria)(Gould) 39, 48
non-human creation, salvation 214
non-human primates
  demonic behaviours 183
  see also bonobos; chimpanzees; langurs;
    male violence
non-human suffering 216
non-humans, male violence among 134,
  161
'non-overlapping magisteria'
  (NOMA)(Gould) 39, 48
non-reductive physicalism 153–4
Northcott, Michael, on genetically
  modified crops 235 n. 52, 237
nucleotides 9

obesity 217 n. 1
O'Hear, Anthony
 critique of evolutionary explanations of
  morality 73–4
 on Darwinism and eugenics 25 n. 22
original sin 6, 164 n. 5, 184–95, 227
 and evolution 215
 theodicy 196–202
 see also sin
'ought'
 and 'can' 156–7, 159
 and 'is' 98, 100–2, 117, 128
 T. H. Huxley's views 30

Page, Ruth, on human relationships with
  the non-human creation 91
pangenesis 7–8
Parens, Erik, on genetic modification of
  behaviour 220
parent–child relationships 124
parental investment 136–7, 177
parousia 209–11
parthenogenetic blastocysts 222 n. 20
'party-gang' organization (Wrangham
  and Peterson) 135
paternal care 137 n. 14
patriarchy 175–6, 178
 and morality 105, 118–19
Paul, Diane, on eugenics 25
Paul, St, on evidence of the Creator's
  work in the world 75
Peacocke, Arthur 59, 59–60 n. 63
 on Christian doctrine and natural science
  55–8
the 'penultimate' (Bonhoeffer) 207–9,
  211
person, concept of 89, 151–2, 153, 159,
  239–40
personal identity 227, 256–7
 and morality 80–3, 85, 88–9, 92–3, 96
 in relation to Christ 92–4
Peterson, Dale
 on adaptationism 142
 on determinism 141
 empirical support for evolutionary ethics
  142
 on genetic predispositions and social
  problems 143–4
 on male violence 133–6, 161
 on original sin 93 n. 94
 on pride 171
 use of parallels between non-human and
  human behaviour 143
phenotypes 15, 148
phenotypic changes 9

Pieper, Josef 209
Pinker, Steven 177
Pleistocene period, importance for human
  development 14
pluralism 159
 and dualism 155 n. 67
Polanyi, Michael 58
political life, relevance of evolutionary
  theory to 24–7
Polkinghorne, John
 free-process defence in relation to
  natural evil 197
 on theology and natural science 58–60
poor, technology as good news to
  229–30
Pope, Alexander 29
Pope, Stephen J., evolution and
  neighbour-love 116–19, 121, 125, 126,
  127
powers, and principalities 179–80
practical wisdom (*phronēsis*) 244
'pragmatic atheism' (McFadyen) 164
pride 228
 Barth's view 93, 169–70, 172–3, 175,
  231
 God's saving work, as salvation from
  93, 165, 170–1, 174–5, 182, 234
 male pride 135, 136, 177
 Niebuhr's view 171
 sin as 170–3, 175–8, 182, 187, 193,
  196, 200, 227, 231
priesthood 90, 91
Priestly creation narrative 84 n. 71
principalities, and powers 179–80
psychology *see* evolutionary psychology

quantum indeterminacy, effects on brain
  processes 151, 152–3

Rachels, James 21, 48
 evolutionary ethics 36, 42–3
 on Moore's critique of Spencer 99
racism, and evolutionary theory 24–5
'radicalism', as unsatisfactory way of
  relating the 'ultimate' and the
  'penultimate' (Bonhoeffer) 208, 233,
  236, 242
Ramsey, Paul, on neighbour-love
  114–15, 127
readiness potential, and free will 146,
  149, 150
reason
 human, and the 'natural', in Bonhoeffer's
  thought 208–9
 practical, first principle of (Thomas
  Aquinas) 105

reconciliation
  Barth's treatment 169–70, 172–3
  see also atonement; salvation
redemption
  Barth's treatment 164 n. 6
  and the doctrine of creation 75
  see also atonement; salvation
reductionism 46, 70–2
  application to evolutionary ethics 33, 42
  and creationism 3–4
  theological alternatives to 246–50
reductionist view of human nature
  Darwinism and 46–7
  versus Christian moral tradition 47–8
Reformed Protestant tradition 3
relationalism 83 n. 69
relationship violence 134 n. 4
repentance 234–5
'reverse engineering' 15–16
Richards, Janet Radcliffe 141 n. 29
  on evolutionary ethics 41
Richards, Robert J.
  evolutionary ethics 101–2, 104
  and the naturalistic fallacy 34
Richerson, Peter J., on cultural group
  selection 70, 74
Ricoeur, Paul 204
Rockwell, Teed 155 n. 67
Rogers, Eugene F. 250
  on the perfection of nature by grace
  117 n. 78
Rolston, Holmes, III
  on evolution and culture 71, 72
  on evolutionary roots of morality 73
  natural theology 86–7
  rejection of the notion of memes 33–4,
  42
Romanes, George 27
Romanes lectures 27
  see also 'Evolution and Ethics' (the
  Romanes Lecture, 1893) (T. H. Huxley)
Rose, Steven
  critique of adaptationism 142
  critique of E. O. Wilson's determinism
  145–6
  critique of parallels between non-human
  and human behaviour 134 n. 4
  described as 'blank-paper Darwinist'
  141 n. 29, 169
Ruse, Michael
  ethical scepticism 101, 102–3, 104
  on evolutionary ethics 35
  on Julian Huxley's evolutionary ethics
  100
  moral hope 37

moral scepticism 44–5
scepticism 34–5, 42
on T. H. Huxley as forerunner of Ruse's
  ethical scepticism 30 n. 33

saga
  Barth's understanding of 77
  biblical saga 187
salvation 5, 173, 228–9, 248
  doctrine of, and human morality 92–5
  Gnostic view of 78
  'penultimate' and 'ultimate' (Bonhoeffer)
  207–9, 211
  scope 211–15, 218
  and sin 165–6
  through Jesus Christ 168, 178
  as transformation 203–6
  see also atonement; reconciliation;
  redemption
sanctification 95
satisfaction theory of the atonement 179
scepticism 46
Schloss, Jeffrey, on altruism and
  neighbour-love 110, 127
Schwöbel, Christoph
  on doctrine of the *imago Dei* 79
  on relational anthropologies 83 n. 69
science *see* natural science
SCNT (somatic cell nuclear transfer) 220,
  222
Scott, Peter, on nature 104–5
Scripture, and ethics, Barth on 108
selection *see* natural selection
selective breeding 161
selfishness, in evolutionary theory 11
sensuality, sinful nature 170–1
serpent (Fall narrative) 93, 172, 189,
  194, 196, 206, 231
sexual roles and relationships 177
sexual selection 7
Simpson, George Gaylord, claimed by
  Ruse as forerunner of Ruse's ethical
  scepticism 35
sin 129, 164–5, 203, 204, 228, 248
  consequences 216–17
  human attempts to ameliorate through
  technology 218–24, 230 n. 38, 235–45
  and the doctrine of creation 75
  doctrine of
  and human morality 92–5, 164–5, 168,
  247
    see also theodicy
  and evolution 243–4, 247
  see also evolution
  as falsehood 181–4, 193

God's response 164–6, 166–9
  see also God
and moral accountability 158
and moral understanding 119, 120, 121
as pride 170–3, 175–6, 182, 193, 231
repentance for 234–5
and salvation 165–6
as sloth 81 n. 61, 175–8, 182, 193
  see also idolatry; original sin
the 'sinful', Bonhoeffer's understanding
  208
Singer, Peter, on moral obligation 109
sloth, and sin 81 n. 61, 175–8, 182, 193
Smith, Adam, influence on T. H. Huxley
  30 n. 33
social Darwinism see Darwinism
social environment, and moral failure
  161
social instincts, as the basis for morality
  72–4
social problems
  causes 17
  and genetic presdispositions 143–5
social welfare, role in natural selection
  24–7
sociality, and evolution 83
sociobiology 2, 13
  criticisms 16, 17–18, 140–5
  and neighbour-love 116–19
somatic cell nuclear transfer (SCNT) 220,
  222
somatic cell therapy 218, 242
Song, Robert
  on the Baconian project 224 n. 26, 225
  on HESC technology 239
Southgate, Christopher
  evolutionary theodicy 202, 232
  humanity's responsibility for creation
  214–15
speech-agency 82
Spencer, Herbert
  The Data of Ethics 24
  evolutionary ethics 97–8, 99
  evolutionary theory 23–4, 26
  criticisms 34, 35
  System of Synthetic Philosophy 23
Spinoza, Benedict de (Baruch) 57
stem cells, human embryonic stem cell
  (HESC) technology 221, 239, 241 n. 72
Stephen, Leslie 36
stewardship 90, 91
Stewart, Jacqui A., on Lorenz's ethology
  74 n. 44
Stoicism, Huxley's account of 28, 29, 30,
  31

Strawson, Galen, denies libertarian free
  will 152 n. 53
suffering, as the consequence of sin 216
supervenience 119–20, 154, 155 n. 67
'survival of the fittest' 23–4
sympathy, as the basis for morality 70

technology
  ethical considerations 6
  and ethics, T. H. Huxley's views 31,
  219
  theological assessments 249, 250
  use to change human nature 40–1, 43
  uses to counter the effects of sin 217
  genetically modified crops 222–4,
    230 n. 38, 235–7
  human genetic modification 218–20,
    242–5
  human reproductive cloning 220–2,
    238–41
  modification of human nature 224
  theological assessments of 229–35
  theological perspectives on 226–9
Teilhard de Chardin, Pierre 50 n. 21
'terminator' technologies 223–4,
  230 n. 38
Tertullian 78
theodicy 6
  in Erasmus' dispute with Luther 156–7
  and evolution 196–202
  and evolutionary ethics 38–40, 43
  T. H. Huxley's critique 29
theology
  and anthropology 172 n. 45
  engagement with biology 48–55, 60–1
  and natural science 55–60
Thomas Aquinas 120 n. 89
  doctrine of analogy 53 n. 32
  on love 116
  on natural law 105, 107
  on nature's perfection by grace 117–18
  on sin and moral understanding
  119 n. 83
time, and the doctrine of creation 76–7
tissue grafting 221
Tooby, John 160
Torrance, Alan J.
  critique of compatibilism 155
  on 'liberty of indifference' 152, 153
  pluralism 159
Torrance, Thomas F., rejection of natural
  theology 87–8
'traitor' technologies 223–4, 230 n. 38
tribalism 125, 126
Trinity 114, 210

and creation 77–9
Moltmann's theology 80
and redemption 193
see also God; Holy Spirit; Jesus Christ
Trivers, Robert L.
on altruism 13
on parental investment 136–7
on reciprocal altruism 67

the 'ultimate' (Bonhoeffer) 207–9, 211
universe
heat death of 77
moral order of 166, 168
univocity 53
the 'unnatural', Bonhoeffer's
understanding 208

value, separation from fact 105
Vanhoozer, Kevin
communicative action 81–2
on God's call and human response 89
Verhey, Allen 210
on the Baconian project 226
virtue ethics 88, 89, 115

de Waal, Frans B. M.
on biological roots of human morality
38, 43, 139–40, 142
use of parallels between non-human and
human behaviour 143
Wallace, Alfred Russel 1 n. 1
on natural selection 24, 25, 25 n. 20
Ward, Keith, on 'explanation' 55
Weismann, August 7–8
White, Roger M.
on Kant's language about evil 191
on Kant's use of '"ought" implies "can"'
156–7, 159
on Luther's and Kant's moral visions
184
on moral judgements 160 n. 78
wickedness, Midgley's account 163–4
Wilberforce, Samuel (Bishop of Oxford),
confrontation with T. H. Huxley
(1860) 22
will, willing 177 n. 62, 192, 215
William of Ockham 120 n. 89
doctrine of univocity 53 n. 32
Williams, George C.
Adaptation and Natural Selection,
rejects group selection 10
adaptationism 142
on determinism 141
on 'immorality' and 'stupidity' of

evolutionary process 39, 43, 138–9,
247
on the material world 85
on natural morality 144
Williams, Patricia A.
on evolution and original sin 193 n. 131
on the free-will defence 197
Wilmut, Ian 220
Wilson, Edward O.
'biologizing' of ethics 43, 99
'biology of ethics' 99–100
determinism 145–6
evolutionary ethics 36, 42, 99–100
on the genetic basis of altruism and
morality 70–1
on moral development 33, 42
and the naturalistic fallacy 34
reductionist anthropology 47 n. 13
on sociobiology 13
wisdom, practical wisdom (*phronēsis*)
244
de Wispelaere, Jurgen, on altruism 66 n. 2
women, empowerment of 161
Woolcock, Peter G.
criticisms of evolutionary ethics 35, 42
moral objectivity 103–4
on moral obligation 109–10
moral scepticism 44–5
world, material world, treatment 84–5
World Anti-Doping Agency 219
Wrangham, Richard
on adaptationism 142
on determinism 141
empirical support for evolutionary ethics
142
on genetic predispositions and social
problems 143–4
on male violence 133–6, 161
on original sin 93 n. 94
on pride 171
use of parallels between non-human and
human behaviour 143
Wright, Robert
on free will 150
on immorality of evolutionary process
138–9
on judicial punishment 159
Wright, Sewall 8, 9
Wynne-Edwards, V. C., on group
selection 10

Zizioulas, John D., on Darwinism and the
doctrine of creation 82